A GUIDE TO
MOTORSPORT CIRCUITS OF THE WORLD

TONY SAKKIS

Airlife

ENGLAND

Copyright © 1993 by Tony Sakkis, Evras Press.

First published in the USA by Evras Press.

First published in the UK in 1994
by Airlife Publishing Ltd.

British Library Cataloguing in Publication Data
  A catalogue record for this book
  is available from the British Library

ISBN 1 85310 518 X

Printed in England by Livesey Ltd., Shrewsbury.

Airlife Publishing Ltd.
101 Longden Road, Shrewsbury SY3 9EB, England

Efforts were made to ensure the accuracy of this guidebook, but it should be noted that schedules, sponsor conflicts, financial, political, and even an occasional typo or two may change the accuracy of the information contained within this guide. We have done our best to stay current but certain things will evolve. We apologize ahead of time for any mistakes — ours or otherwise — which appear here in print. We encourage feedback, and will change the text accordingly. We will not be held responsible for any problems which may occur from incorrect information printed within this guide, and we strongly suggest that you contact the proper officials, whether they be sanctioning body officers or track personnel, before embarking upon your journey.

Thanks to: Jon Beekhuis, Michael Cosgrove, Mark Fogarty, Brian Forster, Wayne Gardner, Robert Garrett, George Goad, Terry Griffin, Mike Harris, Martin Haven, Eduardo Leon, Nan and Bill Lornezen, Gerald McVey, Nao Murase, Rita and Anna Sakkis, Ralph Sheheen, Barry Simpson, Judy Stropus, Shin Sugisono, Steve Whitelock, and scores of other journalists, riders, drivers, PR people, and track personnel who have contributed and whose names now escape...

Special thanks to: Richard Dole, whose incredible photography and sound advice helped turn this book into something special.
And to Evita, who made it her job to see that maps were accurate, and who inspired the book's creation; and to Betty Sakkis who inspired the book's completion.

Photos:
Cover by Richard Dole; all photos by Richard Dole except pp. 195, 198 (Eduardo Leon); pp. 176 (Nan Lorenzen); pp. 92, 161, 208,209, 211 (provided by the tracks); pp. 111, 139, 153, 158, 205 (author).

TABLE OF CONTENTS

How To Use This Guide

This guidebook was designed to make your understanding of world motorsport easier. It is essentially broken into four parts.

The first part, from page 14 to page 24, is a discussion of travel, and ticketing and how to make arrangements from home. It will contain information on tours and provide tips on going it alone.

The second part, from page 25 to page 33, is an overview of some of the major motorsports championships run throughout the world. With a focus of the major regulations and specifications, the section is designed to give you an idea about the series ... and an office address and phone should you desire a more detailed analysis...

Finally, the racetrack section, which comprises the largest body of text from page 34 to page 346, is ordered alphabetically. First by country, then, in the case of the United States, by state, then alphabetically by track name.

Obviously, every effort was taken to ensure that the information contained within these pages is accurate. Yet even with the best intentions, there may be changes or additions. We urge you to perform "due diligence" prior to your trip. Good travelling!

Travel is like riding a bicycle, or like explaining spirituality: you can't ever fully explain what it feels like... or, for that matter, how it works. You *have to* experience it. This handbook is meant to give your mind's eye something to start with.

Entire books can be written about places like Le Mans, Indy and Monaco. And all the pictures and all the words in the world can be placed on the pages, but if you don't experience it yourself, you'll never know what it's like.

Every year just before vacation time you ponder the question of what to do and where to go. Do you sit home and relax and watch the tube for two weeks, or do you do something different this time? A trip to somewhere you've never been maybe? The vacation you've always dreamed of possibly? A trip to the Riviera in May, or a ride into the heat of Daytona Beach in February perhaps?

If you're like most of us, it just seems too difficult. There's the tedious planning needed to survive in hostile environments of vacationland; and there's the research. How could you possibly just take off without having studied everything under the sun about your destination? But well-travelled voyagers don't do the self-destructive over-analyzation, they just do it.

Travelling is not difficult. And most people who travel quite a bit realize that nothing is very far from here. When you realize that anywhere on earth — literally any spot on the planet — is less than three days away, things seem much simpler.

Perhaps you've picked this book up because, hopefully, you want to watch some races at venues other than those in your back yard. Nothing wrong with your own back yard, but you begin to know where all the rusty cans are. Football is the same no matter where you watch it, but racing — well, the track is the playing field, and none of them are level.

If you're truly concerned with the prospect of your journey, and bought this book because you think you'll be given perfect descriptions, close the cover, replace the book in its bag, and return it tonight. It won't happen like that. This guide is meant to give you a feeling of what a handful of tracks around the globe are like. Just a feeling; perhaps an idea of what to expect. But like any personal experience, it may be completely different for you.

Taking it one step at a time, the first problem — the seemingly insurmountable one — is getting to the site of the event in the first place. For those who've never travelled, Europe, Canada, Mexico, and Asia seem so far away; and the first journey seems like such a big step. You may be apprehensive. What will it really be like?

If the prospect of seeing a race in another country scares you enough to consider not attending at all, take a tour. Tours are the effortless way to travel. And rather than not attending at all, are certainly worth the extra money you may spend. They'll take the headaches out of travelling to races, and the worries out of the race fan. Getting from Milan to Monza is a breeze on a tour bus; getting there on public transportation can be traumatic for a novice traveller.

Usually tour companies book the entire trip for you, from air to hotels; with shuttles from the airport to the hotel; and from the hotel to the circuit. Race tickets are also included. Tours can be a kind of home base if everything gets confusing.

Tours are also great if you've done some travelling and know that it's only the racing you seek and don't feel like hassling with room-hunting during the hectic days surrounding a championship event. In most cases, you can book hotels, take advantage of transfers to and from the track, and secure tickets through the tour companies without doing the air portion through them. The media often take advantage of this aspect of tour bookings, and occasionally, as a single traveller, you may end up in a room with an experienced racing reporter with whom you can share ideas (which, I suppose, may be one reason not to book a tour...). Tours also often give you insight into the workings of a race that may otherwise have never been exposed.

Grand Prix Tours was one of the pioneers of American racing tours overseas. Barry Simpson and company know their stuff. All tour guides are fanatics about racing. Some even dabble in writing and photojournalism, and can give you insight into esoteric areas of the sport. They've met most of the drivers — or, at least, know their personal habits intimately — and can give you a better understanding of who's doing what, and why.

In addition, GP Tours also has guest speakers at most races. Phil Hill at Monza, for example. JJ Letho in Monaco, and others. Well-seasoned race fans get new insight from the many speakers GP Tours lines up.

Simpson also has some great angles: a boat in the Monaco Harbor during GP week, or a factory tour on the way to a Grand Prix race. These behind the scenes looks at an event can greatly enhance an ordinary race weekend. Grand Prix Tours can give you more information. Located in Southern California, their number is (714) 646-0327.

The British have a real handle on the racing tour industry. There are more than 700 companies in Great Britain that do nothing but racing tours. In addition there are many other European groups — probably the most renowned being the German Racing Tours Reise. Every bit as good, they should probably be ignored because of the language barrier (if you're reading this, you speak English — so take an English speaking tour).

Of the English tour groups, Page and Moy are probably the most substantially founded. Page and Moy can not only book a tour for you, they can also sell you tickets for Grand Prix races. One of the few English speaking sanctuaries of information about Grand Prix racing, Page and Moy are irreplaceable as a ticket source. Grand Prix Tours often buy their tickets from Page and Moy. Page and Moy offer a selection of packages similar to GP Tours, with all 16 Grands Prix, plus Le Mans, Charlotte, Daytona (the 500), a couple of European FIA Rallies, and Monterey's Laguna Seca for the CART race in November. The company has been operating for nearly 30 years. Their number in Leicester is (44) 533 542 000

Chequers Travel is another British tour company specializing in racing tours. Chequers can be booked very simply, and the company has done enough business to have experienced almost every problem that could occur during a race weekend. Many of Chequer's tours are one-day trips. If you'd like to see just a race, and have no time for qualifying and all the other things which make up a full race weekend, Chequers can get you in and out in a day, and usually far cheaper than you could do it yourself. You can hop on a bus in London, sleep while it crosses the channel, and be in, say, Monaco just in time for breakfast and the race. Chequers also does motorcycle racing, which may give it a big edge in the racing tour arena where bikes are largely ignored. Chequer's number in Great Britain, in Dover, is (304) 204 515; FAX (304) 213 415.

If on a whim you decide you'd like to see a Silverstone F1 race or a World Championship Rally — or better yet, a continental Grand Prix — pick up a copy of *Autosport*, *MotorSport*, or *Autocar and Motor* for auto racing. These will all have a plethora of tour ads in the back, and most are well-run organizations.

For bike racers, Randy Warren's TravelCraft is undoubtedly the best. Warren books rooms for Kenny Roberts' teams; if he can do it for Roberts, he can do it for you. TravelCraft is the most comprehensive motorcycle touring company in the world. They can not only take you to any AMA or WERA race in North America, but any FIM event in the world as well. If all you need is a room, call Randy Warren; if you want the full package, from tickets and ground transportation to airline tickets and accommodations, Warren is your man. The toll free number is (800) 541-1223.

Most of the British companies, as well as Grand Prix Tours, and TravelStar, do a handful of American auto races. But for major American races, Joel Cohen's Tickets Up Front (800) 228-TIXS; or in Indianapolis, 317 633-6400) is probably the best. Tickets Up Front can arrange a complete tour package on any race. They're flexible in what they offer as well as in how they structure their tours. Usually they'll tailor a trip around you by providing assistance for either a single fare or a group excursion. Tickets Up Front travels to a couple of European races as well, but their strength is in American events. You'll be able to secure a ticket, book air transportation, and find hotels and transfers to the track with just one call.

So tours get you to the track quickly, and they whisk you away after the day ends with impressive alacrity. But what if you don't want to be whisked? What if you feel like playing in the pits after the race? What if you want to steal the Marlboro banners? And if you just don't feel like being on a schedule? After all, it's your trip.

And let's face it, half the fun of travel is the adventure. One of the disadvantages of tours are the rigid schedules. Tour companies can find terrific rooms. But travellers often don't want to — or can't — take advantage of the shuttle buses. The fans often leave earlier than the buses do in the morning, and return hours later. Most tours won't stay after the headliners' final practice.

Sometimes things happen too damned early. For F1 you're up at 6:00 am on Friday for prequalifying which starts at 8:00 am, and back on the bus at 2:30 following the first official session. Usually at 2:30 you're just getting up — now you're going to be back in your room?

The more seasoned in the press corps book the same hotels over and over and know the short cuts from that one place, but are lost at any other hotel. The daring members of the media — not all of whom are novice reporters — don't bother with the bookings, rather they just show up Wednesday and look for a room on their own. You'd be surprised what kind of results they have with that technique. Most freelancers, who usually don't know at the start of the season what races they will be covering, have to make the trip without secured accommodations. One way or another they'll find rooms.

A room is always available somewhere. The two variables that make it attractive are the cost and the location. It's easy to get a room for Indianapolis on Friday night of the Indy 500 — if you can drive from Cincinnati.

The first rule of race spectating: make sure you have contingency plans. If you go to Monaco on Wednesday and are unable to find a room that suits you in Nice (not everywhere in Nice is nice), make sure you know what mode of transportation you'll use, and how much extra time it will take to get to the circuit as you move farther from the track.

Sophia Antipolis is just on the outskirts of Antibes a few minutes west of Nice, from here it looks like it would be only a minute or two from Antibes — but Sophia is another 35 minutes from the station . If there's no Plan B you'd have spent extra money on taxis and bus fare. In that instance it would have been easier to stay farther down the coast — or even to have paid extra money and stayed closer.

There are always people trying to save a few dollars on cheap hotels who lose more money because they miss their rides, or are isolated from the crowds and miss the happenings surrounding a race. That's not to say the only way to do it is the easy way. At Sears Point, the Napa Valley ambience is a great reason to get lost and stay in a hotel an hour away.

Planning the trip ahead of time will save you some money. But if your vacation is two weeks away, and you suddenly decide you want to see a Grand Prix or an IndyCar race, well, congratulations — you really are destined to be a world traveller.

Spur-of-the-moment travel is sometimes the best kind of travel. The adventure is more intense, and more exciting without the knowledge of what will happen. Believe it or not, you'll be O.K. You won't have to sleep on the beach, and you won't pay thousands of dollars. At worst you will be mildly inconvenienced. At Indianapolis, you'll need to do some driving. At Le Mans, you'll have to camp in the car, with maybe just a salami and some old bread. But you'll survive. And you'll have fun.

You'll never know what it would have been like unless you do it. If you have the money and you have the time, you're wasting both if you don't get up and go. Zandvoort was one of the greatest places on earth to see a Grand Prix — and now it's gone. How many people said, "next year"? There is no next year. Rijeka was on the calendar for the FIM GP for years, and the drive from Dubrovnik up to Rijeka was literally one of the best in the world. Would you go now during the war? It will never be the same, and if you didn't do it, you missed out on a great adventure that can never be repeated.

If planning something overseas is too traumatic, go to a race here. If nothing else, you can fly in Sunday morning, see the race and leave. It's silly, and its expensive, but it's racing. And next time you see Ernie Irvan spin in front of Davey Allison at Atlanta, you'll know what it was like.

You'll be disappointed to learn that it will cost you $1,300 for a round trip ticket into New York. That's only if you pick up the phone and call United for the cheapest flight to JFK. That's a good hunk of change, and most people pay it.

But the same tickets — literally, the exact same seats — can be purchased for half that amount through charter services. But you'll have to do some homework. Airlines usually sell a good portion of their seats to charter services in advance of the season. Airlines need to know their seats are all spoken for before peak travel time comes around.

The charter services, in turn, use the fares as price-leaders, in an attempt to lure new customers into their offices. The fares are legitimate, and the carriers are usually reputable commercial heavyweights. Almost every major international airline does this, as well as a handful of American carriers. Sometimes the airline is a pure charter service. If you feel uncomfortable with taking a jet overseas on something named "Craig's Airlines", keep looking; you'll find an airline you know and trust.

There are, of course, drawbacks to charter tickets. The major one being refundability. Many of these are completely non-refundable. If there is any possibility of you not making the flight, don't purchase this kind of ticket. Occasionally there is only a slight charge, which still makes the tickets attractive — even if the specter of revision hovers overhead.

But when the charters say "no-refund", they mean it. Pan Am's charter tickets were often not even refundable if you were in the hospital. You'd better have the doctor wheel your gurney to the plane...because you're going, or you'll be $700 soft in the billfold.

So you'll need to plan this trip months ahead of time, but will have to make a decision within hours of finding a good ticket. For a trip in May, plan on making the arrangements in November. It may feel like it's too early. It isn't. You'll be surprised to find that fares sell out as soon as they're published.

Once you find a fare you like, you'll have to book it quickly because it won't last long. Low fares don't sell out within days of their introduction, they sell out within hours. Have some alternate schedules in mind. What if you have to leave Monday? Tuesday?

Although you'll need to make a decision quickly, there's a day or so to back out. If you commit to the ticket, the charter companies will put your name on it. But that's all that can be done over the phone. They need real money to secure the ticket. Even if you give them a credit card number, nothing has been signed. You'll have at least a day to think it over before you finally pay for it.

Another problem is that your trip has to be scheduled around the airport where your plane will land. If you want to be in Italy, don't take a flight into Amsterdam. Many times you'll need to change your schedule depending on what airlines can fly to what city on what day cheapest. Charters usually operate only a few days a week. Depending on the airline, it might cost extra to fly on a Monday — or it may be the only day you can fly. When you plan your trip, make sure you are slightly flexible. Leave some room for revision.

To get information on charter services, get a hold of a major newspaper travel section. Look for the little ads with the great fares. If your paper doesn't have what you're looking for, call a bigger paper near a major airport for travel in the U.S. California, Florida, and any East Coast the daily will all have travel sections that will certainly do the job. You'll have to get to a major hub city anyway for an international flight. You might as well book tickets there too.

―――――――――――――――――――――

Undoubtedly, charters are the best way to go. But if you can't commit to a date, or just can't finalize the trip as a whole, there are several great alternatives. First you can book straight through the airlines — or better yet through a travel agent (travel agencies get paid by the airlines. If the airlines don't pay commission to an agent the money stays at the hangars).

Agents usually will smooth things out for you, running interference while you continue with your life. If you want to use an agent, find one you like personally; they all sell the same services, and the differences come with how you interact during the planning stages. Booking at least 30 days in advance will save you money. A $1,300 fare will probably sell for $950 if you can do it at least 30 days prior to departure — sometimes, too, the prices slide downward as you book earlier than 30 days.

There are also companies offering stand-by tickets a few days before departure. These are great deals but you should never plan a trip on a stand-by basis. If on the spur of the moment you decide to go to Europe to see a race, these are great deals. Otherwise forget using about them.

―――――――――――――――――――――

Once you're there you'll need to get around. The standard answer is the train.

Let's start with Europe: rail passes limit you. You won't be able to stray too far from the train stations; you'll be limited to the bags you can carry at one time; for racing, you'll have to find a way to the tracks from the station; and you'll have to suffer through crowded trains during the height of the racing season, since everybody else on earth is also travelling on the continent by train.

If you're travelling alone, use the pass, but if you have at least one other person with you, rent a car. Car travel is the only way to go in Europe. You'll see things that can never be experienced by train.

Most of the tracks in Europe have bus service. But getting on a crowded bus after a race ends is not easy, nor is it any fun. At some places, like Paul Ricard, the buses are almost impossible to figure out. In Portugal, San Marino, or Monza, you're going to need to take a bus since parking will be a problem. But most tracks are easier to access with a car.

Car travel is cheap too. It will often cost you almost the same amount to buy a train pass as it will to drive for those two weeks. If you can get more people to come along, the costs will drop further.

Most important, if you're a motorsports fan you need to drive on the continent of Europe. If all you can afford is a 1.1 liter Fiesta, you'll have a blast on the smaller roads. If you can step up into a nice cruising car for the highways, then all the better. Before each country's track listing is a description of what to expect as a driver overseas.

If you are heading to Japan or Macau, leave the driving gloves at home. In Macau, you don't have the room for a car; and in Japan you won't want one.

Macau's total land amounts to 5.4 square kilometers. Japan may be large enough for several Cadillacs, but you'd find the going a bit rough. First, the Japanese drive on the wrong side of the road; and second, the traffic in Japan can be horrible — it can take several hours to go just a few miles if you attempt it at the wrong time.

Australia is far easier. They speak English there. Train travel is common in Australia — more than in the U.S., but less than Europe or Japan. Flying around Australia is probably easiest, since the place is so big, and travel takes so long. For information on train travel, call 800 232-2121 for ATS Tour Pacific in Glendale, CA.

For Brazil, or Argentina, cars can be rented for transfer to the circuits, and for tourism, but taxis are plentiful and relatively inexpensive. If you are of an adventurous nature, take a bus to the track — but make sure your passport is in the hotel safe and your money is in your shoe...

North American travel, too, is relatively safe compared to South America. Travel to Mexico should be started in the United States. Most Mexican flights -- even to Mexico City -- fly through New York. Canadian travel is easier, yet a commuter flight to Montreal from New York will probably be cheaper and easier than a round trip to Dorval airport.

Charter flights exist for North American travel, but sorting through the newspapers to save a few bucks is probably not worth the effort. Just keep an eye on the papers for low commercial fares. As with overseas travel, the 30 days advance purchase lowers your fare. It's worth planning in advance for that reason, but you won't have to be as flexible. You should be able to pretty much pick your day and your hour of travel. Sunday evening at Indy may be difficult, but other than that you should have no problems making arrangements.

Unfortunately, getting to the tracks is a real problem once you're in the area. The only way to get to a track in the U.S. or Canada — with a few exceptions — is to drive. That means you need to rent a car, or hitchhike. Most tracks have gigantic parking lots where you can camp — or at least spend the night in your car. But the car is a necessity for most of North America.

Canada is the same as The States, with Montreal, Vancouver and Toronto all having bus service. In Mexico, the Circuit Hermanos Rodriguez is right next to the metro, so public transportation is accessible and simple to use. But most Mexican tracks are in the middle of nowhere. There are buses from the cities, but figuring them out is very difficult. Driving to Mexico is easiest. If you're experience enough to travel by train through Mexico, this guide will be grossly deficient anyway.

For the most part, the easiest way to North America's circuits is to fly and rent a car at the airport or take a taxi.

What about travelling by car altogether? Forget the rental, just drive from home to the track. Good idea if you want to see the countryside, but don't try to save money that way. Consider that a flight from California to Daytona will cost some $350 (give or take). Driving the distance will take six to seven days of serious driving (round trip), and will cost about $300 in gas — that's if you have a fuel-efficient car. So you bring a couple buddies and you split the costs. The money you saved will add back up in the extra six days of hotel. Remember, also, that time you spend at the wheel — especially if you don't like spending 18 hours in a car each day — will be wasted. It would have been better to have worked the extra six days, and flown in on Friday night.

That having been said, there is really no other way to see America than by car. Just don't do it to save money.

Booking a hotel is the hardest part of travelling to any race. The closer you wish to stay to the track the more expensive accommodations will become. If there are inexpensive hotels in the area, they are always booked well in advance.

In the U.S. it's probably a good idea to try to book at a large chain of hotels if possible. They're generally kept at a high level of cleanliness, and you can usually count on them being in a nice part of town. And, when travelling to a new city, it's nice to know something will be familiar.

Motel 6 is by far the cheapest chain in the country. You can call and order a complete listing of all the Motel 6s across the country. The rooms can be booked over the phone with a credit card. All Star Inns is also good. Best Western has more locations than any other chain, probably followed by the Quality/Clarion/Comfort/Sleep Inns. Most chains are happy to help you find a room near your destination. Since most calls are toll-free, go down the list of numbers and check on prices, availability and location relative to the racetrack of your choice.

All Seasons Inns (800) 873-INNS
All Star Inns (805) 687-6364
Best Western (800) 528-1234
Carriage Inn (800) 854-2608
Circle 8 Inn (800) 345-9995
Clarion (800) 221-2222
Comfort Inn (800) 221-2222
Days Inn (800) 325-2525
Doubletree Hotels (800) 528-0444
Econolodge (800) 826-1964
Hampton Inn (800) 426-7866
Hilton (800) HILTONS
Holiday Inn (800) HOLIDAY
Howard Johnson (800) 654-2000
Hyatt (800) 233-1234
La Quinta Inns (800) 531-5900
Marriott (800) 228-9290
Motel 6 (505) 891-6161
Nendels/ Valu Inn (800) 547-0106
Quality Inn (800) 221-2222
Radisson Plaza Hotels (800) 333-3333
Ramada (800) 228-2828
Red Roof Inns (800) 843-7663
Rodeway Inn (800) 228-2000
Sheraton (800) 325-3535
Sleep Inn (800) 221-2222
Super 8 Motels (800) 843-1991
Travelodge (800) 255-3050
Vagabond Inn (800) 522-1555

For Europe there are also several chains. But your best bet is with the smaller unattached hotels and pensiones. France has the largest chains, with Campanile, Ibis, Urbis, and Novotel being the most prolific. All these are relatively inexpensive.

The cheapest motels are the appropriately named Formule 1 Inns -- the European version of a Motel 6 (owned by the Motel 6 chain here in The States). They will be sparsely furnished and fairly bland, but cheap.

There are, of course, Sheratons, Hyatts, Marriotts and other high-line accommodations. These are terrific hotels, but if you're booking a room at one of these because you're afraid of not getting a bed, don't. There are other ways.

Perhaps you'll have trouble in Italy with the two Grands Prix there, but that's likely to be the only place where rooms will be difficult to find upon your arrival. But even there, you'll be able to find something if you get to town by Thursday. All other European Grands Prix — Germany, Hungary, Monaco, Belgium, Portugal and Spain — are easy areas to find rooms. You won't be right in the thick of things, but you'll see the races.

If you want to secure something early by yourself, try one of these chains. All speak some English so it won't be a problem calling, and provided you don't make idle chit-chat, the ones without toll-free numbers will cost you just a small bit of change if you call at the right time. If you're on a real budget, you can stay in a Youth Hostel, although many of them are not safe places to leave valuables while you're off watching the racing. In addition, with a travelling partner, you should be able to get a pensione cheaper.

Best Western (800) 528-2323 (worldwide)
BW International (800) 528-1234 (GB)
Campanile (33) 64 62 46 46 (FR, BEL, NL, GER, SW)
CIGA (800) 221-2340 (GB and Europe)
Concourse (800) 888-4747(FR)
Embassy Hotels (800) 448-8355 (GB)
FiMotel 33 42 436465 (FR)
Formule 1
Hidden Hotels (800) 223-1900 (GB)
Hilton (800) 268-9275 (worldwide)
Holiday Inn (800) HOLIDAY (worldwide)
Intercontinental (800) 225-5843 (GB and Europe)
Josephine Barr, Selected Representative (800) 323-5463 (GB)
Kempenski/Preferred Hotels (800) 223-6800 (GB and Europe)
Leading Hotels of the World (800) 223-6800 (GB and Europe)
Marriott (800) 831-1000 (worldwide)
Melia Hotels (34) 71 234 342 (SP)
Norfolk Capital Hotels (800)641-0300 (GB)
Novotel (also for Ibis/ Urbis) (33)(800) 221-4542 (Continental Europe)
Pullman (800) 223-9862 (GB and Europe)
Ramada (800) 228-9898 (worldwide)
Resinter (800) 221-4542 (GB and Europe)
Sol Hotels (800)336-3542 (SP)
Spain International (800) 336-3542 (SP)
Star Crown Hotels (800) 284-1615 (GB)
Swallow Hotels (800) 444-8355 (GB)
Trusthouse Forte (800) 225-5843 (GB and Europe)
Utell (800) 44 UTELL (GB and Europe)

Tickets for most of the European races can be purchased right at the races. You'll want to be there by Friday morning if possible, but you can usually get tickets as late as Saturday morning (looking for reserved seats as late as Sunday is a gamble). Certainly, looking for seats that close to race day that overlook the pits is wasted energy.

Although tickets are usually easy to find for most European Grands Prix, the exceptions to that rule will be at San Marino and Monaco. These are two races where you'll want to book tickets in advance. You should still be able to get a general admission ticket to Imola as late as Saturday, but at Monaco you'll have to buy the Pelouses Rocher, which are areas of a cliff overlooking Rascasse Corner. Space is limited there and will sell out by Sunday morning, leaving you only a couple of alternatives: you either turn around and go home, or you step up to the plate and buy a private cafe seat. The Rascasse Cafe, Cafe de Paris, or any of the other trackside restaurants will gladly sell you one for $600 or so (they're right next to the track).

For all European races you can purchase tickets either through the track, the Sporting Authority of the appropriate country, or the promoter's office. Or, make things simpler for yourself, and call Page and Moy.

Page and Moy, who as you now know also do tours, will sell you a ticket at face value plus £10 Pounds. They can take a credit card or a postal order, and are extremely reliable. The only problem is getting the tickets. They've had problems with ticketing through the mail, precluding any postal sales unless it's in the UK. You'll either have to pick up the tickets at the track, or go to the Page and Moy's office. Page and Moy's address is 136-138 London Rd, Leicester LE2 1EN, GB, or call (011 44) 5 33 55 25 21.

Unfortunately, Page and Moy will not be able to help you with tickets to Italian races. Unless you book a tour through them, Page and Moy have no tickets for sale at Imola or Monza. Just Tickets sells GP tickets and will likely help when Page and Moy cannot. Write Lincoln Oaks Ranelagh Grove, Broadstairs, Kent, CT10 2TE, or call (011 44) 843 65 160; also try the Italian tour company Bononia Viaggi for tickets to the Italian races: located at Galleria del Toro 3, I-40121, Bologna, Italy, or call (011 39) 51 26 9075.

As a last resort, try the Dutch VVV, which can also provide tickets (the Dutch speak perfect English, and at the VVVs are very helpful), at Alie VVV Bespreek Buros, en telefonisch by VVV Rokin 9-15, Postbus 3696, NL 1001-AL Amsterdam, or call (011 31) 20 204 111.

There are, however, lots of extra tickets for Imola and Monza in existence, and which may be for sale by other tour companies. Once the exact number of people attending a given tour is nailed down, the tour companies can sell you the extra tickets — most of which are better than average. Many magazines and newspapers have ads offering good tickets for decent prices. Buy yourself an *Autosport* and start there.

Tickets for U.S. races are unequivocally cheaper than those in Europe. Unfortunately, they are often more difficult to get.

The Indy 500 sells out in June for the race in May of the following year. Bristol, Daytona, and Talladega are very difficult to find tickets for. There are always a few unreserved tickets put on sale on the day of the race, but the viewing is not terrific. You'll probably see the race, but not as it should be seen.

Call the tracks first. If they're sold-out, ask for suggestions. Most of the track personnel are helpful, and may steer you to a broker in the area. Newspapers are the probably the best bets. If you call the local paper and ask for a copy of the Sunday edition, it will likely have tickets for sale in the classified section.

But probably the best place to find tickets for major America races is Joel Cohen's Tickets Up Front (800) 228-TIXS; or in Indianapolis, 317 633-6400). Tickets Up Front has tickets to most of the major NASCAR events. They may be expensive compared to what the face value of the ticket is, but the tickets are not overpriced. He has tickets to the popular races too: Daytona 500; Talladega; and the Indy 500. For Indy tickets range from $50-$500, and are usually available up to the day of the race. Although the prices will stay the same, the better tickets will be gone as Memorial Day closes in. The same is true with the other popular races: tickets will likely exist as raceday approaches, but the seats will not be the best in the house.

Tickets Up Front is also a tour agency and can help you with either a single trip or a group excursion to any major race in the U.S.. Although the organization runs international tours as well, they are primarily an American event organization.

━━━━━━━━━━━━━━━

Making arrangements from the U.K. is not as difficult or as expensive as it's reputed to be. Telephoning overseas is much cheaper than it once was. Don't worry about calling to check up on your reservations — or even to book a room yourself. If you call at the right times, the bill will be relatively inexpensive.

What follows is a list of the numbers you'll need to call overseas from here, with directions for direct dialling:

Australia: 010+61+ city code (Adelaide 8, Brisbane 7, Melbourne 3, Sydney 2) + number.

Austria: 010+43+ city code (Graz 316, Vienna 1 or 222) + number.

Belgium:: 010+32+ city code (Antwerp 3, Brussels 2, Liege 41) + number; best times to call — 6PM to 7AM U.S. time.

Brazil: 010+55+ city code (Rio de Janeiro 21, Sao Paulo 11) + number; best times to call — 12 Midnight to 8AM U.S. time.

Canada: 010+area code+number; same rules as U.S..

Czechoslovakia: 010+42+ city code (Bratislava 7, Brno 5, Prague 2) + number; best times to call — 6PM to 7AM U.S. time.

Denmark: 010+45+ city code (Copenhagen 1 or 2, Odense 7) + number; — best times to call — 6PM to 7AM U.S. time.

France: 010+33+ city code (Lyon 7, Marseille 91, Nice 93, Paris 1) + number; best times to call — 6PM to 7AM U.S. time.

Finland: 010+358+ city code (Helsinki 0, Turku-Abu 21) + number; best times to call — 6PM to 7AM U.S. time.

Germany: 010+49+ city code (Berlin 30, Bonn 228, Frankfurt 69, Munich 89) + number..
Hungary: 010+36+ city code (Budapest 1) + number.

Japan: 010+81+ city code (Kyoto 75, Osaka 6, Tokyo 33, Yokohama 45) + number.

Macau: 010+853+ number.

Malaysia: 010+ 60+ city code (Johor 7, Shah Alam 3) + number.

Mexico: 010+52+ city code (Guadalajara 36, Hermosillo 621, Jalapa, 281, Leon, 471, Mexico D.F., 5, Monterrey 83, Tampico 121, Torreon 17, Veracruz 29) + number.

Monaco: 010+33+93+number; best times to call — 6PM to 7AM U.S. time.

Italy: 010+39+ city code (Florence 55, Milan 2, Roma 6) + number.

The Netherlands: 010+31+ city code (Amsterdam 20, Rotterdam 10, The Hague 70) + number.

New Zealand: 010+ 64 + city code (Palmerston North 63) = number.

Portugal: 010+351+ city code (Lisbon 1) + number.

Spain: 010+34+ city code (Barcelona 3, Madrid 1, Seville 54) + number.

South Africa: 010+27+ city code (Cape Town 21, Johannesburg 11); + number.

Sweden: 010+46+ city code (Goteborg 31, Stockholm 8) + number.

United States: 010+1+area code+number.

Racing is difficult to understand, even for racers. Yet we wonder with amazement why newspapers don't cover racing more often; or, why, when the papers do cover racing, the accidents and injuries are most prominently featured.

Sports editors are specialists in a field; they are experts in sports. All they do is think about sports. It's not enough that they like sports, they must be able to see through the hoopla around a sporting event and make sense of why it happens.

But go figure racing. There are hundreds of sanctioning bodies, and thousands of series. Motorsports reporting is a full time job, and most papers don't have money to hire a full time motorsports reporter, or time of their own to sort through the garbage races to find a gem. Too many sports editors have been burned by track promoters who've told them that " *this* is the event".

When a local baseball team plays three nights a week, and average attendance is 30,000 a game, there is an obvious need for good coverage. When racing comes to town occasionally and the good shows sometimes only bring in 10,000, how can you blame the papers for not taking the sport seriously?

If you follow racing, you know how difficult it is to keep up with your favorite series. Just following one series is an arduous chore, imagine trying to keep track of several on a daily basis. Newspapers in Charlotte, NC can afford to have several motorsports writers on staff; they have the interest and they have the tracks. In California, the tracks exist, but the interest is, well, let's just say lacking.

Several magazines specialize, and do an admirable job of informing the public. But educated motorsports fans are not as one-sided as most magazines would like to believe. Most NASCAR fans know something about IMSA; most Indy Car fans can tell you who's leading the Formula One Driver's Championships at any give point in the season; Drag racers know that Steve Kinser is back and winning in World Of Outlaws; and AMA fans keep track of just about everything under the sun.

But the average fan has a hell of a time trying to determine the difference between F1 and Indy, or IMSA and SCCA. The unfortunate part of the confusion is that without press the interest won't develop, but without interest there is no media coverage.

Although a plethora of racing series exist in this country, only a few are major players. Not that the other shows are poor. On the contrary, If you watch racing you already know that some of the best racing in the country comes from no-name racers who're competing in insignificant series and contending inconsequential races. But for the sake of argument, we need to put the major series in their rightful places in the sun.

If this is new to you, stay with it a minute. Let's see if we can't straighten things out. What follows is a brief explanation of the sanctioning bodies, the major series, the events of the previous season and an idea of what's to come:

FIA

Federation International du Sport Automobile
8 Place de la Concorde
75008 Paris, France.
PH: 42 65 99 51
FAX: 47 42 87 31

The Federation International du Sport Automobile (FISA) runs Formula One Grand Prix racing, under the supervision of the international governing body, the Federation Internationale l' Automobile (FIA). For every country except the U.S. the FIA is law. The FIA can pull sanctioning and eliminate the country's most popular races if the organizers do not abide by FIA decisions regarding the running of its events. FIA racing is almost nonexistent in the U.S.. The FIA, consequently, has no say in NASCAR or CART, the U.S.'s two most successful series.

FIA sanctions all national Formula 3 and F3000. It also sanctions The

Sportscar World Championship, World Rallying, European Touring Car Championships and hundreds of other international and national series.

In the grand scheme of things the F1 Grand Prix World Championship is the focus of FISA's work. The term "Grand Prix" has been bastardized recently to mean just about everything under the sun. The literal meaning is Grand Prize, and it is, by the truest definition in motorsports, the top formula — or the top set of rules governing a series.

FORMULA ONE GRAND PRIX

Grand Prix cars cannot be purchased. They are created by the "Constructors", and the team that puts cars into the championship points (ten for a win, six for second, four for third, three for fourth, two for fifth and a lone point for sixth spot finish) most often walks away with the Constructor's Championship (and a handy piece of pocket change). The drivers contend a Driver's Championship. The best kept secret in motorsports concerns the F1 purses, and drivers are generally paid a salary, with no claim to prize money.

F1 cars are open-wheeled (no fenders), naturally aspirated (no turbos or superchargers), and are limited to 3.5 liters displacement. The maximum engine size is 12 cylinders, which is becoming the norm these days. They are flat-bottomed, which doesn't allow for aerodynamic aids beneath the car bodies. Wing size, wheel size, minimum weights, and several other limits are imposed by FISA. Horsepower ratings are between 600-750 for cars currently competing. The World Championship is held this year in 16 countries around the world.

Grand Prix weekends — with the exception of the Grand Prix of Monte Carlo (which does not have Grand Prix cars on-course Friday) — are all identical: pre-qualification, when it exists, kicks off the weekend's activities at 8:00 AM Friday morning, and the first practice is from 10:00 AM to 11:30 AM and first timed session is from 1:00-2:00 PM; Saturday's practice session is from 10:00-11:30 and the final qualification is from 1:00-2:00; Sunday's final warm-up begins at 10:00 AM, ending a half-an-hour later, and the race gets a green light at 2:30 PM.

CART INDYCARS
IndyCar
Championship Auto Racing Teams, Inc.
489 Fifth Ave.,
New York, NY 10017
(212) 370-4242
(212) 490-0576

Championship Auto Racing Teams, CART, racing was created in 1978 by Roger Penske and Pat Patrick among others as an American alternative to Formula One, and an enhancement of the USAC (United States Auto Club) championship. Besides Indianapolis, the USAC season was really of little consequence.

The series was determined to run a good portion of its races on road tracks, as opposed to ovals. Eventually, USAC lost control of Indy Cars — except for the Indy 500 which is still sanctioned by USAC.

Indy Cars can and usually are purchased. Engines and chassis may be bought as components, and assembled as the season wears on, but rarely does an Indycar team make its own chassis or engines. Indy Cars, like their F1 counterparts, are open-wheeled. They can and do use turbo-chargers and are limited in terms of turbo boost. As with any open-wheeled cars, there is a strict formula to which the cars need to adhere — weight, width, wheel size, height are all tightly controlled. The cars develop between 700-800 horsepower.

The series is based on a Driver's Championship, and is fought during a 16 race season from April to October. There are two Canadian races, and one in Australia. Weekends are broken up into one practice and one qualifying session per day Friday and Saturday, with the final practice of the weekend occurring Saturday afternoon. Race starts vary on any given Sunday, with the earliest green flag waved at 11:00 AM in Indianapolis, and the latest at 3:00 in Wisconsin.

NASCAR WINSTON CUP

NASCAR
P.O. Box K
1801 Speedway Blvd.
Daytona Beach, FL   32015
(904)   253-0611
FAX: (904) 254-6795

Winston Cup is not Grand National, and NASCAR doesn't always mean Winston Cup. NASCAR is the National Association of Stock Car Auto Racing, and it sanctions hundreds of series all over the country. The premier series is the Winston Cup Championship. The series was once called the Grand National series. The Grand National exists, but is a less prestigious series based on older model cars — although it is often run at the same venues and on the same weekends as Winston Cup.

NASCAR is run by Bill France and family, and is based on close competition above all else. The rules are devised so for a limited amount of money a talented driver can enter a fairly simple race car and win.

Championship points are complicated, and the winner can actually tie the second place man at any given race. But usually the championship is close, and the series champion is usually decided at the final race of the year.

The racing is done in "stock cars", or cars based around American street sedans stock bodies. Except for small rear wings, aerodynamic bodywork is prohibited. The rules are designed to keep competition costs down, so components that are fairly standard on street cars are still not allowed in Winston Cup racing (like, for example, rack and pinion steering). The average WC car costs about $70,000, which is extremely economical considering F1 cars cost as much as $20-million dollars. There are no turbo chargers, tires are purposely kept on the small side, and even air jacks are prohibited.

The series is based on a Drivers Championship, and it is run on 29 weekends of the year, with The Winston, in Charlotte, being a non-championship 30th event.

NASCAR Racing — with the exceptions of the Pepsi 400 at Daytona (a Saturday event), and the Bristol night race — begins Thursday with open practice. The first 25 cars of the grid are set with a single car qualification session Friday, allowing each driver a shot at the racetrack with no other drivers around. Saturday, the remainder of the field qualifies for the remaining spots of the grid. Racing generally takes place Sunday between 1:00 and 3:00.

INTERNATIONAL MOTOR SPORTS ASSOCIATION   GT

International Motor Sports Association
P.O. Box 10709
Tampa, FL   33679-0709
3502 Henderson Blvd.
Tampa, 33069
PH: (813) 877-4672
FAX: (813) 867-4604

The International Motor Sports Association is essentially an American version of the FIA Sportscar World Championship. This one is also in jeopardy like its prestigious European sister. The series is based on sports and sedan racing, with the Grand Touring Prototypes, or GTPs, being the premier class of the series championship.

There are five main categories of IMSA GT (also called Camel GT from apt sponsorship): GTP and Camel Lights (smaller engined GTP cars), which are essentially prototype sports cars (meaning they are fullbodied — as opposed to open-wheeled — and should have the capability of seating two people — although the second person would likely be a contortionist midget); and three classes for stock based sedans which are broken into categories based on engine sizes — GTU cars are limited to engines of 3.0 liter capacity or less and are non-turbocharged. The GTSs can use turbo power or larger normally aspirated engines. And the GTOs are American-built V8s.

GTPs and Lights cars are loosely based around the FIA Group C and C2 rules, and the series recently has, as in Europe, become a showcase for manufacturers like Jaguar, Nissan, Toyota, Chevrolet, and Porsche. The IMSA championship (of which there are actually two in each category — Driver's and Manufacturer's — for a total of ten) is contended over a 12 race season (shortened from 16 last year).

IMSA GTP racing usually starts Friday, with qualifying done Saturday. The morning session Saturday is done as a group, but the fastest eight drivers are locked into the first spots of the grid in an afternoon session of single-car two-lap runs. With the exception of Daytona and Sebring, the racing generally begins at 1:30 Sunday.

SPORTS CAR CAR CLUB OF AMERICA

Sports Car Club of America
9033 East Easter Place
Englewood, CO   80122
(303) 694-7223
FAX: (303) 684-7391

The Sports Car Club of America is America's largest club racing organization, and is both an amateur route into road racing, and a stand-alone pro racing organization.

The SCCA has many different types of racing, from Solo II autocrossing (done in street cars and in parking lots) to the Trans-Am, the premier street-sedan based road racing series.

Trans-Am is contested in street-based sedans, with rules discouraging the use of turbos. Engines are usually V6s and V8s and are usually American based cars such as Camaros, Mustangs, and Olds Cutlasses. The championships (Driver's and

Manufacturer's) are contended over the course of a 16 race season, two of which are held on Canadian soil.

Trans-Am may be the headlining show, but the SCCA prides itself as being a grassroots organization for regular folks who want to go road racing. This is one of the most helpful clubs in the United States, and most of the officials will take time out to educate the less knowledgeable. The club racing, which often attracts some serious teams, are held on both regional and national levels.

When Trans-Am runs as the headlining series of a weekend, SCCA racing is a three-day affair. Practice is throughout the day Friday; Saturday, the "Fast Five" qualifying session is held in the morning (where the fastest five cars are locked in for Sunday's grid), and the remaining spots are up for grabs in the final session Saturday afternoon. Racing generally occurs Sunday at 2:00 PM. When Trans-Am is a support to Indy Cars, the series generally qualifies with Fast Five Friday afternoon, and runs final qualifying and the race Sunday morning and afternoon respectively.

WORLD OF OUTLAWS

World of Outlaws
624 Krona Drive, Suite 115
Plano, TX   75074
(214)   424-2202

World of Outlaws sprint car racing is the premier sprint car association in the U.S.. World of Outlaws sprint cars are openwheeled cars that used to run only on dirt ovals. When some sprint cars ran paved ovals, the WoO was contested only on dirt tracks. That is until 1991. The first asphalt racing in series history went off very well at Kansas' Lakeside Speedway, with Sammy Swindell winning the first on the hard stuff. For 1992 several more visits to pavement are planned. In addition, an indoor stadium race is planned for '92, at the Florida Sun Coast Dome in Tampa.

The cars are winged, or aerodynamically held to the track by means of a spoiler mounted on the top of the car. The wing is deemed a safer form of racing, since in the event of an accident rollovers are not as violent — as the wings act to slow the revolution of a rolling car.

Called outlaws because they appear at local tracks as the biggest show of the year — with the biggest purses — and compete against the locals. The locals, who have a legitimate shot at winning, are usually not the pride of the field. On a track they usually know intimately, they generally finish well down in the pack; Outlaw drivers collect the big purses, pack up, and leave for the next show.

The series is generally contended over the course of a 90 event season, and determines a series champion. Usually, the Outlaw show is a one-night-only show. There are several heats, usually getting underway at 7:00 PM, with the Main starting at about 9:30 PM. For multiple night shows the racing is usually broken up into a series of heats, with mains each night, and a larger purse for the final evening of racing.

UNITED STATES AUTO CLUB

4910 West 16th St.
Speedway, IN   46224-0001
PH: (317)   247-5151

FAX: (317) 247-0123

United States Auto Club racing is not as prestigious as it once was without the Indycar series, but it is still a grassroots racing association, and it is beginning to make inroads into serious pro racing again.

USAC still sanctions the Indianapolis 500, which forms the Gold Crown Championship — the lone event in the Championship. The meat and potatoes for USAC, however, is the Silver Crown sprint car series, which is supplemented by National Championship Midget Championships, Western States Midget Championship, and TQ Midget Championships. The Silver Crown is a nine race series competed at venues around the U.S. (solely on ovals), determining a series champion.

USAC Silver Crown racing is generally run on one-mile tracks, usually during daylight hours. There is one qualifying session where 50-60 cars take a shot at being one of the fastest 20. Those who don't make the top 20 have a last chance race, with the top ten finishers advancing to the feature. The feature race usually begins at 2:30, and is a 100 mile event. For Sprinters and Midgets, the races are usually held at night on Friday or Saturday. Qualifying determines the order of heat races, and the fastest four in each heat race advance to the main, which usually beings at 8:00 PM.

USAC generally releases its schedule later than most of the other sanctioning bodies, and as spring rolls around the new schedule has often yet to be published. For those who require it, the USAC office will be happy to send you a schedule, or will at least tell you where you can pick one up.

NHRA DRAG RACING

National Hot Rod Association
2035 Financial Way
Glendora, CA 91740-4602
PH: (818) 914-4761
FAX: (818) 963-5360

Some 40 years ago the National Hot Rod Association took drag racing off the streets and put it on legitimate racetracks, ultimately breaking its long standing tradition of outlaw status. The NHRA still has a tight rein over how events are run, actually doing almost all of the work at any given racetrack from security to ticketing.

There are three pro classes that make up an NHRA National event; Top Fuel Dragsters; Funny Cars; and Pro Stock. The quarter-mile strip races are won on elapsed time, or the time from the flash of the starting light to the finish line timer. Top speed, and fastest finished doesn't mean anything.

The technology of any of the three classes are usually tied closely to street-going cars — pushed to absolute limits. The engines are still pushrod V8s, but the fine tuning is so close to the limit that an incorrect evaluation of the humidity in the air will lose a competitor the event and can blow up a costly engine.

Funny Cars and TFD are powered by supercharged nitro-methane big block V8 engines with horsepower ratings of nearly 4,000. The Funny cars are

30

front-engined, short-wheelbased car with bodies loosely based on stock cars; dragsters are long wheelbased, rear engined purpose built cars using the same engines as those found in the Top Fuel Dragsters; Pro Stock are big block V8s that are run without nitro-methane. The championship is held over a 20 race season, and decides a series champion in each of the three categories.

Friday and Saturday of any given NHRA race weekend is composed of sportsman drag racing plus the three classes of Pro racing running two qualification passes per day, totalling four runs. The racing slots 16 total finalists into Sunday's program. Sunday's Eliminator divides the field from 16 to eight, to four, to two and, finally, produces an event winner in each class, usually by 6:30 Sunday evening.

FIM GRAND PRIX WORLD CHAMPIONSHIP MOTORCYCLE RACING

Federation Internationale Motorcycliste
Chemin William-Barbey, 9
CH- 1292 Chambesy, Switzerland
PH: (011 41) 22 758 1960
FAX: (011 41) 22 758 2180

The FIM is essentially the motorcycling counterpart of the FIA, although the two are not related. The FIM runs several championships, but the premier series in the Grand Prix World Championship for 500cc motorcycles.

The Grand Prix World Championship is held with 500cc bikes, 250cc machines, 125s, and a Sidecar Championship. There was an 80cc championship but it was eliminated in 1990. The World Championship is contested in a 12 to 16 round championship, in 11 different countries for a World Champion Rider. All championship bikes are built by commercial manufacturers, and the factories are heavily involved in the racing. Americans have dominated the competition for the past few seasons. In 14 years Americans have won 11 World Championships.

The FIM also runs a Superbike Championship (essentially a division run on machinery closely related to street production bikes), which is run separately from the GP Championship, and is 15 rounds of racing contested in 15 separate countries.

FIM riders occasionally have a free practice day Thursday, although that wasn't the case several years ago. Practice for each group officially begins Friday, with a provisional grid being set Friday afternoon for each class of bikes. The final grid is set Saturday afternoon, with five bikes per row. Racing takes place Sunday, with the 125cc bikes out first before noon; the 250s run next, also usually before or right at noon; the 500cc class generally follows the 250 bikes at about 2:00; and Sidecars end the day at between 3:30-4:00 PM. Races are usually short — about 45-55 minutes.

AMERICAN MOTORCYCLIST ASSOCIATION

American Motorcyclist Association
33 Collegeview
P.O. Box 6114
Westerville, OH 43081-6114
PH: (614) 891-2425

The AMA sanctions many quality series, and produces some of the best racers in the world. Unfortunately the riders don't seem to stay in the AMA long, choosing to head instead to Europe and a ride in the FIM championships on like machinery.

AMA championships can be broken into three categories: oval dirt track racing; road racing; and motocross. The AMA Grand National has been the AMA's staple for most of its 44 year history, with a 17-race championship run on dirt ovals (a half-mile or longer).

Road Racing Championships are mainly concerned with Superbike racing (based on street motorcycles) and 250cc Grand Prix Machinery — the Road Racing Championship is based on nine national races producing a series champion.

500cc and 250cc National Championship Motocross Series are contested at both indoor and outdoor motocross dirt tracks (that are off-road style terrain). Indoor champions are called AMA Supercross races, and a season consists of 14 events to produce a series champion; the outdoor motocross racing is run over the course of seven events to produce series champions.

WERA MOTORCYCLE RACING

Western Eastern Roadracers' Association
P.O. Box 21960
Hilton Head Is., SC   29926
(803) 681-WERA

The Western Eastern Roadracer's Association took a big jump in 1990 with the Formula USA series, and looked poised to knock the AMA off the top of American bike racing. Although WERA has been sanctioning events for 18 years, most have been forgettable seasons. But in 1990 WERA's Formula USA found television coverage for all 10 races on its calendar, and that alone was enough to lure Kenny Roberts away from the AMA to WERA in 1991. The run-what-you-brung series is contested around any size or configured bike that can be designed, but the premium is usually on handling and stopping.

Racetracks

AUSTRALIA

Australia is a favorite of the well-travelled and a popular first choice for the novice. There's just something about an island (in reality, a continent) populated by people who have a reputation for friendliness, who produce some of the best beer in the world, and who also speak English that seems to tempt travellers. From cities like Sydney to green forests around the Snowy River, and from tropical jungles to the desolate Ayers Rock flatlands, Australia holds fascination for travellers. For race fans, the continent is becoming one of the best places to watch a race.

With Jack Brabham and Alan Jones (and now Gary and David Brabham), the country has heroes in Grand Prix racing. But recently other areas of motorsports have inspired a bigger interest in Australian racing. Geoff Brabham won the IMSA GTP Championship three years in a row; Dick Johnson, the National Championship winning sedan driver, has moved to NASCAR and American stock car racing; and three Grand Prix Motorcyclists are putting Australia on the map in motorcycling — most notably, Wayne Gardner, Australia's first World Champion Grand Prix rider (1987 500cc GP World Championship), has created an unquenchable thirst for GP bike racing.

For both bikes and cars, Australian events are probably the finest on each calendar. And the enthusiasm that surrounds each race is astounding. The boom in racing is obvious from the proliferation of hot bikes and cars on Australian roads — most notably, with American-style stock car modifications. Australians, remember, drive the big sedans on the left side of the road.

Australia isn't like Asia, where everything is intimately placed along the roadside so you're compelled to calculate the distance between the wrong side of your car and the immovable objects it so narrowly misses. Australia has lots of room.

The cities have their confining qualities, of course, but are far more modern, and generally are built for real cars, and real driving. Once you get away from the big cities, driving in Australia is as easy as driving across Texas — although with fewer armadillos.

Armadillos may be scarce, but kangaroos, cattle, and horses are not. Given the choice, most people would rather hit an armadillo. Kangaroo crossing signs abound. At first they may seem cute, but you'll understand the significance of the signs soon enough.

Most rental car companies suggest using extreme caution when driving in the Australian countryside at night. They use language stronger than just suggestion if you mention the Outback. It is very dangerous to drive the Outback at night, and if you state your intent to do that, the rental people will argue adamantly with you, compelling you to reconsider. Take their advice.

You don't need an International Driver's Licence to operate a car in Australia as long as you have a valid drivers licence. Speeds are held to 110KPH and 60KPH in the cities.

Tourist Information: **Australian Tourist Bureau**, (213) 552-1988.
Sporting Authorities: **Confederation of Australian Motor Sport**, 382 Burke Rd., Camberwell, Victoria, 3124, Australia. PH: (61) 3 889 3746; FAX: (61) 3 809 1862; **Motorcycling Australia**, 1/10 Hoddle Street, P.O. Box 142, Abbotsford, Victoria 3067. PH: (61 3) 416 3199; FAX: (61 3) 416 2743.

Adelaide Grand Prix

c/o Grand Prix Board
300 Rundle St.,
Adelaide. 5000
South Australia

PH: (61) 8 223 1111
FAX: (61) 8 232 4144

Location: Southern coastal Australia, in Adelaide, on Highway 1.

Circuit: 2.349 mile road course; 16 turns.

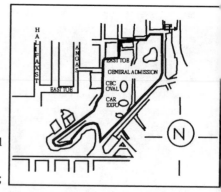

Major races: FIA Formula One Grand Prix World Championship.

Crews look forward to the Australian Grand Prix at Adelaide — the last race of the season — during the entire competition year. In general, Australians try to make the GP corps feel at home, and the Adelaide crowds do whatever they can to promote the city, the race and the country. The place becomes one big party while the GP is in town, with Fosters Beer becoming the king of the city.

Although the Australian Grand Prix has been academic for the past several years with the championship having been decided in Japan, it was, again in '92, a controversial final race. For two years the streets for Sunday's race have been completely flooded. In 1990 it was enough to have had Alain Prost forfeit his spot on the grid, citing very hazardous spots of deep standing water. In 1991 (Prost had been fired by Ferrari and so again did not participate in the Australian GP, which was controversy enough), there was talk of boycotts due to the dangerous conditions caused by the deluge, but the race was started as planned and stopped at half distance. In 1992, Mansell and Senna had a coming together in their last race together, putting each other out on the 14th lap.

The race is run through the streets of downtown Adelaide, comprising several major thoroughfares and a few Rymill Park roads (around which the circuit runs). Run on Wakefield Road, East Terrace, Rundle Road, and Dequetville Terrace, the race is contested right through downtown Adelaide.

The Casino is just a half mile from the circuit. Once used as the central train station for the South Australian city, the casino/train station has been the hub of Adelaide's night life for more than 150 years.

The trains no longer run, but the crowds in and around the place still make it seem that way. If you arrive early, you'll have no problem getting into the casino, but if you get there fashionably late, be prepared for a serious wait. The doors are monitored and only a certain number of players are allowed in at any one time. It's not uncommon for gamblers to wait outside five hours or more to lose some money. But beware: there's a dress code.

Although several other distractions endure to keep you occupied throughout the duration of your stay, you're here for the GP. There are several great places to watch the racing at Adelaide. If you feel like stepping up for good seats, it's going to cost you —$350 Australian. The best places are in the chicane at the end of the start/finish straight, or above the pits at the start.

There's a good deal of general admission here, but if you want to see racing all three days, use the seats. The "bronze" bleachers, on the Brabham Straight on Adelaide's backside, give you a decent view (try for the stands closest to the right-hander coming off the Alan Jones Straight). The "silver" seats are good, but for a few dollars more you can have the "gold". This is a popular race — for both

Australians and foreign travellers — so buy tickets ahead of time if you want good ones.

Adelaide Grand Prix organizers have a system where many Australians offer their homes for temporary use as a bed-and-breakfast for the race. So far, only about 2,000 people per year have utilized this system, although rooms exist for far more.

The houses are inspected by Grand Prix officials and are listed on an improvised star rating according to their size and proximity to the circuit. "Grade A" is the best, featuring large and generally conveniently located houses, with large bedrooms, and a smaller "sitting" room usually available as well. "Grade B" offers a bit less privacy, but is still usually in a larger home, with good sized rooms; "Grade C" is an average size Australian residence on a typical urban block, with shared bathroom.

There are also, of course, many hotels in the area, and if the Grand Prix Association is unable to give you any help (which is unlikely, since they're structured to help with accommodations), you can call the B & B Scheme. Or contact the Australian Grand Prix Office, Box 1111 P.O., Norwood, SA 5067, PH. (008) 61 232 4112 or fax to (008) 232 0442.

Tickets are available through the standard international ticketing outlets, but Adelaide, more than other circuits is set up to accept overseas ticket applications and sales through its ticket office. Write to the Australian Formula One Grand Prix Office at P.O. Box 1111, Norwood, SA 5067. The phone is 618 223 1111; Fax (08) 232 4144.

Amaroo Park
Australian Racing Drivers Club
Annangrove Rd
Annangrove NSW 2156, Australia

PH: (02) 679-1121
FAX: (02) 679 1184

Location: Eastern Australia, 40 miles northwest of Sydney, off Windsor Rd.

Circuit: 1.16 mile road course, seven turns.

Major races: Shell Australian Touring Car Championship; Formula Holden Australian Driver's Championship.

Small but fairly fast, Amaroo Park has been dominated by the Australian

sedan star Dick Johnson. Its major races are, aptly, the Australian Touring Car Championships — of which there are several rounds per year here.

There are no grandstands at Amaroo Park, so you'll want to walk about and watch from trackside. There is limited access on the north side of the circuit, so most people prefer to stay on the south side, in or about the paddock area. There is no access, either, to the inside of the track. So except for the Honda Corner and the quick uphill left-hand Nissan Skyline kink just past start/finish, you'll see nothing but right-handers, and will only be able to watch them from left to right.

Amaroo Park sits in a natural amphitheatre with surrounding residences built on five-acre residential blocks. The historic towns of Windsor and Richmond are a half and hour from Amaroo and are worth a look. Parramatta, the best place to stay while watching the races, is also about 30 minutes away. There is no camping here.

Bathurst Mount Panorama

Australian Racing Drivers Club Ltd,
Annangrove Rd,
ANNANGROVE, NSW 2154, Australia

PH: (02) 679 1121
Track: (063) 311 600
FAX: (02) 679 1184

Location: 130 miles west of Sydney, between Orange and Lithgow, on the Great Western Highway, on the southwest outskirts of Bathurst.

Circuit: 3.86 mile road circuit; 15 turns.

Major races: Tooheys Bathurst 1000.

Built in the 30's and known most of its life as a dirt road, Bathurst's Mount Panorama — and the road that traverses the mountain — is now the site of what's become the most popular race in Australia.

Bathurst was the original site of the Australian gold rush in 1851. And the road, which is closed now only once a year (the track once hosted a motorcycle race, which has disappeared), winds through what was a miners' paradise for 25 years of the strike. The six kilometer loop has held races since before World War II, and was the site of the 1938 Australian Grand Prix. It is now the Tooheys 1000 for Touring Cars.

The circuit is run in a counter-clockwise direction, and rises some 460 feet in its six kilometers. The most popular viewing areas of Bathurst are at the top of the hill at the Nissan Skyline, or in Hell Corner, just at the end of the Pit Straight. Skyline is an Australian version of Laguna Seca's Corkscrew, where all the drivers see for an instant is sky, and they commit to a corner they can't see until they're in it.

Grandstands exist — the most notable being the ones at Caltex Chase and on Pit Straight — but for the most part, the race is meant to be seen from the embankments surrounding the road. There's a shuttle bus from the pits to the top of the hill, using the access road to the top of Mt. Panorama, and two foot bridges allow access to the center of the circuit.

This is a big event in Australia. The F1 race is probably second in terms of prestige to Bathurst's touring car race. Because of that, rooms will be very

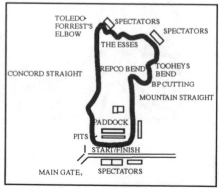

hard to find. Track officials urge you book a year in advance if possible. Try Bathurst first if you find yourself in town in time for the race, but don't be surprised if you have to stay in Orange or Katoomba — each nearly an hour away.

If you have the wherewithal to book early, contact the Bathurst Tourist Information Centre at (63) 33 62 88. There is camping at the circuit, at the top of the mountain. For advance booking, contact the Australian Racing Drivers Club at Amaroo Park, at Annangrove Rd., Annangrove NSW 2156, Australia; PH: (02) 679-1121; FAX: (02) 679 1184.

Calder Park Raceway
Calder Highway,
Keilor 3036,
Victoria, Australia

PH: (03) 390 1222
FAX (03) 390 2767

Location: Fifteen miles south of Melbourne on Highway 79 (Calder Highway).

Circuit: 1.44 mile National Circuit oval/ 2.57 mile Grand Prix Road course (six turns)/ quarter-mile dragstrip.

Major races: NASCAR/AUSCAR Championships; Australian Touring Car Championships.

Calder Thunderdome runs no major international championships yet. But the situation is bound to change.

The popular facility opened in 1988 at an expense of $50 million dollars, and since its February inauguration the track has almost tripled its yearly attendance. It's expected to continue the upward growth curve for well into the 90s.

Calder has an oval, a dragstrip, and a road circuit. The Australian Touring Car Championships contend two rounds of the championship on the small road circuit, and drag racing is beginning to attract crowds as well. The new NHRA championship will hold its first season of international drag racing at Calder in January of 1994, and the alcohol Funny Car-based championship looks to be a popular series.

But the place is primarily known as Australia's only oval. Having hosted

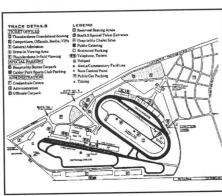

two non-championship American NASCAR events in 1988, Calder is unique. Australia is the only country outside the U.S to have hosted a NASCAR race, and several top name Winston Cup drivers ran the Calder race in '88 (the track record, incidentally, is still held by American Dave Marcis). Since that time, the interest in NASCAR racing has caught on in Australia. If it develops into a full-fledged international series, Calder will be in the heart of it.

The oval hosts five of seven rounds of the NASCAR/AUSCAR championship races. Incentive for racing at Calder's new circuit is a $50,000 check due the series champion who promoters would like to think is headed to the U.S. and for a ride in a Winston Cup car. So far it hasn't happened that way, but the interest is certainly there.

Although there are a few places to stay along the Calder Highway south of the track, the best place to stay is in Melbourne. For more information on rooms in the Calder area, contact the Melbourne Tourism Authority at 20th Lvl 80 Collins St. Melbourne, VIC 3000, (3) 654 -2288; or fax (3) 654-8195.

Eastern Creek Racetrack
Horsley Rd.,
Eastern Creek, NSW

Office: 105 Miller St.,
North Sydney, NSW   2060

(PH) 2   923-4234

Location: Six miles west of Sydney, just off the Great Western Highway 44 at the Doonside exit, adjacent to the Western Freeway 32.

Circuit: 2.358 mile road circuit; 12 turns.

Major races: FIM Grand Prix Championship; Road Racing Championship.

With the explosion in motorsports Down Under, and the growing trouble between government sponsored tracks and tobacco-sponsored entries, the Phillip Island facility and some of the other newer venues are becoming virtually unusable, and new sites have been sought. Sydney has been in need of a major facility for some time, and a consortium led by Sir Jack Brabham was formed to find a suitable place for Australia's motor sport.

Adelaide has been under fire for tobacco sponsorship from some of the citizenry recently, and it appeared that Eastern Creek would eventually steal all the action. But in 1992 the track had lost virtually all its major races, with Phillip Island witnessing the return of the Motorcycle Grand Prix, and the WSPC abandoning Australia -- as well as everybody else --altogether. In 1993, however, it was back in action with a round of FIM Grand Prix racing.

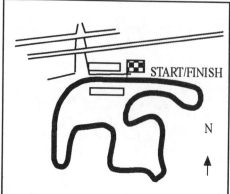

Eastern Creek was completed in the middle of 1990, and held its first race in July of the same year. In '91, it hosted the first race of the WSPC Championship as well as the second round of the FIM World Championship.

Pundits feel Eastern Creek will eventually host several varieties of international racing regularly, including Karting — on what is touted to be a World Championship Kart facility — and drag racing — on the quarter-mile dragstrip (which will be raced the wrong direction on the road circuit which will run counter-clockwise). The NHRA international Alcohol Funny Car series will contend a round of the championship in January of 1994. In addition to two smaller club and kart tracks, twin 18-hole golf courses are being groomed for the crowds which will appear for the racing. A swimming pool also exists for drivers and riders.

Located in a sparsely vegetated, hilly area just west of Sydney, the track is well situated. Built off two major thoroughfares, the track is easy to get to and easy to find. Seeding and turfing for general admission areas have been completed, and there is camping for spectators (contact the track for more information).

Parramatta is the closest place to stay, but don't count on lots of places when the GP returns. There were enough rooms for teams in '91, but not nearly enough for fans. Sydney is probably the best. For more information on lodging, call or write the Sydney Convention and Visitors Bureau, Lvl 13 80 William St. Woolloomooloo, NSW 2011, (2) 331-4045; Fax, (2) 360-1223. Or call the track.

Lakeside Raceway Pty Ltd

Office: P.O. Box 74 (29 McDougall Street, Milton) Paddington, QLD. 4064

Track: Lakeside Road, Dakabin. QLD Pine Rivers Shire (UBD REF J1 Map 2)

PH: (07) 369 8444
FAX: (07) 369 9272
Track: (07) 285 3333
Track Fax: (07) 285 3304

Location: 15 miles north of Brisbane

Circuit: 1.44 mile road course; six turns.

Major races: Shell Australian Touring car Championship; Formula Holden Australian Driver's Championship.

The warm, green Pine Rivers Shire Recreation Area is home for Lakeside Raceway, and the track actually sits just a few feet from the shores of Lake Kurwongbah.

The Pine Rivers Shire area is a resort and recreation hotbed which attracts tourists from all over the country. Racing may be a big attraction, but it is not king here. Grass skiing (the real draw of folks to the area), fishing, swimming, camping, sailing and general outdoors amusement is the allure for most who travel to Lake Kurwongbah. But Lakeside is certainly one of the most beautiful tracks in Australia. If not in actual track layout, then certainly in setting.

The track itself is a favorite among Australian racers. Like most Australian tracks, it's short, but it's fairly fast. Recently resurfaced, the

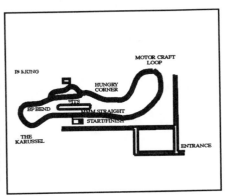

quicker cars can get through in about 50 seconds with speeds at about 100 mph — which would be far faster were it not for the slow Karussel.

Spectator access is limited to banks alongside the racing surface. The best places are on the hill just past the Karussel in BP bend, where you'll be able to see most of the first half of the track; or try the hill at the final turn at Ford Corner.

In addition to the asphalt racing, Lakeside also offers several good Hovercraft races in the dam, which is just a few hundred feet north of the track.

Lakeside is 30 minutes from downtown Brisbane, so accommodations will be no problem in Brisbane in a pinch. But try to stay near the lake, perhaps in Petrie, Narangba, or Kallangur. Contact the Pine Rivers Shire Council at 220 Gympie Road, Strathpine (PH: 205 2322) for more information.

Mallala

Sporting Car Club of SA
51 King William Rd.,
Unley 5051, South Australia

PH: (08) 373 4899
Track: (085) 272 323
FAX: (08) 373 4703

Location: South Australia, 55 miles north of Adelaide.

Circuit: 1.56 mile road circuit; eight turns.

Major races: Shell Australian Touring car Championship; Formula Holden Australian Driver's Championship.

Mallala is located in a flat farmland outside the country town of Mallala, which was an old RAAF airbase. The track is fairly isolated, set some 12 miles away from South Australia's Barossa Valley, home of a handful of quality Australian wineries. Mallala's 600 inhabitants are not the track's only spectators — the venue generally attracts an average of 15,000 per race.

Nearly defunct when a new South Australia track was created in 1970, competitors lamented the passing of the challenging but forgiving circuit. In 1982 the track reopened, and has since been a success, hosting an Australian Touring Car Championship round as well as a round of the Formula Brabham open-wheeled series. The track is very safe, with wide run-off areas, making it one of the better places for Australian youngsters to learn to drive racecars.

There are accommodations between Adelaide and Mallala, but probably the best place to stay is in the Barossa Valley. If you're already staying in Adelaide, the drive is less than an hour, and there is really no need to move closer to the circuit.

For more information on local lodging call the Adelaide Hills Regional Tourist Association, P.O. Box 308 Hahndorf SA 5245, (8) 389-6200.

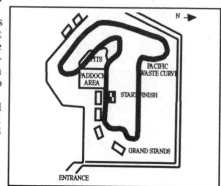

Oran Park Raceway

Box 28
Narellan, NSW 2567

PH: (046) 46 1004
FAX: (046) 46 1674

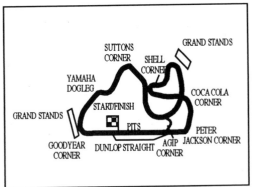

Location: In New South Wales, on the eastern Australian coast, 40 miles southwest of Sydney, off the Hume Highway.

Circuit: 1.53 mile road course; eight turns.

Major races: Shell Australian Touring car Championship; Formula Holden Australian Driver's Championship; Australian Truck Racing Championship.

Oran Park was built by the New South Wales Road Racing Club in 1960 (known then as the Singer Car Club). Club members actually constructed the track by hand, and its first failures were as a direct result of the amateur workmanship. It took 18 months to finish construction — which included nothing but the track itself. The track surface was substandard, and cracked and broke up quickly in its first few seasons. The control tower was an old double-decker bus!

Since those poor first seasons the track has become one of the best in NSW. It now has permanent facilities, and is attractive to manufacturers for testing. It's used 350 days of the year, and has a four-wheeled test track on the property — giving it the added distinction of being a test track for off-road manufacturers. Six advanced driving schools are also located here.

Truck racing is quickly becoming the feature attraction at Oran Park. Six-ton big-rigs pitted against each other on the tight 1.2 mile road circuit make for some interesting events. Truck racing is usually held March through October, and now includes classes for sports utility vehicles.

Located in Narellan, the best places to stay to see racing at Oran Park are in Liverpool, in the western suburbs of Sydney; Campbelltown, which is nine miles southeast of the track; Bankstown, just east of Liverpool, near Sydney; or Sydney itself.

For more information on lodging, call or write the Sydney Convention and Visitors Bureau, Lvl 13 80 William St. Woolloomooloo, NSW 2011, (2) 331-4045; fax, (2) 360-1223.

Phillip Island
Phillip Island Motor Sports Pty Ltd
RMB 500 GP
Cowes VIC 3922, Australia

PH: (059) 52 2710
FAX: (059) 52 3160

Location: 78 miles southeast of Melbourne, on Back Beach Road, on Phillip Island.

Circuit: 2.71 mile road circuit; 12 turns.

Major races: FIM World Championship Motorcycle Grand Prix; FIM World Superbike Championship.

Although the circuit on Phillip Island lost the FIM GP in 1991 to Eastern Creek, the race returned for another run in 1992. Victorian regulations against tobacco advertising in motor racing had prompted an evacuation of Phillip Island by the GP. It continued, however, to host the FIM Superbike race. In '93, it only hosted a Superbike event; the GP moved back to Eastern Creek.

The recently constructed circuit tops the list in all areas for GP riders. Japan may be the most prestigious, but Phillip Island is the most fun. But the place is usually cold in April, the month of the Australian GP. How cold? Phillip Island is a major tourist area for penguin watchers. The October running of the Superbike Championship should be pleasant, however.

The circuit has been done up right, and has earned a great amount of praise from riders. This track is fast — odd for a new circuit. It has a very fast straightaway at start/finish and only one tight turn. Designed by the same person who laid out both Adelaide's F1 circuit and the new track in Sydney (where the FIM GP moved in '91), it was done with no expense spared. Permanent garages are in place and there are plenty of great spectator areas — in both general admission and seated grandstands.

In addition to the advertising constraints and the cold weather, there are very few places to stay. A short ferry ride puts you in Victoria, but you'll still be an hour from Melbourne. There are rooms on the island, but plan on camping if you want to stay on the island (there are several camping areas around the track).

For more information on camping, call or write the track; or contact the Mornington Peninsula Tourist Information Center for more information on lodging and other tourist attractions: 54 Playne St. Frankston, VIC 3199, (3) 783-3222; or fax (3) 783-4930.

Sandown Int'l Motor Racing Circuit
c/o Light Car Club of Australia,
46 Queens Rd, Melbourne,
Victoria 3004, Australia

PH: (63 2) 529 2199
Track: (63 3) 546 1785
FAX: (63 3) 51 5369

Location: 15 miles northwest of Melbourne, between Princes Highway 1 and Springgate Road.

46

Circuit: 2.41 mile road course, 11 turns.

Major races: Sandown 500 for Touring Cars.

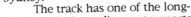

Mercedes posted a track record here in 1988 when the circuit hosted its most noteworthy event, the final round of the '88 FIA World Endurance Championship. But since then the Sandown has been mostly overlooked in favor of either Adelaide, Phillip Island or Sydney.

The track has one of the longest histories in Australian motorsports, with racing having been run in the area since 1907. The present circuit was built in 1961 and the first race was held on the asphalt on 1963. It was upgraded in 1984 to full championship standards but only saw international competition three times.

There are two tracks that are used at Sandown; the first, a 3.1 KM, is the pre-Championship layout; the latest version, the 3.9 KM circuit is the one more commonly used nowadays. There is only one main grandstand at Sandown — that, located at start/finish, with a seating capacity of 10,000. Most of the track can be seen from the main grandstand.

Located in Springvale, a Melbourne suburb of some 85,000 inhabitants, the track is easy to find. Only some 15 miles from Melbourne city-center, the facility is just off the Princes Highway. Although the main entrance is off the six-laned Princes Highway, the area is often congested during major events — such as the Sandown 500. So even though parking is abundant, getting into the place can be a bit of a problem.

To alleviate traffic problems, the track, which runs around a horse racing track, is blessed with a Main Eastern Railway station. The Railway, and the appropriate Sandown Park Station, makes it easy to travel either from Victoria or Melbourne without driving.

The best place to stay is in Melbourne. For more information on rooms in the Sandown area, contact the Melbourne Tourism Authority at 20th Lvl 80 Collins St. Melbourne, VIC 3000, (3) 654 -2288; or fax (3) 654-8195.

IndyCar Grand Prix
Level 7, 64 Ferniy Ave.,
Surfers Paradise, Queensland   4217
Australia

PH: (61) 75 88 6800
FAX: (61) 75 31 6611

Location: Eastern coastal Australia, on the Gold Coast, 60 miles south of Brisbane, in Surfers Paradise.

Circuit: 2.7 mile road course; 11 turns.

Major races: CART Indy Car World Series Championship. NASCAR Championships.

Before the race through the streets of Australia's famed Gold Coast ever saw an Indy Car, it had already become one of the most controversial races in the world.

CART, being of a rebellious nature, decided to ignore the FIA's warnings about moving "minor formulas" across international boundaries for championship racing in 1991. The FIA had threatened both the Confederation of Australian Motor Sport and ACCUS with retribution if the IndyCars headed to Australia for a championship race.

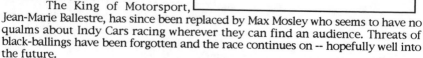

START/FINISH

The King of Motorsport, Jean-Marie Ballestre, has since been replaced by Max Mosley who seems to have no qualms about Indy Cars racing wherever they can find an audience. Threats of black-ballings have been forgotten and the race continues on -- hopefully well into the future.

The Gold Coast Grand Prix, like any other race in Australia, was successful before the fact. And in the wake of all the criticism and cynicism the race was a success. The street race organizers expect much better turnouts the longer the race continues to be run. Bookings and ticket sales need to be done ahead of time.

This is a fast street circuit, with speeds of 180 MPH achievable on the straights, and an average speed of 120 MPH around the track. The start sits on a terrifying length of nearly straight asphalt which spans over one mile. It then circles back, through the middle of the heavily congested Surfers Paradise resort area, down along the Nerang Slough, across the river and back to start/finish. So the back straight essentially runs along the beach, with the backs of the grandstands just a few feet from the breakers on the sandy shores.

Although the map in this guide shows the kink in the beach-side Main Beach Parade as a chicane, the new circuit actually uses an "S" turn.

There are grandstands on both sides of the track, with excellent pedestrian access (the path behind the esplanade on the beach will allow foot travel from one end of the beach to the other). The course itself is a good one for fans — better, in fact, than most street circuits. Raised spectator seating is available so that all the track passing directly in front of the stands is visible.

Staying in Surfers Paradise wouldn't be extremely difficult in March if you plan ahead. But for this race, considering the beautiful weather and the race, there will be a shortage of accommodations close to the circuit, even though the place boasts of more than 20,000 rooms. The immediate area is prepared for floods of tourists, but not as many as the organizers are expecting. You might have to find a hotel, apartment or motel a few minutes away. If you find yourself on the Gold Coast but still have no place to stay and wish to see the race, Brisbane should suffice. It's only an hour away, and getting in and out should be no problem. Try Surfers Paradise anyway, you could be pleasantly surprised — but don't count on it.

For more information, contact the Australian IndyCar Grand Prix office hotline and accommodation service directly through the track, or the Queensland Travel Center.

Symmons Plains

Tasmanian Motor Racing
Box 92A
Launceston TAS 7250

PH: (003) 31 5195
Track: (003) 98 2244
FAX: (003) 31 3496

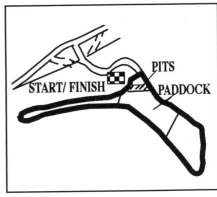

Location: On the southern coast of Australia, in Tasmania, just 20 miles south of Launceston on Highway One.

Circuit: 1.44 mile road course; four turns.

Major races: Shell Australian Touring Car Championship; Formula Holden Championships.

Four major meetings are regularly held at Symmons Plains, with the average attendance here established at about 17,000 per race. Two Holden Championship meetings run here, as well as a round of the Sport Sedan Championship, and the popular Shell Ultra Car Touring Car Championships.

The track is filled to capacity during the quartet of major national races, and the place is generally active the rest of the year. If not cars, motorcycle racing or club functions are likely occurring at this farmland venue.

No grandstands exist at Tasmania's only racetrack, but there are plenty of good general admission areas where spectators can see a majority of the track. Try the Dunlop hump, or the Coca Cola Straight.

The track has been around for 30 years, and track officials plan on bringing the facilities up to international levels in the future, with the hope of attracting more domestic Championship events — as well as a possible international race or two. Rooms are best found in Launceston. Contact the track for more information, or call the Australian Tourist Commission.

Wanneroo Park

WA Sporting Car Club
Unit 2, 75 Hay St.
SUBIACO WA 6019
PH: (09) 381 4432
Track: (09) 405 1717
FAX: (09) 382 2278
Track Fax: (09) 405 4487

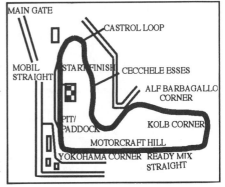

Location: 15 miles north of Perth, off Wanneroo Rd, on Wattle Ave.

Circuit: 1.46 mile road circuit, five turns.

Major races: Shell Australian Touring car Championship.

Wanneroo sits in a rural bush area just north of Perth. Perth is essentially where the bush begins in western Australia. And it can get hot here.

The track has some good elevation changes, and winds up the hill and then down to a quick 180 degree corner. Like most Australian circuits, it is short and tight.

There are no grandstands at Wanneroo, but there are plenty of viewing areas on the grass banks around the circuit. Try the Yokohama Corner, or the area from the Castrol Corner through the BP Corner. There are a few rooms in the area — most notably in Mindarie, some six miles from the track; or stay in Perth, which will have plenty of accommodations.

Call the Western Australian Tourist Center at 772 Hay St., Perth WA 6000, (9) 322-2999; or fax to (9) 481-0191.

Willowbank Raceway
Office P.O. Box 536
Mt. Gravatt, Qld 4122
Australia

PH: (61) 7849-6881

Circuit: Quarter-mile dragstrip.

Major races: Australian WinterNationals Drag Racing

Location: 50 KM from the center of Brisbane, on Champions way and Cunningham Highway (which becomes the New England Highway, eventually heading down the eastern coast of Australia west of Brisbane)

Located in a semi-wooded area, Willowbank Raceway owners took out just enough trees for a strip, with the result being a scenic track with just enough space for a dragstrip. It is often described as one of the prettiest racetracks in Australia.

Willowbank is one of the tracks in the NHRA's new international series slated for December of 1993, and the only major track on the east coast that is a purpose-built strip. It is the only track with national event status, hosting one of the country's biggest drag races (the biggest are the Grand Finals in Melbourne, at Calder, and the Finals at Eastern Creek, and this place runs the June Winter Nationals).

There are currently two grandstands — one was just built —and a grass mound which can hold a good sized crowd. So far, the biggest was 11,500 people.

Camping isn't officially allowed at Willowbank, but some people do camp in the parking lots overnight. The track won't kick you out, but would prefer that you camp up the street at a proper campground on Cunningham hwy. Or you can stay in Ipswich (90k pop)which is 15KM towards Brisbane; or a half an hour west you can get anything you want.

Winton Motor Raceway
Benalla Auto Club
Box 249
Benalla, VIC 3672, Australia
PH: (057) 66 4235
FAX: (057) 66 4249

Location: Six miles northeast of Benalla, at Winton, on Old Hume Highway, 115 miles from Melbourne.

Circuit: 1.25 mile road course; nine turns.

Major races: Shell Australian Touring car Championship; Australian Production Car Championship; Motorcraft Formula Ford Festival; Australian Truck Racing Championship.

PIT LANE

START/ FINISH

RACE CONTROL

Owned by Benalla Auto Club, Winton Motor Raceway has risen from the humble origins of club racing in the 1950s to become a major national racing facility in Australia. Used mostly as a testing facility, it sees daily use by several major manufacturers for tire testing, dealer conventions, and other assorted corporate functions.

The track sits on 400 acres of beautiful rolling hills. The place is known for its brevity and quick turns, where drivers have almost no time to relax. Besides the Shell Ultra Touring Car Championship, the Formula Ford Festival also highlights the season calendar. Usually held in August, the FF Festival is one of the biggest racing events in Australia.

Winton regularly attracts large crowds, most of whom watch from the spectator mounds located around the course where they can create their own seating. The grandstand area past start/finish is a favorite, and the tricky turn-one, which is a decreasing-radius right-hander, has a blind exit which makes for some good action.

There are rooms in the immediate area, in Glenrowen, Benalla, Wangatatta, and Milawa — all of which are within 15 miles from the circuit. You can call the track for more details or for a short list of hotels at the above number; or try: Winton Motor Raceway, Fox St., Winton, VIC, 3673, PH (57) 66 4235; or try the Goldburn Tourism Association at High St. Nagambie VIC 3608, (57) 94-2647.

AUSTRIA

A drive east through Germany is the most natural route into Austria. And of the nations in Europe, Germany and Austria are more culturally linked than any other two countries of the continent.

But Austrians are quick to point out that they are not Germans. Their countries are clearly separated. And unlike Belgium and Holland, borders until recently were not open, and one must stop each time across the frontier. The language is German; the cities look like any in Germany; but these are Austrians, proud of Austrian achievement, and detached from German successes or failures.

Anyway, Austria has had a better share of successful racing drivers. There haven't been many Austrian drivers (only five Austrian drivers have contended F1 in the past 40 years). But what few there have been were successful indeed. Niki Lauda, the greatest Austrian driver, won the World Championship three times; Jochen Rindt won the Championship posthumously in 1970; and more recently there has been Gerhard Berger, who now offers Austria its best hope of a World Champion since Lauda.

Austrian highways are fast in the summer, but should be negotiated with care during the winter. The Autobahns, unlike their German counterparts, are usually posted with speed limits of 130 KPH — although like the rest of Europe, nobody seems to pay any attention to the signs. Most roads are toll-free. Although the Brenner pass from Innsbruck to Bolzano, Italy is a pay road (as are several other long tunnel roads) most are free. As in Switzerland, there are some major tunnels — sometimes 15 miles long or more. Road conditions are some of the best in Europe, with wide shoulders and nice surfaces.

Austrians adopt the German etiquette of driving. But flashing the high-beams at slower cars is no longer accepted, so Austrians generally leave the headlights on while in the fast lane, moving to the left as they pass, and back into the fast lane when needed. Speed limits drop to 50 KPH in cities, and 100 on the smaller roads away from town.

The International insurance, or green card, is required in Austria for anyone driving a car. For renting a car an international drivers licence is necessary.

Tourist information: **Austrian National Tourist Office** , at Osterreichische Fremdenverkehrswerbung at Margaretenstrasse 1, 1040 Vienna, PH: 575 714.

Sporting Authority: **Osterreichischer Automobil., Motorrad-und Touring Club,** 1015 Wien, 1-3 Schubertring, Postfach 252. PH: 222/71199; FAX: 222/7131 807.

OsterreichRing GmbH,

OsterreichRingstrasse 2
A-8724 Spielburg
Austria
PH: (43) 35 77 22 928/ 35 77 24 599
FAX: (43) 35 77 22 928-13

Location: Central Austria, roughly between Salzburg and Graz.

From Salzburg, take Autobahn A10 and Bundesstrasse 96 east toward Vienna. Follow Bundesstrasse 96 until it becomes Schnellstrasse 36 shortly before Knittelfeld — the site of the circuit — following signs to Zeltweg; From Vienna, take Autobahn A2 South to Schnellstrasse 36 until you reach "Zeltweg Ost" exit.

Circuit: 3.7 mile road course; six turns

Major races: FIM Superbikes; GM-Lotus Euroseries; National motorcycle and drag racing.

Aside from the FIM Superbike race in July, Osterreichring hosts no major races — at least none with the stature of the F1 race. Nevertheless, it's too good a circuit to be off the major calendars for long. One of the fastest circuits on the

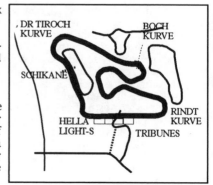

Grand Prix schedule when the GP cars ran here, it will eventually find a premier series to entertain.

The Ring was built in 1969, and renovated in 1988 — ironically just after it lost the FIA Grand Prix. The Grand Prix ran here first in 1964 on a temporary circuit. Reception as it was in Zeltweg, the track was constructed shortly afterward, and the first Grand Prix was run on the permanent track in 1970.

Osterreichring, or the "O" as it's called, has been continually updated, with the latest addition a widening of the start/finish area, and some 20,000 new seats — of which 3,000 are covered.

The track is set in a beautiful landscape, and has been called one of the best in the world for race fans. It is astoundingly fast, and very challenging. Drivers generally like the circuit. There's good runoff here, and it is considered a safe track. The FIM has granted homologation (certification for FIM events) through 1994.

Start/finish is located in a valley, with both the final corner and the first corner carved into a hill. The dramatic crest at the top of the rise following the start has been the site of some great action, as the drivers keep their throttles wide open over the blind brow, and then try to position themselves for the downhill Hella chicane, which is now actually the first corner.

From there, the track is wide open to the Tiroch Curve; then down a gear and back up to full speeds — sometimes as high as 360KPM into the difficult Bosch Curve. Back up the hill, around to the left where one of the most challenging curves in racing, the Jochen Rindt Curve, awaits racers. Jochen Rindt Curve, named after the first Austrian F1 World Champion (1970), is a fast off camber right-hander that needs to be taken just right to keep control and without losing speed.

Grandstands are located at start/finish, in the Hella Ss, and in the Bosch Curve. Most people however, prefer to wander around the infield and watch from there.

Camping is mostly done in the infield or at the far end of the track near Tiroch, and at the approach to Bosch Curve. The infield is hilly and one can see the track from most campsites. The area at the far end is also hilly, and even though there is usually a great crowd, you can actually find plenty of places to camp where you can have a little privacy — although most of the areas are open fields of grass.

Parking is no problem here, although getting into the area can be a bit of a problem since it's on a two lane road.

On off days, you can take a tour of the track in your car, or, if you have a bit of disposable income available, you can rent a racecar for the afternoon. Several schools convene here, and there is plenty of testing and training going on as well.

There are now plenty of smaller hotels, guesthouses, and bed and breakfasts. In the past few years, the rooming shortage that had always been a problem at Zeltweg has been corrected with the construction of more hotels and inns. Still, during a major race it may be very difficult to find space. Right now there are now major international auto races, however. Most of the smaller rooms are available in the beautiful Aichfeld Valley a few minutes from the track.

Camping is probably the best alternative to driving to the Ring for the major races. Some 22,000 people a year used the camping areas during the Grand Prix years, and the campsites are usually located so that from your tent you can watch racing.

For more information, including maps and hotel listings, call The Austrian National Tourist Office at Osterreichische Fremdenverkehrswerbung at Margaretenstrasse 1, 1040 Vienna, PH: 575 714.; or call the Fremdebverkehrsverband Knittlefeld at (43) 3512 6464.

Salzburgring

IGMS Salzburgring,
Molckhofgasse 3,
A-5020 Salzburg, Austria

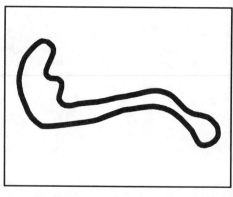

PH: (43) 662 848734/
(43) 662 848735
FAX:(43)662848734-4

Location: 10 miles southeast of Salzburg, Austria.

Circuit: 2.63 mile road course; five turns.

Major races: FIM Grand Prix Motorcycle World Championship — 125cc, 250cc, Sidecars, and 500cc.

Few on the FIM GP motorcycle circuit would not argue that Salzburgring is the most beautiful track in GP racing. But there are few riders who would defend the place.

The twisty, fast track, which has nice elevation changes and a good variety of corners, has had safety problems in the past — especially with armco that runs right up to the track in some places, and which can be fatal to motorcyclists.

At the top of the hill, on the back side, time can be gained for those who have the guts to keep the throttle open a bit longer. The consequences of a mistake, however, can be mortal in that area. Improvements are quickly being made, and hopefully will satisfy riders. The circuit is truly an impressive one. From the restaurant in the middle of the track, to the excellent viewing areas afforded spectators, Salzburgring is one of the best for fans.

The best places to watch racing are located at either end of the facility. From the steep hills that surround the track you'll see all the track from several places, but the best places are in the two tight corners linking the front and back portions of the track together.

Salzburg can be a problem when looking for rooms during the GP- usually held in May. It's best to book ahead, or arrive early. If you're unable to locate a room in Salzburg, try Linz, which is about 70 miles distant — but, on the Austrian Autobahn, can be reached in 45 minutes.

For more information, including maps and hotel listings, call The Austrian National Tourist Office: NY, (212) 994-6880; LA, (213) 380-3309; Chicago, (312) 644-5564; Houston, (713) 850-8888.

BELGIUM

Belgium is an interesting mix of Germanic and Latin, with the result being a combination of orderliness and passion. Northern Belgium is Flemish and the language is Dutch; and southern Belgium is French, with French spoken there. A local dialect is also occasionally used by some of the older folks in the north.

One of the worst feuds in Europe is between the northern and southern Belgians. As youngsters pledge their allegiance to either faction and refuse to learn the language of the other half of the country, a national economic stumbling block has been created. But the fighting is rarely done on a physical level, and the tolerance of age usually shines through.

Belgian Roads are more German than French, although the southern Belgian road signs, near Spa, will be in French, where the northern signs will tend to be written in Dutch. The country's two official languages make things slightly confusing, although, like Holland, English is generally spoken in Belgium. So if you have a problem, just ask.

The speed limits in the north are obeyed much more often than those in the south. Autobahn travel is limited to 120 KPH, while the smaller roads are traveled at 90, and the cities are limited to speeds of 60.

Northern Belgium is usually travelled at the speed limits, and vehicles using the road at a much higher rate of speed are good targets for the Polizei, who hang out in green-and-white Porsches in Belgium and southern Holland. The southern part of the country begins to feel the French influence, and the speeds tend to creep up a tad more. The Autobahn is suddenly referred to as the Autoroute, and the French rules of driving apply more than the Dutch.

The French, like in most Latin countries, use the left blinker as they pass on the left, keeping it blinking until they return to the right lane. As always, the left lane is only used for passing. And unless you're getting near 300 KPH, keep right except for the brief instants you need to use the left lane to pass.

Keep the left blinker flashing to indicate only a temporary run in the right lane until the mission is accomplished. If you find it difficult to overtake a particular vehicle — perhaps on a hill — and find a faster vehicle in your mirrors, switch the left blinker to the right side, indicating that you'll be moving over as soon as possible.

Tourist information: **Belgian National Tourist Office**, in Belgium at the Town Hall in Brussels, at 513 8940.

Sporting authorities: **Royal Automobile Club de Belgique**, 53, Rue d'Arlon, 1040 Bruxelles. PH: 2/230 20 35; FAX: 2/230 75 84; **Federation Motorcycliste de Belgique**, 550 Chaussee de Louvain, Bte 7, 1030 Bruxelles, Belgium. PH: (32 2) 736 9912; FAX: (32 2) 732 0128.

Circuit de Spa Francorchamps,
55 Route de Circuit,
4970 Francorchamps,
Belgium

PH: (32) 87 27 52 58/ or 27 51 38
FAX: (32) 87 27 52 96

Location: Eastern Belgium, 22 miles from Liege, and 13 miles from the German border.

From Paris, take the Autoroute A4 to A31 North (which becomes E25 once inside Belgium) and follow it to the N62 road East into Spa; From Liege, take A25 to N62 into Spa.

Circuit: 4.31 mile road

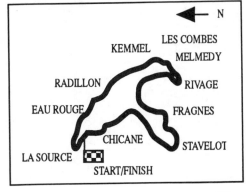

course; 11 turns.

Major races: FIA Formula One Grand Prix World Championship; FIM Grand Prix Motorcycle World Championship — 125cc, 250cc, 500cc, and Sidecars; FIM Superbike Championship.

As the longest track on the F1 calendar, Spa-Francorchamps has its unique problems. Not that length means much generally, except maybe in terms of course-marshalling. But at Spa, it means a lot: it often means rain at one end of the track, and a dry surface at the other.

From La Source to Malmedy the distance is nearly two miles, and frequently the track forces drivers to make a decision about rain or slick tires on a grid that doesn't give a good indication of what the other end of the track will hold. That has always been the danger at the scenic Belgian venue.

This circuit alternated as the site of the FIA Belgian GP with Zolder until 1983 when Spa was finally repaved and shortened a bit. It was postponed the same year it returned while the track finished curing. In fact the whole caravan showed up and went home Saturday when the track began cracking. The race was run later in September.

The FIM GP circus, as of 1991, was not scheduled to return to the fast racetrack. Problems in 1990 concerning insurance — the organizers apparently failed to secure the correct insurance by the free practice day Thursday — saw the cancellation of Thursday's free practice day.

In addition, tickets had also almost doubled in the past few years. And the track, which was one of the favorites of the GP crowds, became a very poorly attended event. Whatever the problems, they still seem to continue, since although the race ran in '92 it did not run during the '93 season.

The track itself is one of the most interesting on each GP circuit, with the long left-hander going into the Bus Stop Chicane, the La Source hairpin, and the

long Kemmel straight being three of the best viewing spots in all of racing. The area surrounding the track is nicely forested, but not as thick as, say, Hockenheim where there is almost no way to see daylight. Getting into the track is a bit confusing, since it's mostly a temporary circuit. You'll enter at Eau Rouge (don't forget to stop at the stores where you'll probably want to buy miniature F1 cars), and walk to your seats from there. Be prepared for a walk.

There are really no bad seats at Spa. In fact, save your money and just get general admission tickets and wander around. The general admission tickets are expensive here, but well worth the money. Eau Rouge can't be watched from any stands — there aren't any that overlook that stretch of track, and you'll want to see that.

Paths that follow the track run nearly all around the place, so you'll be able to walk and watch at the same time. If you must find a seat, there are new grandstands down from the pits, which offer fairly good viewing areas, and are as close as you'll get to start/finish. Down from the hairpin, in Francorchamps Grandstands, is also a decent place to watch a race. But unless it's a personal tradition to buy a reserved seat, just go general admission here.

The circuit itself is easy to get to, and is only one hour from Brussels. If you get here late you may need to book that far away. Taking public transportation is a good idea since you'll do some walking anyway. If staying in Liege, the train to Spa is a 30 minute ride. The train leaves you in Spa — but the race is in Spa-Francorchamps. You'll still have to take a bus to the entrance of the circuit. But the bus from the Spa station doesn't quite go far enough. It's therefore better to take the train two extra stops to Verviers and take that bus to the circuit.

For information about rooms in Liege, Spa, or Brussels, call the Belgian Tourist Offices listed at the beginning of this chapter.

Zolder
**Omloop Terlamen Zolder
Kontroleteron,
B-3540 Zolder, Belgium**

**PH: (32) 11 423943/ 11 425279
FAX: (32) 011/25 21 44**

Location: Central Belgium, roughly between Liege and Brussels.

Circuit: 2.6 miles, nine turns.

Major races: German Formula 3 Championship; GM Lotus Euroseries; Europa Truck Cup; Benelux Opel Lotus Championship; German Touring Car Championships.

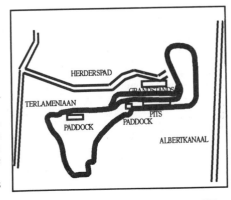

Zolder has fallen out of favor with just about every major international championship series lately. The changes in the track surface, plus the sparse run-off, have put this venue in the dangerous category with the drivers.

Zolder alternated with Spa as

the home of the Belgian GP for several years. But Gilles Villeneuve lost his life, and those who come to Zolder have no choice but to remember the talented Canadian. A memorial in his honor hovers over the exit of the pits. Now Zolder's claim to fame is a German Touring Car race.

The track is still a classic bit of racing. The downhill past start/finish is a good place to watch, and has always made for great action at the start of a race as the cars enter a fast left-right combination in a group; the fastest part of the track is now between Bianchibocht and the chicane on the backside of the circuit.

The track is centrally located, so getting to the area is theoretically not a problem. But if you've never been there it will be a major headache. From Brussels, take E40 to A2 East, where it will eventually become E314. Zolder is not listed on many maps, but it will appear within three miles of the junction of A2/E314 and E313. There are plenty of places to stay — although Zolder will not be one of them. Brussels is 35 miles west, Antwerp is 30 miles northwest, and Liege is 20 miles south.

For rooms, contact the Belgian tourist office listed at the beginning of the chapter.

BRAZIL

Brazil is the land of equality, where people are judged by character rather than money or skin color. Brazilians are often of Caribbean ancestry, and the distinction between white and black is less important here than anywhere else in the world. In order to be called black in Brazil, you must be very, very dark — but even then, nobody really cares.

Brazil is where one can literally be reborn. Personal history is insignificant in Brazil, it's a place where nobody asks where you've been, and few care where you're going. There's a belief among pickpockets that theirs is a profession that actually provides a service. To have one's possessions, and one's identity taken away is said to be liberating. Stories of travellers remaining in Brazil indefinitely after being robbed abound; and the victims essentially become Brazilian until they decide to be rescued.

The atmosphere in Brazil at nightfall reflects the character of the country. Work is obviously undertaken in order to enjoy the evenings. Recreation becomes complicated enough that it's not simply a pastime, but an obsession. Brazilian race fans are more fanatic than any others, following Ayrton Senna, Nelson Piquet, and Mauricio Gugelmin around the world to watch them race.

The country has some of the best racers in the history of the sport. Certainly, Senna is the hero of Brazil now, but all motorsports personalities are deified in Brazil. There was Emerson Fittipaldi, Nelson Piquet, Raul Boesel, and, of course, Ayrton Senna.

Unfortunately, the country's love of the sport does not spur the economy. The 1990 version of the Brazilian Grand Prix saw the unveiling of one of the best tracks in the world. All the stops were pulled out at Sao Paulo's Interlagos, as the Brazilian round fell to Alain Prost... yet again.

Getting around in Brazil is usually not difficult. Driving in Sao Paulo or Rio is not really as bad as say, Rome, Tokyo, or Mexico City. In fact, most of Brazil is fairly refined when it comes to motoring. Driving through Sao Paulo or Rio at night, however, is a different story.

In Brazil's bigger cities, as in all Latin American urban centers, robberies at traffic lights are commonplace. If things continue as they were in 1990, it will be even worse. Even the Police often suggest not stopping for the red lights. Do not stop for what may look like a bad accident. In many cases, it will have been staged in order to get you to stop. If there are several people in your car — preferably large males — you might consider it, but only if you feel there is a legitimate problem. Otherwise, keep going. Tell someone in your hotel once you arrive, but leave it to someone else. If it's daylight, you can relax a bit, but beware of similar traps on semi-deserted roads.

Because of these robberies, traffic is sometimes unpredictable. Self-preservation is a great reason for running a red light. Be careful. Speed limits are 110KPH on the larger roads and 60-80 in the city areas. Lots of drivers — especially taxi drivers think themselves the next World Champions, so the limit is usually ignored.

Tourist Information: **Brazilian Tourism Authority,** in Brazil at the **Office of Tourism** at Pca do Republica 154, Sao Paulo. PH: 259 2000.

Sporting Authorities: **Confederacao Brasileira de Automobilismo,** Rua da Gloria, 290 — 8 Andar, Grs 801/802, Cep 20241, Rio de Janeiro, Brazil. PH: (55) 21 221 4895; FAX: (55) 21 242-4494; **Confederacao Brasileira de Motociclismo,** Av. Paulista 2073 — edificio Horsa I, 6 Andar — Conjunto 623, Sao Paulo SP, CEP. 01311-300. PH: (55 11) 284 8185; FAX: (55 11) 287 8832.

Autodromo Goiania
Grande Premio do Brazil
KM 6 Estrada de Bela Vista

PH: (62) 241 4122

Location: 50 miles east of Brasilia, on the Brasilia Highway.

Circuit: 2.38 mile road course, eight turns.

Major Races: hosted a round of the FIM World Championships for 500cc and 250cc motorcycles, but now no major races.

Goiania was well-liked by FIM Grand Prix motorcycle ranks, and was considered a safe circuit. It was challenging by design, and the atmosphere around the track was always enjoyable — which is normal in Brazil. Riders looked forward to the event, traditionally held as the last round of the Championship in September.

The only problem, and the one that finally lost the race for Goiania, was the track surface. The old track hadn't been resurfaced in some time and cracks and bumps were severe. Considering the beautiful new Interlagos circuit in Sao Paulo, and the economic situation in Brazil, the Goiania circuit will probably not be repaired in the near future, much to the disappointment of the FIM GP rider corps.

Located in the middle of nowhere, its closest big city is Brasilia, which is some 130 miles northwest of the track. Although Goiania is a beautiful place, there is probably not much reason to visit it unless racing is happening. The FIM Grand Prix was its raison d'etre. The national formulas

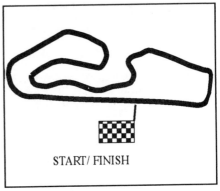

START/ FINISH

are good, but are probably not worth the visit. If you do make it there, Goiania ha
plenty of rooms, or try Trindade, 20 miles west.

Interlagos
Autodromo Jose Carlos Pace
Av Sanadoir Teotonio
Vilelia 259, Sao Paulo, Brazil.

PH: (55) 521-9911

Location: Nine miles south of Sao Paulo, between Diadema, and San
Bernardo Do Campo.

Circuit: 2.6 mile road course; 12 turns.

Major Races: FIA Formula One Grand Prix World Championship.

Interlagos, alas, hasn't had the best of luck. The multi-million dollar
facility is possibly the best FIA Grand Prix track in the world. Its only problem is
the country in which it is located.

With the deterioration of Rio's track, it was necessary to upgrade either
Jacarepagua or Interlagos. Since Ayrton Senna hails from Sao Paulo, it seemed a
better idea to showcase Brazil's best in the hero's home town.

Unfortunately, its return in 1990 will not be remembered fondly by
anyone present at its reopening. The economy was in the critical stages when the
travelling caravan got to town. The new president had taken control of the country,
and was finally cognizant of the severity of the economic situation. Within hours
of that revelation, the F1 teams arrived for the first race on the new Interlagos.

First, Goodyear's tires were seized — apparently because the tire company
needed to pay a new tax just imposed on foreign tire makers; second, nobody knew
how much anything cost. There was no currency exchange allowed, so nobody
knew how much they were paying. Taxi drivers refused to take dollars, or Marks,
or Pounds, so nobody could go anywhere. The hotels charged everything to the
guests' rooms, then had the guests pay on credit cards as they left following the race
— but they never knew exactly how much they were paying.

To make matters worse, the corner curbing — which was excellent for the
automobiles — was unacceptable to the FIM. The motorcycling establishment
asked the track to make changes in
the curbing. When it was not done,
FIM officials cancelled the Grand Prix
slated for the end of the season. Any
chance of the investment breaking
even was lost at that point.

Although 1991 and 1992
were far better than 1990, there are
still major problems inherent in seeing a race there. The best that can be
said about Interlagos, other than
praising the track itself, is that the
situation can only get better.

Paulists are usually a bit less
emotional than the Cariocas — al-

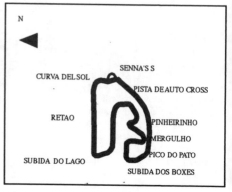

though they are still Brazilians, and still possess the same passion for motorsports. But Sao Paulo itself is more a serious city than Rio. It's a manufacturing city, and has less of the distractions of Rio's beaches — and less of the allure of its sister city, which is some 260 miles northwest.

From downtown Sao Paulo the circuit is only a few miles away. Although tours are the best bet, it's not as easy to find tour companies that go to Brazil anymore.

Regardless, being the adventurous soul you are, just hop in a taxi and head to the track from your room in downtown Sao Paulo. Even if you get taken — figuratively — for a ride by the driver, it should cost you no more than $20 or so — less, if the driver wants to charge you the right rate. Like Rio, there are also plenty of cheap buses. You can take the subway as far as the Jabaquara Station, and take a taxi from there (which is only three miles from the track). Car rental is not a bad idea either. It will likely cost you less than the taxi rides in the long run, plus you get the freedom of leaving whenever you want. Driving in Brazil is not as bad as many places.

Getting tickets to the Grand Prix is not as difficult as the Italian races, although there is at least as much interest in racing in Sao Paulo as in Imola. The people don't have the kind of money the Italians have, however, so grandstand tickets are available up until Saturday. To find tickets, it's easiest to go to a branch of the Unibanco, which are littered throughout Sao Paulo as well as the rest of Brazil.

Try for seats overlooking the off-camber down-hill first turn. From there you'll see most of the track as well as the pits and the start. Sao Paulo has plenty of rooms, and even during the Grand Prix there should be no problem getting one — but you'll want to stay in a good hotel here, so book early if possible.

Rio de Janeiro
Autodromo Circuit Nelson Piquet
Av Ambaixador Aberlardo Bueno,
Baixada de Jacarepagua, Brazil

PH: (55) 213421313

Location: 20 miles west of Rio.

Circuit: 3.125 mile road course; 11 turns.

Major Races: Long-time host of the FIA World Championship Grand Prix, now no major races.

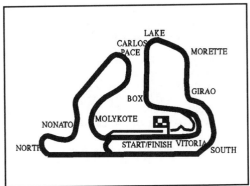

With its plaguing problems, many of which came from the weather in Rio, Jacarepagua is now dormant. But the GP moved not because of the heat but because of the sub-standard track conditions. The track surface was poor, and the overall condition of the circuit was bad.

Recently renamed Circuit Nelson Piquet, it was considered one of the most challenging tracks on the GP calendar. With the high temperatures, high humidity, terrific G-forces on the circuit, bumps, and the vocal Brazilian crowd, it was a true achievement when someone other than a Brazilian won the race — as, in fact, was usually the case here.

With the move to Sao Paulo and Interlagos in 1990, the circus seems to miss the clowns who appeared in Rio. The F1 establishment wasn't too pleased with the new city — although the track itself is a real dream, with facilities better than the best in Europe. But only Rio is Rio, and it seems possible the GP could possibly return here someday — even though economics look to be an insurmountable stumbling block.

The track is located away from downtown Rio about 20 miles. There are really two ways to get to the track. The first is to take either Rua Ana Neri or Ave Brazil to RJ 089, then south to the track; the other way, which takes longer, is past Copacabana and Ipanema, across the Jacarepagua Bay, past the municipal airport and north to the circuit.

You won't want to stay close to the track. Stay on the beach. There is camping available at the circuit, for those who wish for a bit more adventure.

Since there's no GP here, there are no tours anymore. You'll have to find your own way to the circuit if staying in the city. Barring rental cars, you'll have to take a taxi, which will probably cost you $20 or so; or if you feel bold, take a bus, which will only cost you about three-cents — but watch your wallet!

CANADA

Canada may be just north of the U.S., and Canadians may be very similar to Americans, but motorsport is appreciated far more in Canada than in the United States.

Even the smallest tracks set enviable standards of attendance. And although the U.S. can boast of the Indy 500 and NASCAR racing, Canada's interest in motorsports is universal; and Canadians are as enthusiastic about Indycar racing as they are in Drag racing, motorcycle racing, or FIA Grand Prix racing.

Canada's interest in motorsports may not be climbing as far and as fast as it could, due mostly to sponsor and sanctioning disagreements — which were so irreconcilable in 1987 that the Canadian Grand Prix was eliminated from the FIA World Championship.

The Canadian Automobile Sports Club and the new Grand Prix organizer, Mr. Benoit Mailloux, continue trying to sort out control of Canadian motorsport. Some of the older tracks were confident enough in the direction of Canadian motorsports to have begun renovation aimed at bringing several major international races to Canada -- but 1993 was a barren season, with almost no organized racing.

In terms of getting around, Canada is identical to the United States. Highways and speed limits are essentially the same — except Canadians use KPH rather than MPH. Speeds are limited on the major roads to 110. Remember that from Vancouver to Toronto is sparsely populated, so the roads aren't eight-lane expressways. From Windsor or Sarnia, Ontario to Quebec, the roads are wide multi-laned and fast — although if you drive fast you'll be cited.

Canadian police seem to just pop out of your trunk. You'll never know where they come from. Do yourself a favor: drive at the speed limit.

Police in Canada use radar. But if you use a radar detector, you'll be cited, and the detector will be confiscated — so leave it in the trunk, or don't bring it at all.

Once past Toronto, heading east, the signs will be written in French more than English. Once you're finally inside Quebec signs will be written totally in French.

Sporting Authorities: **Mr Benoit Mailloux,** Rue Saint Pierre, Montreal, Quebec H2Y 2L6. PH: (514) 842 9512; FAX: (514) 845 6573/ **ASN Canada (FIA):** (416) 479-4000. **Canadian Automobile Sports Club,** 693 Petrolla Rd., Downsville, Ontario, Canada, M3J 2N6. PH: (416) 667-9500; FAX: (416) 667-9555; **Canadian Motorcycle Federation** , Box 448, Hamilton, Ont., L8L 8C4. PH (1 416) 522 5705; FAX (1 416) 522 5716.

Tourist Information: **Alberta Tourism** (800) 661-8888; **BC Tourism** (800) 663-6000; **Travel Manitoba** (800) 665-0040; **New Brunswick Department of Tourism** (800)562-0123; **Newfoundland Department of Development, Tourism Branch** (800) 563-6353; **Nova Scotia** (800) 565-0000; **Ontario Ministry of Tourism** (800) 268-3735; **Prince Edward Island** (800) 565-0267; **Tourisme Quebec** (800) 444-7000; **Saskatchewan** (800) 667-7191; **Northwest Territories Travel** (800) 661-0788; **Centre Information Touriste,** 1001 rue du Carre Dorchester, Montreal (514) 873-2015.

Atlantic Motorsports Park

P.O. Box 3010 South
Halifax, Nova Scotia
B3J 3G6

PH: (902) 429-7528
Track: (902) 758-2237
FAX: (902) 468-5635

Location: Eastern Nova Scotia, 35 miles from Halifax, on Highway 102 North, in Shubenacedie.

Circuit: 1.6 mile road race course; 11 turns.

Major races: CASC Regional racing; AMCRA Motorcycle Championships; Castrol National Superbike Championship.

Unfortunately, Atlantic Motorsports Park's challenging track doesn't get as much use or recognition as it should. Because of its location in Nova Scotia the place is usually deserted, and the sharp turns and tricky elevation changes are usually wasted on the sparse crowds.

Not that there's no interest in Halifax. There is. But the area isn't well-populated. There's not much here to sustain the high-dollar world of racing. Bike

racing is the biggest draw. The second biggest is the Canadian Championships for Remote Control Cars, which are also held here on a very high-tech remote control racetrack.

For the true-to-scale racing, most people drive their cars through the tunnel and park, watching the track from the infield. A few grandstands offer some semblance of spectatordom, but most who watch are found scattered around the track. When you come into the circuit,

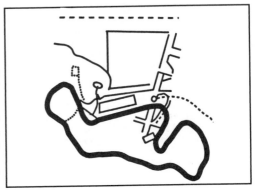

you'll buy a ticket, which allows you to stay for the weekend — and you can camp for free if you like. In fact, if you request it, you can get free firewood as well.

The 377 acres of Atlantic Motorsports Park has a motocross track as well as a karting track, and racing occurs 16-20 weekends a year. Although much of the track was resurfaced in 1992, testing is still relatively inexpensive here. By the way, the track record, which was set in the '70s, was posted by none other than Gilles Villeneuve.

If you don't fancy camping, Halifax or Truro are the best places to stay — Truro being about 25 miles north while Halifax is south a few minutes. Call the Nova Scotia Tourist Office at (800) 565-0000.

Mont-Tremblant
P.O. Box 480
Mont Tremblant,
Quebec, Canada
JOT 1ZO
PH: (819) 425-7871
Fax (8190 425 9183

Location: In Quebec, 60 miles north of Montreal, in the village of Mont-Tremblant.

Circuit: 2.65 mile road course; 14 turns.

Major races: FF Championship

A major Laurentians Mountains ski resort area during the winter, Mont Tremblant is green and spectacular during the summer. The place is popular — and not just for the racing.

Mirroring the surroundings, the track has lots of the area's elevation changes, and is a picturesque circuit. Lake Moore is next to the track and can be seen from the cockpits of the racecars at certain spots.

One of the most fantastic places in Canadian motorsports to watch the racing is from outside of Namerow Corner. The steep corner is quite sharp going uphill, and exits downhill. Fans can stand on a rock cliff and watch from just a few feet from the track — you can see most of the rest of the track from there as well. Turn two is also good, as it gives a view of the top of the hill where the cars get light then try to hold it together while going into the downhill quick turn three — sometimes sideways. This track is the home of Jim Russell International Driver's school, and presents quite a challenge for its students. New for 1993 was the Nissan Performance Driving School — in addition to a skidpad, which both schools will use.

Stay in Mont Tremblant if you book early, but don't be concerned about it; the entire place is filled with hotels. St Jovite is very close and you should be able to find something there. There is also plenty of camping in the area. For more information contact Tourisme Quebec at (800) 444-7000.

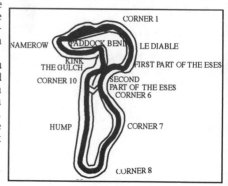

Gilles Villeneuve Circuit

Bassin Olympique
Ile Notre-Dame
Montreal, Quebec
H3C 1A0
PH: (514) 392-4731/
(514) 392-9022/ (514) 871-1421

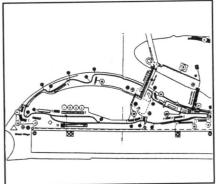

Location: South eastern Quebec, in the Saint Lawrence River, just east of Montreal, on Ile Notre Dame.

Circuit: 2.75 mile road course; 13 turns.

Major Races: FIA Formula One Grand Prix World Championship; Honda Michelin Challenge Championship; Players GM Championship.

Circuit Gilles Villeneuve is what remains of the '67 World Exposition and the '76 Montreal Olympics. When the Expo vacated in '68, the island was abandoned, and the track lay dormant for nine years.

In 1976 the island saw life again as the Montreal Olympics stopped for three weeks during the summer. The Olympic Basin on Notre Dame Island was created for rowing competition, and roads were paved for access to different spots on the island.

When the Olympics ended, it again lay dormant — until the idea to build a permanent racing circuit was approved. Relics of the two great temporary events still remain on the island, including the Olympic Lagoon and one of Bucky Fuller's first domes — or at least remnants of the structure.

Circuit Gilles Villeneuve will continue its relationship with the Formula One Grand Prix circus indefinitely, making it the only North American stop for the F1 World Championship in the future. Many in the European press corps felt it would be missing in 1992. The opinions on the expected move were based mostly on perceived safety problems.

Although the place is generally a safe venue, during the FIA World Sports Car race in 1990 a manhole cover, which was located on the track, managed to come loose and was sucked up by a passing prototype. The errant cover — which weighed well over 100 lbs — landed on the track and shattered, sending heavy shrapnel into the air. The result was pileup that destroyed two cars and very nearly killed Porsche driver Jesus Pareja. The WSC race, which was the first prototype race in Montreal, disappeared, but the F1 race was never affected.

Track officials removed most of the manhole covers in 1991 and made minor modifications to the pit lane entrance, which was a complaint of the F1 drivers. The 1992 track was slightly longer (4.43 KMs now; vs 4.3 KMs for the old). In addition, turns 14 and 15 were slightly altered.

In 1992 the race was to be one of the highlights of an otherwise dull season when Ayrton Senna snatched the lead of the race on the first lap and Nigel Mansell tried everything he could to get by, eventually taking himself out of the race by sliding into the sand traps on an ill-fated passing attempt. The 1993 season, with Michael Andretti in F1, the race was packed with Americans looking for the same kind of drama with their man. Unfortunately, it was not to be.

Montreal is exceptionally good for the novice traveller. It's Quebec, and very French. There's a large percentage of Quebecois who speak absolutely no English, so the adventure will be as complete in Montreal as it would be in France.

But the second language in Montreal is English, so there will always be someone there to help you if you don't speak French very well.

The track is also a great one for first-time fans. Access has been severely limited in past years, but spectating areas are still good no matter where you sit. And finding your way around the facility is easier than most GP tracks.

The areas on both ends of the track are terrific, each giving a nice view of the cars as they enter and exit the two tightest corners on the circuit. At the far end of the circuit, near the garages, you'll have a great view of the cars entering the tightest corner on the track from the fastest section. Just past start/finish is probably the most popular area, and seats are relatively inexpensive there. The tight section past the pit exit provides a perfect stadium area where the cars enter for a slow left/right sequence.

From downtown Montreal, getting to the track is probably easier than any other GP circuit. The Metro goes from Montreal directly to Ile Ste Helene, which is just 300 yards away from Ile Notre Dame. If you choose to drive, you'll park way on the other side of Ile Ste Helene, and the walk is a half-mile farther — parking is expensive as well. Remember, the Metro station was constructed especially for events on the Notre Dame, and it will accommodate heavy traffic. Compared to Monaco, or Mexico, where trains stop right in front of the circuits, Montreal is still far easier. Once you step off the Metro there is no confusion as to the direction of your seats, or how to get to certain spots on the circuit.

Rooms in Montreal are relatively plentiful, although the best downtown rooms are booked well in advance — and can be a tad expensive. You can stay farther west in Montreal, and it will be cheaper, although it will require some public transportation. You won't want to drive downtown to park for any length of time, however, since parking downtown is expensive. An alternative to staying in Montreal is Longueil, on the east side of the St. Lawrence. The Metro runs as far as Longueil, so you still won't need to drive. It's also generally a tad cheaper. For more information on accommodations call the Montreal Tourist Office at (514) 873-2015.

Mosport's International Speedway

P.O. Box 205
Peterborough, Ontario K9J 6Y8

PH: (416) 513-0550
Track: (705) 743-3850
FAX: (416) 513 0566

Location: Southern Canada, 50 miles from Toronto, on Highway 20, east of highway 57, beside Mosport Park.

Circuit: Half-mile paved oval.

Major Races: ACT & Super Modifieds.

Mosport's International Speedway sits next door to its famous Canadian namesake, Mosport Park.

Mosport's International Speedway, which leases the land from the larger raceway, was a dirt track when it first opened. But the racing didn't go too well on the dirt surface, and it was quickly paved. Its biggest show is the stock car ACT (American Canadian Tour) race which is set in mid-September. There is a weekly show (Saturday) with three classes; Street Stock; Late Model; Sportsmen; and OSCARR Late Models.

The 7,000 seat oval shares Mosport's land, and it does have camping like its big sister.

Mosport Park

Office Address: 825 Denison st.
Unit 16 Markham
Ontario, CAN L3R 5E4

R.R. #5
Bowmanville, Ontario,
Canada L1C 3K6

PH: (416) 513-0550
FAX: (416) 513 0566

Location: Southeastern Canada, approximately one hour east of Toronto.

From Toronto, take Highway 401 East to Bowmanville. Once in Bowmanville, take exit 431, or Waverly Rd, North to Durham Rd 20, and then East 7 miles to Mosport Park.

Circuit: 2.46 mile road course; ten turns.

Major Races: SCCA Trans-Am Championship; Formula Atlantic Championship.

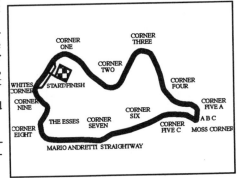

Opened in 1961, Mosport has been the leader in Canadian motorsports. Just about everything now considered traditional in Canadian motorsport has roots in Mosport Park.

In 1967 Formula One, Indy Car and Can-Am races were contested for the first time on Canadian soil at Mosport. The first event ever held at Mosport was won by Stirling Moss at the Players 200 Sports Car race.

Manfred Winkelhock's fatal accident here in 1985 and a decreasing international financial pie conspired to keep the track from hosting any major international events from 1986 to 1990.

But recently extreme measures have been initiated to correct the problems. In fact, Mosport officials geared up to standardize the facility in time to comply with the 1992 homologation rules for FIM Grand Prix motorcycle racing — but were left off the latest schedule anyway.

Mosport has recently affected changes which include wide run-off areas and large gravel pits, removal of most of the armco barriers, as well as the demolition of a 500 foot stretch of concrete wall. Somewhere near 50,000 cubic yards of earth were moved in the renovation process. Canadian motorsport, as popular as it is, has inspired the investment, and Mosport looks to be one of the premier venues in Canada again. The SCCA Trans-Am was the first longtime series to make its return in 1992, and the championship was on the '93 schedule as well.

Camping is Mosport's forte, and most of the hilly 720 acres of Mosport Park can be used for camping — which is free with the price of admission. For more information on Mosport's camping, call the track.

Staying near Mosport is best done in Toronto. There are other areas closer, but Toronto is the easiest to find rooms, and most convenient — especially for late arrivals. For information on Toronto hotels, or accommodations in surrounding areas, call the Convention and Visitors Association of Metropolitan Toronto at (416) 368-9821 or (416) 368-9990.

Race City Speedway
750,   333 11th Ave SW
Calgary, Alta,
T2R 1L9, Canada

PH: (403) 264-6515
FAX (403) 237-8271

Location: On the outskirts of Calgary, just southeast of the city.

Circuit: 2.0 mile road course; 10 turns/ quarter mile dragstrip/ half-mile high banked oval.

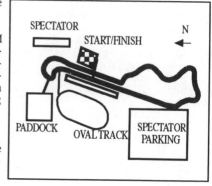

Major races: Players Ltd GM Motorsports Series; Formula Atlantic; Formula Ford 1600; Castrol Canadian Superbike Nationals; ASA Stock Cars; Shell Rotella T 18 Wheeler Weekend; Molson Canadian Funny Car Nationals; NHRA drag racing.

Race City Speedway reflects the terrain of Calgary: it's flat and dry. Actually, there are some ever-so-slight elevation changes on the racing surface in an otherwise flat area.

The track is interesting in that it not only has several variations of racing, but they're all juxtaposed. The main straight of the road circuit — which is also the dragstrip — lies just 100 feet from the oval track, and the back stretch of the road course is only separated from the front stretch by a retaining wall. So from the top of the grandstands, during practice on the road course, you'll watch the oval in operation, while the road cars go two directions in front of you. On many weekends spectators can see two events for the price of one as both road course and drag racing may be running while stock cars race on the oval.

The '93 season marked the second year of stock car racing, with ASA and CASCAR West weekends being the highlights. The biggest race is usually the ASA Players 500.

The best place to watch road racing is from the north end of the racetrack, where you can see almost the entire track. Another good place, recently opened, is at the south east end of the road course, which permits close up viewing of all the turns at the south end. There are no grandstands, but there is a small hill where you can park your lawn chairs.

The area has plenty of hotels which will be no problem for late arrivals — even during racing.

Sanair International
St Pie, Quebec,
Canada J0H 1W0

PH: (514) 772-2426
FAX: (514) 772-2236

Location: Eastern Canada, 30 miles east of Montreal, on Route 10, at exit 55 off highway 10 or 123 off highway 20.

Circuit: .89 mile oval/ .3 mile oval / quarter-mile dragstrip/ 1.25 mile road course; eight turns; Go kart track.

Major races: NHRA Le Grandnational; ACT stock cars; Ten Wheelers National.

Sanair Speedway is an odd mixture of six different disciplines of motor

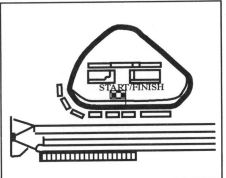

racing. The biggest event at the rural facility was NHRA's Le Grandnational which was held on the dragstrip. Now gone due to fuel politics, the venue has seen better times, once holding a round of the Indycar Series Championship.

Unfortunately, Sanair will always linger in American's minds as the place where Rick Mears had his terrible accident, breaking both his feet as his car hit the Sanair guardrail in 1984. The small oval in the little town of St. Pie has probably seen its best days now. Indycars will never return.

But across the street, at the road course/dragstrip things are still going relatively strong. The drag racing draws 60,000 people annually, and the road track, with its Ten Wheelers racing brings in a good crowd. The late model ACT racing also draws 10,000 people to the oval as well.

The road race track is used mostly for motorcycle racing, which is popular as ever. But, keeping within Canadian tradition, conflicts between sanctioning bodies and sponsors keep the place more empty than full.

The best places to stay will be in St-Hyacinthe or Granby, although there are several small towns in between Montreal and Sanair which will have rooms — St. Pie, not being one of them. Call the Tourisme Quebec office at (800) 444-7000 for more information on accommodations.

Shannonville Motorsport Park
RR #2
Shannonville, Ontario, Canada
K0K 3A0

PH: (613) 969-1906
FAX: (613) 966-6890

Location: 11 miles east of Belleville, off the Windsor/Montreal Highway #401, about 120 miles east of Toronto.

Circuit: 1.4 mile road course/ 1.2 mile road course.

Major races: WERA Formula USA/ RACE Canada Challenge; Firestone Firehawk.

Shannonville hosted a round of the Can-Am held here in its waning years, but most of the recent racing has been strictly Canadian national championship caliber, with the biggest events being two rounds of Canadian F2000 series.

Shannonville Motorsport Park is comprised of several tracks at one venue. The "Nelson track", which is the original circuit, is the shortest road circuit. The other variation, the "Bertrand Fabi" track, named after the young Quebecois who was heralded as the next Gilles Villeneuve and who was tragically killed while testing an F3 car in Great Britain, is the longest version.

The area surrounding the circuit is very flat. Indeed, there are almost no elevation changes on the track, but it is a twisty layout nevertheless. It offers a great deal of runoff, and is a favorite with motorcycle racers, holding several Canadian national and regional races. The F.A.S.T. Motorcycle School, one of North America's few bike schools, calls this track home, and the Nissan Schools and the Bridgestone Racing School also use Shannonville as their base of operations. In 1993, "Pay-Per-Lap" public lapping commenced, allowing the public to experience what a race lap feels like in the family beater.

Viewing is done from one place:

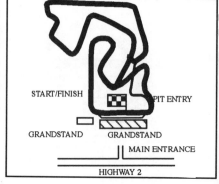

70

the grandstands. From there you can see the entire track — with the possible exception of the extreme left side which is partially blocked by trees if you sit in the wrong place. It's a very technical track, so drivers concentrate on being very smooth here.

The best place to stay is Belleville, which is 11 miles away. Kingston is also relatively close — about 30 miles. Camping is also available — both at the track and in the surrounding area, and admission is free, with firewood included. Call the track or the Ontario Ministry of Tourism at (800) 268-3735 for more information on accommodations.

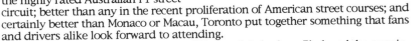

Molson Indy Toronto

Exhibition Place, Toronto, Ontario Office: Molson Indy Exhibition Stadium Gate 9, 4th Floor, Toronto, Ontario, Canada, M6K 3C3

PH: (416) 260-9800 FAX: (416) 260-9400 Tickets(416)260-4639

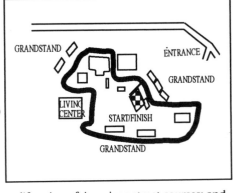

Toronto's Indycar track has been touted as the best street circuit in the world. Considered better than the highly rated Australian F1 street circuit; better than any in the recent proliferation of American street courses; and certainly better than Monaco or Macau, Toronto put together something that fans and drivers alike look forward to attending.

The track encompasses part of Toronto's Lakeshore Blvd, and the remainder is run through the Exhibition Fairgrounds, which open for legitimate business a couple of weeks following the race in August.

The circuit is very fast and very wide, which is why it's a favorite of drivers. It's smack in the middle of Toronto, and offers great viewing for a street course, which is why it's a favorite with fans. Originally, it was difficult to move about the circuit by foot. But changes have been implemented which have just about eliminated that.

Buses or the tram run right to the entrance of the Exposition grounds. But from anywhere in downtown Toronto, it's just a fifteen minute walk to the track. There's really no reason to rent a car here. It's too convenient to take public transportation, and parking can be a problem.

Toronto's only drawback is the cost of rooms. The best places — the most convenient places — are expensive. There are plenty of rooms available, but they can cost you. Track officials seem to feel that future races might be much better for travellers' pocketbooks due to the relationship with the Canadian dollar. Even so, if you're travelling on a budget, try the outskirts of town in southwest Toronto, Mississauga, or Hamilton, which is an hour away. The Convention and Visitors Association of Metropolitan Toronto at (416) 368-9821 or (416) 368-9990. Information on public transportation can best be found through either of these numbers as well.

Trois Rivieres

c/o Grand Prix Players
P.O. Box 120 C
Trois Rivieres, Quebec,
Canada
PH: (819) 373-9912
FAX: (819) 373-9678

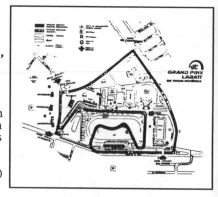

Location: Midway between
Montreal and Quebec City on the north
shore of the St Lawrence River, 60 miles
from Montreal.

Circuit: 1.6 mile road course; 10
turns.

Major races: SCCA Trans-Am Championship; SCCA Formula Atlantic
Championship.

Trois-Rivieres' temporary street circuit is something of an annual
tradition in Quebec, and the city-center Exhibition area has been used as a Trans-
Am track for some 15 years off and on, with Canadian national championships
being held prior to that. Racing was interrupted for a couple of years for financial
reasons, and the temporary track was lengthened at one time, but has been
returned to its original form lately.

As a street circuit, it has obvious limits for spectators. One of the best spots
to watch racing is at the first corner where you'll see down the main straight
through the last few corners, as well as into the pits. Or try Depallier corner — the
hairpin. There is a slight elevation change, but it is not important for spectators.
One noteworthy point about Trois-Rivieres is that the curbs are filled with asphalt,
so drivers can use the sidewalks for racing!

With a population of 350,000, Three Rivers is not a small town, and
finding rooms will be no problem. Call the office of tourism, Tourisme Quebec at
(800) 444-7000.

Vancouver Indy

777 Pacific Blvd. South
Vancouver, BC
Canada V6B 4Y8

PH: (604) 684-4639
TICKETS: (604) 280-INDY
FAX: (604) 684-1482

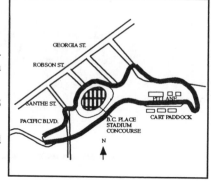

Location: In the Heart of Vancouver on the Old '86 World Expo site, run
around the Pacific Place.

Circuit: 1.7 mile road course; 13
turns

Major Races: CART Indycar World
Series Championship.

As with Montreal's F1 event, Vancouver's site is perfectly suited for racing, utilizing a semi-permanent piece of pavement in amusement park-style venue.

The track runs along Pacific Blvd. North and Pacific Blvd South around the BC Place Stadium, which hosts the BC Lions Football team. With the exception of Pacific North and Pacific South Blvds, the rest of the track is purpose-built for the Indycar race. The site is completely flat.

Vancouver officials boast of one of the best general admission circuits in the world, with several good viewing areas for roaming fans. There are, of course, a good number of grandstands which are limited to start/finish and the turn-three hairpin. Reasonably clear of buildings, Vancouver's seated fans can see a great deal of the track.

There are 1.3 million people in Vancouver, so you'll find everything you could ever want within a few miles of the Downtown Core — Vancouver's main downtown hotel district.

A handful of first-class hotels exist within walking distance of the track — mostly located on Georgia or Burrard streets, four or five blocks away. But the majority of the rooms available for this race are in The Core, which is about a mile away.

Downtown filled up quickly in '91, '92 and '93, and the situation will likely be the same for the next running. Officials suggest booking at least six months in advance. If you find yourself in the area on Thursday or Friday of race weekend there will still likely be rooms available — but not downtown. Suburbs of Vancouver can accommodate overflow, with the best spots found in Burnaby, Richmond, and North Vancouver.

There are good bus services from the Downtown Core, and the Skytrain runs from Burnaby. There are also shuttles and buses from the Downtown Core. The Vancouver International Airport is just a few minutes from the track. Granville St. goes from the airport down to the entrance of the circuit. There is no overnight camping near the circuit.

Call the Vancouver BC Tourism for more information on booking rooms at (800) 663-6000; for Skytrain, bus, or shuttle transportation from your hotel to the track, call the BC Transit at (604) 261-5100.

CZECHOSLOVAKIA

Czechoslovakia is not exactly steeped in motor racing tradition, and Czechoslovakian road vehicles are not known to be the sportiest in Europe. Czechs are compelled to be primitively utilitarian in their motoring.

But events held in the country and the interest in them certainly belie those facts. Brno is a very successful racetrack, attracting huge crowds — most of whom own neither a car nor a motorcycle.

Due to the scarcity of autos there is also an undersupply of roads in Czechoslovakia. There is really only one major road through Czechoslovakia — from Prague to Brno and down to Bratislava. The others are short versions of the Autoroute from the outskirts of both Bratislava and Brno which head east. The main road, which is very good, is designated by the #1, the abbreviated routes are designated #2; all others use two numbers, and are small and usually narrow.

The Autoroutes have speed limits of 110KPH, and are generally obeyed. Smaller roads have a limit of 90KPH, and should be respected as well. Cyrillic signs are confusing, so keep your English map handy. Although passing is done on the left only, and one only ventures into the left lane to pass, there will be very few exotic cars cruising through there, so things are a bit more relaxed than, say, a romp in the fast lane in Germany. The standard green insurance card, and an international drivers licence are necessary for your trip by car. You'll need a visa to enter the country.

For more information on Czechoslovakian or Eastern European travel, call Tatra Travel at (212) 737-5972, located at 1489 2nd Ave, New York, NY 10021.

Tourist Information: **Czechoslovakia Travel Bureau**, 10 East 40th St., #1902, New York, NY 10016, (212) 689-9720.

Sporting Authorities: **Ustredni Automotoklub CSSR**, Opletalova 29, 116 31 Praha1. PH: 423969-971-975; **Ceskoslovenska Motocyklova Feder-ace**, 21 Opletalova, 110 00 Prague, 1. PH: (42 2) 267 883.

Grand Prix CSSR-Brno,
Automotoklub Brno
65743 Brno,
Basty 8,
Czechoslovakia

PH: (42 5) 76 23 45
FAX: (42 6) 76 21 31

Location: Southwestern Czechoslovakia, 40 miles from the Austrian border, 100 miles from Vienna.

From Vienna take National Route 7 toward Mikulov/Brno, or take the D1 Autoroute from Prague. The circuit is seven miles northwest of Brno, on route E50/E65.

Circuit length: 3.35 miles, 13 turns.

Major races held: FIM Superbike Championship.

With the political climate in Czechoslovakia as it is now, things are much lighter at the Autodromo Brno. Although the region has improved dramatically recently, the Czech FIM GP is still a step back into the bleak recesses of eastern European history. Democracy and socialism may have invaded Czechoslovakia, but change is coming at a snail's pace. The inefficiency of communism is a hard habit to break, and the apathy of track staff and officials can still be stifling. The 1994 and beyond rounds of the motorcycle GP World Championship were not confirmed, but are expected to be on the schedule again eventually.

The track itself is an excellent venue — good for both fans and riders. IRTA (International Road Racing Teams Association, the motorcycling equivalent of FOCA) has given Brno its blessing, assuring the GP will continue to return; and there are glances from the FIA for a possible auto race at the circuit eventually.

Located just 20 minutes from downtown Brno, rooms are easy to find and very cheap. Since most fans are locals, the rooms are generally available up to the last minute.

Seats are inexpensive if you

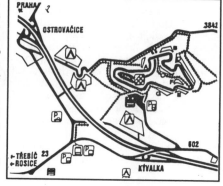

must have a reserved seat, but there are really no bad spots from which to watch racing. There are three grandstands for those who buy tickets, but the entire place is set in the midst of manicured earth made ready for spectators.

The track starts at the top of a hill and winds down into a valley, then back up the hill through the other side of the valley. Bike racers tend to like faster tracks, since the slow ones cause more wheelspin out of the tight corners, which is an invitation for a spill. Here, they have no qualms. The track is a medium speed circuit with corners that are neither too slow nor too fast.

Some riders expressed an opinion that the track was a bit on the boring side to ride, since it has all constant radius turns, and each corner is very similar. It's banked in places (giving spectators an incredible view), and the fast line is the precise, unspectacular one.

There are huge campgrounds on the outskirts of the circuit if you want to rough it. Buses are available from Brno to the track. Before you go, call the Czechoslovakian Office of Tourism.

Most

Automotoklub Banske Stavby Most,
Gottwaldova 2957,
434 93 Most, Czechoslovakia

PH: (42) 2 796906

Location: 60 miles northwest of Prague near the junction of National Routes 27 and 15, 11 miles from National Route 8, and six miles from the East German border.

Circuit: 2.58 miles, 10 turns.

Major races: FIM Superbike Championships; FIM European Road Racing Championships; European Interseries Cup.

If it were possible to purchase stock in a racetrack Most would be a hot trader. No major European automobile races run here yet, although its recent renovation indicates that it may be vying for a major event.

Up until 1992, following the new construction, the best the Czechs had managed to pull off had been a European Championship road race for bikes. But those, as well as the smaller national races, have been phenomenal successes. So in 1992 the place broke into the big league and became host to the 9th round of the FIM Superbike Championship — but it rained, and the race was cancelled. Although it did not appear on the 1993 calendar, the track is likely to host a major two-wheeled event soon. A GP perhaps...?

Although Brno's track is built on the site of a major Czechoslovakian city, Most is just 50 miles from Prague, Czechoslovakia's biggest city. With the re-unification of Germany, Most, which sits just eight miles from the East German border, will see an

START/FINISH

influx of German fans coming across the frontier to watch what will likely be the best European Championship motorcycle races of the season and one of the best Superbike races on the continent.

In '91 the place attracted a round of the Interseries Cup, and that might have started the ball rolling for Most. It hosted some good sized sports car races in the early '80s, but has been away from the fray until recently.

The problem with Most is finding information on rooms. There is little in the area to book, and getting through by phone is more difficult than trying to call Santa Claus. Czech officials have so far been unwilling to accommodate the west — not because they resent Westerners, but because the Czech system is steeped in inefficiency.

Camping will be your best bet. Plan on sharing your campsite with a lot of people, since the camping areas will fill to capacity — and then some. There are good general admission areas here, and seats will likely be available as late as Saturday of the event.

For more information, call the Czechoslovakia Travel Bureau, 10 East 40th St., #1902, New York, NY 10016, (212) 689-9720. Or call the track — and be prepared to wait.

DENMARK

Denmark has a few good drivers, and one major racetrack, but it's not known for being tremendously motoring-oriented. Depending on where you wish to go in Denmark, you can do more sailing here than driving. Most people enter Denmark through West Germany, although from Great Britain there are several ferries that deposit you and your car on the western Jylland coast.

From Germany's A7 North, which becomes E3 once inside Denmark, there are two ways to reach Copenhagen. The first is the ferry from Fynshav to Bojden and another boat ride from Korsor to Slagelse, and then a short drive to Copenhagen; or drive up north past Kolding to the E66 through Odense to Korsor and the same ferry ride to Slagelse. The distance and time are about the same, provided you time the ferry just right. The expense is minimal, so that shouldn't make much difference, and the scenery is good either way.

The speed limits in Denmark are slow: 100 KPH on the major roads, and 80 and 60 in the minor stretches. Your licence plate needs its country of origin on it or you will need to purchase a sticker indicating the country in which your car was rented, and you should have the European green insurance card, as well as an international driver's licence.

Tourist Information: **Danish Tourist Board** in Copenhagen, at the Tourist Information Office on Hans Christian Andersen Blvd. 322 (PH: 111 325); or contact Hotelbooking Copenhagen at least three days ahead of time for a list of hotels anywhere you plan on being in Denmark at Kiosk P, Central Railway Station, DK-1570, Copenhagen V. PH: 451 122 880.

Sporting Authorities: **Dansk Automobil Sports Union**, Gersonsvej 25, P.O. Box 69 2900, Hellerup, DK. PH: 31 62 80 22; **Dansk Automobil Sports Union,** Brondby Station 20, 2605 Brondby, DK.. PH: (45 42) 45 55 55; FAX: (45 42) 45 89 84.

Jyllandsring
A Jyllands-Ringen,
Resenbro, Denmark
8600 Silkeborg, Denmark

PH: (45) 1 06 853322

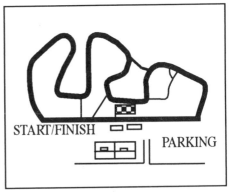

Location: Central Jylland region of Denmark, just east of Silkeborg, about 25 miles west of Arhus. From Arhus, take Regional Route 15 West to Silkeborg, and follow the road out of Silkeborg east toward Resenbro, where the track is located.

Circuit: 1.05 mile road course; seven turns.

Major races: Scandinavian Opel Lotus Championship; National Formula Ford, Saloon, motorcycle, and truck racing championships.

Jyllandsring once hosted the Danish GP, but no major European championships are held here anymore. The track is small, and relatively unchallenging. Its forte is its forgiving nature, making it one of the best for new drivers.

Several schools call this home, one being a bus and truck driver's evasive driving school — where students learn how to get the big barges sideways, then correct the spins.

The track is almost completely flat, rising just a few feet in the corners of the back portion of the circuit. There are no grandstands, but the spectator mounds alongside the circuit provide excellent views of all the action. There is no infield, so from anywhere around the track you'll see all the racing.

Only a few minutes away from Silkeborg, accommodations are best found there. Contact the Tourist information office in Silkeborg for more information on rooms at Torvet 9, P.O. Box 950, DK-8600 Silkeborg; PH. (86) 82 19 11.

FINLAND

Finland has only one major racetrack, but it isn't used for any major international racing. One only has to look at the number of Finnish rally drivers to see that the heritage of Finnish racing is not based on pavement racing, but on dirt racing. Even Keke Rosberg was known for his ability to drive an ill-handling car well on bad surfaces — he was trained in drifting cars on loose surfaces. The best rally talent in the world comes from Finland, and the country's large expanses of woodland, and miles of unpaved (and unpavable) roads gives Finland's drivers excellent surfaces on which to practice their skills. Many of the Finnish and Swedish roads are sand and oil.

Most roads are challenging — all are set in beautiful surroundings. One of the most scenic drives in all of Europe is the overland journey from Sweden up the Gulf of Bothnia and into Finland through Oulu. Driving to Helsinki from Sweden takes only a half-day when travelling by ferry but will take at least two days if taking the land route. If you're in a hurry, take the ferry, which leaves several times a day from Norrtalje to Turku. But if you can afford the extra time the longer route is far superior. The coastal road is asphalt. Speed limits in Finland are 120KPH for the major roads, 100 for the minor roads, and 60-80 on the smallest roads. An international driver's licence is recommended, and a country of origin sticker is required for the car, as well as a green card for proof of insurance.

There are hundreds of rallies in Finland, and they take place year-round. 1,000 Lakes Rally takes place in August, so if you plan on being in the area, give the Finnish Auto Sport Federation a call for the ever-changing location of the staged rally — or the dates and times of any of the Finnish national rallies.

Tourist Information: **Finnish Tourist Board**, called the Finland Travel Bureau, which is located at Kaivokatu 10, in Helsinki, or ask for the City Tourist Office in any major hub city.

Sporting Authorities: **Finnish Automobile Sport Federation**, Radiokatu 12, 00240 Helsinki, Finland. PH: 158 2462; FAX: 158 2492; **Suomen Moottoritto r.y.**, Radiokatu 20, P.O. Box 27, 00240, Helsinki, Finland. PH: (358 0) 158 2250; FAX: (358 0) 147 742.

Kemora Racing Circuit
68700 Veteli, Finland

PH: (358) 68626266

Location: Western Finland, between Oulu and Kokkola, approximately 230 miles north of Turku.

From Turku, take the National Route 8 north toward Kokkola.

Circuit: 1.7 mile road course; nine turns.

Major races: Scandinavian Opel Lotus Championship; Finnish Road Racing Championships; Truck Racing; Kemora Endurance racing.

Built in 1983, Kemora started life as a very short circuit. Originally constructed at .9 miles in length, it was extended in 1986 to its present size, and a final renovation was finished at the start of the 1992 season, which brings the circuit to 2.6 miles total length. Runoff is adequate, and road surfaces are wide and smooth.

Kemora hosts a performance driving school, as well as a very small motor museum... which may now be blessed with as many as a half-dozen vintage cars. On the outside of the track a small Go-Kart circuit sees as much action as its big sister, and a skidpad is also a popular fixture here.

There is a lone grandstand, located on the long straight — on the new portion of the track. But the best place to watch racing is from the top of the pit boxes, which are open for racing. There is also limited access to the areas surrounding the circuit.

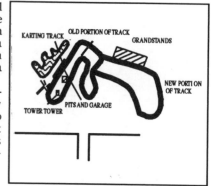

The main problem with Kemora is its weather, which is usually cold and rainy. The best place to stay is at the track, in the campsites. Campers can take advantage of RV hookups and showers. There are several places to buy meals in the pit compound. For more information call the track, or the Finnish Office of tourism.

FRANCE

The French are credited with popularizing the automobile. Indeed, Panhard, Peugeot, Renault, Delage, and several other historic names inspired interest in the automobile in the late 1800 and early 1900s.

Frenchman Nicolas Cugnot is recognized as the first inventor to have conquered the quest for a self-propelled vehicle with a horseless steam tractor in 1770, while Etienne Lenoir is credited as the inventor of the automobile, with patent records showing a coal-gas fueled carriage in 1863.

Regardless of who invented it, the French made the automobile stylish, and the outgrowth of the interest in the automobile was racing. The Nice Hillclimb was largely responsible for what eventually became the Monaco Grand Prix. And France has Le Mans, which is the most significant motor racing city in the world, outside Indianapolis.

The first Grand Prix was held in Le Mans in 1906, and the oldest endurance race is still held there — the 24 Hours of Le Mans. France, in fact, is the home of the FIA, making it probably the most important country on earth in terms of international motor racing.

Driving in France reflects the interest in racing. In the U.S. German roads have the reputation for being the fastest in Europe. For Europeans, however, France is generally known to be the place where speeds are highest. The French Autoroutes have relatively high tolls, so locals and most commercial vehicles use the smaller local roads. The congestion in the cities is very rarely found on the Autoroutes (except outside Paris, where it's as bad as the worst cities in the world), and the roads are every bit as good as the German Autobahns.

You'll have to pay attention in France. It can be very dangerous if you don't concentrate on your driving. There's a speed limit on the Autoroute of 130KPH. But it's almost universally ignored, except maybe in the south on the Riviera, where it is at least acknowledged to exist. The police sit on the sides of the road in many places, with cars flying by at over 160, and they won't even move. Of course, exceeding the speed limit is against the law, and motorists can technically be cited.

Rene Arnoux was stopped recently for allegedly driving his Ferrari at a speed approaching 300KPH. It took the police some time to finally catch him! But those are the speeds at which these roads can be driven. Especially in Central France, between Paris and Avignon, the left lane is the property of some very fast cars. You might be cruising at 160, and passing a car in the left lane with alacrity and be caught by a faster car as if you were anchored.

Remember to keep the left blinker flashing if you do venture into the fast lane — no matter how fast you go. Even the supercars keep their blinkers on, conceding that there still may be faster cars out there, and that they're watching their mirrors too.

The smaller roads are more dangerous. They too have speed limits — but are also generally disregarded. The limit is usually 90KPH, unless otherwise posted. The small French roads have what are jokingly called "chicken lanes". Most roads have three lanes: one headed each direction, and one for either direction to pass.

That means that the central lane will be shared by the fastest cars in either direction. Make sure you have some perception of speed and distance, because 160 KPH — which drivers often have to achieve to pass — equals 320KPH, or 192 MPH.

That's faster than most people are used to calculating, and it can bring two cars together pretty fast, with disastrous results.

Paris is another interesting motoring adventure. If you're heading to Rome, make sure to take a trip through the center of Paris to prepare yourself. Otherwise, leave the car at the hotel and don't use it again until you leave the city.

For the adventurous, try the Arc de Triomphe. It looks like a parking lot at a baseball stadium, with hundreds of people frantically trying to get out as fast as possible — and all going different directions. If you can master the circle around the arch, and can get to your destination on the first try, you may be alright in Rome.

Roundabouts are entered from the right, yielding to traffic coming from the left. Everybody watches their right side. Like the U.S.'s version of a rear-ender, if you have damage on your left fender, it's usually assumed to be your fault. Be alert!

Also, the toll roads are very expensive. It isn't odd to find stretches of road where you'll have to pay $20 or more for a toll. Keep that in mind when you plan your trip through the French countryside. The Autoroutes are faster, but it may cost you $150 to get from one end of the country to the other. The smaller roads are usually the best way to see the countryside anyway.

Hotel information can be found by using the standard "i" information centers, which are usually located near the main train stations in any given city, and also along the Autoroutes. An experiment in 1990 with a toll free number for hotels, restaurants, and tourist information has proven successful, although there are no firm commitments for '91 or beyond. The free phone number, good from any phone in France, was 05 20 12 02. It's likely to remain the same indefinitely, but call the French Government Tourism Office here in the U.S. for confirmation before you leave.

Tourist Information: The **French Government Tourist Office**. Try the main center in Paris, which can link you to any of the other major hub cities of France — located at #127 Ave Champs Elysees, Paris. There are generally all-inclusive hotel and pensione guides available from the local offices, and the main offices here can give you information on how to get a hold of one of the listings.

Sporting Authorities: **Federation Francaise du Sport Automobile**, 136 rue de Longchamp, 75016 Paris. PH: (33 1) 47 27 97 39; FAX: (33 1) 47 04 53 76; **Federation Francaise de Motocylisme,** 74 Av. Parmentier, 75011, Paris. PH: (33 1) 4700 9440; FAX: (33 1) 4700 0837.

Circuit d'Albi
Route de Toulouse
F-81990, France

PH: (33) 63 54 94 00
FAX: (33) 63 38 96 01

Location: Southwestern France, roughly between Toulouse and Montpellier.

From Toulouse, take National Route 88 North to Albi; From Montpellier, take Autoroute A9 West to N112 North to Albi; and from Paris, take A10 to Bordeaux to A62 to Montauban (N999 East), and N999 to N88 into Albi.

Circuit Length: 2.2 miles; eight turns.

Major races: French Formule 3 Championship; French Supertourisme Championship; FormuleRenault Championship;

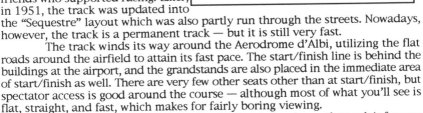

FRANCE CIRCUIT D'ALBI

PARKING

START/FINISH

PARKING

LE SEQUESTRE AIRSTRIP

CHICANE DU SEQUESTRE

In 1930, Albi's track was a street circuit which hosted a Grand Prix race. Even then, the circuit was blindingly quick, with an average speed for the race of almost 80 mph.

In 1933 the Saint-Juery circuit was constructed by a group of friends who supported racing. Later, in 1951, the track was updated into the "Sequestre" layout which was also partly run through the streets. Nowadays, however, the track is a permanent track — but it is still very fast.

The track winds its way around the Aerodrome d'Albi, utilizing the flat roads around the airfield to attain its fast pace. The start/finish line is behind the buildings at the airport, and the grandstands are also placed in the immediate area of start/finish as well. There are very few other seats other than at start/finish, but spectator access is good around the course — although most of what you'll see is flat, straight, and fast, which makes for fairly boring viewing.

Most of what runs here these days is historical racing — the track is famous for its classic car racing. There are usually enough rooms in Albi, or along 88 in either direction. You shouldn't have to travel all the way to Toulouse for rooms, but if so the Office de Tourisme is located at Donjon du Capitol, 31000 Toulouse; PH. 61 23 32 00. Or try the toll-free "green number" from anywhere in France at 05 20 12 02

Charade
Circuit de Montagne
d'Auvergne,
62 Rue Bonnabaud
6300 Clermont Ferrand
PH: (33) 73 939929
FAX: (33) 73 93 80 06

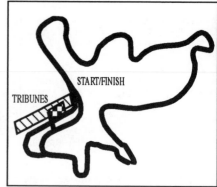

Location: South-central France, three miles west of Clermont-Ferrand on National Route 89, just off Rural Route 21.

Circuit: 2.4 miles, 22 turns.

Major races held: Major races: French Supertourisme Championship; Porsche Cup; Formule Renault Championship; French Formula Ford; Clio Championship; Alfa-Romeo Sport Prototype .

Now known as the Circuit Charade, this historic track's old name and parts of its old racing circuit will likely continue to be more famous than the new venue. Charade's previous title was Clermont-Ferrand, and it was the intermittent site of the F1 World Championship from 1965 to 1972, with brief departures to Le Castellet, Le Mans, and Reims.

The old track was a long and very twisty piece of asphalt — some 5.3 miles and 33 corners to the place. The new track is less spectacular, but more along the standards of the F1 fraternity with its current length.

The five-plus miles of track used to wind up through the town of Charade, through the really twisty bits at the base of Mont Miel, around Puy de Grave Noire, and past Puy de Charade and Autodrome back to the start.

Somewhat emasculated, the new track is contained to the southern base of the hill around Puy de Charade, winding past Autodrome, and Champeaux-Bas. The old track is utilized for about 70 per cent of the circuit, running from just above the second turn of the old circuit due east to connect with the final nine corners — the new addition has eight turns to it. Although very challenging, the new Charade is not as impressive as its older sister.

Organizers had hoped to lure the French GP here, but with the new contract with Magny-Cours -- and the cancellation of the GP altogether -- that situation looks unlikely for the near future.

Although new facilities have been built, there is still only one grandstand — that, located at start/finish. Viewing is good here, except that the far end of the track is still heavily forested, so you'll likely stay somewhere near the final few corners or the first third of the track.

A new access road has been recently completed to the south of the circuit, so getting in and out will be slightly easier. It is not a problem so far, but if some of the more noteworthy series come through — such as the French F3 Championship — it can get congested.

Although Charade has some rooms, it's best to stay in Clermont-Ferrand. For more information, call or stop by the Office de Tourisme, 69 Blvd Gerovia, 63000 Clermont Ferrand; PH. 73 93 30 20. Or try the toll-free "green number" from anywhere in France at 05 20 12 02.

Circuit Auto-Moto de Croix-en-Ternois

ASA Ternoise
BP No 24,
62130 St Pols/Ternoise,
PH: (33) 21 03 3013/
030224/FAX: (33) 21 03 2720

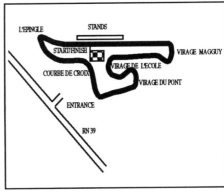

Location: Northern France, roughly between Paris and Lille, or between Arras and St Pol sur-Ternois on National Route 39, 30 miles from the A1 off RN39 toward the exit Saint Pol Sur Ternoise, where the track borders the RN39.

Circuit: 1.18 miles, 7 turns.

Major races: French Formule 3 Championship; French Supertourisme Championship; Porsche Cup.

Croix en Ternois sits on a featureless hillside in the rural farmland just off the RN39 National Route. And although racing is usually good, there's really no other reason to visit the place.

There are no grandstands at Croix en Ternois, and except for the areas atop the few permanent garages just across from start/finish, spectating is done from the manicured earth embankments alongside the circuit. Because of its relatively featureless surroundings, as well as the hillside location, most of the track is visible from anywhere. So just standing on the dirt shoulders should yield you a good shot of the racing.

Although the racing generally attracts good crowds, most of the fans are locals. The area is not a tourists' paradise, so rooms will not likely be booked in advance. There are, however, only a few rooms available in St Pol. You'll be able to do some makeshift camping in the parking facilities which surround the circuit, although there only about 10 trees in the whole place, so don't figure on a nice forested campsite. If you need a real room and aren't able to find one in St. Pol, try Arras or Le Touquet, which are each about 15 miles in either direction on the RN39.

Circuit Dijon-Prenois,

c/o M. Chambelland,
BP 8 21380,
Missigny, France

PH: (33) 80 353222/
80356057
FAX: (33) 80 35 33 22/
80356166

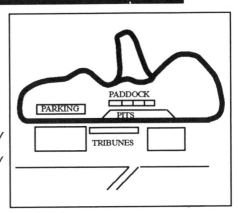

Location: Eastern Central France, 10 miles north of Dijon off the N74.

Major races: French Formule 3 Championship; French Supertourisme Championship; Porsche Cup; Formule Renault Championship; French Formula Ford; Clio Championship; Alfa-Romeo Sport Prototype Championship; 905 Championship; Coupe Ex Championship.

Circuit: 2.36 mile road course; 7 turns.

Dijon's surfaces have not been maintained over the years, and the abuse to race cars was one reason why the FIA moved Formula One away from the centrally located French track. The circuit has a reputation for being very fast, and race laps are very quick — just over one-minute per lap in an F1 car.

It hosted both a round of the FIA Prototype Championship and a FIA F3000 race in 1991, but has not appeared again on either calendar recently, and will likely never see a Grand Prix again — especially while Paul Ricard and Magny-Cours are so hot on one-upping each other and the French government is so hot on eliminating racing of all kinds..

The track hosted the Grand Prix five times from '74 to '84, the most noteworthy date being the '79 race, where on the final lap Gilles Villeneuve and Rene Arnoux banged wheels several times in what's classified as one of the most spectacular battles in all of modern day Grand Prix racing.

The two, fighting for second spot through most of the race, came together in what looked more like a Mickey Thompson Off Road race than a Grand Prix. Villeneuve led from the start in his Ferrari 312 T4, with Jean Pierre Jabouille and Arnoux falling behind in their Renault Turbos. Past mid-point, Jabouille passed Villeneuve and Arnoux followed suit. It appeared to be a Renault 1-2. Villenueve, in the Ferrari 312 T4 with badly worn Michelins, set sail to break up the dominance at the French showcase race, and passed Arnoux on the final lap — and was subsequently re-passed by Arnoux. Although Villeneuve finally triumphed, finishing second, the next several corners of that lap were nothing short of a shoving match, with the two drivers interlocking wheels and battling on the dirt and grass as much as on the pavement. Whenever Dijon is the site of a major televised race, the opening clips usually replay the fight for second place from the '79 race.

Dijon is a very viewable circuit, and there are some excellent spots from which to watch the racing. The main tribunes at start/finish are spectacular, since the faster cars are really moving as they flash past the pits. But probably the best seats are smack in the middle of the track behind the pits. Sitting between the "S" Sablieres and the Parabolique you'll see a good bit of racing as the cars make the drive up toward the Parabolique Hairpin, and then watch them as they climb the hill toward Courbe Des Gorgeolles.

The track is covered with brush inside, and there are no grandstands on the outside of the circuit. There is access to Petite Combe and the off-camber Courbe De Pouas — which is probably the most critical and difficult corner on the circuit — although no grandstands exist in the immediate area.

This track is hardest on left front tires, and understeer here will certainly lose the favorite his race. If you keep an eye on the cars as they negotiate the Parabolique you'll be able to see those who are going to have trouble as the race goes on.

This is the home of the Winfield Driving School which is said to be one of the best drivers schools in the world. The school boasts of having put Alain Prost on the top. Regardless of Winfield's impetus, Prost got his break through the school with a sponsored ride. If you write for information, the school will be happy to send you some things — including hotels in the area, which will be handy even if you decide not to attend.

The best places to stay for a weekend at Dijon is in Dijon itself. The track

84

and the school will send you lists which will have hotels all over the immediate area. But even for a GP weekend Dijon should be no problem if you book early. For the minor series — which are currently running here — you should be able to appear on Friday and have no complications whatsoever.

For more information, call or stop by the Office de Tourisme, located at Place Darcy, 21000, Dijon; PH. 80 43 42 12. Or try the toll-free "green number" from anywhere in France at 05 20 12 02. Or call the track.

La Chatre
Circuit Regional Automobile
Mairie de la Chatre,
La Chatre 36400, France
PH: (33) 54 48 03 53/ 54 48 26 48

Location: Central France, between Limoges and Chateauroux, approximately 150 miles south of Paris.

From Paris, take Autoroute A10 to A71 to National Route 20 toward Chateauroux, turning east at Local 943 to La Chatre, then following the signs to Bourges and the circuit, located on 940.

Circuit: 1.45 mile road course;12 turns.

La Chatre is no longer on any major European series schedules. Too bad. The street/permanent circuit is very challenging and very safe. Built just off the main road — and incorporating some of the 940 highway — La Chatre is a nice, slightly hilly track with lots of run-off and great viewing. There is paltry space on the tarmac of the tight track, however, limiting the fields to 20 starters.

The 940 highway loops right on the way to La Chatre from Bourges, and the track, built on the northwest side of the road, incorporates the right-hand 940 sweeper — which is the fastest part of the circuit.

Oddly enough, the only viewing areas are on the far side of the track, in the Pelouse Nord — which is set on a hill so that the entire course can be seen — or the Pelouse Sud, which limits spectators to the turn leading onto 940 and little else. There is almost no other spectator access.

The start/finish line used to be located on the short straight adjacent to the long 940 sweeper. But the design made for poor starts, so it was recently moved so the pits (which remained in the same place) are now entered off the 940, to the right, rather than from the short chute.

Parking for the races is done either on the other side of the Pelouse Sud, or behind the track near the Pelouse Nord. There is plenty of parking, since most of the racing is not of national championship caliber.

The best place to stay is in La Chatre, and the Office de Tourisme there is very helpful — either when you arrive or before you leave on your trip. It's located at Square George Sand, 36400 La Chatre; PH. 54 48 22 64. Or try the toll-free "green number" from anywhere in France at 05 20 12 02.

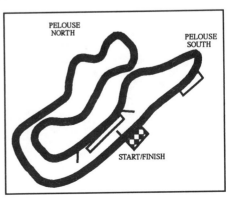

Le Mans

**Circuit de La Sarthe,
c/o Automobile Club de
L'Ouest,
Circuit des "24 Heures"
Les Raineries 72040
Le Mans   Cedex 19,
France**

**PH: (33) 43 40 24 24
FAX: (33) 43 40 24 25**

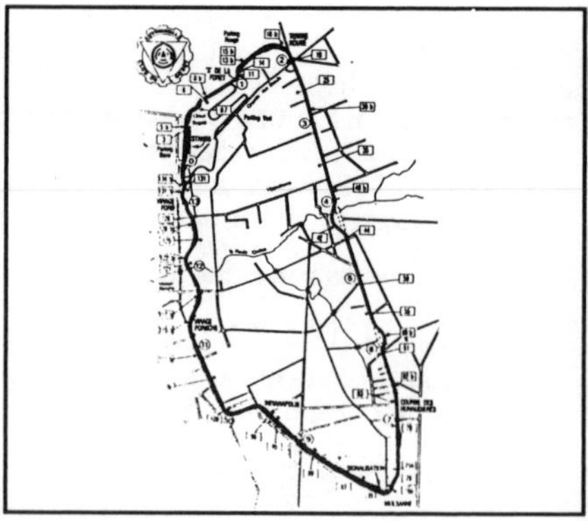

Location: Northwestern France, approximately 120 miles from Paris.

From Paris, take the Autoroute A10 to A11 west to Le Mans. Circuit is clearly marked.

Circuit: 8.4 miles; 12 turns (full circuit)/ 2.63 miles; 11 turns (Bugatti circuit).

Major races: 24 Hours du Mans for Sports Cars (full circuit); FIM World Endurance Championships; French Formula 3000 Championship; French Formule 3 Championship; French Supertourisme Championship; Porsche Cup; Formule Renault Championship; French Formula Ford; Clio Championship; Alfa-Romeo Sport Prototype Championship; 905 Championship; Coupe Ex Championship; 24 Heures Camions Truck Racing; 24 Heures Karting (24 Hour Kart race).

Le Mans is one jewel of what Eddie Cheever once called the "Triple Crown of racing". The trio being the Monaco Grand Prix, the Indianapolis 500, and the 24 Hours of Le Mans. Of the three, Le Mans is the oldest of the three, and is certainly the most fun.

Le Mans is history, and those who aren't the least bit interested in racing before they attend the classic 24 hour happening, will be fascinated as the checkered flag falls Sunday afternoon.

Three days of English radio broadcasts will educate anyone with ears, and

by the time the ordeal is over the unindoctrinated will be experts. If somehow one could attend the event without watching any of the on-track action, there is still night at Le Mans.

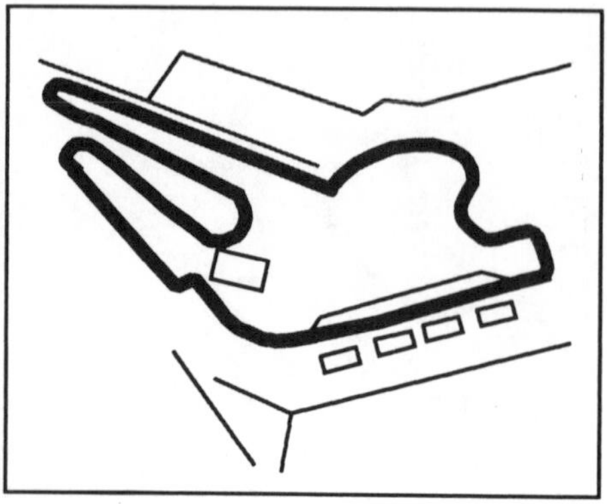

When the sun goes down the real show begins. The Amusement park lights come up, complete with midway sideshows and fairground barkers. The partying at Le Mans can bruise even the best livers, and the damage is evident Sunday morning when the sun comes up on the swollen heads of those who overindulged.

There is nothing like an endurance race for the ardent fan. That's the one time fans can participate in racing. When the tedious lapping of cars sends the average fan to bed or to the the bar, the serious racefan stays; waits; watches. The drama of a race car at speed is intensified at night. The hot glow of overworked engines gives spectators a view they wouldn't ordinarily have during the day; the headlights gobble up ground at 300 feet per second, and the cars appear to be silent at that speed — until the sound catches up.

But night racing at Daytona, Spa, or Sebring is not like night racing at Le Mans. Le Mans is a happening. There's no description that adequately explains what happens here. If you can see only one race in Europe, it must be the 24 Hours of Le Mans.

1992 was a disaster for the circuit. And it turned out that the Auto Club de l'Ouest was right: the World Sportscar Championship was doomed with FISA's regulations. In fact, the race itself has been hurt in the process. The fight with FISA that saw the club's control of their own race slip from their hands was one of the worst that either faction fought. So much so that the organizers of the race canceled the FIA-sanctioned F3000 event in anger and sued FISA for damages resulting in a poor turnout of cars at the 24 Hours. They won the suit, but received a very small award. The contract guaranteed a full field, and it was far from full when the flag dropped.

For 1994 and beyond, the Automobile Club de L'Ouest is allowing just about anything to run in the event, and so far the reports suggest that races will run full grids once again.

There's really only one way to watch the race, and that's to camp at the circuit. Plenty of spaces exist which can be reserved early through the Auto Club de l'Ouest, by mail, by phone, or in person at any of the ACO's offices (there's one in Paris). You should have no problem arranging a campspot Saturday morning in-person either.

Camp as close to the track as possible, but don't worry about it, since you can't see anything from any campspot anyway — it just makes it easier to get trackside if you are close. The areas on the outside of the Dunlop Curve are

probably the best, since you can get to and from the track with relative ease.

Almost everything is general admission at Le Mans — unless you're fortunate enough to be invited to the pit-suites, or if you purchase a paddock pass — and the track offers incredible viewing areas anyway.

Most viewing is done from the start/finish up to the entrance of the Mulsanne. The area around the famous Dunlop Bridge is good, although a bit neutered since the chicane was added in 1987. Even though the speeds are lower in the Dunlop Curve, the kink created a natural stadium area which is very dramatic at the start.

But the downhill, past the Dunlop Bridge in "S De La Foret", is one of the most incredible sequences in all of racing, with the cars braking ever so slightly on the downhill left-hander, then hard on the loud-pedal for the right turn toward Tertre Rouge.

If you can arrange it try to make it out to the Mulsanne Straight. Once the longest in racing at over three miles, race cars once achieved speeds of nearly 250 MPH there. The new chicanes may have their critics, but speeds that high do not make for forgiving accidents — and at night the situation was worse.

It will take a while to get to the one spot where you can watch the action on Mulsanne. You'll likely take a bus out to the restaurant on the Mulsanne — which is the most popular eatery in all of France for the the weekend. Since you can't walk there from inside the track, it's best to see the Mulsanne sometime Thursday during practice.

Remember to bring a clear plastic ticket holder to the race with you. Your ticket will need to be visible at all times during the weekend — plus, each time you go from trackside to the campgrounds or outside the circuit you'll receive another ticket which allows you back inside the circuit. The system keeps tickets from being passed through the fences, but it also means if you lose yours you'll be purchasing another one.

There are hotels in Le Mans, or you could go farther away to room, but why? Come for qualifying on Thursday, leave Friday's free day for Paris, then return early Saturday morning with your sleeping bag. You can get as sophisticated as bringing a tent-trailer with all the modern utilities, or you could brave the night with a bottle of red wine and catch a few winks in the warm morning hours.

Getting out of the circuit can be a mess. It might be wise to plan dinner at the track, leaving after the crowd does. Plan on two hours. Once you hit the Autoroute, however, you'll never even know there had been a race that weekend. Leaving early doesn't really work either, since lots of people do that.. and you wouldn't want to miss anything anyway, right?

If you must, call the Office of Tourisme at Hotel des Ursulines, rue Etoile, 72000 Le Mans, France. PH: 43 28 17 22. Or call the toll free "green number" at 05 20 12 02 from anywhere in France.

Circuit International de Nimes Ledenon
30210 Remoulins, France

PH: (33) 66 37 11 37/ (33) 66 37 27 75
FAX: (33) 66 37 15 92

Location: Southern France, between Nimes and Avignon, next to the city of Remoulins.

From Paris, take Autoroute A6 South, turning to A7 South, then onto A9 South, bearing west at Remoulins on National Routes 981/86 to the track; from Marseille, take A7 North to National Route 100 to Remoulins, following 981/86 past the city to the track.

Circuit: 1.86 mile road course; 15 turns.

Major races: French Formula 3 Championship; French Formula Ford; Clio Championship; Coupe Ex Championship; Motorcycle Championships.

Ledenon's undulating track nicely follows the contours of the hills around the city of Remoulins, and although the track's length and width (nine meters in most places, fifteen in others) would allow it to host a World Championship event, it has yet to put out the money Magny-Cours or Paul Ricard have, and in fact is not interested in attracting a GP.

The track is challenging, and has several good places from which to watch racing. There are grandstands in a few spots about the course, so even minor race outings have enough permanent seats to make it worth the visit.

A second circuit is beginning to make a name for itself as well at Ledenon. Alongside the old circuit is a new road course, which varies in both elevation and layout, utilizing none of the old Ledenon circuit. The second track, a 2.1 mile 14 turn track is much faster than its twisty neighbor, but it is considered a good venue for both spectators and competitors.

There are plenty of places to stay here. Remoulins has a handful of rooms, or Nimes will be wide open.

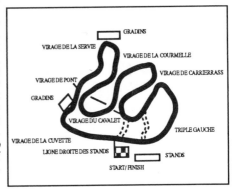

The nearest Office of Tourisme is located at 6 rue Auguste, 30000 Nimes — which is 20 minutes west of the track; PH. 62 28 00 80. Or try the "green number".

Magny-Cours
ASA du Nivernais,
Circuit de Magny Cours,
5840 Magny Cours, France

PH: (Office)(33) 86 58 17 33/ (Track) 86 212074
FAX: (33) 86 21 20 28

Location: Central France, between Dijon and Bourges, just south of Nevers.
From Paris, take the Autoroute A6 to National Route South to 151 South, bearing south on N7 to the track, just past Nevers.

Circuit: 2.4 mile road course; 14 turns.

Major races: FIA Formula One Grand Prix World Championship; FIM Grand Prix Motorcycle World Championship; French Formula 3 Championship.

Magny-Cours came from out of nowhere in just three years to host the country's premier racing event in 1991, the July running of the French Grand Prix. The event was a success. And as expected, rooms and traffic were a problem.

1992 was even worse for ingress and egress, with the truckers' strike in full force absolutely choking traffic into and out of the track while protesting a new law that would revoke their licences for too many traffic tickets. Their means of protest was to park the trucks bumper to bumper in the middle of the highway, clogging all major arteries.

Magny-Cours held the FIM Motorcycle Grand Prix 500cc and 250cc races in 1992, and most of the field hated the place. Some teams felt it was a fairly dangerous layout and didn't find it suitable for motorcycle racing.

However, the place in general, is impressive. Known as the "technopolis" of France's heartland, the racetrack is only the hub of the fixture, which includes full shop and testing facilities (most notably used by Ligier's F1 team), several driving schools, and a technical school, which will offer France's first academic degree in Sports-Engineering.

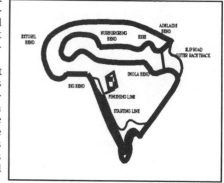

Located outside Nevers, just south of the Loire Valley, Magny-Cours was completely rebuilt from an existing circuit with impetus from both Jacques Laffite and Rene Arnoux. The layout was inspired by some of the most difficult corners on several tracks around the world — and each corner is aptly named in honor of the cloned racetracks.

Magny-Cours officials boast of a 75% viewable track from grandstand seating. In fact, the best seats here are probably not at start/finish, but in the seats at the Golf Kink (which bounds Magny-Cours' golf course on the west side) or at the Adelaide Corner.

The track has since been repaved and the surface, which was once criticized by Guy Liger for being so smooth nobody could get any traction for racing, is now the standard for racing surfaces.

The French government is heartily endorsing the new racetrack — to the horror of Paul Ricard and Dijon officials, who'd hoped to hold either or both the motorcycle and automobile Grands Prix.

The problem with this racetrack is access and the accommodations. It may have been difficult to find rooms near the circuit at Paul Ricard, but they were available. Here the rooms are few and far between, and even booking ahead will likely be a major headache.

Nevers has plenty of rooms for the smaller races. But when either Grand Prix returns it will be critical to start looking early. The track can send you a nine-page booklet on accommodations in the area (you can reach the track easiest by fax at the number listed in the top margin); if you have trouble getting through or are looking for a room as the date closes, call the French Office of Tourisme at 31 rue du Rampart, 58000, Nevers; Ph. 86 59 07 03. Remember the Green Number while in France. If you get off a plane in Paris on Monday and call the toll-free number immediately, you may get lucky. The number is 05 20 12 02.

Plan on doing some driving. You may not have to for smaller races. The places to look first are, obviously, Nevers, then la Charite-s-Loire, Autun, Bourges, Montlucon, or Vezelay, and finally Vichy.

If things get ugly, and you can't find a room in the area for some reason or another, consider taking the train. There's a station in Nevers and there are major routes which will leave you in town several times daily from farther destinations — and will likely be beefed up for the major races. Likewise, there will probably be shuttles available on race weekends.

Parking will be no problem since there's plenty built into the technopolis, but the roads will likely be very congested. There's no Autoroute. Which means all traffic is expected to arrive and depart the races on four small, two-laned roads. Paris is only 85 miles away, but the drive will take you two hours on a light traffic day — much longer on a GP weekend when the truckers are on strike...

UTAC Autodrome de Linas-Montlhery,

F-91310 Montlhery, France

PH: (33) 69 011047
FAX: (33) 69 01 78 45

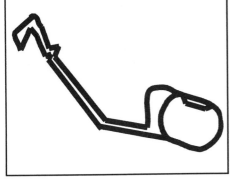

Location: 20 miles South of Paris, on National Route 20

Circuit: 2.12 mile road course, with five turns; or 1.5 mile oval.

Major races: French Super-tourisme Championships; French Clio Championship; Formula Ford; Coupe Ex Championship; Alfa Romeo Sport.

Run by UTAC Labs, the French organization which oversees safety and homologation standards for the French auto industry, Montlhery sees more testing than racing. But the facility is one of the best in France. The oval, which is incorporated into each of the three major variations of the circuit, is as impressive as any American superspeedway, with an admirable 33 degree banking on each end of its 1.53 mile oval.

The track is driven in both directions during testing. But it's used clockwise only for French national racing (as is the standard on European road courses). There is a four-turn extension and a couple of chicanes added for variety. The oval portion will likely become one of the regulars if the FIA Oval Racing Championships ever comes to pass. The road track is 2.12 miles but the total length of the road racing test track is 4.0 miles.

The infield is a manufacturer's testing grounds, with skidpads, permanent ruts, cobblestones, and a collision and impact testing track. Beneath the oval — the racing surface stands several stories off the ground — are labs and offices. In fact, the main feature is not the track but the huge testing facilities just north of what should be Turn One.

One lone grandstand overlooks the start/finish pits, so most of the viewing is done from the grounds surrounding the circuit. Most people prefer to watch from the infield — or you can walk out on the road portion of the track which is south of the oval.

The road portion is almost completely flat and not really worth the effort since the place is well forested and viewing is limited. Parking is done in the infield, and the area can accommodate the entire field with their equipment and a full house of spectators.

There will likely be rooms available in Montlhery until Saturday during a race weekend. But if you fail to find something there, Paris is only a few miles north, and between the city itself and the track lies the Paris Orly Airport, which will have plenty of rooms in a pinch. For more information call or stop by the Office de Tourisme, located at Place de l'Hotel de Ville, 91310 Montlhery, France; (1) 69 01 70 11. Or try the toll-free "green number" from anywhere in France at 05 20 12 02.

Nogaro
Circuit Automobile Paul Armagnac, BP-24, 3211 Nogaro, France

PH: (33 62) 090249/090208
FAX: 33) 62 69 05 44

Location: South western France, roughly between Bordeaux and Toulouse, 110 miles from the Spanish border.

From Bordeaux, take Autoroute A62 East 135 miles to National Route 931/124, bearing south to Nogaro; from Toulouse, take N124 North to Nogaro.

Circuit: 1.89 mile road course; six turns.

Major races: FIA Formula 3000 Championship; French Formula 3.

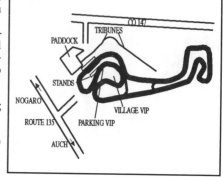

Circuit Paul Armagnac sits on a flat plain in southwestern France, equal distance from Bordeaux and Toulouse. The climate of the Nogaro track is warm and predictable, and the area is known for its food and drink.

Track officials boast of an 80% viewable circuit, and several great grandstands for spectators. The seating capacity here is 35,000 — although the stands are seldom filled to capacity. The stands wind from the final turn to halfway down the racetrack, with both sides of the track visible from at least half of the seats.

In addition to the seats, the circuit has some excellent viewing areas at trackside, which is 100% accessible. Most fans prefer to walk about and watch from the fences.

The track was constructed in 1960, and offers every amenity that circuits like Paul Ricard or Dijon have — without the bigger shows the other two lay claim to.

There are several rooms in Nogaro, but you may have to stay a few miles from the track. You can try Eauze or Condom, a few miles north, or Aire-sur-l'Adour, a short drive to the south. For more information contact the Office de Tourisme at Place Bossuet, 32100 Condom; PH. 62 28 00 80. Or try the toll-free "green number".

Circuit Pau-Arnos

sa Cecidil,
32 av Jean Mermoz,
6400 Pau, France
PH: (33) 59 327209/59816188

Location: 13 miles from Pau

Circuit: 2.0 mile road course; seven turns.

Major races: French Formula 3 Championship.

Pau-Arnos was developed in 1987 as a counterpart to street racing through the heart of Pau city-center, which has been held there since the '30s. The new permanent circuit is touted as being the most picturesque in France, and the climate of Pau is a good selling feature of the venue.

Climbing and falling some 160 feet in its two miles, it boasts very fast sweepers and tight twisty bits — both of which are provided with good run-off. There are six variations of circuit which can be used, from a .4 mile loop to the 2.0 mile championship track.

Nicknamed the "snake in the green body", the track snakes its way through the beautiful grassy valley which comprises the 600 acres of track land. Starting on a ridge, the track dips into the valley and winds its way back around to the top of the hill again.

Grandstands are located on the outsides of the corners, so most of the racing will be visible from anywhere, and the start/finish stands are the best of the bunch.

There is camping in the area,

and Pau is still the best place to find a room. The Office of Tourisme for Pau is located at Place Royale, 64000 Pau; PH. 59 27 27 08. Or try the "green number".

Circuit Paul Ricard
ASA Circuit Paul Ricard,
Route Nationale 8,
F-83.330 Le Beausset, France

PH: (33) 94 90 76 90/ (33) 96 90 76 27
FAX: (33) 96 90 72 75

Location: Southern France, between Marseille and Toulon.
From Marseille take the coastal road to Toulon and take National Route 8 to the circuit in Le Beausset, or take the A50 Autoroute to N8 and come into Le Beausset from the north.

Circuit: 2.37 mile road circuit; six turns.

Major races: FIM Superbike Championships; French Formula 3 Championship; Alfa-Romeo Sport Proto Championship; 905 Championship; Clio Championship; Formule Ford; Formule Renault.

Even more than Monaco, Paul Ricard was once the Grand Prix to see if you were looking for racing on the Riviera. Monaco is crammed with "wannabes", many of whom could care less about racing.
But Paul Ricard is unassuming. It is southern French hospitality without the pretension of the eastern Cote d'Azur. It is also very French. Unlike Nice or Monaco, where everybody speaks English, Bandol and Toulon are more European resorts. Of course, many people speak English, but you'll have to struggle more in French than in, say, Monaco. But the people are generally friendly, and will wait patiently as you try to communicate.
Unfortunately, Paul Ricard is no longer on the GP schedule, and for now its biggest race will be the FIM Endurance Championship. Like, Monaco, however, Paul Ricard is no gem in terms of room availability. The weather during both the Superbike and the FIM Endurance Championships is excellent, and the resorts will be filled. For even the smallest race, there will be a good drive from your room to the track.
Other than getting to the circuit, which can take some time, Paul Ricard is one of the nicer tracks in Europe. Getting into the track is a headache — what with only one small road to the circuit and
one main entrance. But once inside, it's well laid out and easy to walk about. There aren't as many general admission spots from which to watch as at other permanent courses, and those that are good generally are packed all weekend long. It might be a good idea to find seats early.
One of the best places to watch is either the Mistral straight, which was the longest in F1, where cars got up to 200 MPH and tap the brakes for Signes, or just past the Mistral in Signes — although the sun

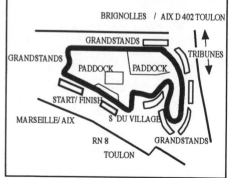

94

sets on the Signes stands in the afternoon, and it gets very hot.

A stay in the area during F1 races was a problem. Even if you got to the circuit on Wednesday — when, at most places, you'd still be able to find some rooms somewhere — almost nothing was available in the area. Things have changed, and it's not as vital that you do homework anymore. But it is still recommended. If you choose to do so, the local tourist agency has a terrific handbook on every hotel or room in the region. You can write or call early and set it all up.

If you do plan early, try for a room in Bandol. It's one of the most beautiful spots on the Mediterranean, and worth paying extra. Toulon and Marseille should be easier and cheaper. Le Castellet is still out of the question, no matter how far in advance you do your planning, and no matter how small the race is.

If you find yourself with no place to stay, one word will get you through the ordeal: camp. Camping is one of the best ways to inexpensively see a race at Paul Ricard. There are plenty of places within two miles of the track — although the ones just up the road will be booked early just like the rooms in Bandol. But there are many terrific areas within just a few minutes of the wooded track.

For more information, call the Agence Regional Tourisme et Loisirs of the Conseil Regional Provence-Alpes-Cote d'Azur, CMCI, 2 Rue Henri Barbusse, 13241 Marseille - Cedex 01, or call (33) 9108 6290 (telex: 402 986 F), or call the track.

Circuit de Pau
ASAC,
Basco-Bearnais,
Palais d'Aragon,
F-64 Pau, France

PH: (33) 59 27 01 94
FAX: 59 27 61 69

Location: Southwestern France, at the foot of the Pyrenees (Atlantiques) Mountains, 72 miles from the Spanish border.

From Bordeaux, take the Autoroute A62 South to National Route 932 to 134 into Pau, where the track is located in the center of town.

Circuit: 1.7 mile road course; eight turns.

Major races: FIA Formula 3000 Championship; French Formula 3 Championship.

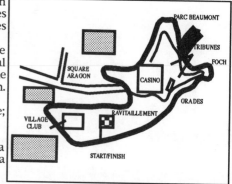

Pau has been hosting a race through its streets since the 1930s, but only recently has the race become a must-see event for motorsports fans. The atmosphere has always been a bit more serious than at Monaco where the Grand Prix has been more of a happening than a race.

But at Pau, where a great driver will usually outshine a good machine, racing has always been the key. Always run as an F2, F3, and F3000 race rather than the more prestigious F1 camp, the quaint town has attracted the real die-hard fans who appreciate the minor series. And for drivers, this is the jewel of the season. There seems to be as big a to-do around the F3000 race, without the insanity associated with Monaco.

The race is run through what would be considered a second version of Monte Carlo's Casino Square. Pau, however, has far more twists in it than Monaco, and the access is far better here than at its famous Riviera sister.

Most of the access here is general admission. And even though the race's popularity is beginning to curtail spectator access, it is still far better than Monaco. Grandstands exist at start/finish, and are probably the best seats if you feel like being stationary for the weekend. Or try the Foch corner at the far end of the racetrack; or Railway Corner, or Alain Prost Tribunes. If you're going to walk, be sure to watch from the twisty bits around the casino, which are set up so you'll see most of the action from GA areas.

Pau is considered one of the best places in France for those who enjoy good cuisine. Across the board, Pau is regarded as one of the most exciting dining cities in the country.

Be sure during the weekend to stroll the Avenue de la Pyrenees, which separates, by terrace, the top and bottom halves of the city of Pau. Standing a hundred or so feet above the lower portion of Pau, the city spreads out before you and then the valley rises into the snow-capped Pyrenees and the Spanish frontier. It is a truly beautiful sight. The casino, in typical European fashion, is a bit on the classy side, and there is a mild dress code. It's worth a look.

There are several great hotels in Pau which sit right along the racetrack, and from which you can watch the racing. Like Monaco, they will be booked well in advance. Unlike Monaco, they will not be untouchable, and if you get cracking early you'll be able to secure one of them.

The nearest Office of Tourisme is located at Place Royale, 64000 Pau; PH. 59 27 27 08 (FAX: 59 27 61 69). Or try the "green number".

Circuit Rouen les Essarts,

ASAC Normand,
46 rue General Giraud,
F-76000 Rouen, France
PH: (33) 714983/ 719520

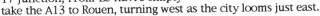

Location: Northern France, 40 miles from the English Channel, between Le Havre and Paris.

From Paris, take Autoroute A13 West toward Le Havre, heading north to Rouen at the National Route 17 junction; From Le Havre simply take the A13 to Rouen, turning west as the city looms just east.

Circuit: 3.4 mile road course; six turns.

Major races: French Formula 3 Championship.

Rouen hosted the French Grand Prix five times intermittently from 1952 through 1968. Jacky Ickx won the finale in '68 in a Ferrari, and Dan Gurney won the event twice; once in a Porsche, and once in a Brabham.

The racetrack has changed several times during its years, using public roads throughout the seasons which invariably changed. The track has always utilized the forested roads just west of Rouen, and the inherent danger in a forested track eventually led to its abandonment by the GP circus. The race was finally put to rest following Jo Schlesser's death in a Honda in 1968. The track continues to evolve as the roads are updated (in 1971 the racing was actually run on the A13 Autoroute), and the current version is a 3.4 mile road course. There's talk of eventually constructing a permanent circuit here.

Due to its temporary nature, grandstands exist only near start/finish, and in the hairpin. Most of the circuit is seen on a corner-by-corner basis. There are few places where one can see more than one or two turns at a time. Probably the best place to sit is in the grass at the Rouen/Elbeuf Hairpin, or in the start/finish Tribune just off the A13.

Rouen has plenty of rooms and will likely still have accommodations even during the French F3 race. You will likely have difficulty if you arrive Saturday, but other than that there should be no problems. The nearest Office of Tourisme is located at Place de la Cathedrale, 76000 Rouen; PH. 35 71 41 77. Or try the "green number".

GERMANY

German drivers may not have the best records in international racing competition, but German engineering is usually the standard of excellence in automotive technology, and German road cars are known as the best performing road cars in the world.

Historically, Germany's forte has always been building cars. The pre-war days of the Auto-Union (now Audi) and Mercedes domination illustrated the mechanical ingenuity of German designers. Porsche, Mercedes, BMW, Audi, and Volkswagen (with the exception of the Porsche TAG and BMW engined F1 cars) all have roots in sports and sedan racing. German manufacturers have always striven to succeed on the track to enhance new car sales, and the road car has been a direct beneficiary of the advancements made on the track.

When Michael Schumacher burst upon the FIA Grand Prix scene in 1991, Germany became known home to the driver likely to become one of the best in history, having won a Grand Prix race on the first anniversary of his debut in a Grand Prix car. Schumacher is Germany's best hope for a German World Champion.

Motorsports fans need to plan an airline flight into Germany for the driving alone. If you want to watch racing, you'll certainly want to know how it feels to drive a highway that has no speed limit. It's an interesting concept.

True, most of Germany does not have a speed limit. That doesn't mean you can always drive your car as fast as you like. If everybody wanted to go to the most private beach in the world, it wouldn't be very private anymore would it? Same with the Autobahn. If everybody wants to drive fast, and everybody uses the highways, you won't go very far very fast will you?

Germany has the reputation for fast highways. But the Autobahn is often congested, making speed runs difficult. At best, in those conditions, fast driving is unsafe. The best time to drive German highways is at night, in which case you'll have to be deadly careful; or between 10:00 am and 2:00 pm. Rush hour exists in Europe just as it does anywhere else. It doesn't matter how fast your car can go if you're stuck with a million other people who're reading the paper and heading to or from work.

The Autobahn, unlike the fast French Autoroute, is also sticky when it comes to what cars can be driven on the highway. People considering a used car purchase for their trip should pay heed: there are some very strict rules concerning safety. One of the things you'll notice about Germany is the lack of old cars. After a certain point, they're simply considered obsolete.

That goes for highway safety as well. Highway police patrol the highways in their Porsches looking for unsafe drivers. Remote cameras exist to photograph cars, looking for safety violators. Several years ago, a driver lost his licence for life when a picture was discovered of him kissing his girlfriend while on the road.

On the other hand, Germany has the best driver information systems on any highway anywhere. Accidents are promptly described on stationary billboards along the Autobahn, and the emergency squads are there very quickly to take care of the injured, or just to clean away the mess.

The traditional German way to drive fast is to stay left, with one eye on the mirror, watching the breaks in traffic to the right for that marauding 560 SEC which occasionally rockets past. The high beams were once employed when a car in the fast lane didn't appear to be moving right quickly enough, although that practice is now illegal. Now, however, fast drivers usually keep the headlights on and use the French system, with the left turn signal continuously blinking to get slower cars' attention.

Horror stories of drivers staying too long in the left lane, or not moving over when the faster cars appear, abound. Many have been shocked to find out how bold some of the German drivers are. Occasionally, if you insist upon staying in the fast lane, you'll get an aggressive tap from behind by the car in tow — that at 160KPH! Use your head.

Tourist Information: **German National Tourist Office**, 747 Third Ave., New York, NY 10017. PH: (212) 308-3300; or 444 So. Flower St., Suite 2230, Los Angeles, CA 90071. PH: (213) 688-7332. The toll free number is (800) 637-1171.

Sporting authorities: **Obertste Nationale Sportkommission,**

Waidmannstrasse 47, 6000 Frankfurt/Main 70. PH: (49) 69 633 0070; FAX: (49) 69 633 0073. **Obertste Motarradsport Kommission** Waidmannstrasse 47, 6000 Frankfurt (MAIN), 70. PH: (49 69) 963 1530; FAX: (49 69) 631 4466.

Avus Berlin (Brandenburg)

ADAC Berlin e.V., (Brandenburg)
D-1000, Berlin 31,
Bundesallee 29/30

PH: (37 2) 30 86 86 284
FAX: (37 2) 30 86 86 289

Location: Suburbs of West Berlin.

Circuit Length: 2.928 miles; two turns, two chicanes.

Major races: German Touring Car Championship.

Avus holds no major international championships. But the historical significance of the track — where the Auto-Unions and silver Mercedes strutted their prodigious pre-war power — makes the site worth the visit.

Avus sits in Charlottenburg, a western suburb of what used to be West Berlin. The Avus Autobahn linked the center of West Berlin to the rest of the west via Hanover. The Avus Autobahn (named after the track, not vice versa) was really the best way out of West Berlin to West Germany by car.

The racetrack was incorporated by the Autobahn, and the roadway was actually built upon the racetrack. The new track is now a true highway which is shut down one weekend a year for racing.

The 43-degree banking (nicknamed the "wall of death") that linked the two awesome straightways no longer exists at the Berlin venue, but the site of the incredible 1937 Grand Prix season, where the fastest race in history was run at an astounding 171 MPH, still elicits images of the dominance of Germany's racing cars in the years of the sport before the war. Do your homework before going, the experience is better with knowledge of the era.

The track may not be the most challenging, but it is obviously very fast. Braking is at a premium. And although the slow parts are where the action is in passing, the best places to watch are really along the main straights where you can see the speed of the cars.

Most of the off-track action happens at the Nordkurve, and that is where all the grandstands are located. Across the street from the main grandstands is the Deutschelandhalle Messegelaende am Funkturm — or the exhibition center — which will likely have entertainment coinciding with the racing on the track. And the tribune at the Nordkurve is likely your best should you desire a real seat. The Halensee stop for the tram is the closest were you to take public transportation from city-center.

With the German frontier

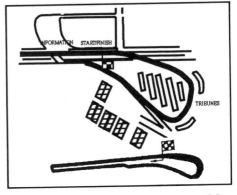

99

now open, and no visas necessary, the track is even more accessible. For information on hotels or other tourist information, contact the Berlin Verkehrsamt, at the Europa Center; PH. (030) 21 234; Fax 21 23 25 20. There is camping about 12 miles from the center of Berlin, and the Berlin Verkehrsamt can tell you more should you wish to pitch a tent.

Diepholz
AMC Diepholz e.V im ADAC,
Postfach 11 07
2940 Diepholtz, Germany

PH: (49) 5441 2155 + 4312
FAX: (49) 5441 8460

Circuit: 1.7 miles, 8 turns.

Location: Northwestern Germany, approximately 50 miles east of the Dutch border, about 20 miles north of Osnabruck.
From Hamburg, take the Autobahn A1 South to local Route 69 South; from Dusseldorf, take the A1 North to Steinfeld, and follow signs to Diepholz.

Major Races: German Formula 3 Championship; German Touring Car Championship; Carrera 2 Porsche Cup.

Diepholz, like several other German racetracks, is built upon a German airbase. Called, appropriately enough, Diepholz Airbase, the place is completely flat, and is a fairly fast circuit. It has one of the tightest hairpins in racing, and it is that feature which makes it unique, and which probably keeps it on the German F3 Championship calendar. Other than its hairpin, the track is simply two straights with either esses or chicanes, with a loop at one end connecting the two together. 1992 saw the addition of a tight chicane which lengthened the circuit somewhat.
The track celebrated its 26th year in 1993, and in its time it has been upgraded very little. It is not the greatest for spectators. Remember, this is a functioning military base, and the commanders of the place do not fancy people walking around the grounds. With no way to get trackside, race-watching is limited to the stands.
Diepholz is really in the middle of nowhere, so rooms will not be plentiful. The demand for the few which exist, however, will be low, so finding a vacant room will likely not be a problem.
The best places to stay are in Lembruch, near the tourist area around the Dummer See Lake; or around Diepholz/Vechta, driving the few minutes to the track. Information on hotels or other tourist activities can be found by contacting the Verkehrsamt in either Osnabruck (at Markt 22/23, PH: 0541 2 23-22 02) or at Diepholz (at Rathausmarkt 1, PH: 5441 909 1.

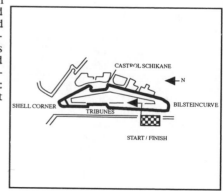

Hockenheim

Hockenheim-Ring GmbH,
D-6832 Hockenheim, Germany
PH:(49)62 05/ 70 21 24
FAX: (49) 62 05/ 1 41 22

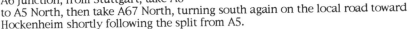

Location: Southwestern Germany, 15 miles from Heidelburg, between Stuttgart and Frankfurt.

From Frankfurt take Autobahn A67 South, turning south to Hockenheim shortly before the A5/A6 junction; from Stuttgart, take A8 to A5 North, then take A67 North, turning south again on the local road toward Hockenheim shortly following the split from A5.

Circuit: 4.22 mile road course; nine turns.

Major races: FIA Formula One Grand Prix World Championship; FIA Formula 3000 Championship; German Formula 3 Championship (two rounds); FIM Grand Prix World Championship; FIM Superbike Championship; GM Lotus Euroseries Championship; German Touring Car Championship; Carrera 2 Porsche Cup.

Hockenheim assumed the chores of hosting the German Grand Prix while Nurburgring was being rebuilt, and it was generally assumed that the new Nurburgring would replace Hockenheim as the permanent site of the Formula One Grand Prix once Nurburgring was completed. But the dull new circuit at Nurburgring cemented the Hockenheimring as the permanent home of the German GP, which quickly signed a five-year deal with FOCA for a race. The track also saw the return of the FIM Motorcycle Grand Prix in 1993.

Hockenheim has been described as two circuits that work independently of each other, and which require different set-up: the first, the twisty slower portion from Bramskurve 2 through the stadium past Sachs and out past the fast right-hander to the Bramskurve 1; and the second, the ultra-fast circuit from the entrance of Bramskurve 1 through Ostkurve to the entrance of Bramskurve 2.

The second part, the fast part, is almost unviewable. To see anything you have to walk through the Black Forest and back to the Ostkurve. If on the way you decide you want a look at the track — good luck. Trying to find the track from the infield roads is impossible. You'll know the cars are there, somewhere — you'll hear them. But you won't know how to get to the edge of the track to watch. The only legitimate general admission tickets are in Ostkurve, and the place is almost an hour-and-a-half walk from anywhere.

The slow part, however, is a delight. It's set up as a stadium, and almost any seat in the place can watch almost the entire sequence of turns. Obviously, the best seats will be those directly in front of start/finish, but there is really no bad seat in the grandstands.

Buy tickets ahead of time here if you can. The veteran fans know the same things you just discovered, and tickets are hard to find because of the demand. Getting tickets at the track is not impossible, but the fact that the ticket sales booths are also hard to find makes a difficult situation worse come race weekend.

If you get there late you'll also have a problem finding a room — at least one that's close. Heidelburg is a good alternative, although it's about an hour away.

The track is right off the main road, so getting in and out is not a major problem here. If you get there ahead of time, try the hotels in the Black Forest. There are some beautiful places there worth the extra time if you get there early.

For information on hotels or other tourist information, contact the Heidelburg Verkehrsamt at Freidrich Elbert Anlage 2, PH. (06221) 10 821; FAX (06221) 15 108. Or try the Mannheim Verkehrsamt at Banhofsplaz 1; PH. 0621) 101011.

Mainz-Finthen
**Hesse Motor Sports Club e.V. Im AvD,
Sekretariat,
Postfach 3142,
6200 Wiebaden, Germany**

**PH: (49) 61298572
FAX: (49) 61 29 8317**

Location: Central Germany, 25 miles from Frankfurt.
From Frankfurt AM Main International Airport, take Autobahn A3 to A60 West to Mainz.

Circuit: 1.45 mile road course; seven turns.

Major races: German Formula 3 Championship; German Touring Car Championship

This flat circuit's biggest event is the German F3 race, and is reportedly not in good standing in even that arena. Another in the list of German airfield circuits, Mainz-Finthen calls an American Army base home. Like Wunstorf and Diepholz, it is a short, fast track that has little room for passing and less margin for error.

Also like Wunstorf and Diepholz, the officers who oversee the place don't appreciate fans wandering about on a military base, so access is limited — more so here than at the other two establishments. The races here have been severely limited since the Persian Gulf conflict, and the races have been cancelled, then returned to the calendar, then cancelled again. It was not scheduled for racing in 1993.

The best places to stay are either in Mainz, or in Finthen: either town has only a few inns, but since there will not be the greatest desire to watch racing here — there won't be the biggest waiting list either. For information on hotels or other tourist information, contact the Mainz Verkehrsamt, at Banhofstrasse 15; PH. (06131) 233 741.

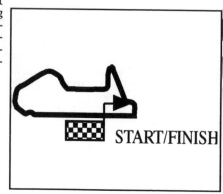

START/FINISH

Norisring

MC Nurnberg,
30 Ziegenstr 97,
D-85 Nuernberg,
Germany

PH: (49 911) 533327
FAX: (49 911) 533328

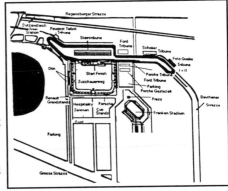

Location: Southeast Nurnberg, in Dutzendteich, around the Steintribune.

Circuit: 1.42 mile road course; six turns.

Major races: German Touring Car Championships; German Formula 3 Championship.

In a country known for tedious attention to detail when it comes to its motor racing and racetracks, Norisring is one of the oddest circuits in Germany. It seems completely out of place here.

A temporary street circuit, Norisring is very short, very fast, and very, very wide... except in the places where it needs to be wide.

The track runs around the Steintribune, in southeast Nurnberg. The main straight runs directly past the Steintribune structure, where Hitler rallied support for his cause as tanks paraded up and down the street. Across the immense strip of asphalt is a park complete with baseball diamonds and green playing fields. At the far end of the circuit sits a rural area as an anachronism to the expanses of commercial structures which have been built just across from the racetrack.

With its weird mixture of styles, Norisring appears to have been air-lifted and dropped into a college setting somewhere. The main straight looks out of place in a racing context, and the street looks out of place in a civic context. Nothing here seems to fit.

But the racing is fantastic. The crowds that appear at the short circuit are nothing less than sellouts. The venue used to host a round of the Prototypes some years back, but now must be satisfied with the German Touring Car Championship — which may actually be a better draw than the old WEC races.

The Steintribune holds some 25,000 people, and is where most fans try to sit — if nothing else, just the atmosphere here makes it worth the trouble. From the Steintribune you'll see at least half the track (which isn't saying much).

If you fancy some real action, try Tribune I or II down at the first turn. The goliath front straight, which can hold some 10 cars side-by-side, narrows into a hairpin that can barely take two at a time. The run down to the hairpin is ultra fast, and the guys with good brakes will be the pride of the field here. Obviously, it's where all the bumping and passing goes on.

You really need a seat here since the track is almost completely flat and so very short. From any elevated platform you'll see a good portion of the track. Buying tickets can be done as you exit the Dutzendteich railway station... the parking lot of the station is literally bounded by the racing surface.

Nurnberg has rooms, but most Germans just take the train into the circuit from elsewhere. Since leaving from the station will be difficult no matter where you are staying, you may as well pick your spot based on comfort and cost rather than convenience. Everything is conveniently located to Norisring.

For additional information contact the Nurnburg Verkehrsamt at Frauen-

torgraben 3/Postfach 4248; PH. (0911) 23360; FAX 233 666; call the German
National Tourist Office at (800) 637-1171; or contact the track.

Nurburgring GmbH,
D-5489 Nurburg/Eifel, Germany

PH: (49 2691) 2041/2031/2032
FAX: (02691) 30 21 59

Location: Western central Germany, near Koblenz.
From Koln, BAB 61 to Wehr to N412 to N258 or BAB 48 to Ulmen to N257,
N258. The old circuit winds past Adenau, but the new track entrances are farther
south, either on N412 or N259 which intersect N257 within two-miles of Adenau.

Circuit: 2.82 mile road course; 11 turns; North Loop: 14 mile road course;
73 turns.

Major races:: GM Lotus Euroseries Championship; German Formula 3
Championship (three rounds); German Touring Car Championship.

Nurburgring was taken off the World Championship FIA calendar shortly
following Niki Lauda's horrific crash in 1976. Although it was then — and remains
today — one of the most incredible racetracks ever built, it was just too fast and
too dangerous.
"There were so many sections of the Nurburgring where you were just a
passenger," wrote Jackie Stewart. Indeed, the length of the track and the variety of
the turns and speeds made it the most challenging in the world. Few drivers liked
the track, but it was an institution. When Lauda nearly died in '76, the establishment realized that marshalling a 14 mile track was impossible, and it was
abandoned.
Now re-worked, and shortened to its current length of 2.82 miles, the track
has little of the old circuit in it emotionally — although it does incorporate some
parts of the old track. It does not inspire bravado like the old track did. It hosted
a F1 race again in 1985, but the event was short-lived and the switch back to
Hockenheim came shortly afterward. The new circuit, in the opinion of most
drivers and fans, is boring.
The bikes ran here until 1992, then also abandoned the place for
Hockenheim. For them it's a terrific track safetywise. With the exception of
Holland's Assen circuit, Nurburgring is
probably the safest on the FIM calendar.
Wide runoff and deep sand pits make
it forgiving for the GP riders, and the
racing is every bit as good as at any
other place for the two-wheeled aficio-
nados.
The new ring is touted by track
officials as the track where the spectator is "king". Except for the area on the
back part of the track, the circuit is
completely surrounded by grandstands. Although the area around the
first corner is good, probably the best
areas are in the downhill heading

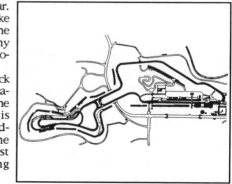

toward the Dunlop Hairpin, where you'll see the riders for a decent amount of time before they disappear over the brow headed toward the Yokohama curve.

Even though there is no F1 racing currently, there are still reasons for F1 nuts to come to Nurburgring. There's the Nurburgring Racing Museum that's worth a look, and the old track can be driven in your street car for 13 Marks when there's no racing on the new circuit. But be careful — most people fancy themselves of Fangio blood and drive as if they were real racecar drivers. The new circuit can also be toured in either a bus or in a racing taxi — at speed.

The new circuit may be boring, but it's always busy. There are concerts in the area between the new and old circuits, with some big-name entertainers. Plenty of club meetings take place here, and there's a Kart track, developed by Zakspeed, which also holds several international caliber events throughout the season.

Camping is available during events, and better ideas concerning what campsites are available and what the costs are can be found by calling the Campingplaz Mullenbach Office at 2692 224.

For accommodation information, contact the Verkehrsamts in Koblenz (at Hauptbanhof/Postfach 2080; PH. (0261) 31 304), or Bonn (at Muenstrerstrasse 20; PH. 77 34 66). Or call the track's hotel listing service at 2641 50 15.

Singen

ADAC Sudbaden e. V.
Am Karlsplaz 1, 7800
Freiburg, Germany
PH: (49) 761 368 80
FAX: (49) 761 258 26

Location: 20 miles from Lake Constance, in southwestern Germany, three miles from the Swiss Border, off rural route 34.

Circuit: 1.68 mile road course; 13 turns.

Major Races: German Touring Car Championships

This new circuit ran its first race in 1991 through the streets of an industrial suburb with a round of German Touring Car racing. The course is essentially flat, but contains some fairly challenging corners.

In 1993 the track ran the top two national series, with German Touring Car Championships and German F3 running the same weekend. Rumor suggests it may host a round of F3000 racing eventually.

Located in the mountainous region around Lake Konstanz, there are plenty of places to stay for racing. Singen itself has a handful of rooms. Planning ahead would be a good idea in anticipation of the GTCC returning to the circuit. So would staying farther out. Uberlingen will likely have places to sleep; and Radolfszell has a few inns.

For more information call the Konstanz Verkehrsamt at (49) 75 31 284 376, or Bahnhofplatz 13, 7750 Konstanz.

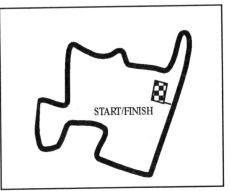

START/FINISH

Wunstorf

ADAC Niedersachsen Sa-
chsen-Auhalt (Sportabteilung),
Hindenburgstr 37,
Hannover 1, Germany
PH: (49) 511 8500311

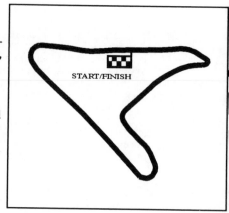

START/FINISH

Location: Northern central
Germany, eighteen miles from Hannover.

From Hannover, take Auto-
bahn A2 West to National Route 441,
then two miles to Wunstorf.

Circuit 3.14 mile road circuit; five turns.

Major races: German Formula 3 Championship; German Touring Car
Championship.

Another German airbase used for racing, Wunstorf is essentially a triangle
with a slight bend in one side, and is not the most challenging racetrack in
Germany. It is very similar to Diepholz in almost every respect.

Without the chicanes that blight two sides of the triangle, it would be
downright boring — for both drivers and spectators. The track is faster than
Diepholz because its chicanes are not as tight.It is a fairly long track, and so just
getting from one side to the other to watch racing is a headache.

Formula cars have problems running here because of the prospect of
hitting the airport landing lights, which still exist in their appropriate places about
the circuit. There have been efforts to eliminate the lights, but the military doesn't
exactly promote the plan. It will likely be run as it is.

The tribune at start/finish will give you the only view worth speaking
about, and for the German Touring Car Championships, the 10 minute break
between races will yield any fan who sits there a great look at the pandemonium
that goes on there.

You can stay in Hannover, which is 20 minutes from the track; in
Steinhude — near the Steinhuder Meer lake; or in Garbsen. Information for hotels
can be found by contacting the Verkehrsamt Hannover, at Ernst August Platz 8; PH:
(00511) 168 2319.

BRITAIN

Great Britain is the headquarters of racing worldwide. Not only do Brits
have the largest tally of wins in GP racing since 1950, but almost every chassis run
on road race tracks today comes from England. Almost every competition sports
and open-wheeled racecar is made by British hands.

The British are not obsessive about their racing like the Italians, but almost
everybody understands what's going on in British racing. Ask an old lady if she
knows who Nigel Mansell is, and she'll likely tell you for which team he last drove
and when his last victory was.

McLaren, Williams, Tyrrell, Lotus, Lola, Penske and just about any other chassis manufacturer make their wares in Britain, usually employing countrymen to implement the technology. So at any given racetrack, the predominant language in the paddock and along the pit complex will be English -- spoken with a distinct British accent.

In fact, the same situation exists in motorcycling, where there are far fewer dominant British teams in the two-wheeled World Championship than the four-wheeled series. Competitive or not as manufacturers, British motorcycle mechanics are in serious demand, making up a good percentage of the caravan that meanders over the globe for nine months of the year.

And lest we forget, the man touted as one of the greatest all time race car drivers in the world is British. Nigel Mansell captured the Formula One Driver's Championship after coming up short three previous seasons, then promptly stunned the world by retiring from Grand Prix racing and moving to America to contest the IndyCar championship -- which he easily won. He became America's most talented "rookie" ever, changing the face of the series and tripling exposure world-wide the day he announced the move to The States from Europe.

So with the rich history surrounding the world's first concrete closed circuit (Brooklands) and the amazingly fast Silverstone as well as Donington, Brands Hatch and all the smaller national and club circuits, Britain is blessed with a structure which will continue to produce World Champion drivers as well as championship caliber designers and crewmen. Britain is, after all, a significant component in the history of motor racing.

Britain is also the home of road-going motoring. It's where the MG was born and where motorcycling was made popular. But racing and mass produced vehicles have long since gone separate ways. Most car companies of Great Britain have been swallowed by larger multi-national companies, and the British motorcycling industry, which was so dominant in the '50s and '60s, no longer exists. Motoring pride comes from racing now, not manufacturing.

Tourist Information: **British Tourist Authority.** In London, you'll find a BTA in Victoria Station, Harrods, or Heathrow, which will put you in touch with any major hub city in Great Britain.

Sporting Authorities: **RAC Motor Sports Association Ltd.**, Motor Sports House, Riverside Park, Colnbrook, Slough SL3 0HG. Great Britain. PH: (44) 753 681 736; FAX: (44) 753 682 938; **Auto Cycle Union**, ACU House — Wood Street, Rugby, Warwickshire CV21 2YX. PH: (44 788) 540 519; FAX: (44 788) 573 585.

Brands Hatch Circuits Ltd,
Fawkham, Nr Dartford,
Kent, DA3 8NG

PH; (44) 0474 872331
FAX: (44) 0474 874766

Location: about 20 miles south-west of London, near West Kingsdown.

From the peripheral M25 (if going southeast), take M20 to A20 North, where the track can be found two miles from West Kingsdown; if coming southwest on the peripheral M25, take M26 East, and come back west on the M20 to A20 and West Kingsdown; from central London follow A20 from Greenwich into West Kingsdown.

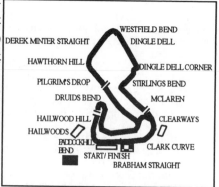

Circuit: 2.6 mile road course; nine turns.

Major races: British Formula 3000 Championship (three rounds); British Formula 3 Championship (three rounds); British Touring Car Championship.

Brands Hatch no longer hosts a round of the FIA World Championship, and for most regulars on the Grand Prix trail, it was either a favorite or a real handful. Jackie Stewart said he never got a Grand Prix car to handle here; and Niki Lauda finally, late in his career, began to understand the peculiarities of the place, and actually took a liking to it following years of frustration.

The track is located in a bowl-like amphitheater, naturally created in the English countryside. The short "Indy" circuit can be seen from almost anywhere in the immediate area, and may soon be in use again — if FISA's Oval Car Championship seeds ever bear fruit.

The longer Grand Prix track requires a trip into "the country". It's in a forest. But unlike many wooded circuits, there are several great viewing places, which are both easy to get to and which afford excellent shots of the cars.

There are spectator banks at Paddock, Druids, or Clark Curve, but the areas at Dingle Dell, Hawthorn's Westfield, and Stirling are probably the best. Have a walk around the picturesque circuit and see if you can't find somewhere better.

The nearest railway station is in Swanley, which is only about a mile from the main entrance of the circuit, and a bus runs during the bigger races. A hotel outside the gates allows those with a bit extra disposable income to walk, although the cheapest accommodations are further out — London is probably the easiest place to stay.

For accommodation information in London, contact the London Tourist Board at 26 Grosvenor Gardens SW1 ODU, PH: 71 730 3488.

Cadwell Park Racing Circuit,
The Old Manor House,
Cadwell Park, Louth, Lincs,
Great Britain

PH: (44) 0507 343 248
FAX: (44) 0507 343 519

Location: Northern England, 10 miles northeast of Horncastle off the National Route 158, approximately 100 miles north of London.

Circuit: 2.17 miles/ 1.47 miles (Club Circuit); nine turns.

Major races: British Formula Ford Championships; 750cc Superbikes.

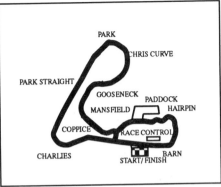

Cadwell Park is a picturesque track which has held some great national formula races, although its width will always keep field sizes small, and prevents it from ever being in the limelight again. The tight, narrow, twisty circuit got drivers airborne in a fast, cresting right-hander called "mountain". It was often described as driving on a country road somewhere.

There are several rooms in Horncastle, or try Woodhall Spa, or Louth — all a few minutes from the track. For more information call the track or the British Tourist Authority.

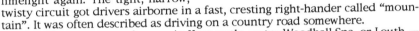

Castle Combe Circuit,
Chippenham, Wiltshire, SN147EY, Great Britain

PH: (44) 0249 782417
FAX: (44) 0249 782392

Location: West central Britain, between London and Bristol, off the M4 about 80 miles west of London.

Circuit: 1.84 mile road course; five turns.

Major races: British Formula Ford.

Castle Combe is one of the toughest circuits in Great Britain, and is considered one of the best tracks in England to watch racing — although there is little else here besides club racing.

There are few similarities to the bigger circuits — in other words, you're going to have to rough it here. But the inconveniences will probably be worth the trip. In recent years the place was very fast and very bumpy, and is not for the weak at heart. Still a circuit for the brash, it is slated for resurfacing in 1993, and will be faster than ever. Like the old Formula Ford races in the US — or the Sports 2000 racers of late — the club racers are very aggressive here and often do things pros wouldn't dare try. Castle

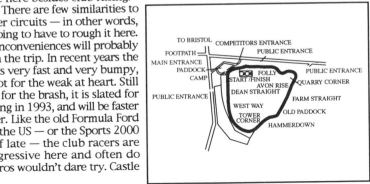

Combe often attracts 10,000 or more to a club event.

The best places to watch the drivers try to keep some control over the difficult circuit are Quarry, Tower and Camp — which are three of the best corners in British racing. Spectator access is fantastic at these corners as well.

It is about an hour-and-a-half from London, and a car is probably the best way to get here from London. There are several hotels in the area, and probably the best place to stay is in Chippenham, which is five miles away. The track can help with a Fixtures and Guide for the circuit, which should be available with a call. Or contact the Chippenham Tourist Information Center at The Neeld Hall, High St., Wiltshire SN153ER, PH: 249 657733.

Donington Park
Castle Donington,
Derby, DE7 2RP

PH: (44) 0332 810048
FAX: (44) 0332 850422

Location: Central Great Britain, between Leicester and Derby, approximately 80 miles from London.

From London, take the Autoroute M1 North past Leicester to A6, or East Midlands airport, heading west. Turn left at 453 to the track.

Circuit: 2.5 mile road course; eight turns.

Major races: FIA Formula One Grand Prix World Championship; FIM Grand Prix Motorcycle World Championship — 125cc, 250cc, 500cc, and Sidecars; FIA World Sports Prototype Championship; FIA Formula 3000 Championship; FIM Superbike Championship; British Formula 3000 Championship; British Formula 3 Championship; Esso British Touring Car Championship (2 rounds).

Probably the most up to date circuit in Great Britain, Donington Park has recently been handed a nice gift in the form of a World Championship round of the FIA Formula One Grand Prix World Championship. Usually overshadowed by Brands Hatch and Silverstone, the former was passed over when Autopolis was unable to host the '93 version of the Asian Grand Prix, and the race was renamed the European Grand Prix and moved to Donington.

The venue is excellent, with extraordinary run-off areas so both bikes and cars are in as safe an atmosphere as possible, given the relative dangers of the sport. Located in the British countryside, the track is also one of the most beautiful in Britain.

Deep sand pits trackside rate the circuit number-one with the FIM riders, and the special surface keeps the track as dry as one could ask. The composition is such that water drains through the track. Like Silverstone, this

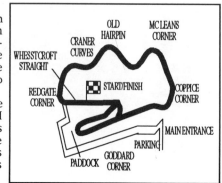

track has been used since the early days of the sport, and is constantly being updated. Unlike Silverstone, Donington has decent elevation changes; it is also generally safer.

This was the site of the last GP in Europe before WW II, and the Donington Collection Museum contains a great exhibition of Grand Prix cars. It's worth a visit, as is the castle near the track.

The track is quick, and its good elevation changes make it great for fans. Try watching from the Craner Curve, an incredibly fast downhill sweeper; or take a look from McLeans, the fast over-the-brow right hander that both enters and exits in an off-camber manner.

If the two hour drive from London is too far, there are several good hotels in the immediate area. Try Derby, or Nottingham for rooms; or for camping, the Peak District National Park is only 20 miles away. Call the track for more information, or contact the Nottingham Tourist Information Center at 14 Wheeler Gate Nottinghamshire, NG12NB, PH: 602 470661; or the Derby Tourist Information Center at the Central Library, The Wardwick, Derbyshire DE11HS, PH: 332 650 523.

Isle of Man Tourist Trophy

TT Auto Cycle Union
ACU House, Wood Street
Rugby, Warks., CV21 2YX

PH: (788) 540519
FAX: (788) 573585

Location: On the Isle of Man, located between Great Britain and Ireland in the Irish Sea.

Circuit: 37 .75 mile road course; 79 turns.

Major Races: The Isle Of Man TT.

Of all the tracks in this guide — of all the races listed in this book — the Isle of Man Tourist Trophy is the most incredible and most outrageous. It's the longest, the most dangerous, the most unpredictable, and the oldest motorcycle race in the world. The Isle of Man TT is simply the most unique race on the planet.

Once run as part of the FIM Grand Prix Motorcycle World Championship, the race was finally deemed too dangerous in 1976, and lost its World Championship status. TT organizers pleaded, but the FIM put an end to the race — relenting somewhat, and agreeing never to run a Grand Prix during the two weeks of the TT. To this day, no GP is run during those two weeks — but few GP riders compete in this dangerous race anymore.

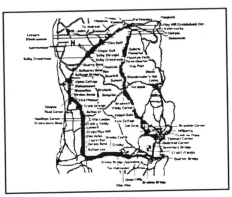

The Isle of Man TT is run over the two weeks that straddle Spring and Summer. The first week of the TT Fortnight is relegated to practice —usually held during the last week in May. Racing is held the first week in June, with the final day taking place mid-June.

Practice is held three times a day. The first practice of any given day is at first light, at 5:00-6:30; afternoon practice happens between 2:00-4:00; and, finally, evening practice caps the day off at 6:00-8:00 pm. Practice starts Monday and runs through Friday. Racing then begins Saturday, followed by the craziest motorsports day in racing, "Mad Sunday".

Mad Sunday could be an event in itself. The circuit, from Ramsey and climbing into the mountains ending at Creg-Ny-Baa, is opened up to the public — which is allowed to go as fast as they like for that one day. Huge crowds gather at the Gooseneck Hairpin, a sharp left-hand uphill 180 degree turn, as the one way traffic hits the difficult turn with no speed limit. Most of the accidents happen here. Fortunately, the general public doesn't ride fast parts of the circuit with the same reckless abandon as the slow bits, so there are very few serious injuries.

On Monday, the real racing resumes. The race is done in stages, and, in fact, is not really a race at all but a time trial. Starts are staggered every 10 seconds. The bikes are numbered in the same order as they start. So by watching the numbers and calculating the intervals you can see who's fastest by comparing him to rider ahead of him.

The lap record was set in 1992 at 123.61 mph — meaning riders hit speeds of over 180mph in some places on the streets! The reason this place is so different is that there are no barriers like you'd see at an automobile street race. It's as simple as closing off the roads with saw-horses and holding a race. Spectators can sit on hedgerows as riders sweep literally within inches of their feet.

There are many great places to watch the racing. Obviously the best way would be to spend the qualifying week moving about the track, then watching from the select spots the following week. Some of the better viewing is at the bottom of Bray Hill, a relatively slow (70 mph) downhill corner; try Glen Crutchery Rd, a main road which leads onto St Ninians Crossroad; probably the most photographed is Bradden Bridge (which even has grandstands located in an old churchyard that can be secured for about $2.00 dollars a seat) where most riders — and some sidecars — get airborne.

This is not a simple race to get to. It takes about four-and-a-half hours via the Ferry from Heysham to the Isle of Man (you can take a train to Heysham, which is located near Liverpool, from London). You can do it quicker by taking a Manx Airlines flight from London's Heathrow to Ronaldsway Airport on the island.

Because of interest in off-shore investment (The Isle of Man is not a part of the GB tax structure), there are not as many rooms available as there once were. Those hotels which are not booked for business people — who are finding the TT more and more of an inconvenience — are often being converted to offices. Things are bleak, but not impossible.

Stay in Douglas if possible. The Douglas harbor and the promenade is lined with hotels — probably 200 hotels are in the immediate area. If not there, try Onchan, Peel, Ramsey, or Castletown (where the airport is located). If you find yourself on the island and just can't find a hotel — don't fear. Just put on your adventurer's outfit and camp — or stay in one of the tent villages. Farmers often rent fields, barns, and sheds, so you'll have no problem. Just don't count on room service. And be prepared for rain (weather updates can be found by calling 16633 while on the island).

Public transportation is excellent and can be found by calling the Isle of Man Tourist Board. If things on-track get too complicated, call the TT Hotline at 16688 for the latest TT news; or for more information call or stop by the Department of Tourism at Sea Terminal, Douglas, Isle of Man, (788) 686766.

Knockhill Raceway

Dunfermline, Fife, KY12 9TE
Scotland
PH: (44) 0383 723337
FAX: (44) 0383 620167

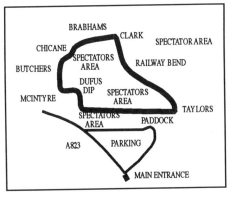

Location: Southern Scotland, about 50 miles east of Glasgow, near Dunfermline, on A823, four miles from the M90.

Circuit: 1.3 mile road circuit; seven turns.

Major races: British Formula Ford 1600.

Knockhill is known as Scotland's best racetrack. Since there are no other tracks in Scotland, the description is probably accurate. A Scottish Superprix was held here in '87, and, although there are ambitious plans for a major event here, nothing has yet materialized.

The track is open seven days a week from February to December, and is used mostly for testing and corporate functions. It does, however, hold a full schedule of racing, and has a full spectrum of activities. Knockhill has cars — both open and closed wheeled varieties — as well as motorcycle races, Karts, car/bike races, it also has a couple of schools that hold classes on the facility grounds.

There are no grandstands for spectators, but there is a good view afforded pedestrians who wish to walk up to the fences. There are also three elevated spectator banks. The best viewing, however, is left to those who drive their cars into the circuit and who park beside the track. Camping is available here, and hotels are available in Dunfermline (contact the Dunfermline Tourist Information Center at Glen Bridge Car Park, Chalmers St., Fife, PH: 383 720 999), if you don't wish to camp.

Mallory Motorsport Park Ltd,
Kirkby Mallory, Leicestershire,
Great Britain

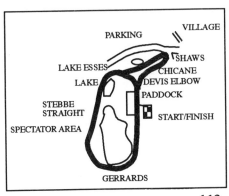

PH: (44) 0455 42931
FAX: (44) 0455 48289

Location: Central Great Britain, just 12 miles east of Birmingham off A47.

Circuit: 1.35 mile road circuit, five turns.

Major races: British Vauxhall Lotus Championships.

Mallory Motorsports Park is essentially just a loop around a small lake, with what is arguably one of the tightest hairpins in racing — and certainly the tightest in Great Britain.

The corner is so critical — and so different for the rest of the track — that many drivers set their chassis from the cockpit on entry to the hairpin, then re-adjust it after the exit for negotiating the rest of the track.

Spectator viewing is terrific with a view of most of the track from anywhere on the circuit. There's general practice each Wednesday morning. Leicester and Hinckley are the easiest places to stay, at eight and four miles from the circuit respectively. Contact the Leicester Tourist Information Center at 6 St Martins Walk, Leicestershire LE15DG, PH: 533 626305.

Oulton Park

Brands Hatch Circuits Ltd,
Oulton Park,
Little Budworth, Nr Tarporley,
Cheshire, Great Britain
PH: (44) 082921 301
FAX: (44)082921 378

Location: Northern Great Britain, in Cheshire, about 20 miles south of Liverpool.

From Liverpool, take A533 to A49 to Tarporley; from London take the M6 toward Liverpool, exiting at the junction of M6 A54/A535, heading west on A54 to A49.

Circuit: 2.77 mile road course; eight turns.

Major races: British Formula 3 Championship (two rounds); British Formula 2 Championship; Esso British Touring Car Championships.

Oulton Park is located in a forest, and set up with elevation changes, utilizing both tight, twisty bits and long, fast portions. The track has been described as mini-Nurburgring. There's not a lot of run-off here so it will likely never be the world class circuit it once was. The death of Derek Warwick's brother, Paul, which reportedly occurred at Knicker Brook corner, hasn't helped the track's reputation any.

Spectators will have difficulty watching the whole race at once, and corner by corner viewing is really the only way to see Oulton. There are stands in four sections around the track — mostly near the paddock and start/finish.

The track is used for testing quite often, with open practice on Tuesdays, Wednesdays, and Fridays. Hotels can be found in Chester (contact the Chester Tourist Information Center at Vicars Lane, Cheshire CH11QX, PH: 244 351 609) and Tarpoley.

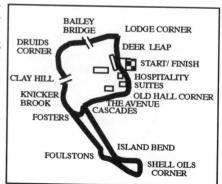

Pembrey

**The Welsh Motorsports
Centre, Pembrey
c/o BARC, Thruxton
Andover, Hants
PH: (44) 264 773794
Track: (44) 554 891042
FAX: (44) 264 773794**

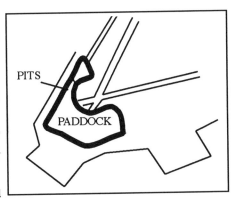

Location: Southern Wales, 10 miles off the 48 Junction, off the M4, approximately 15 miles northwest of Swansea.

Circuit: Six/eight turn road circuit; 1.1 miles; 1.5 miles

Major Races: Club racing

Pembrey is making a comeback. It has recently been used for testing F3 cars, F3000 machinery, an occasional bike or two — and sometimes an F1 team. The track is miles from anything. Consequently, it allows testing and practice on virtually any day of the week throughout the season.

The track is a combination of very quick and very slow corners allowing the maximum of each variation of corner. The Speedway Straight through the ultra-quick Woodlands and into Forest Curve tests the faster machinery, and the Hatchet Hairpin and Dibeni Bend challenge the handling of all cars in preparation for smaller tracks. The 500 acres of Pembrey make access easy and viewing good.

There are not many places to stay in the area, and the few that are close are filled quickly. The track lists three inns within a few miles, and will be happy to give you more information should you desire it. A short ride down to Swansea — or better still, Mumbles — will be worth the drive west to Wales. Rooms in Swansea can be found by contacting the Swansea Tourist Information Center at Singleton St., West Glamorgan St., SA13QN, PH: 792 468 321.

Silverstone Grand Prix Circuit

**Silverstone Circuits Ltd,
Silverstone, nr Towcester,
Northants, NN12 8TN, Great Britain
PH: (44) 0327 857271
FAX: (44) 0327 857663**

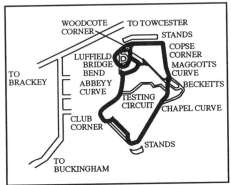

Location: Central Britain, between London and Birmingham, about 30 miles north of Oxford and about 14 miles south of Northampton.

From the north or southeast, take the Autoroute M1 to Junction 15A (Northampton), proceed south on the A43 (Towcester/Oxford) approximately 10 miles to Silverstone Village, which is a few miles past Brackley before Towcester, and follow the signs to the track.

Circuit: mile road course; 3.2 mile course, 18 turns.

Major races: FIA Formula One Grand Prix World Championship; FIA Formula 3000 Championship; British Formula 3000 Championship; British Formula 3 Championship (six rounds); GM Lotus Euroseries Championship; Esso British Touring Car Championships.

The old Silverstone was feared by most Grand Prix drivers. Unlike Monaco, where the fear stemmed from the inherent danger in the racetrack, Silverstone was just fast -- very fast. The old U.S. airbase was basically flat and very quick, with an average speed over its nearly three miles of nearly 150 MPH -- at just over one minute per lap. Run-off room was always a concern -- Stowe and Club being both the fastest and the least forgiving. Tire barriers on the outside of the fast corners have claimed a few cars.

But the circuit underwent major renovation in the winter of 1991, with slower bits being carved into the long, fast strips of asphalt. The track was certainly not unsafe, but stood improvement.

The efficiency of the Royal Auto Club Motor Sports Association is unimpeachable and is probably what has kept the GP at Silverstone for so long. In 1989, on the first lap of a Formula Ford race, a mid-pack shuffle caught one driver out, and put him on his roll bar. The remaining cars sidled by, and the course marshalls abandoned their posts to attend to the youngster. Following a quick check to see if he was okay, he was removed quickly, but gently, walked to the ambulance, which by now was on the track, and taken away; in the meantime, the car had been flipped back onto its wheels, and pushed off the track behind a barrier; the marshalls rapidly picked up all the debris, swept the track, ran back to their posts, and were ready again as the cars came around for the second lap -- less than 90 seconds later!

The efficiency of the organization is the same regarding entry and exit of the track during the GP weekend. There are standard procedures, and designated roads for entering and exiting Silverstone depending on the times you want to do it. Silverstone is not a simple circuit to get into or out of. There is really only one small two-laned road to the circuit. Once you're some miles away, the choices are better regarding where you can go, but in the immediate area it should be a mess -- but it isn't. If California's Laguna Seca could organize like this, they'd be a sure bet for the permanent home of the U.S. GP.

That being said, the Brits are this conscientious because they've had practice. There's just as much enthusiasm for Nigel Mansell in Britain as there is for Ferrari at Monza -- and that comes with a serious interest in motor racing in Great Britain. With only a few exceptions, any given driver sits behind the wheel of an English designed, English prepared, or English owned car. The English, in general, tend to be statisticians more than the Italians, and can rattle off past winners of the British GP as if they were just thinking about it -- which they may have been.

Silverstone, contradicting what was said earlier, is not really as flat as one is often told. There are, in fact, some inclines which make it interesting to watch. The circuit, in general, is a good one to view a race. The area from the exit of Chapel Curve to the entrance of Abbey, which is in a natural bowl, can be seen from anywhere in the immediate area. That area is also one of the best places to get a feeling for the speeds.

With a General Admission ticket you can walk the entire track, except the area on the start/finish straight where grandstand guards will keep you out (unless you have a ticket). You may wish to join the exclusive club in the stands, and if you do, be sure to book early or you will be out of luck. No matter, viewing is good everywhere, and there are some absolutely priceless spots in general

admission to watch the race. But don't get confident about getting any of them. For qualifying and practice, the grass overlooking the track is only half full. On race day that's far from the case, and you'll have to be there very early to secure a spot. Even if you get there in time, be sure to have someone guarding your spot if you need to use the bathrooms. Squatters have rights, and you may never be able to get back to your well-chosen, but inaccessible, spot.

However, if you do go general admission, try to sit so you can see the huge television screens which are placed about the course. They're extremely handy. You can get the best of both worlds — if you bring a radio too... well, you've got it made.

Make sure and put a few dollars' wager on the race. There are Ladbroke's parlors all over, and even a booth at the track — and Mansell will certainly be the favorite.

The start/finish grandstands, with their Guinness Stout and Rover car ads plastered around, give you the feel of Britain, and are terrific if you need to watch the pits and the start. The covered grandstands are just a bit claustrophobic, however, and once seated most people tend to stay there for the whole weekend — and you certainly want to spend at least half that time watching from somewhere else. If you decide you want those you'll have to contact the circuit early, because they'll be gone — otherwise you'll be fine buying tickets upon arrival.

Staying around Silverstone is not really as much of a problem as one would think. Although the nicest, cheapest, and closest inns always fill up in advance, nothing (except for one or two small inns) is within walking distance of the track, so it's just a matter of how much further you'll drive (a handful of buses are available, but are so complicated that the mode is probably not worth pursuing). Northampton is closest, but fills up quickly. Oxford is about a half-an-hour away in light traffic and has lots of bed-and-breakfast houses available during that time — and it's worth a visit anyway.

For a list of Oxford Hotels and Guest Houses, or information on how to book, contact: Accommodation Secretary, Kathleen Brennan, Falcon Guest House,

90 Abingdon Road, Oxford; PH (865) 722995. Or call the Oxford Tourist Information Center at 865 726 871 (located at St. Aldates, Oxfordshire OX11DY). For more information on accommodations in Northampton, contact the Northampton Tourist Information Center at 21 St. Giles St. Northamptonshire NN11JA, PH: 604 22677 34881 EXT. 404.

Snetterton Circuit
**Brands Hatch Circuits Ltd,
Snetterton Circuit, Snetterton,
Norwich, Norfolk, NR16 2JU
PH: (44) 0953 87303
FAX: (44) 0953 87822**

Location: Eastern Great Britain, approximately 80 miles North east of London, 20 miles south west of Norwich.

From London, take the Autoroute M11 to A11 to the track, which is located on A11.

Circuit: 1.95 mile road circuit; seven turns.

Major races: British Formula 3000 Championship; British Formula 3 Championship.

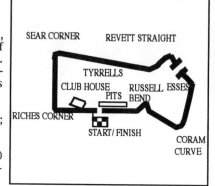

Snetterton, in recent years, has become a popular F1 testing place. Although it has much less going for it than Donington, Brands Hatch, or Silverstone, it's a challenging place, with a varying degree of cornering speeds and corner geometry. Another airport circuit, the fast corners are blighted with sparse run-off. Van Diemen is located here, and others seem to be attracted to the track since Silverstone has become an expensive raceshop-mecca.

There are several buses which serve the track and nearby trains connect the area to the rest of Great Britain. The nearest hotel facilities are in Snetterton, Thetford, and Wymondham. The nearest Tourist Information Center is in Thetford, located at White Hart St., Norfolk, IP241AA, PH: 842 752 599.

Thruxton Circuit Ltd,
**Thruxton Circuit, Nr Andover,
Hants, SP11 8PN, Great Britain**

**PH: (44) (26) 477 2607/ (026477) 2696
FAX: (44) (26) 477 3794**

Location: Southern Britain, 60 miles west of London, 35 miles north of Southampton.

From London, take Autoroute M3 South to A303 west, passing Andover on the way to the circuit, which is a few miles west of Andover.

Circuit: 2.36 mile road course; nine turns.

Major races: British Formula 3000 Championship; British Formula 3 Championship; British Touring Car Championships.

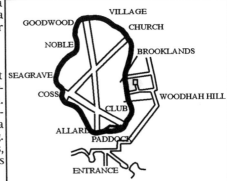

Thruxton is another flat British airport circuit. Unlike Silverstone, run-off here is not a concern. At Thruxton, an unhooked car usually has a football field's worth of a slide to go before hitting anything. There are a few ultra-fast corners, and some tight, twisty sections, so it's a challenge to drivers.

Big grandstands afford a view of most of the track — although you won't be able to walk any closer to the track than the grandstands. Thruxton is traditionally known for having the final big race — albeit non-championship race — of the season, the Televised Thruxton Weekend.

Hotels are available in nearby Andover and Salisbury, and special rates often apply for those who are using the circuit — but usually must be applied for in advance through the track. Other than that, Winchester or Southampton are your best bets. For more information on lodging, contact the Tourist Information Center, located in Southampton at Above Bar Precinct, Hampshire SO94XF, PH: 703 221 106.

HUNGARY

Hungary is best seen first from a boat heading down the Danube. Driving from Austria is the most frequent means of passage into Hungary, but the jewel of Hungary is Budapest, and the trip down the Danube to Budapest is much nicer than the drive. Time-wise, however, it's better to take a car.

There are four border crossings from Austria into Hungary. The southernmost crossing is the most widely used. The #10 road from Vienna is probably the best way into the country and gives you a better feeling of security since that's where most people enter, and you can essentially travel in an anonymous convoy.

The place is rather stark. Communism is not big on advertising, and the lack of ads makes the place feel a bit less inviting. Things are changing, but slowly.

From the eastern outskirts of Gyor, the road gets wider and faster. Up to there it's two-laned, but becomes four-laned for the 85 mile trip into Budapest from Gyor.

The limits are posted at 100KPH on the major roads and 80 on the smaller ones; most people drive at the posted speeds — although for the GP things are relaxed a bit. You'll need a European green insurance card, and an international driver's licence. Remember, also, that you'll need a visa for Hungary. You should have no problem getting one in Vienna, provided you apply 24 hours ahead of time. You can get them at the points of entry as well, but it is recommended that you do it ahead of time. From the U.S., contact the Hungarian Consulate General , 8 E. 75th Ave., New York, NY 10021.

Tourist Information: **Hungarian Travel Bureau** , IBUSZ, 630 Fifth Ave., #2455, New York, NY 10111. PH: (212) 582-7412.

Sporting Authorities: **Magyar Auto-es Motorsport Szovetseg** , Romer Floris u.4/a, 1024 Budapest, Hungary. PH: (36) 1 115 8469; FAX: (36) 1 115

3089; **Magyar Auto-es Motorsport Szovetseg,** Dozsa Gy. u. 1-3, 1142 Budapest. PH: (91 44) 235 1684.

Hungaroring
2146 Mogyorod, Pf10,
Gazdasagi Tarsasag,
1136 Budapest, Hungary

PH: (361) 532640/533924
FAX: (361) 183 7320

Location: 12 miles north east of Budapest; 155 miles from Vienna

Circuit: 2.49 mile road course; 14 turns.

Major races: FIA Formula One Grand Prix; Europa Truck Cup; GM Lotus Euroseries.

Hungary has changed dramatically since its first international race in 1986. It originally seemed as if the race would be a disaster. Officials apparently had little idea as to how a Formula One race should be run, so it was disorganized; the Hungarian Government wasn't sure how to treat the swarms of guests, so they treated them like Hungarians — badly. And to top it off, it was too hot for most of the northern Europeans.

Things have gotten better since then. The government has relaxed with the new climate in Eastern Europe. But Hungary's change was evolutionary more than revolutionary, so things still remain similar to what they were before the fall of European communism in '89/90. The grip has only been loosened by a few degrees. There are still some things you aren't supposed to see, places you cannot walk, and certainly places you wouldn't want to walk anyway.

The Danube flows between the two cities of Buda and Pest, and it is really a very attractive place. But, like most Eastern Bloc countries, the lack of color is oppressive.

With the GP circus, things lighten up somewhat, but the entire event is an adventure. For the unindoctrinated traveller, the race is really designed to be done with a tour. Finding a room in Hungary once inside the country can often be very difficult.

With the bad points put in their proper perspective, Hungarian travel is probably one of the better adventures in Europe. The place can be reached from Vienna by jetfoil, which is just a four hour trip down the Danube. There is also train service from Vienna, but river travel is far more spectacular.

When you reach Kaleti Station in Buda, you'll want to find a room. The equivalent of Intourist is adjacent to the station, and the office workers all speak English. They can arrange rooms, tours, sell race tickets, and will give you instructions to your hotel, and to the track as well. They will likely tell you how to take the trolley,

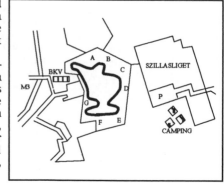

but the cost of a taxi is dirt cheap. There are only a handful of taxi drivers who speak English, so make sure everything is written down in Hungarian for them. If you've come by car, the track is well marked and you should have no problem finding the place without ever trying to communicate.

Tickets are hard to find ahead of time, because this is really a big deal in Hungary. There is limited information on how to get them, where to get them, and where the seats are once you do get them. Try for tickets opposite the pits — general admission will be a zoo. You'll have an easier time getting the most expensive tickets than the cheapest ones.

Unfortunately, the major race here is in jeopardy. The FIA Grand Prix costs the country a great deal of money, and as this guide was being prepared there were rumors that it would eventually be cancelled — in fact, it was a surprise to most that it appeared on the '92 and '93 schedules.

The first Hungarian FIM GP was run in 1990, and was surely a money maker. But apparently there have been safety problems for the bikes. The track itself is very safe, with lots of run-off, but there are some major problems with the heights of the berm, as well as the painted lines on the circuit (which are deadly for bikes and which caused the race's cancellation in 1991).

You need a visa, but can pick one up fairly easily in Vienna just before leaving for Hungary; or call the Tourist Bureau. For more general information, call the HTB at (212) 582-7412.

IRELAND

Motoring in Ireland is not taken as seriously as in Britain where the country is very cognizant of motor racing. But with Eddie Jordan and a handful of Irish riders and drivers — Niall McKenzie and Martin Donnely being the most famous — Ireland is becoming more interested in the sport.

Like Great Britain, Ireland uses right hand drive cars. In the cities drivers tend to be less aggressive, but on the country roads — most of which are very narrow — drivers tend to drive very fast.

The Naas Dual Carriageway from Dublin south is one of the only four-laned roads in Ireland, and it is only 20 miles long or so. The rest is a maze of single-laned roads.

The Irish demand etiquette on the road and will forgive an occasional faux-pas from a foreigner if you acknowledge your mistakes. Like most European countries they will flash their headlights at oncoming traffic to signal a constable who may be sitting down the road waiting for those who are travelling above the speed limit. Police are not as malicious as they are in the U.S., but they will give tickets.

Dublin to Liverpool is 4.5 hour ferry trip but some of the best Irish scenery is from Roslare to Dublin, and you can catch a ferry from Roslare.

Tourist Information: Irish Tourist Board, 757 3rd Ave., New York, NY 10017; PH: 800 223-6470

Sporting Authorities: **Royal Irish Automobile Club**, 34 Dawson Street, Dublin, IRE; PH. 1 775 141; FAX. 1 710 793; **Motorcycle Union of Ireland**, 24 Ballyminstraugh Road, Killinchy, Co Down, Northern Ireland BT23 6RE. PH: (44 238) 541 716; FAX: (44 238) 541 142. 770688

Kirkistown Race Circuit,
Rubane Rd, Cloughey, Northern Ireland

PH: (44) 0232 244938
FAX: 232 247135

Location: Northern Ireland, about seven miles from Belfast.

Circuit: 1.53 mile road circuit; seven turns.

Major races: British Formula Ford; Irish Opel Lotus Championship.

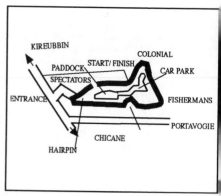

Kirkistown is Northern Ireland's only permanent racetrack. At one time it was an RAF base. At just a mile or so from the coast, it's unique in Ireland in that its average climate is warm. It's usually clear here, with very little wind. The same reasons for its choice as an airbase are why the place is so nice for racing.

Its problems do not concern Summer racefans, but are still worth noting: The area is located on flat reclaimed land, and during the "Spring tides" (which are really floods during the Fall), the concrete in the bowl portion of the track expands some 3/8ths of an inch, making racing impossible at that time of year.

Still, it is one of the nicest spots in all of Ireland, and has the lowest average rainfall of any spot on the island — both north and south. There are plenty of places to stay near the track, and rooms are rarely filled when the bigger FF races come through. Des McAuley, the track manager, is a friendly guy who'll give you his opinions on a good place to stay in the area, or call the Belfast Tourist Information Center at 232 246 609, or 232 320202, or 8494 520 84.

Mondello Park Motor Racing Circuit Ltd,
58 Haddington Rd., Dublin 4, Ireland

Location: Eastern central Ireland, 20 miles from Dublin on the N7.

Circuit: 1.24 mile road circuit, six turns.

Major races: Irish Opel Lotus Championship (seven rounds); Formula Ford Festival.

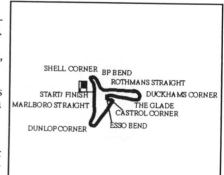

Mondello Park is the Republic of Ireland's only permanent motorsports venue. At one time it hosted F5000, but now only Formula Ford. The Park hosts the Irish Formula Ford Festival, and the wild atmosphere inspires race car drivers to literally drive their race cars to the track on city streets for competition.

Dublin will have plenty of rooms during even the biggest race here. For more infromation call the Irish Tourist Board — Board Failte, by its domestic title — at 14 Upper O'Connell St., Dublin 1; PH 74 77 33; or Baggot Street Bridge Dublin 2, PH: 765 871.

Phoenix Park
Irish Motor Racing Club Ltd,
12 Robin Villas,
Palmerstown, Dublin 20, Ireland

Location: Eastern Dublin, Northern Ireland.

Circuit: 2.12 mile road course, seven turns.

Major races: Irish Open Lotus Championship; Irish Motor Racing Club racing.

Phoenix Park's circuit — located in a city park — is only open once a year for the meeting of the IMRC along with a round of the Irish Lotus Championship, but judging on the safety features — of which there are few — once a year is enough. Built in 1929, the park has beautiful relics of days past — most of which act as obstacles to avoid in the case of a spin.

Dublin will have plenty of rooms should you find yourself in Ireland during the May race date. For more information contact the Board Failte — the domestic name of the Irish Tourist Board — at 14 Upper O'Connell St., Dublin 1; PH 74 77 33; or, Baggot Street Bridge Dublin 2, PH: 765 871.

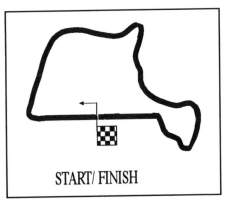

START/ FINISH

ITALY

Italians are known for being auto racers. And there's a good reason: try driving there. It feels as if you're racing for your life.

If you fancy yourself a bit of a racing driver you must rent a car in Rome. To do it right, pick the thing up at 4:30 PM Friday and drive across town.... but make sure you get the optional insurance.

Of all the countries with FIA sanctioning, Italy comes closest to being the nation with the most perfect motorsports fans. The entire country gets behind racing, and auto racing is discussed anywhere, and anytime. Ferrari is not a manufacturer, it's a religion.

Italians' passion for driving spills onto the road. Drivers in Italy use the streets to practice. There may be lines on the road, but lanes don't exist, and there are no rules. You are only governed by your own sense of ethics and fair play. If you don't play fair, don't worry, nobody will think you malicious. If you do play fair, you'll be squished. It is probably an unhealthy place to drive for too long.

However, since rules don't actually exist (or, anyway, nobody pays any attention to them), you can do just about anything you want - at least in Rome. Don't be alarmed if in heavy traffic the guy in front of you makes a left turn from the far right lane. U-turns from the left lane; left turns from the right lane; driving on sidewalks; and cutting people off like they don't exist is the norm in Rome.

The rest of the country is pretty straightforward. In fact, Italy is probably one of the strictest countries in Europe when it comes to speeding. The police sit on the Autostradas waiting for derelict drivers to come screaming past, whereupon they simply point their finger.

There is no shriek of a siren; no heart-stopping blue and red lights... just a friendly little paddle with a red dot on it, and a smiling Italian, who'll point at you, and motion for you to pull to the side of the road. If it happens to you, you'll understand why you feel compelled to pull over. There's just something so civilized about the method.

Keep in mind that there are Carabinieri — or military — who usually park up the road a spell, waiting for the guys who try to run away. When you see parades of people tapping their high beams, slow down. It means there are police ahead.

The speed limit on Italy's Autostradas is 130KPH in the winter, and drops to 110 in the summer months when the accident rate climbs. There are still places, like on the A10 from Ventimiglia to Genova, that are playgrounds for fast cars manned by drivers who don't mess around with anything as meaningless as a speed limit. But for the most part, people drive near the limits.

The cities, other than Rome, are pretty easy to conquer — except when trying to find directions. There is usually no rhyme or reason to the city plans. Remember that most of the country is very old, and they weren't thinking in terms of automobiles when they planned the streets. Florence is difficult; Milan is difficult — in fact, most cities are generally confusing. So be patient.

Finally, tolls are an unexpected irritation for most travellers. Most guidebooks don't warn of the expensive road hazards. Except for a few brief stretches around Rome and Terni, the only major piece of road that isn't a toll road is from Salerno to the Straits of Messina. Ninety per cent of all Italian Autostradas, or main highways, have tolls. Unlike France, there are few alternate routes in Italy. It will be expensive to drive in Italy — and gas is more expensive in Italy than anywhere else in Europe, averaging about $1.50 a liter (almost $6.00 a gallon).

Tourist information: **Italian Government Tourist Office**; In Italy look for the Compagnia Italiana Turismo (CIT) located in Rome at the Piazza Della Repubblica.

Sporting Authorities: **Commissione Sportiva Automobilistica**

Italiana, Via Solferino 32, 00185, Roma, Italy. PH: (39) 6 494 1024/1026; FAX: (39) 6 494 0961. Or, for San Marino, **Federazione Auto Motoristica Sammarinese,** Via M. Moretti 5, Saravalle, 47031, Rep. San Marino. PH: 549 900 757; FAX: 549 905 958. For motorcycles, use the **Federazione Motociclistica Italiana,** 70 Viale Tiziano, 00196, Roma. PH: (39 6) 323 3815; FAX: (39 6) 3685 8160.

Autodromo Pergusa
Ente Autodromo Pergusa
Piazza Garibaldi, 8
94100 — Enna, Sicily

PH: (39 935) 25660/36069

Location: Central Sicily, just off the A19 on Rural Route 290, between Catania and Palermo.

Circuit: 3.6 mile road course; 14 turns.

Major races: Italian Formula 3 Championship; FIA Formula 3000 Championship.

Enna Pergusa is becoming the Pau of the South. The hot Sicilian weather brings F3000 fans from northern Europe, and the beauty of Sicily brings the sightseers who co-habitate with migrant race fans. The long racetrack is not the easiest to view from any one place, and it is not exactly the most challenging layout, so the race itself will never be a Monaco or a Pau, but the venue will certainly rank as one of the most interesting.

The track encircles a lake, appropriately named, Lago di Pergusa, and is more a long series of right turns than a road course. Without the three sets of chicanes it would almost be an oval, and from the tribune on the north east side of the track one can see most of the track across the lake.

The tribune fills quickly for the F3000 race, and finding a ticket ahead of time will be nearly impossible unless you speak Italian and can call the circuit directly. But there are several areas around the track which will provide good views of the racing — although nothing will do the job like the raised tribune.

Rooms for Enna will be a bit hard to find during the F3000 race, but if you call ahead of time, or show up in person a few days prior to the race, you will likely be successful in your search.

Try Enna first, where the National Tourist Office is located at Piazza Garibaldi, 1, PH: (0935) 21 184; then try Pergusa; or Agrigento, about 25 miles west, at the ENIT office at Viale della Vittorio, 255, PH: (0922) 26 926; or Catania, some 45 miles east, at the office at Largo Paisiello, 5, (095) 316 407.

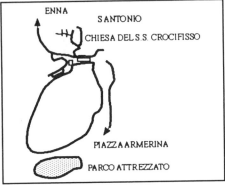

Imola

Autodromo Dino Ferrari
40226 Imola, Italy
Office: Automobile Club
Bologna,
Via Calori 9/d, 40122,
Bologna, Italy

PH: (39) 522158/522159
FAX: (39) 51 55 25 18/ (39)
542 30 420

Location: Northern central Italy, 20 miles south east of Bologna.
From Bologna take either the Autostrada A14 South to the Imola exit, or take the Regional Route 9 straight to Imola — which bypasses the tolls.

Circuit: 3.13 mile road course; 12 turns.

Major races: FIA Formula One Grand Prix World Championship; Italian Formula 3 Championship.

When Gerhard Berger's Ferrari hit the wall in the Curva di Tamburello in the 1989 San Marino Grand Prix Imola showed its true colors. The reaction by the fire marshalls was instantaneous. Before the car came to a stop — in fact, before the car had even burst into flames — the fire marshalls were running toward the Ferrari with their fire bottles. When the car erupted into flames, it may have seemed like an eternity to those who watched, but it was attended to with lightning quick precision.

"We think we've got it covered at Silverstone," said one British journalist following the impressive work on Berger's car, "but the Italians have got it on all of us, haven't they?." Imola's potential disaster gives a good look at the Italian track, and how things really work at the Italian venue.

But, remember, it's still Italy.

The San Marino GP caters to the Italian crowd. Things may have been serious in Berger's time of need, but — as long as a Ferrari is still running anywhere on the track — things are identical to Monza. In fact, Monza is mild in comparison. The difference between Monza and Imola is that Imola is traditionally held on a major holiday, freeing people who ordinarily wouldn't have attended the GP.

Imola is a different breed of race. This is Ferrari's circuit. Dedicated some years ago, the Autodromo Dino Ferrari is a Ferrari shrine. One English fan went looking for a Williams T-shirt, and discovered there were none available anywhere; if it's not red it doesn't sell.

Throngs of police wander the grounds whose only job is to whack tree-dwellers out of their perches with clubs. It doesn't seem to help much since they just climb higher. If those monkeys don't impress you, try the caged ones. How many tracks have a zoo on the property?

It may be hard to get used to Imola, but once you go, it will be the race you'll want to see over and over again.

The bad things about Imola are essentially the same things that are bad at Monza. Access to and from the track is via one long road to the side of the main entrance, and following the conclusion of the race, it can take hours to get out.

Hotels in Imola might as well not exist, since you can't get any of them

126

anyway. Rimini is best, but you may not be able to find anything there either. By the way, Imola is a good distance from San Marino. Don't go to San Marino looking for the track, it's nearly an hour away.

The really frightening thing is ticketing. There is a distinct possibility that you'll find a room and not be able to get tickets — even general admission tickets. Try calling the track office, although don't get upset if you don't get through. Then try the Auto Club in Imola or Page and Moy. And, if things get tight, consider going to the track Tuesday to pick up tickets. You really shouldn't have a major problem with general admission, but show up Saturday morning to buy Sunday's passes anyway — just for safe measure.

The city most apt to have rooms will be Bologna. You can call the Bologna tourist office, where they'll certainly be able to put you in contact with a hotel on pensione with rooms for the GP, or you can call the Italian Tourist Offices here, which will help you with a list of hotels in the area — either way, you must then call the hotel yourself from here. If you get to Bologna by Wednesday, you should have your pick of the mid-range places. Any later, and you're asking for trouble.The Italian Government Travel Office in Bologna is located at Via Marconi 45, PH: (051) 237-413.

Autodromo Magione

AMUB Magione
Localita Bacanella
06063 — Magione — PG
Perugia, Italy

PH: (39) 75 84 03 03

Location: Central Italy, between Florence and Perugia, approximately 80 miles north west of Rome.

From Rome, take the Autostrada A1 to Orte, bearing east toward Perugia. Pass Perugia heading toward Magione, where the track is located; from Florence, take A1 to National Route 75 to Magione.

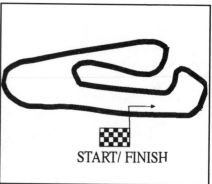

START/ FINISH

Circuit: 1.03 mile road course; six turns.

Major races: Italian Formula 3 Championship.

Magione is generally abandoned during the year, except for a handful of national caliber automobile and motorcycle series and the single Italian Formula Three event in April. Good for spectators, and great for sightseers, the track is short and uncomplicated, but not unchallenging. It's used more for testing than anything else.

Rooms can be found in both Florence and Perugia if nothing closer to the track is available. For Florence, the Italian Tourist office is located at Via Manzoni, 16, PH: (055) 247-8141 or (055) 247-8142; the Perugia office is located at Via Mazzini, 21, PH: (075) 35341.

Misano
Autodromo Santamonica
Via del Carro 27a,
1-47046 Misano Adriatico(FO),
Italy

PH: (39 541) 615159/616221

Location: Central-eastern Italy, between Ancona and Rimini, on the Adriatic Coast, about 160 miles from Rome.

From Rome, take the Autostrada A24 East to A14, past Ancona to Cattolica; From Bologna, take A14 South to Cattolic (two miles from Cattolica).

Circuit: 2.16 mile road course;10 turns.

Major races: FIM Grand Prix World Championships; Superbikes; Italian Formula 3 Championship.

START/ FINISH

Misano had had its share of controversy in the past. In 1989, the slippery conditions made the track very dangerous, and the top FIM riders boycotted the race, citing the hazards of the slick track surface. It was run anyway. Italian Pierfrancesco Chili won that event — at this writing his only 500cc victory. Unfortunately for Chili, his career will always be linked to the empty victory which was only contended by the smaller teams which couldn't afford to stay out of the race, and Misano will probably always be remembered by bike racers for the race that shouldn't have been. Again in 1990 weather played a part, as rain stopped the race with 10 laps to go.

The track is actually very good. It's safe and there's excellent run-off. It's actually 30 meters short of the minimum for an FIM GP, and that fact was conveniently overlooked — until 1992. The race was been cancelled in favor of Mugello. Officials had planned on eventually adding a loop to it to enhance the layout anyway, they were simply forced to do it sooner. In 1993 the GP caravan again breezed through this picturesque summer resort and the racetrack was back on the 1993 FIM GP calendar.

There's plenty of spectator banking and several good grandstand areas, although the majority of viewing is done from General Admission areas. One of the best places to watch the racing is in the Tifolica, a tight left-hander which is critical as it sweeps onto the fastest parts of the track.

You'll likely have to stay a few miles away in Rimini for the race, although you'll still need to get here early. If not Rimini, Bologna or Ancona will be best — although a good hour's drive. There are camping facilities in the area, and although they need to be reserved ahead of time for the bike races, there should be no problems now for F3. The Bologna tourist office will be able to put you in contact with a hotel or pensione. The Italian Government Travel Office in Bologna is located at Via Marconi 45, PH: (051) 237-413; for Ancona, the office is located at Via Marcello Marini, 14, PH: (071) 201 980.

Autodromo Nazionale Monza,
20052 Monza Parco, Italy

PH: (39) 39329 866
FAX: (39) 39 32 03 24

Location: Northern Italy, 12 miles from Milan City-center.
From Milano, take National Route 36 North to Monza.

Circuit: 3.6 mile road course; six turns.

Major races: FIA Formula One Grand Prix World Championship; FIA Formula 3000 Championship; FIM Grand Prix World Championship — 500cc, 250cc, 125 cc and Sidecars; FIM Superbike Championship; Italian Formula 3 Championship.

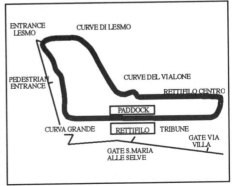

Monza is madness. That's why Monza is worth the headache.

There are few races which contain the emotions like a day with the Tifosi at the Autodromo di Monza. If, perhaps, you can be there when Ferrari wins, well, the whole trip will have been worth ten times what you spent. Like in 1988, when, under the dark cloud of McLaren domination, Ferrari swept with a 1-2 win. The place went crazy that day.

It's impossible — in fact, dangerous — to be anything other than a Ferrari fan at Monza.

Monza is getting lost for hours, hearing the cars, but never knowing how to get trackside; it's being Italian for a weekend; not caring when, or if the buses will come to bring you back to your hotel in Milano; it's being loud, having fun, and heckling anything and anyone. It's the biggest party of the Italian racing year.

Monza has the reputation for being uncontrollable. The reputation it has with fans running onto the track the minute the cars cross the finish line typifies Monza. Police try to stop the enthusiasm, but it never works. Grandstands built to hold 10,000 people — that are in such disrepair, that they shouldn't even hold 1,000, — will be overrun by 12,000 fans, hanging, sitting, or swinging from the structures.

Finding a ticket at Monza is relatively easy, since nobody seems to pay for tickets here anyway. Finding a good ticket is not nearly as easy, and as with all GPs, it will cost you. One of the best places to watch is in Lesmo, where there is a spectacular natural arena of action. Television never does this area justice, and the seats are really terrific. Anything near Parobolica is spectacular as well. Start/finish is rather boring though, and probably not worth the extra money. No matter where you are, you'll hear what's going on out on the track from the shouts from around the circuit!

With the prospect of an FIA Oval Track Championship on the horizon, the old banking at the Monza oval may be refurbished — which would be quite an incentive to visit Monza if the GP cars are not to your liking. The old banking still exists, and while walking through the infield you'll come upon it. Although fenced off, a look at the historic sections is worth the effort of struggling through the forest.

Staying in Monza, and getting to the track is a real problem. If you have any brains at all, you won't even think of driving. It takes forever to get in, and twice that to get out — if you can even find a parking space once you get to within a mile

of the track.

Don't plan on staying in Monza. It's impossible. If you do some homework you can stay in Milano, which is only a few miles away, but will take you an hour by bus, or 40 minutes by train. The buses start leaving the train station in Milano at about 5:30 AM (buy your ticket across the street from main entrance to the Milano train station in the coffee shop) and the ride is effortless. Getting back, as you can probably already imagine, is no picnic. Plan on staying for a couple of hours until the crowd thins out, or pack yourself into a bus for an hour-and a-half (figuring on extra traffic) of pure hell.

Milano will fill up quickly too. Even the small penziones will fill up, so get to the track as soon as possible (like Wednesday). If you want to do it right, call the Italian Government Tourist Office and ask for a copy of their list of accommodations for the Milano area. They'll be happy to help you. Calling to reserve your room from the U.S. during economy hours is very inexpensive.

The number in Milano's downtown Galleria the Italian Tourist office, which can give you a list of hotels and possibly help you book your room — if its not too close to GP (Wednesday is fine, but any later the office will be mobbed and the office staff will not help), is PH (02) 870 016. The office is located at Via Marconi, No. #1.

Mugello
SAIM S.pA
Autodromo Internazionale del Mugello
(Office) Scarperia (Firenze), Via Senni, 15
50038,   Italy

PH: 055 8495800
FAX: 055 8495808

Location: 20 miles north east of Florence. From Florence, take Rural Route 65 North to 503 toward Scarperia, following the signs to the track.

Circuit: 3.1 miles, 13 turns.

Major races: FIM Motorcycle Grand Prix; FIM Superbike Championship; FIA F3 Championship; Italian Porsche Championship; Italian Formula 3 Championship

In 1991, Mugello hosted only an Italian Formula 3 race, and it was far from being a major circuit.

But renovation was carried out on the Florentine track by Ferrari and the venue is now poised to take on the world — or the World Championship at any rate. This track now has the potential to handle any motorsports event safely and in a stylish blend of contemporary design and good old-fashioned challenging racing.

In these days of safe and sterile tracks Mugello offers a change. It was created with safety as the foremost requirement, but at the same time its altitude changes and its fast layout make it a drivers track as well. The old circuit was retained in the renovation, but the entire track was resurfaced and widened, providing billiard-smooth asphalt. Long sand traps were added where bushes and shrubs once stood, and a ring road spans the perimeter, providing emergency vehicles a quick way in and out — and motorcyclists a chance to breathe easier. It hosted some World Championship motor races in 1992, and may host the San Marino GP again eventually. Nevertheless, the Superbike World Championship will go to Monza. Odd.

The new pit complex is modern enough for any international meeting. Since the track winds up and down a hill in a manner of switchbacks most of it can be seen from anywhere you plant yourself.

There are a few hotels around the track, and considering its current status rooms will likely be much more scarce than in the old days. Florence proper is only a few minutes away and is certainly worth a few extra days... even during racing season. For Florence, the Italian Tourist office is located at Via Manzoni, 16, PH: (055) 247-8141 or (055) 247-8142 and a trip to the train station or a stop on the Autostrada prior to arriving in Florence will yield a room through the booking agents at the tourist offices, provided you're prepared to pay a commission.

Autodromo Vallelunga,
Vallelunga ACI Sport SpA,
1-00063 Campagnano di Roma
(Via Cassia, bivio Km34.5),

PH: (39) 6 904 1009/ 6 904 1027
FAX: (39) 6 9042197

Location: 20 miles North of Rome, between Via Flaminia (Rural #3) and Rural #2, near Campagnano di Roma.

Circuit: 1.98 mile road course; six turns.

Major races: Italian Formula 3 Championship; GM Lotus Euroseries Championship.

Vallelunga's FIA F3000 race returned in 1993 after missing the 1991 season as well as an acrimonious relationship with 3000 drivers in 1992 (the teams didn't like Vallelunga's crowds much, it seems). Motorcycles dominate Vallelunga's action these days, although there is a great deal of car testing and a few decent sedan races as well.

Located in northern Rome, in the Olgiata section, the area is famous in Italy for its golf course, the appropriately named Olgiata Golf Course. The Viterbo is near the track, but most of the area is new buildings and lots of Roman greenery.

Most of the short track is not visible to spectators, and the portions which are don't exactly bring the fans

AUTODROMO VALLELUNGA

to their feet. Its proximity to Rome makes it an easy racetrack to find at the last minute, and certainly worth a visit during a May or September Italian F3 date.

The short track is an Italian version of the local American suburban/rural dirt track, with the weekend warriors coming out to watch a good day of racing without a care for who participates. The lone grandstand, which sits in the infield near start finish, only seats some 7,000 people. But it's a good place to park yourself to watch the racing — you'll see most of the track from the top rows of the stands.

The track has good elevation changes, starting on a downhill slope, then winding back up the hill on the backside of the course, and ending with a quick turn back onto the start/finish line. Although spectator access is not as good as it could be parking is abundant, so you should plan on seeing Rome and driving the short distance for the races.

Rome is the best bet for rooms. The National Government Tourist Office is located at Via Parigi, 11, in Rome. PH: (06) 461 851.

Autodromo Varano
Circuit Riccardo Paletti
So. GE.SA. S.r.l.
Via Emilia Est, 13
43100 — Parma, Italy

PH: (39) 59 843974

Location: Central Northern Italy, between Bologna and Milan, 20 miles south west of Parma.

Circuit: 1.1 mile road course; five turns.

Major races: Italian Formula 3 Championship.

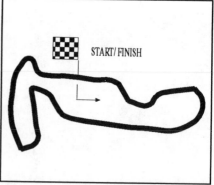

This stiflingly short racetrack, originally called Varano Melagari, was constructed in 1970, and was built as a 550 meter circuit which ran around a small football field. Two years later officials extended the circuit to the existing 1800 meter length. In 1982 Riccardo Paletti, whose parents had some control in the circuit, died in an F1 car in Montreal. The track was subsequently renamed after the late Paletti.

Based on the old football field theme, the place is almost completely flat, although challenging enough to host Italian F3 and viewing is good from most places. Built alongside the Ceno River — which is more a slough than a river — getting about the place is difficult. Access from the east is impossible due to the entrance road and fences; access from the west is restricted by the river; and there are no roads to the north, so your walk will originate from the main parking lot on the south portion of the property. Due to this, most of the viewing will be from the south end of the circuit.

Rooms for Varano are best found in Parma, just a few minutes drive from the circuit. The closest Italian Tourist office is located in Parma at Piazza 5, Parma, 43100, or call 5 21 33 959; The Italian Government Travel Office in Bologna is located at Via Marconi 45, PH: (051) 237-413.

JAPAN

Japan finally became an integral part of the motorsports in 1987 when it hosted its first FIA Grand Prix since 1976, and only the third in its history. The Japanese have been on the forefront of auto racing technology for the past few years in automobiles and the past dozen or so in motorcycle racing.

Japan's races are very well organized, and, like everything Japanese, is immediately a standard to which all others aspire to achieve. Japan is car-crazy, and Toyota is king in the Asian market. Japanese, however, separate racing and motoring — similar to Americans — and the two disciplines of motoring don't come together very often. German cars are certainly admired for their engineering in Japan, but are far more appealing due to their expense and the status of ownership than for their performance. Japanese are generally more preoccupied with the machinery and the image of motoring than with sport.

Conditions on the road reflect some of the culture's notions of racing, but for the most part the two realms will be forever separate. Ask a Japanese his suggestions regarding car rental in Tokyo and he'll give you a condescending smile, suggesting you have no idea what you're getting into.

If you fancy a bit of adventure it's something worth doing. But not in Japan. If you want adventure, rent a right-drive car in Australia and drive across country. Japan is not a motoring adventure, it's an invitation for an ulcer.

The Japanese drive on the left side of the road, in cars that range in variety from golf-carts to Mercedes limos — and which are always much closer together than you'll want to see them. The Japanese are not the greatest drivers on earth either. What they lack in skill they often try to make up for in bold driving.

Driving in the rural areas is not a problem, except that you won't know where the hell you're going since many signs are written only in Japanese characters. The traffic in Japan can be horrible, taking several hours to go just a few miles if you attempt it at the wrong time. Finally, the speed limits in Japan are only 100 KPH on the highways, and everyone seems to drive at the limit — even if the cars are capable of three times that speed.

Tourist Information: **Japan National Tourist Organization** , in Tokyo, 6-6, Yurakucho. 1-chome, Tokyo. PH: (0476) 32-8711.

Sporting Authorities: **Japan Automobile Federation** , 3-5-8 Shibakoen, Minato-ku, Tokyo, Japan. PH: (81) 33 436 2811; FAX: (81) 33 584 3525; **Motorcycle Federation of Japan,** 2-16-7-7F Dai 2 Okano Bldg., Higashi-Nihonbashi, Chuo-ku, Tokyo 103. PH: (81 33) 3865 84 41; FAX: (81 33) 3865 84 40.

Autopolis International Race Course
1110-12 Kaminoda, Kamitue-Village
Hitagun Oita, Japan 877-03

OR: **Nippon Autopolis Co., LTD.**
1110-12 Kaminoda, Kamitsue-Village, Hitagun
OITA, 877-03, Japan

OR: **Ginza Wall Building**
13-16, 6-Chrome, Ginza, Chou-ku
TOKYO, Japan

PH: **(Autopolis) 0973-55-1200; (Nippon Autopolis Co.) 0973-55-1111; (Tokyo) 03 3541-0011**
FAX: **(Autopolis) 0973-55-1201; (Nippon Autopolis Co.)** 0973- **55-1212; (Tokyo) 03-3541-0199**

Location: In southwest Oita Prefecture, about 15 miles from Asomachi, and 20 miles from Kumamoto City.
Take the Kiushu Expressway to the Ueki exit, and follow the signs about 50 miles to the track.

Circuit: 2.94 mile road circuit; 14 turns.

Major Races: All Japan Formula 3000 Championships; All Japan Touring Car Championships.

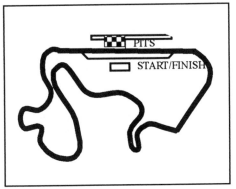

"I've seen the future," a British journalist said recently, "And it is called Autopolis."
Japan's newest circuit, which has been advertised on the sides of some very expensive For-

mula One race cars, is the prototype of racing circuits. Estimates of construction costs are upwards of $500-million dollars. Unfortunately, a good deal of it was never paid. Granted a round of the FIA World Championship in 1993, the circuit found itself with no way to pay collection agencies and creditors as they closed in on the circuit. The Asian Grand Prix — which would have been the second race in 1993 for Japan — was necessarily cancelled and the race moved from there to Donington in Great Britain.

The Autopolis was constructed in a similar fashion to the Technopolis at Magny-Cours — only on a much, much larger scale. Sitting in the middle of a green isolated mountainous area, Autopolis rises like a city. It is such a huge compound that it appears from the sky to be just that — a city. The area is like a journey into a Colorado mountain ski area. Craggy volcanic-looking peaks mark your way, and the track itself sits some 3,000 feet above sea-level. But as you enter the facility — usually from the top of the hill — nothing can prepare you for the expanse. The paddock and the press facilities, located on the main straight, are big enough to put the average racetrack inside the grounds — and that's just the paddock!

The press facilities at Autopolis make Daytona, Indianapolis, Monza, and Silverstone look like Boy Scout Clubrooms. Three stories tall and two hundred yards worth of glass and metal can easily accommodate the biggest crowd of journalists and PR types.

The permanent seats are so far located in the first and final turns — and more are apparently being planned. As it is now configured, Autopolis should accommodate some 150,000 fans — and another 250,000 will eventually find room, perhaps standing along the banks.

The track dips into a bowl, which provides a natural viewing area. Most of the track is visible from anywhere. It has more than adequate run-off and is considered a very safe, yet very challenging track.

The best place to watch is from the end of the massive straight. The stands in the corner offer a view of this very difficult first turn. Although it is a very fast corner, a good deal of passing will be done on the approach to the right-hander. The grandstands provide a great view of the cars as they enter the ultra-fast sweeper and enter the next straight flat-out in preparation for the tight 90 degree right-hander. Although these stands don't hold as many spectators as the grandstands in the final turn, they're covered, and it's here where the tickets will be at a premium. In addition, there is another stand located on the outside of the first corner at the apex, and another seating area at the far end of the track at the 8th turn.

The stands in the final corner are very impressive. Looking like a baseball stadium, with seats following the curve of the final turn, and made of hard plastic and color-coded based on price. There are some 20,000 seats available here. From this vantage point you'll be able to see a great deal of the track — except the start/finish area. And in the infield near the final turn you'll be able to walk back and forth in the general admission areas, watching the action on both sides of the track. There is a cafeteria in the infield which will provide a view of the racing action from the dining room. The cafeteria holds 2,500 people.

But it is not just motorsports that makes Autopolis impressive. And the brochures contain little information about the racing aspect of the venue. What Autopolis is is a "unique fusion of culture, sport and art". The area has been undeveloped on purpose in order to keep the outdoors feeling of the rugged surroundings. The streams and forests of the Aso area have been consciously preserved so it feels like a retreat.

Autopolis is run like a club. For members there is a wide variety of activities — including but not specifically geared toward racing. There is a golf and tennis club, riding stables, a water sports complex, two hotels, and a museum.

The museum, by the way, is not a motorsports museum, but a fine art museum housing some quality works from Picasso, Monet, Renoir, Van Gogh, and others.

From the air, Autopolis is a mass of wide racing roads and a maze of well-placed access roads with at least five tunnels which allow access under the track surface to the infield. A smaller karting and test racetrack also fill the infield. There is, of course, a dragstrip and an air strip. For one reason or another, major series are still not finding their way to the circuit.

There are only a few events scheduled here at Autopolis — and no FIA or FIM World Championship events yet exist.

The track will be happy to help you find a room, and you should call, write or fax a note to them for more information on lodging.

Fuji International Speedway
Oh-Mika, Oyama-cho,
Sunto-gun, Shizouka Pref.,

PH: 055-78-1234

Location: South central Japan, on the island of Honshu, 80 miles south west of Tokyo.

From Tokyo, take the JR Tokaido train to Gotemba, then the Tomei bus to the speedway; or take the bus straight from the Tokyo station to Gotemba, transferring to the track.

Circuit: 4.41 kilometer road course; seven turns.

Major Races: Japanese Sports Prototype Championship; Japanese Formula Three Championship.

Fuji, for as long as it exists — indeed, for as long as there is a Japanese F1 Grand Prix — will always be remembered as the one that lost the World Championship for Niki Lauda in October,1976. The first ever Japanese Grand Prix saw Lauda back from the horrible Nurburgring accident, and within seven points of clinching his second World Championship for Ferrari. In the pouring rain, he lapped two circuits and withdrew; the championship, he said, was not worth his life. At the airport he heard over the news: James Hunt had taken third and secured the points needed to overtake Lauda and win the championship.

Fuji ran a WSPC round until 1989, when Suzuka monopolized all Japanese rounds of World Championship competition. It did host five of eight rounds of the 1992 Japanese Sports Prototype Championship, and two rounds of the championship in 1993.

The picturesque racetrack sits at the base of Mt. Fuji, and, amid the high-tech world of Autopolis and Suzuka, Fuji will always have a claim to Japanese racing sentiment due to

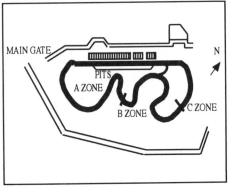

137

its ambience. Fuji elicits memories of the younger days of racing, with a very narrow pit lane — like Le Mans, and very small garages. It is rarely sunny here, since it sits so close to the mountain, which gives it an even more dramatic atmosphere.

The circuit is fast, with a long start/finish straight of nearly a mile in length. The straight has an elevation change, and the cars enter it headed uphill, with a crest in the center, and a long downhill to the first turn. The track then winds down around the hill through a twisty bit of track, then back up the hill to the end of the start/finish straight again.

The main grandstand runs the full length of straight, and because the straight is higher than the rest of the circuit you'll see most of the track from the stands.

Although seats are probably the best way to spend a weekend at Fuji, the general admission tickets — which allow you to walk about the infield — will yield you good view of the circuit as well.

Now that there are no major races here at Fuji, finding a room will be much easier than it has ever been. You can also stay in Tokyo and drive the 100 miles — two or three hours — on race day. Parking is plentiful, and access is decent — even for the bigger races.

For more information on rooms call the Shinwa Travel Service Company, 261-3 Hiragaki, Fuji, Shizuoka, 416, Japan. PH: 5 4 563 3711.

Mine Circuit (was Nishi-Nihon Circuit)
Nishi-Aho-cho,
Mine City,
Yamaguchi Pref, Japan

PH: 08375-8-0321

Location: Southern Japan at the south eastern tip of the island of Honshu, 100 miles south west of Hiroshima, and approximately 450 miles from Tokyo.

From Tokyo, take the Ogoori train via JR Shinkansen, transfering to Sanyo Main Line at Asa Station, then to Mine Line for Mine station, and a taxi to the track from there.

Circuit: 2.83 mile road circuit, eight turns.

Major races: Japanese Formula Three Championship; All Japan Motorcycle Road Racing.

Mine City Raceway is an interesting track that sees probably less use than even Nishi-Sendai but it has lots of potential, and may eventually be used as more than just a Japanese F3 track.

The circuit was reconstructed during the winter of 1990/91, and the entire circuit, which was then called Nishi-Nihon, has changed as well as the name. The circuit layout has changed significantly, and new grandstands are already springing up all over the course. Now the track is run

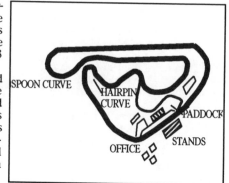

counter-clockwise rather than clockwise.

Mine City has plenty of rooms near the circuit — although the distance from the hotels will still be nearly a half-an-hour's drive. Try Shinonseki City, Ube City, or Onoda City. Although there are currently plenty of places to stay, if the ambitious work being done does in fact attract a major series the rooms may not last.

The Japan Travel Bureau can be reached at (81) 3 276 7875 (disregard the 81 if calling from Japan).

Nishi Sendai Hi-land Raceway,
**12 Hayasakayama Nikkawa,
Miyagi-Cho Miyagi-gun,
Kiyagi-ken, Japan**

**PH: (81) 022 395 2120
FAX: (81) 022 395 2330**

Location: Northern Japan on the island of Honshu, 240 miles north of Tokyo.

From Tokyo, head toward Sendai on the JR Tohoku Shinkansen, then transferring on the JR Senzan Line to Nishi Sendai Hi-Land, and a short taxi ride to the track.

Circuit: 3.76 mile road course; 15 turns.

Major Races: Japanese Formula Three.

Nishi Sendai is a popular test track, although at the bottom of the list in terms of prestige in Japanese tracks. It did, however, host a round of the 1987 FIA World Endurance Championship. The track is worth a look while visiting the historically significant Sendai City, built by famous Date Family.

For more information on rooms, call the track or contact the North Japan Overseas Travel Company LPD, Kahoku Bldg., 1-14-35, Ichiban-cho, Sendai, Miyagi, 980, Japan. PH: 22 227 6106.

Sugo Land Sugo Circuit
**Sugo, Murata-cho,
Shibata-gun, Miyagi Pref, Japan**

PH: (81) 0224 83-3111

Location: Northern Japan, on the island of Honshu, 150 miles North of

Tokyo.

From Tokyo, Take the Tohoku Driveway through the Murata Interchange, following signs to Sugo Sportsland (aprox 4 hrs); By train, take the Tohoku Hinkansen line to Sendai, then the local bus to the track.

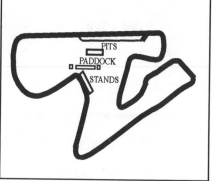

Circuit: 3.74 mile road course; 11 turns.

Major Races: FIM Superbike Championship; Japanese Sports Prototype Championship; Japanese Formula Three Championship.

Sugo was once in the race for the first rights to host a Japanese GP. Considering that there was no Japanese Grand Prix at all in either cars or bikes until 1987, officials at Sugo worked hard to attract the first FIA GP. Obviously, they failed to secure either GP. In 1991, '92 and '93 the FIM Superbike Championship made an appearance at Sugo, and will likely continue to be a part of the Championship.

More work is now being done to attract FIM GP motorcycles. However, it seems unlikely that the FIM would move from Suzuka, since Suzuka is safe, and proven. — even though Sugo is used by Yamaha as a test track, which gives it some clout in motorcycling.

Sugo has some pretty interesting devices here for racers including a weather forecast board which constantly changes during a weekend to help teams make the right choices in set up — and to help fans choose the right apparel. There is also a golf course on Sugo grounds, as well as eight tennis courts, and a swimming pool.

Camping is available at the circuit, and there's a hotel on the property — although it will be quickly booked for the bigger events. For more information contact the Sugo organization, or contact the Tokyo office (located at the Yoei Bldg., 4F, 8-8-5, Ginza, Chuo-ku, 104; PH 03 575-4771), or at the Sendai branch (at the Fukuda Bldg., 1-4-1, Ichiban-cho, Sendai-shi, Miyagi-ken 980; PH 022 266 8401.

Suzuka International Racing Course
Inao-machi, Suzuka City,
Mie Pref., Japan
7992 Ino-cho
Suzuka-shi, Mie-ken,
510-02

PH: (81) 593 781111/ (81) 593 701 465

FAX: (81) 33 436 4559
TELEX: 2227048

Ticket info: (81) 33 582 3221; FAX: (81) 3 582 3023

Or write to: Suzuka Circuit Co. Ltd., Akasaka Twin Tower, East Tower 16F, 2-17-22 Akasaka, Minato-ku, Tokyo, 107

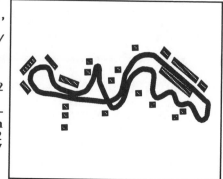

Location: South central Japan, on the island of Honshu, on the Ise Bay, 210 miles south west of Tokyo, in Suzuka City.

From Tokyo take the train to Nagoya via the Shinkansen line, at Nagoya transferring to the Kintetsu-Shirako line, then a 15 minute bus ride to the track.

Circuit: 3.5 mile road course; 11 turns.

Major Races: FIA Formula One World Championship; FIM World Endurance Championship; FIM Motorcycle Grand Prix World Championship — 500cc, 250cc, 125cc, and Sidecars; Japanese Sports Prototype Championship; Japanese Formula Three Championship.

Suzuka's Japanese Grand Prix is one of the best on the calendar for both two and four wheeled GP racing. The Japanese take pride in their Grand Prix, and the track brings no complaints from either set of racers. Considering that Honda had dominated Formula One since 1985 and a Japanese bike has beaten Europe's best every year since 1975, there is good reason for the Japanese to pull out all the stops for a perfect track and excellent treatment. And in 1992, for the first time since its inception in 1976, the Japanese Grand Prix was not the site of controversy.

Big news, that.

Because in 1976, Niki Lauda protested the wet conditions and lost the championship to James Hunt; in '77 Ronnie Petersen and Gilles Villeneuve tangled, and the resulting crash killed two people. When the GP returned in 1987, Nigel Mansell, who had a realistic shot at the championship, crashed in practice and forfeited the crown to Nelson Piquet — who failed to finish both the Japanese and the Australian GPs.

In 1988, with only one win needed at the 12th round of the championship following a domination of the previous events, Senna couldn't finish a race, and the championship was suspiciously decided four races later at Suzuka, the Honda test track; in 1989, Alain Prost and Ayrton Senna collided. Senna continued, albeit with a push-start and a shortcut through the escape road, and Prost had the title locked up with Senna's disqualification — or he didn't, depending on who you asked. Again Japan proved to be the deciding race of the championship, and altered the future of McLaren, which subsequently lost Prost to Ferrari, and a great deal of respect from the rest of the field. And in 1990, the turn-one shunt between Prost and Senna — which sealed Senna's second world championship — will be a hot topic of ethics in racing for some time to come. But in 1991, in the most controversy-free race yet, Senna clinched the championship. Again, in 1992, the race was relatively trouble tree.

Controversy aside, the Japanese Grand Prix is one of the best on the calendar, as far as organization and money spent on making sure the show is good. The event is so popular the Japanese have to enter a lottery to buy tickets. The track tries to make everyone from fans to media feel at home. Although the Australian GP, which is organized with the same intensity as Japan's GP, usually appeals more to Westerners than Japan, the trend is changing. The Japanese spend the most money on racing, and the tendency is carried over to the racetrack in Suzuka.

Suzuka's GP bike race is nearly as popular, but its biggest and best two-wheeled show is probably the Suzuka 8 Hours, which pits the best Grand Prix riders in the world against each other on 750cc motorcycles, rather than the 500s they're used to. The machines cost a fortune, since they're specially prepared for this event, and the riders are paid huge fees for the one-off race. Held mid-July, the race is hot and humid. It starts at 11:30 a.m. and ends in darkness. In 1992, Wayne Rainey won his final 8 Hours for Honda with teammate Daryl Beattie on an ill-handling RVF750.

For media there is nowhere better than Suzuka. All that is required is a phone call to the Public Relations department of the organizing Committee, in

141

Tokyo. The PR department handles all the arrangements for rooms in Suzuka, and will, depending on how early and how close to the main hotels you book, provide transportation to the circuit. But for the rest of the world, life is a bit more difficult.

Since all the rooms in Suzuka City are completely booked by the track for press, crews, and circuit workers, there is literally nowhere in Suzuka for spectators to sleep. The best bet is probably Nagoya, although there are rooms in Tsu, Tu-Shi, Yokkaichi, and several other smaller cities in the immediate area.

It would seem that attending the Japanese Grand Prix is difficult. The language is a problem, the hotels are expensive, and the circuit is in the middle of nowhere. But if you simply call the Japan Travel Bureau before you leave, things will become infinitely easier. Even tickets are easier for foreigners to get than for the Japanese.

The Japanese, you'll find, are gregarious when it comes to foreign travelers, and will go to great lengths to make your stay easier. Most Japanese understand that their culture makes Westerners uncomfortable. And although they may not change their habits for you, they'll certainly help find somewhere that will suit you.

Renting a car for Suzuka is probably not a wise idea since from even as close as Tsu, a commute at the wrong time can take several hours. Japanese drive on the left of the road, and on the right of the car. In addition, even European drivers tend to be intimidated by Japanese motorists. And the signs — which will obviously be in Japanese — will confuse even the fiercest road warrior. Train is the best mode of travel in Japan, and getting from anywhere is easy once you've gotten the specifics from the JTB on how and where.

The Japan Travel Bureau can be reached at (81) 33 276 7875 (disregard the 81 if calling from Japan). For working press (you'll have to go through FISA for accreditation for F1 events) call the PR division at the circuit at (81) 33 582 3221; or fax (81) 33 582 0323.

TI Circuit AIDA
T&I Corporation co., LTD
1210 Takimiya Aida-ch0
Aida-gun Okayama
Japan T701-26

PH: 8687 4 3311
FAX: 8687 4 2600

Location: 75 miles from Osaka; and the same distance from Hiroshima.

Take the Tomei Expressway to the Meishiri Expressway to the Chugoku Expressway to Aida.

Or: take the Shinkansen line to the Okayama Prefecture and Aida.

Circuit: 1.94 mile road course; 12 turns

Major races: All-Japan F3; All-Japan Touring Car championships; National Motorcycle racing.

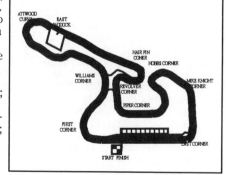

The TI circuit was inaugurated in December of 1990 but was only occasionally used by the Japanese motorsports fraternity. In 1992, however it saw several national races, with the Japanese F3 and All-Japan Touring Car Championships being the biggest of the season.

The climate at TI is mostly mild and makes it good for racing most of the summer. Run-off is good, with gravel beds located on the outside of the corners. The corners, by the way, have been named after famous race car drivers -- none of whom are Asian. There are grandstands at start/ finish and the best place to watch is from there, although there is a separate paddock at the east end of the race-track which also offers a good view of the slow, challenging Attwood Curve Hairpin. The track rises some 40 feet, with the highest spot at Hobbes Corner and the lowest at Attwood curve.

The best places to stay will be in Okayama City or in Mimasaka-Onsen, where there are hot springs. You can fax the track for more information or call the Japanese Auto Federation or the Japanese Tourist Bureau, listed at the beginning of the chapter.

Tokachi International Speedway

Tokachi Motor Park co.,
477 Kowa Sarabetsu
Ksai-gun Hokkaido
Japan, T089-15
PH: 0155 21 3910
FAX: 0155 21 2910

Circuit: 3.08 mile road course; 16 turns.

Location: On Hokkaido, near Sapporo, 20 minutes from Obihiro Airport.

Major races: All Japan prototype championship.

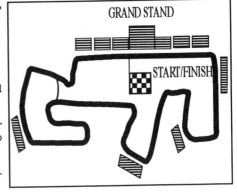

Japan's newest motor racing circuit, Tokachi International Speedway, was just completed in October of 1992, and construction of the grandstands, pits and drivers' salon was postponed until after winter of 1993 (and finally completed in May of 1993). Winter sees some two feet of snow drop on the surrounding area. In 1992 there were no activities, but in future years Tokachi will conduct a great deal of winter testing.

Although they are not in place, the entire track will be visible from the proposed grandstands. The track, like the surrounding area, has just slight elevation changes. The track rises some 40 feet in its three miles, with a maximum grade of two per cent.

For now, you will be able to find rooms at Obihiro City, which is about 25 miles from the track. But when racing starts it will likely be much harder to find accommodations.

Tsukuba Circuit

Oaza-Muraoka,
Chyokawa-mura,
Yuuki-gun,
Ibaragi Pre.

PH: 02964-4-3146

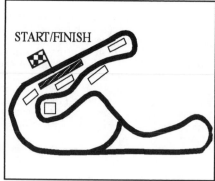

START/FINISH

Location: Central Japan, on the island of Honshu, 80 miles north of Tokyo.

Form Tokyo, take the Joban Expressway to the Yatabe Interchange to the track.

By train, take the JR Johban Line to Toride and the SODO Station, and a short taxi ride to the circuit.

Circuit: 1.21 mile road circuit; seven turns.

Major races: Japanese Formula Three.

In the grand scheme of things, Tsukuba is every bit as good as the best in Europe. But sitting in Japan, so far away from all the Europe based super-series, Tsukuba is as close to getting a shot at the F1 GP or the FIM GP race as Cloverleaf Speedway is to getting a Winston Cup race. Actually, Cloverleaf probably has a better shot at the Winston.

Tsukuba is a small circuit in a suburban area of Japan which is gaining in popularity because of growth in the nearby community. Now a hub of Japanese technology, the Expo '80-inspired eastern "Silicon Valley" has exploded in growth from an insignificant rice field to a major electronic technology center. The track sits in the middle of it.

The open area leaves plenty of room for expansion on both sides of the fence. But the track is more popular now because of the sheer number of people who now live in the immediate area, and it's becoming more valuable as real estate... and may be in jeopardy.

Mostly used as a motorcycle track — complete with one of Japan's premier motorcycle racing schools — Tsukuba is completely flat, although not unchallenging. It has a good variety of corners, and has decent run-off. Like most Japanese tracks, the pit facilities are top-notch, and there are private garages. In the motorcycling vein, there is also a small motorcycling test track adjacent to the larger circuit.

There are several grandstands around the circuit, but they are limited to about 1,000 fans each, except for the main tribune at start/finish. The best seats are at start/finish, and from the higher tiers you'll see a good part of the flat circuit including the challenging Dunlop Kink.

The Japan Travel Bureau can be reached at (81) 3 276 7875 (disregard the 81 if calling from Japan), or contact the JTB Discover World Inc., 4-1-11, Kudan-Kita, Chiyoda-ku, Tokyo 102. PH: 33 263 1450.

MACAU

Located on the south eastern coast of China, Macau is considered the Monaco of the East. The small Portuguese-owned peninsula is one of the gems of Asia. Like Monaco, it's the only place in the area where gambling is legal. It, too, is becoming one of the most expensive places in the world to own real estate. The peninsula is only 2.5 miles wide, and 1.06 miles long.

The country is actually comprised of two islands and the Asian peninsula.

144

The islands are linked to the city of Macau by twin bridges. It is some 40 miles from Hong Kong. Since Hong Kong doesn't allow gambling, the high rollers migrate to Macau to lose their money. Macau's legalized gambling inspires even bigger crowds during its famous race weekend — which usually happens at the end of November.

Weather here is neither humid nor dry, and generally hovers at a very comfortable 70 degrees. The Macau Government Tourist Office will be very helpful should you be planning a trip to the small country; there are several handbooks available for the MGTO that will list all hotels and restaurants. A valid passport is all that is required for a visit to Macau.

Tourist Information: **Macau Tourist Information Bureau**, 3133 Lake Hollywood Dr., P.O. Box 1860, Los Angeles, CA 90078. PH: (213) 851-3402; FAX: (213) 851-3684. or in Macau at the **Macau Government Tourist Office**, Edificio Ritz, Largo do Senado, 9. PH: (853) 315566; FAX: (853) 510104. There is a hotel reservation center at the Hong Kong Airport as well as a Macau Information desk.

Sporting Authority: **Grand Prix Organizing Committee**, c/o Macau Government Tourist Office, Edificio Ritz, Largo do Senado, 9. PH: (853) 315566; FAX: (853) 510104.

Macau
Circuito Da Guia,
Edificio Ritz,
Largo do Senado, 9.
Macau
PH: (853) 556235
FAX: (853) 590986/342454

Location: On the Macau Peninsula, in Macau City Center, 40 miles west of Hong Kong.

Circuit: 3.8 mile road course; 19 turns.

Major Races: Formula 3; non-championship motorcycle Grand Prix racing; Group A Saloon Cars.

Macau's eclectic racing program continues to draw some of the best drivers and riders in the world. A non-championship F2 and Formula Pacific race for many years (and now a championship F3 race), the open-wheeled action continues to headline the event. But the place has much more than that.

Although past contenders of the F3 race in Macau have been guys like Ayrton Senna, Martin Brundle, and Stefan Johansson, motorcycle racing is at least as noteworthy. In past years, Ron Haslam. Kevin Schwantz and Didier de Radigues raced here.

There are actually several different classes of bike and car racing on the Guia circuit — and many are amateur racers on street machinery. The racing is generally good, no matter who's out there.

In addition to the bikes and

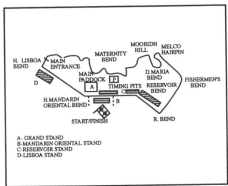

A- GRAND STAND
B-MANDARIN ORIENTAL STAND
C-RESERVOIR STAND
D-LISBOA STAND

the Formula cars, a series of sedan races takes place through the narrow streets — including some SCCA IT type racing, some vintage racing, a spec series with pro and celebrity racers, a touring car race, and a wild supercar race which is held essentially with street stock exotics.

Practice for the racing begins Thursday, and the first race is Saturday. Motorcycling begins the Saturday morning racing program, while the two 15-lap legs of the F3 race and the 30-lap Group A race are highlights of the Sunday program.

The circuit starts on the waterfront and proceeds to the famous Lisboa corner, where first-turn skirmishes inevitably happen at least once a year (Lisboa is actually the second turn but the first is taken flat out, and is not considered a turn at all). The entrance to Lisboa Corner is really one of the few places where overtaking can be done with any precision. The approach to Lisboa also provides one of the few good spectator areas.

The course winds right, and up the hill where there is no run-off whatsoever, then back to the Melco Hairpin. The hairpin is so tight a standing yellow flag is posted there prohibiting passing all weekend long. From Melco the track comes back down the hill to the harbor, and back onto the fast front section of the track.

There are really only three spectator areas; one from the penultimate corner, through which the track extends to start/finish (and which has reserved grandstands); a second at Lisboa Corner; and the third is open plan seating in front of Macau's reservoir, between R and Reservoir bends. Racing is good, spectating is decent, but like its European sister in Monaco, the racing is less an attraction than the scene in general.

Remember: there are really only two ways into Macau unless you come through China, and that's by boat or helicopter, and into the main terminal, which is located inside the circuit. Life gets very rough for those who arrive during the races. No matter which day you wish to arrive (unless it's Wednesday or earlier). Plan on being there before 8:00 a.m. or after 4:30 p.m. if you want to stay in Macau. The recent addition of the "flyover" connecting city-center with the inside of the circuit has made transportation from the terminal to your hotel a bit easier — but expect delays if you arrive while the racing is on.

If you arrive at the ferry terminal while cars are on-course, there will be no way to move your baggage to your room. If you're travelling light, you'll have no problem getting to your hotel. There are pedestrian bridges which, with a little luck, will get you to your room fairly rapidly. But it's impossible for cabs to get around in the middle of the racing. If you can manage it, arrive Wednesday.

Getting to Macau is simple: just catch either an East Asia Airways helicopter, a jetfoil, a hydrofoil, jumbo catamaran or the high-speed ferry across from Hong Kong, which is 40 miles away. All forms of transport depart from the Macau Ferry terminal, located at the Shun Tak Centre in central Hong Kong island. The ferry, which is cheapest will take about 90 minutes; the jets, hydrofoils or jumbo cats will take about an hour; helicopter flights take about 20 minutes. Tickets are available at the Macau Ferry terminal or through leading travel agents.

No matter what, you'll have to book a room in advance. Macau might as well be an island. surrounded on three sides by water, and by Red China on the fourth, there's nowhere else to stay. If you wish, you can take a boat in to Macau for the racing each day and stay in Hong Kong — and you may have no other alternative if you get there late. But that would get very expensive for four days of racing.

The Lisboa, which sits on the corner whch bears its name, is one of the biggest hotels — and the one with the best casino. Everything is close in Macau, and the track winds through it all, so don't worry about where you're staying. Although Portuguese is the official language of Macau, English is spoken in most places. If you wish to take a tour of Mainland China, you can set it up through your hotel while you're staying in Macau. The concierge will give you travel tips, and will make the jaunt enjoyable.

For more information, contact the Macau Tourist Information Bureau at (213) 382-2353; or from Hong Kong, go to the Shun Tak Centre (PH: 540-8180) for more personalized information.

MALAYSIA

Johor Raceway
Sport Communications
SDN BHD — Room 7, 16th floor
Kompleks Tun Abdukl Razak
Jalan Wong Ah Fook
8000 Johor Bahru
Johor Darul Ta'Zim, Malaysia
PH: (60) 7 237397
FAX: (60) 7 232489

Location: On the southern tip of the Malaysian Peninsula, 19 miles south east of Johor Bahru city center, about thirty miles north east of Singapore.

Track: 2.32 miles, nine turns.

Major Races: FIM Superbikes.

1992 marked Johor's introduction to major road racing. Although the circuit hosted the World Endurance Championships in 1991, the switch from the relatively minor FIM series to the premier class transformed it from an insignificant regional racetrack to a major international venue --with a shot at an F1 car race. Unfortunately, in '93 it only hosted a Superbike race.

Shah Alam circuit hosted the FIM GP in 1991, and by all estimations it was successful, safe, and comfortable for both riders and fans who travelled to the circuit. For that reason the GP circus returned to Shah Alam.

The track, like Shah-Alam, is built with plenty of minor altitude changes. The undulating terrain is challenging, with several slow corners — notably, Lucky Strike Corner and Shell Corner — and a very fast long straight.

But these days the track's merits, at least to the teams, are listed based on comfort and convenience. The hospitality suites overlooking start/finish are air conditioned, the 32 lockable garages and wide pit lane allow crews to work on the bikes in relative comfort and privacy. Shower facilities are available to crews, as is a club with a swimming pool.

The best places to watch racing are from the main grandstands where you'll see a good deal of the track, from Lucky Strike Corner, and from Shell Corner. No matter what, the climate should be hot and sunny, so even if you decide to walk around you should have a decent view and an enjoyable time.

Johor Bahru has many good hotels available, the best being at city center. For more information you can call or write the track, where your questions will be answered with alarming alacrity. Or you can call the Malaysian Tourist Office.

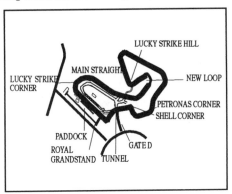

Shah Alam Motor Racing Circuit
Shah Alam Motor Racing Association
40000 Shah Alam
Selangor, Darul Ehsan, Malaysia

PH: (60) 3 5508780
FAX: (60) 3 5504726

Location: Central Western Malaysia, just off the Federal Highway, Kuala Lumpur Klang, which is 13 KM from Subang Airport.

Circuit: 2.3 mile road circuit; 13 turns.

Major races: FIM Grand Prix World Championships; Selangor Automobile and Motorcycle Championships.

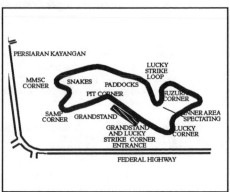

Shah Alam sits in the Klang Valley, just 20 minutes from Kuala Lumpur, and about ten minutes from the Subang International Airport.

The circuit has recently been resurfaced and was widened, giving it an excellent rating by international participants. For the first time in 1991, it hosted a round of the FIM Grand Prix World Championship, as well as a round of FIA Prototype racing. But for 1992 Shah Alam played backseat to Johor, which hosted its first GP. Due to the general affinity of the place by the riders, Shah Alam again hosted a GP in 1993.

The circuit, and surrounding Shah Alam Motorsports Paradise complex, offers good racing and great views for spectators, although there's currently only one grandstand structure. The course is a fast one, with two rising sections on either sections of the track — one in the Suzuki Corner, and one at the "Snakes". The altitude at each end is certainly not breathtaking, but it makes the course more interesting.

The best places to watch are from either the Electrolux Hill, where, while sitting on the grass, you'll see most of the track; in the final turn, where you'll see the downhill out of the Suzuki Corner through the Lucky Strike Corner and down the start/finish straight; or in the start/finish grandstands, where you'll see about 70% of the racetrack. Admission is cheap — about $40 Malaysian dollars for a grandstand seat at the Superbike race.

Bus, train, and shuttle taxi services exist during the racing season, and the track officials, who speak perfect English, can give you more information on how to use each if you request it.

Shah Alam has several five star hotels within minutes. For Hotel and all-inclusive booking packages call (60) 3 550 8788 or (60) 3 559 9710; or fax (60) 3 550 4726 or (60) 3 559 6168 at Shah Alam Motorsports Paradise Racing Circuit, SAMP Complex, 40000 Shah Alam, Selangor Darul Ehsan, Malaysia.

148

MEXICO

Although Mexicans are passionate about motor racing, unlike Brazilians or Italians Mexicans have no almost no interest in racing personalities. It's the racing itself that appeals to Mexican fans. Most Mexicans have an interest in actually doing some racing, and watching is usually as close as they'll get to really participating. There are several Mexican auto racing magazines which, oddly, generally sell better than the typical road car magazines.

The Carrera Panamericana was one of the most fascinating — as well as one of the most dangerous — races in the world, and it captured the imagination of the country. In the Carrera's heyday, Mexican racing was prolific. Racing took place in the streets, under government supervision, and almost every town had a road race at least once a year.

It was not the accidents at the Carrera that ended Mexico's street racing, but the death of Pedro Rodriguez some fifteen years later (killed in a prototype race in 1971 in Germany), coupled with the events of the Mexican Grand Prix in 1972 that sealed Mexico's fate. Effective in 1971, street races were outlawed. Mexico's fiery enthusiasm in Motorsports was quickly extinguished.

But recently the fascination has returned. Partially spurred forward by the Grand Prix (which returned in 1987) Mexico has seen an incredible explosion in racing. From five tracks in 1983, Mexico now has 19 racetracks. New circuits are being constructed at a rate of two a year.

Mexican racing and Mexican racetracks are becoming more popular with Americans as well, since entry fees are cheaper and licensing is easier. Additionally, renting racecars in Mexico is substantially less expensive than in The States. Drivers who only want to race occasionally, and who consider competition an infrequent form of recreation, can mix racing with a Mexican vacation.

As in no other country on earth, Mexico is consumed with interest in grassroots racing. Local tracks and Mexican drivers are the rage. Mexican FIA F3 is run with Honda and Alfa-Romeo engines, with British chassis; Mexicans can't even buy Alfas or Honda, and they have almost no interest in the series. Most feel Mexican racing would be even more popular if the FIA bowed out and allowed IndyCar racing into Mexico, but even IndyCar racing is less interesting to Mexicans than local racers on local tracks.

Mexicans like to drive. They're generally adept, too, at getting their cars in and out of traffic without hitting anything. Mexico City is not quite Rome, but it takes a courageous driver indeed to drive through the congestion. If you miss making a turn in Mexico City, you may literally be gone for 10 miles before you get a chance to flip a U-turn. To make matters worse, traffic is horrible.

Red lights seem to be only a suggestion to slow down. One-way streets seem to indicate a short-cut going the wrong direction. If you drive from the U.S. to Mexico City you may, by the time you reach the capital, have enough experience to survive, but it is still advisable to leave your car somewhere safe — like your hotel parking facility — and take a taxi or the Metro.

In Mexico City, and most major Mexican cities, just keep up with traffic and do as everyone else does and you'll be okay. But on the highways, where you're often alone, you must be careful. Pastures often bound highways and cattle wander onto the roads. Children play by the sides of the roads too, so expect to see balls, or kids themselves, at any moment.

The situation is not that dangerous if you remember that you need to stay at or below the speed limits. At a decent speed, you'll have time to react. That's one of the reasons most Mexicans don't speed on the highways. It's tempting to stick your foot in it on some of those beautifully straight, flat, and relatively wide roads — but don't. That goes for driving at night. Unless you're around Mexico City, try to keep off the roads when it gets dark. Clean, cheap rooms are everywhere in Mexico, so stop and enjoy.

Mexico's roads are generally good, at least as far as the major arteries go.

During the rainy season, which batters the northern Gulf Coast, through Central Mexico and into all of Southern Mexico, the roads can often be plagued with deep ruts. But that condition is a rarity, and the roads are usually clean and fast.

Except for a toll road from Cordoba to Queretaro — on the middle of which sits Mexico City — the country is limited to a network of two-lane highways. Most Mexican Highways have wide, safe shoulders, and well-maintained road surfaces.

A knowledge of Spanish is helpful. But not if you get pulled over by the police. Unless you speak the language fluently, don't try conversing with the police. You'll just get yourself in trouble. If asked to pay a fine, you may be tempted to tell the officer something inappropriate in Spanish ... which will cause more trouble. It's simpler to speak English — which is your language — and hope the communication barrier will keep you from saying anything completely improper, with the end result being your timely — and hopefully inexpensive — release.

One tip: Mexicans are usually treated with contempt, at least by Americans. Once you understand that the majority of the people will give you half of anything they own once they get to know you, you'll hopefully treat them with some dignity. If you treat them with the respect they deserve, you'll never have any problems.

Sporting Authorities : **Federacion Mexicana de Automovilismo Deportivo**, A.C.. Av. Patriotismo 586, COL: Sa Pedro de Los Pinos, 03800 Mexico, D.F.. PH: (52 5) 598 33 16/ 598 33 26; FAX: (52 5) 611 38 18. Or **Promotodo**, Av. Constituyentes #251, COL: Daniel Garza, Mexico D.F. 11840; PH: (52 5) 272 9438; FAX: (52 5) 277 3976. Or for the bikes, try **Federacion Mexicana Motociclismo**, Av. Rio Churbusco Puerta 9, Ciudad Deportiva Magdelena Mixhuca, Mexicao, DF. CP. 08010; PH (52 50 5192 040; FAX: (52 5) 3966 919.

Tourist Information: Mexican Government Tourist Office, 10100 Santa Monica Blvd., Los Angeles, CA 90067, PH: (213) 203-8151 or (213) 203-9335; In Mexico, contact the **Mexican office of Tourism** at President Masaryk 172, Col: Polanco, Mexico D.F., Mexico. PH: 250 0123.

150

Autodromo Aguascalientes

Office: Promotodo, Av. Constituyentes #251, COL: Daniel Garza, Mexico D.F. 11840; PH: (52 5) 272 9438; FAX: (52 5) 277 3976.

Or: Jose Luis Gonzalez 5 de Mayo No. 314 Col: Centro Aguascalientes, Ags CP 20000 PH: (52 491) 485-91

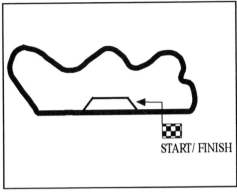

START/ FINISH

Location: Central Mexico, 11 miles east of Aguascalientes, on Route 70 toward Ujuelos, in Aguascalientes State.

Circuit: 2.4 mile road course; 9 turns.

Major Races: Marlboro Cup Championship (Chrysler F2; Phantom); Delval Truck Cup; Tecate Sport Prototype Cup.

As a fairly long circuit by international standards, Aguascalientes is considered one of the fastest in Mexico. It has only one tight turn — but even that one can be negotiated at better than 50 miles per hour. Its one drawback, a major factor in race strategy, is the track surface. The pavement here is very abrasive, and tire wear is a problem.

The track has proved itself valuable to the city, inspiring a good deal of local support for the handful of major Mexican races it holds. Although it sits nearly 6,000 feet above sea level, it's very hot and often humid. Aguascalientes is populated by 750,000 or so people, and rooms, although not plentiful, are easy enough to find — albeit not always modern and spotless.

While here, try to visit the Casa De La Cultura, which is one of the largest art schools in the country. If you're in town for April racing, the fiesta de San Marcos showcases students' work, and the entire place becomes a celebration of art. There are also, of course, bullfights, cockfights and several other indigenous Mexican attractions.

For information on hotels in the area, call (491) 51155 or 60347; or write the Secretario de Turismo at Plaza Patria 141, Aguascalientes, AGS 20230.

Moto Autodromo de Cancun

Office: Federacion Mexicana de Automovilismo Deportivo, A.C.
Av. Patriotismo 586
COL: Sa Pedro de Los Pinos
03800 Mexico, D.F.
PH: (52 5) 598 33 16/ 598 33 26
FAX: (52 5) 611 38 18

Location: KM 7.1 Carretera Aeropuerto Cancun Quintana Roo.

Circuit: .852 mile road course; 10 turns.

Major races: Montana Championship.

About ten miles from the the lush resort city of Cancun City, the newly inaugurated Moto Autodromo de Cancun waits for Mexican racing to discover its newest jewel. Opened February, 1992, the track is still being readied for major racing as this guide goes to press. Its location from Mexico's fastest growing resort community will likely make it a very popular track.

The area is well known for its luxury hotels, so staying here when racing comes through will be no problem — although it may be a bit on the expensive side. Make sure you leave some extra time to relax at the clear, warm Caribbean shores and take a look at some of the Mayan archeological ruins. For more information, contact the Mexican Government Tourist Office, 10100 Santa Monica Blvd., Los Angeles, CA 90067, PH: (213) 203-8151 or (213) 203-9335.

Autodromo Chihuahua

**Office: Promotodo,
Av. Constituyentes #251,
COL: Daniel Garza,
Mexico D.F. 11840;**

**PH: (52 5) 272 9438;
FAX: (52 5) 277 3976.**

**Track contact: Sr. Cruz Borriga
Prolongacion Av. Tecnologia 10313
COL: 24 de Junio
Chihuahua, CHI 31128**

**PH: (52 14) 19 00 17
FAX: (52 14) 19 00 17**

Location: Northern Mexico, in Chihuahua State, 7 miles west of Chihuahua.

Circuit: 1.1 mile road course;12 turns.

Major Races: Marlboro Cup Championships.

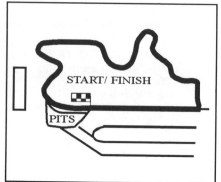

152

Considered one of the better Mexican circuits in terms of both safety and track surface, Chihuahua has reasonably wide run-off areas and smooth surfaces. A Promotodo track, the goals at Autodromo Chihuahua are to continue renovating the circuit until it's on par with the best in the U.S.

Most Mexicans consider this the third best in the country, with only Mexico City and Monterrey being more accommodating to racers. It was built in 1988 for the Marlboro Cup, and new pits have already been added. The dry desert capital city of Chihuahua has a population of 800,000, and rooms are easy to find.

There are now grandstands located at start/finish which hold approximately 6,000 people. Earth embankments also offer good views of most of the track, and more seats are expected.

For information on hotels in the area, write the Secretario de Turismo at Libertad Y Calle 13, 1st Floor, Chihuahua; or call (14) 159124.

Autodromo Internacional de Guadalajara
Office: Mar Caribe No. 2440
Col: Country Club
Guadalajara, Jalisco, Mexico

PH: (Mr. Hugo Desdier, track official): (52 36) 168-644

Location: Western central Mexico, in Jalisco State, three miles from the Guadalajara International Airport.

Circuit: Paved tri-oval.

Major Races: Marlboro Cup for automobiles and motorcycles; Montana Cup Super Formula K Championships; FIA Formula 3 Championship; CAR 90 Resistencia Endurance Championships.

Mexico is experiencing an explosion of interest in motorsports, and this Guadalajara tri-oval is on the forefront of the renewed fascination in racing.

The tri-oval is a unique animal to Mexicans. The idea of watching cars contend the entire track from one seat is certainly not new, since most Mexican tracks are fairly modern. The new tracks, unlike most European tracks, were designed with the show in mind. But an oval — or tri-oval, as the case may be — is a completely different concept in Mexican racing.

The four major promoters and sanctioning bodies, which are fighting for control of the lucrative surge of Mexican interest in racing, will only agree on one thing: that the tri-oval is probably the most spectacular track in the country. Besides the Autodromo Hermanos Rodriguez in Mexico City, which is owned by the government, this is probably the most used track in Mexico.

The track itself is very hard on tires. Abrasive track surfaces and good loading on the slight banks make tires a major concern here. It does not provide the creature comforts like the tracks of Hermanos Rodriguez or Monterrey, but its uniqueness makes it one of the best places to watch

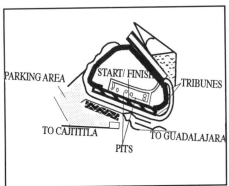

153

Mexican racing.

"The City of Roses", as it is known in Mexico, is famous for its Mariachi bands, and the sounds of the uniquely Mexican music will be omnipresent. The Mercado is the biggest in all of Latin America, and everything from dried fish to diamonds can be purchased here very inexpensively. Located between Javier Mina and Avenida Rodriguez on the east side of city center, the market is worth at least a half-day's look. Check out the Plaza de los Mariachis as well, where roving musicians will entertain you for a few minutes or for the evening.

For information on hotels in the area, write the Secretario de Turismo at Morelos 102 Guadalajara, JAL, 44100; or call (36) 140123 or 131196.

Autodromo Hermanos Rodriguez,
Federacion Mexicana de Automovilismo Deportivo, A.C.
Av. Patriotismo 586
COL: Sa Pedro de Los Pinos
03800 Mexico, D.F.

PH: (52 5) 598 33 16/ 598 33 26
FAX: (52 5) 611 38 18

Location: Central Mexico, in eastern Mexico City, a few miles south of the International Airport, off Calzada Chabacano.

Circuit: 2.75 mile road course; 15 turns.

Major Races: Marlboro Cup Championship (Chrysler F2; Phantom); Delval Truck Cup; Tecate Sport Prototype Cup; Mexican Formula 3 Championship.

The Autodromo Hermanos Rodriguez is no longer the proverbial albatross around the neck of the Mexican racing establishment. Memories of the unlucky 1970 Mexican Grand Prix no longer linger, and the new Hermanos Rodriguez circuit, and its organization, is as good as any. Racing historians shudder with the memory of the race two decades ago, when fans literally sat on the sides of the track surface, and where Jackie Stewart almost hit a dog in practice.

These days, it's dust, bumps, smog, and Montezuma's Revenge that worries drivers.

Recently, with the explosion of interest in motor racing in Mexico, more races have been run on the circuit, eliminating the slippery conditions caused by an unused track surface — which was probably the biggest complaint prior to 1989.

But there's still nothing that can be done about the bumps. When resurfaced, the track still returns to its former rippled self. Built on a dry lake bed, the whole city is constantly dipping and moving as the wet earth below expands and contracts with the changes in temperature.

Ultimately, the circuit condition cost Mexico its crown jewel, the F1 race. The GP was cancelled for the 1993 season and, as of this writing, it is not

START/ FINISH

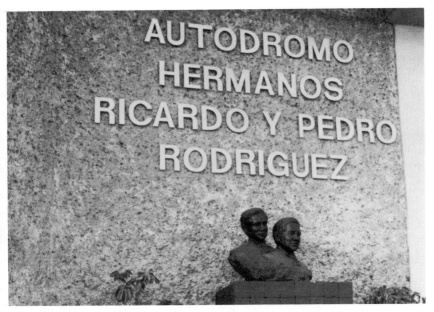

scheduled to return. But with the recent cancellation of the French Grand Prix, who knows? Regardless, the first ever FIM Superbike championship ran its finale at Hermanos Rodriguez in October, which was equally significant.

Never mind the track. Unless you're a driver you shouldn't care. Mexico is one of the best places in the world to see an international race. Most Europeans

generally hate the place, but few seem to have tried to understand what Mexico is about, and prefer to eat European food and find European conveniences — of which there are few. For Americans, Mexico is infinitely easier to understand.

When Americans travel to Europe, they tend to try to blend in — albeit usually unsuccessfully. In Mexico, Europeans are generally more obtrusive than Americans, and the focus is rarely on them. Most Americans — at least, Californians, Arizonans and Texans — have a good understanding of the culture. With a little sense of adventure, most Americans will have a great time in Mexico's capital city.

The circuit is excellent for spectating. Tickets are relatively inexpensive and, with the possible exception of the seats opposite the pits, most areas are still available raceday, or at any rate Saturday. The "Esses" or Retorno is a good place to watch, but make sure you walk past Curva Penaltada — the slightly banked right hander is very fast and very spectacular, especially at the exit.

Zona Rosa is where everybody wants to spend their nights. If you like rubbing elbows with the beautiful people, you'll want to stay there as well. The best Hotels — the Galleria Plaza, Krystal, and Century — are all very affordable during race week. The Aristos Hotel, just outside the Zona Rosa on El Paseo de La Reforma, is usually a race sponsor, and generally where the race headquarters and registration is located.

The drivers and riders are rarely hassled in Mexico outside the circuit, so they're most approachable here. You can literally have coffee with Doug Polen — although maybe not at the same table. If you want to be more adventurous, stay in Zocalo. It is real Mexico; very quaint and inexpensive.

Don't bother with a rental car — taxis are cheap, buses are plentiful, and the metro, which is one of the cleanest and easiest in the world to use, will drop you just outside the circuit for just ten cents (from Zona Rosa take Linea 1 to Pantitlan, transferring to Linea 9, then riding two stops to CD Deportiva). Besides, you need to be more aggressive than a Roman to keep pace with Mexican drivers.

Remember: Don't eat the lettuce, or any fruit or vegetable with a high liquid content; order your drinks without ice; drink only purified water or bottled drinks; and whenever in doubt, make sure your food is served piping hot (the heat will kill the germs in your food)... and stay away from the taco vendors unless you have an iron stomach.

You can arrive in Mexico without a room, and will have absolutely no problem finding good clean accommodations as late as Saturday. Check with the Airport hotel information booth as you leave the baggage carrousels at Mexico City International Airport. For more information about Mexico City, call or write the Secretaria de Turismo at President Masaryk 172, Col: Polanco, Mexico D.F., Mexico. PH: 250 0123.

Autodromo de Sonora
Office: Promotodo, Av. Constituyentes #251, COL: Daniel Garza, Mexico D.F. 11840; PH: (52 5) 272 9438; FAX: (52 5) 277 3976.

Track contact: Oscar Mazon
Veracruz y 14 de Abril
Col: San Benito,
Hermosillo, Son. CP 83190

PH: (52 621) 419-00/ (52 621) 404-65

Location: Northwestern Mexico, in Sonora, five miles from Hermosillo, less than two miles from the Hermosillo International Airport.

Circuit: 1.2 mile road circuit; six turns.

Major Races: Marlboro Cup Championship (Chrysler F2; Phantom); Delval Truck Cup; Tecate Sport Prototype Cup.

El Autodromo de Sonora is another in a long line of Promotodo tracks. Set in picturesque Hermosillo, this city's track was just recently put into operation. Built in 1986, the circuit has already been modified, with a slightly longer version just having been completed.

The organizers boast a pit area which can accommodate 700 cars, and parking which can handle an additional 2,000 vehicles. Modern grandstands, restaurants, and restrooms are also on the top of the convenience lists. Adjacent to the track, off-road races are often contested. The main straight is also used as a drag strip occasionally.

Drag racing was once done in a reverse direction from the road race circuit, and there was a concern for safety since the armco overlaps the wrong direction. But the situation has been remedied, and the staging is now done close to start/finish, with the starting line at the start/finish stripe.

Hermosillo has plenty of rooms and is quite a charming city, with tree-lined boulevards and Mexican-tiled sidewalks. There are a handful of famous golf courses in

START/ FINISH

the area, and the nearby lake provides a nice backdrop for a stay in the area wh'
racing.

Information on hotels in the area can be found by writing the Secretar
de Turismo at Palacio Administrativo, Tehuantepec Y Comonfort, Hermosillo, SC
83260; or call (621) 72964 or 70857.

Autodromo Internacional de La Jolla

Federacion Mexicana de Automovilismo Deportivo, A.C.
Av. Patriotismo 586
COL: Sa Pedro de Los Pinos
03800 Mexico, D.F.
PH: (52 5) 598 33 16/ 598 33 26
FAX: (52 5) 611 38 18

Location: Northern Mexico, 21 miles south of the border at Ciudad Juarez/
El Paso, just off the Pan American Highway 4.

Circuit: 2.2 mile road course; 15 turns.

Major races: Mexican F3; Marlboro Cup Championship (Chrysler F2;
Phantom); Delval Truck Cup; Tecate Sport Prototype Cup.

La Jolla opened its gates for its first race, a Mexican Formula Three event,
in September of 1991. 1993 marked its second full year in operation. Rumor
suggests that it will be a major force in Mexican motorsport, at least rivaling
Monterrey.

La Jolla was built with the show in mind and the entire track can be seen
from the stands, which exist along start/finish straight. It seats some 20,000, and
more stands are being considered. Corporate and VIP suites have not yet been built,
but are also forthcoming. The circuit is as modern as any in Mexico, and the sandy
runoff makes it a safe venue as well.

This track may just end up being known as not just the finest private
facility in Mexico, but the best in the southwest. The goal here is to attract as many
teams from north of the border for testing at the area's only permanent road racing
facility. Other than Phoenix and the test track at Fort Stockton, TX (which is a
private corporate testing facility) La Jolla is the only permanent facility in some
500 miles — and the only road course.

The 1992 season at La Jolla didn't quite work out as planned. The
tentatively scheduled SCCA Trans-Am
race never came to be, and the track
still looks forward to hosting a major
U.S.-based championship to make it an
international venue.

If and when that happens,
teams would likely stay in El Paso and
be shuttled back and forth to the track
by bus. There will likely be shuttles for
fans as well. If not, there are 2.2 million
people between the two border cities —
and plenty of hotels.

El Paso, like Juarez, is hot and
dry. El Paso, unlike Juarez, has a huge
auto theft problem. It may be wise to

START/ FINISH

get insurance on your car and drive it into Juarez rather than leave it in El Paso — at least there you can keep an eye on it.

For information on lodging, call the Mexican Government Tourist Office at 10100 Santa Monica Blvd., Los Angeles, CA 90067. PH: (213) 203-8151, or (213) 203-9335. In Mexico or El Paso, contact the Mexican Office of Tourism at (52 161) 20170 or (51 161) 40123.

Autodromo De la Laguna

Promotodo, Av. Constituyentes #251,
COL: Daniel Garza,
Mexico D.F. 11840;
PH: (52 5) 272 9438;
FAX: (52 5) 277 3976.

Track Contact: Jorge Segura
Boulevar independencia # 1578 pte.
Torreon, Coahuila, MEx   27170
PH: (52 17) 16 61 13

Location: Northern central Mexico, in the State of Durango, 27 miles west of Gomez Palacio and one mile off Route 40.

Circuit: .9 mile road course; seven turns.

Major races: Marlboro Cup Championship (Chrysler F2; Phantom); Delval Truck Cup; Tecate Sport Prototype Cup.

Promotodo's mastermind, Michel Jourdain, realized his Autodromo De La Laguna wasn't moving in the proper direction, so he sold the facility in 1990. But with the renaissance in Mexican racing, Jourdain saw the wisdom in keeping the property, and recently he bought it back and is investing in the circuit to bring it back to national status.

It is a flat circuit, with little run-off, and, in the past, had almost no spectator facilities. That situation is changing now. Grandstands are being built, but the few hills where you can watch the action will have to suffice for the time being. Spectator amenities at the hot dry circuit will likely improve by next season.

There are a handful of rooms in Gomez Palacio, or Matamoros will have plenty of good accommodations. Hotel information can be found at the office of the Secretario de Turismo at Blvd. Miguel Aleman 250 Oriente, Gomez Palacio, COAH; or call (17) 141556 or 144434.

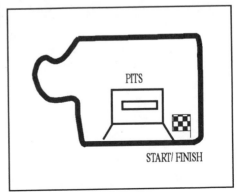

Autodromo de Leon

Office: Promotodo, Av. Constituyentes #251, COL: Daniel Garza, Mexico D.F. 11840; PH: (52 5) 272 9438; FAX: (52 5) 277 3976.

Track contact: Luis Esquivil Aztecas No. 202 Col: Bugambilias Leon, GTO., Mexico

PH: (52 473) 464-53/ (52 473) 420-84

START/ FINISH

Location: Central Mexico, in Guanajuato State, nine miles from Leon, on the road to Santa Ana Del Conde.

Circuit: .73 mile road course; 4 turns.

Major Races: Marlboro Cup Championship (Chrysler F2; Phantom); Delval Truck Cup; Tecate Sport Prototype Cup.

The Autodromo Leon is one of the shortest full-width road courses in North America. It was constructed in 1977 and is ancient in terms of Mexican motor racing, which has seen a tripling of its racing facilities in just the last seven years.

Originally, the track was longer, and the layout included a hairpin. Obviously, a track as short as this one is can't afford to have many quick turns — at least not for full sized cars. It was straightened — actually shortened 35 meters —and repaved in 1985. Now instead of doubling back on itself to form two hairpins, it now makes one 90-degree turn, which also eliminated another pair of curves.

The track is completely flat but there are several good spectating areas both on the sides of the small hills which surround the track, and in the two grandstands located just before start/finish and just before the final turn.

Guanajuato has plenty of clean, inexpensive rooms within a few miles of the track. For information on hotels in the area, write the Secretario de Turismo at Conjunto Commercial Estrella Local 13 Blvd Adolfo Lopez Mateos, Leon, GTO.; or call (471) 65310.

Autodromo de Monterrey

c/o Doris Jimenez
Ave. Ruiz Cortinez 620 Ote.
Ciudad Guadalupe, N.L., Mexico

PH: (52 83) 79-37-06

Location: Northeastern Mexico, in Nuevo Leon State, 10 miles north of the city of Monterrey on Route 85 toward Nuevo Laredo, 235 miles from the Laredo/ Nuevo Laredo border.

Circuit: 1.92 mile road circuit; 11 turns.

Major Races: Marlboro Cup Championship (Chrysler F2; Phantom); Delval Truck Cup; Tecate Sport Prototype Cup.

Monterrey's racetrack almost manages to transcend the feud between the four major racing promoters — but not quite.

Owned by Filiberto Jiminez, this track is second in prestige only to Mexico City, and is a logical place for major international racing. Its length makes it a likely place to run a major motorcycle race, and it is safe enough to host any premier series. There are rumors of IndyCars heading to Mexico, and it would likely be for this track that Indycar drivers would cross the border.

But FIA control of Mexican racing prohibits the move. The logical expansion of American racing into Mexico, and vice versa, is held up by threats from the FIA that the GP will be pulled if Indycars compete on Mexican soil. About the only thing the four groups agree upon is that Indycars should eventually come to Mexico. But the Abed Brothers, who promote the F1 race in Mexico City, are not quick to see their race eliminated. With no movement there, the situation has remained a stalemate — and Monterrey, which is a venue waiting for an international event, continues to host exclusively Mexican formulas.

The track is very fast, wide,

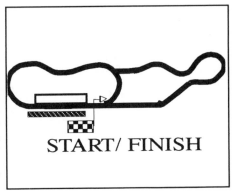

START/ FINISH

and was remodeled in 1987, earning the name "The Desert Princess of the North" It has air conditioned suites, and a restaurant on the facility grounds. There are almost 800 hotel rooms in the area — ranging from three to five star quality, and the Monterrey International Airport is close to the circuit.

As Mexico's third largest city, it feels as congested as Mexico City or Guadalajara. Like its sister cities, it's probably best if you leave your car in the hotel parking lot and travel to and from the circuit by taxi.

The journey from Texas to Monterrey is fairly effortless. The few miles' worth of drive south of the U.S. border is relatively uneventful until it rises into the Sierra Madre, and deposits you into the basin of the city.

Accommodations are both inexpensive and clean; and meals range from tacos at the vendors' stands to French cuisine. Try the Secretario de Turismo for more information on rooms at Edificio Kalos 4th floor, Zaragoza Y Constitucion, Monterrey, N.L., 67100; or call (83) 444343 or 401080.

Pachuca

Office: Promotodo, Av. Constituyentes #251,
COL: Daniel Garza,
Mexico D.F. 11840;
PH: (52 5) 272 9438;
FAX: (52 5) 277 3976.

Track contact: Luis Del Rincon
Matamoros No. 500
Pachuca, Hgo. CP 42000

PH: (52 771) 207-50/ (52 771) 427-31

Location: Central eastern Mexico, in Hidalgo State, five miles from the City of Pachuca, on route 130 toward Tulancingo.

Circuit: 1.1 mile road circuit.

Major Races: Marlboro Cup Championship (Chrysler F2; Phantom); Delval Truck Cup; Tecate Sport Prototype Cup.

Pachuca is perhaps not the greatest of tracks in Mexico. It's short, and not the best in design. But it was resurfaced recently, and is now wide enough to do some serious racing. Although there's no real problem with the circuit, it just lacks any qualities that make it noteworthy.

Nevertheless, it is always packed to the brim with spectators, and the Marlboro Cup is a big deal here. Its proximity to Mexico City (45 miles) makes it easy for both fans and racers to travel to Pachuca. The Teotihuacan Pyramids are a few miles away, literally on the road to the track from Mexico City, and are certainly worth a stop going to or from the circuit.

Since most of the fans are locals, Pachuca's few rooms should suffice for the racing. For more information on hotels in the area, write the

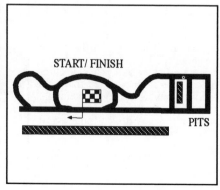

Secretario de Turismo at Allende 406, 1st Floor, Pachuca, HGO. 39500; or call (771) 23253 or 23276.

Autodromo Potosino

Office: Promotodo, Av. Constituyentes #251, COL: Daniel Garza, Mexico D.F. 11840; PH: (52 5) 272 9438; FAX: (52 5) 277 3976.

Track contact: Xavier Campos Juan del Jarro No. 105 Barrio de Santiago San Luis Potosi, S.L.P. 78028, Mexico

PH: (52 481) 290-16

Location: Central Mexico, in San Luis Potosi State, 14 miles east of the city of San Luis Potosi in Villa Zara Zaragoza, on route 70/110 toward Tampico.

Circuit: .77 mile road course; five turns.

Major Races: Marlboro Cup

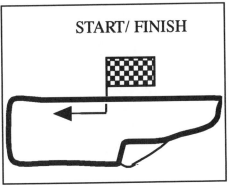

START/ FINISH

163

Championship (Chrysler F2; Phantom); Delval Truck Cup; Tecate Sport Prototype Cup.

El Autodromo Potosino is another brief Mexican road circuit. At just under eight-tenths of a mile, there's not much in the way of thrilling top speeds. But, as with any Mexican track, the place is popular, and racing is generally good in that atmosphere. For the Marlboro Cup races, 50,000 people usually congregate upon the dirt embankments!

The track was resurfaced just recently for the F2 cars, which form part of the Marlboro Cup. It is not the best of circuits, but has most of the modern conveniences, and good spectating areas.

Your best bet for a room will be in San Luis Potosi. Hotel information can be found by writing the Secretario de Turismo at Manuel Jose Othon No. 130 — Altos, San Luis Potosi, SLP. 78000; or by calling (481) 23143 or 42994.

Autodromo de Amozoc, Puebla
**Track contact: Cesar Gonzalez
Cinco Pte. No. 2308
Puebla, Pue.**

PH: (52 22) 48-54-27

Location: Central southern Mexico, in the State of Puebla

Circuit: .9 mile road course; eight turns.

Major Races: FIA Formula Three Championship; Montana Cup Super Formula K Championships; CAR 90 Resistencia Endurance Championships.

Puebla is owned by the Abed brothers, the same family who promote the Grand Prix at Hermanos Rodriguez. The feud between the Abeds and Promotodo precludes the popular F2 cars (and anything linked to the Marlboro Cup) from running here. The Abeds promote F3, and this is the biggest venue for both the F3 series and the track.

The track was built in 1985 by Promotodo and later sold to the Abed brothers. It has one of the best surfaces of all Mexican racetracks. It was not only resurfaced recently, but was altered a bit. It's anyone's guess which layout is used most often, as there are several variations of track which are often utilized. Until 1990, the version most used was the tight track, which employed the first available left turn, then doubled back into itself, and looped back around to make a 180 degree left turn onto the start/finish straightway.

At the end of the '90 season, with the championship still to be decided, the main variation of the track cracked and broke up badly in

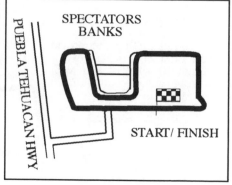

164

some places. The final round of the championship was thus held on Puebla's oval.

Puebla is not yet a tourist's paradise — but it is rapidly becoming one. Very small and compact, the picturesque city is enclosed on all sides by mountains. It's known for being the site of some of the oldest buildings in the western hemisphere, making it a popular attraction for Mexican vacationers.

There are a few rooms here but it is best to book ahead. Information on hotels can be found by writing the Secretario de Turismo at 5 Sur No 1301, 5th Floor, Puebla, PUE. 72000; or by calling (22) 375013 or 374026.

Autodromo de Queretaro

Office: Promotodo, Av. Constituyentes #251,
COL: Daniel Garza,
Mexico D.F. 11840;
PH: (52 5) 272 9438;
FAX: (52 5) 277 3976.

Track contact:Luis Martinez (52 42) 13 59 68

Location: Central Mexico, in the state of Queretaro, nine miles north of the city of Queretaro.

Circuit: .84 mile road course; six turns.

Major Races: Marlboro Cup Championship (Chrysler F2; Phantom); Delval Truck Cup; Tecate Sport Prototype Cup.

Queretaro is where Maximilian was executed, and where plans for the War of Independence were formulated. It's old Mexico, and isn't exactly the most accessible place on the earth, either locally or nationally.

Queretaro's racetrack is a small, slow track which still manages to reel in thousands of spectators when the bigger Marlboro Cup racing comes through. Located seven miles off the main road on a winding dirt trail, shuttles exist to take spectators to the track, but you must do some serious homework if you're to find where they are and how to catch them. There are some 750 hotel rooms in the area. For more information, write the Secretario de Turismo at Cinco De Mayo No. 61, Queretaro, QRO. 76000; or call (463) 40179 or 40428.

Autodromo Del Norte de Saltillo
Office: Promotodo, Av. Constituyentes #251,
COL: Daniel Garza,
Mexico D.F. 11840;

PH: (52 5) 272 9438;
FAX: (52 5) 277 3976.

Location: Northern central Mexico, in Coahuila State, on the outskirts of the city of Saltillo.

Circuit: 1.4 mile road course; nine turns.

Major Races: Marlboro Cup Championship (Chrysler F2; Phantom); Delval Truck Cup; Tecate Sport Prototype Cup.

Opened in 1988, Saltillo is designed so spectators can see the entire road racing circuit from any seat. Saltillo is another Promotodo track. And, as with most of Promotodo's designs,

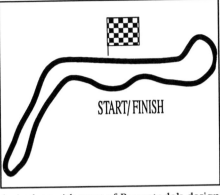

START/FINISH

the track has been laid out with the show in mind.

There are plenty of grandstands — which are usually full when the Marlboro Cup or Montana Cup races come through town. There are also liberal general admission areas built upon strategically placed, man-made dirt embankments.

For drivers, the track is challenging but safe. There is liberal run-off room in the appropriate places, and on the straights there are nice smooth concrete barriers — which are high enough so fans can watch from just a few feet from the track.

The mile-high elevation can be a problem but the temperature is usually mild to warm. Founded in 1555, it has Colonial Spanish influence and is worth a look for history buffs. For hotel information, call (841) 54444 or 58390; or write the Secretario de Turismo at Centro de Convenciones, 2nd Floor, Saltillo, COAH.

Autodromo Parque Tangamanga
San Luis Potosi

Office: Federacion Mexicana de Automovilismo Deportivo, A.C.
Av. Patriotismo 586
COL: Sa Pedro de Los Pinos
03800 Mexico, D.F.

PH: (52 5) 598 33 16
FAX: (52 5) 611 38 18

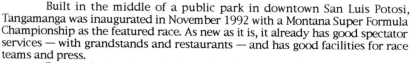

Location: In the Parque Tangamanga II, downtown San Luis Potosi.

Circuit: 1.38 mile road circuit; eight turns

Major races: Montana Championship

Built in the middle of a public park in downtown San Luis Potosi, Tangamanga was inaugurated in November 1992 with a Montana Super Formula Championship as the featured race. As new as it is, it already has good spectator services — with grandstands and restaurants — and has good facilities for race teams and press.

Because the Autodromo is located inside the city, the best place to stay will be in SLP, and there are plenty of rooms. Contact the Mexican Government Tourist Office at 10100 Santa Monica Blvd., Los Angeles, CA 90067, PH: (213) 203-8151 or (213) 203-9335.

Autodromo de Tulancingo
Bosque el Angel
Office: c/o Sr. Angel Herrera Yanez
Carretara Mexico Tuxpan Km 90
Tulancingo, Hidalgo

PH: (52 775) 30973

Location: Eastern Mexico, on Carretera Mexico-Tuxpan KM 90.

Circuit: .84 mile road course; nine turns.

Major races: Endurance championships.

Located in tropical forests of Mexico, Tulancingo is unique and agreeable for adventurers. Inaugurated on

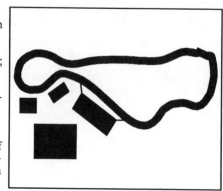

May 22, 1990, Tulancingo has very few services for either fans or teams. There are no grandstands yet, but a small seating structure was expected by the end of 1993 near the paddock complex. There is no control tower, but it, too, is about to be located. Six kilometers away from Tulancingo City, there will be plenty of rooms in Tulancingo. For more information, contact the Mexican Government Tourist Office, 10100 Santa Monica Blvd., Los Angeles, CA 90067, PH: (213) 203-8151 or (213) 203-9335.

Autodromo Veracruz
c/o Gerardo Sanz
Ciruelos No. 80
Col: Floresta
Veracruz, VER.
PH: (52 29) 37-45-84

Location: Southeastern Mexico, in Veracruz State, six miles northwest of the city of Veracruz, on Route 140 to Jalapa.

Circuit: 1.5 mile road course; nine turns.

Major Races: Marlboro Cup Championships for Automobiles and motorcycles; FIA Formula Three Championships; Formula Ford 1600 Championships (two rounds).

For drivers, Veracruz is probably the least liked circuits in all of Mexico. Carved out of a hilly area, the track has little runoff and is very fast, leaving little room for error and lots of things to hit in the event a mistake is made. The surface itself is dusty and dirty.

But it's one of the best places in Mexico — or possibly North America — to watch a race. Veracruz is one of the most beautiful resort spots in Mexico. A true trading port of historical Mexico, it's old Mexico, with unspoiled beauty — unlike places such as Americanized Puerta Vallarta, or Acapulco.

The oldest colonial city in Mexico (est. 1519), it has a great deal to offer tourists. The Gulf Coast location brings Veracruz warm tropical air, and the hillsides around the racetrack are surrounded by green grass — which pretty much stays that color throughout the entire summer. The track is only three miles from the Gulf of Mexico, and the Atlantic Ocean.

There are fantastic spectating areas at the circuit. From the top of the hill you'll see most of the circuit. You can also get fairly close to the track in several places, safely watching the action from only a dozen feet or so away. Marlboro has built hospitality suites at the very top of the hill, and if you have contacts, that's absolutely the best place from which to watch the race.

Rooms in Veracruz range from Five Star to budget, and unlike most of Mexico, the port doesn't cater to foreign tourists. You'll likely need some Spanish here. Be careful not to arrive during the Lenten Mardi Gras;

START/ FINISH

it may be impossible to find any accommodations. For more information, contact the Secretario de Turismo at Bajos Palacio Municipa, Veracruz, VER. 91700; or call (29) 361088 or 329942.

Autodromo Zacatecas
Track Contact: Guillermo Sigg
PH: (52 492) 23875/ 21898

Location: 13 KM from the city of Guadalupe Zacatecas heading toward Cosio Aguascalientes at KM 13.

Circuit: 1.14 mile road course; nine turns.

Major races: Mexican endurance racing.

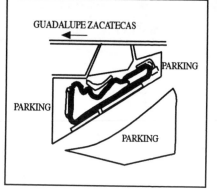

The Autodromo Zacatecas sits in the valley of the original colonial city of Zacatecas, and the surrounding area is rich in Mexican history. Open since 1987, the circuit itself has very little of the district's history. The track is slowly being developed, but as of this writing is still without spectator facilities. There are spectator embankments, but no stands yet exist and the circuit has never sold out its tickets.

Like most tracks in Mexico, the entire track can be seen from just about anywhere on the spectator embankments. The small valley in which the track sits produces extreme temperature changes and it will be either very hot or very cold here. During the racing season, it will be quite warm, so beware. The track sits some 7,000 feet above sea level so it can make you a bit dizzy as well if you are unaccustomed to the thin air.

Zacatecas will have enough rooms for even the biggest F3 and F2 races. Information on accommodations can be found by contacting the Tourist Board in Mexico at (52 492) 20170 or (52 492) 26 757.

MONACO

If you can only see one Grand Prix race, it should be Monaco. Its description as a storybook kingdom fits Monaco perfectly, and the crowded little country still grows bigger, with the confusion of Monaco's maze of tunnels and the hum of major construction ever present.

There are only a couple of ways into Monte Carlo. In fact, there are only a few dozen streets in the whole country. During a race weekend, the streets become a veritable traffic jam of exotic-car drivers trying to be seen during the Grand Prix. Since the whole country would be inoperative for four days, the roads open up between sessions each day of the race weekend.

Monaco, at any other time, is worth a visit by car. You can come in from either the A8 Autoroute, due north, which winds down the precariously twisting road; on the narrow semi-flat road from Cap d'Ail; or, from Ventimiglia and via Highway 1.

It is certainly worth a drive up the hill on Highway 1 toward Ventimiglia at least once. The view from there is one of the best on the Riviera, and the Monaco harbor is a phenomenal sight, with the beautiful blue of the Mediterranean in the background. Drive slowly, and make sure the brakes are in good working order.

Driving in the city may be easier when the GP isn't running, but parking will never be simple in Monaco, no matter what time of the year. There are far more cars than there are spaces to put them, and the spots you do find will cost you a pretty penny. Unless you're staying in Monaco, it's best to park your car elsewhere and take the train.

Tourist Information: **Monaco Tourist Office** at (33) 933 08701, or write, 2A Boulevard des Moulins, 98000, Monaco; or in The States, call (212) 759-5227.

Sporting Authority: **Automobile Club de Monaco**, 23 Blvd Albert 1er, BP 464, 98000, Monaco. PH: (33) 93 15 26 00; FAX: (33) 93 25 80 08.

Circuit de Monaco,
Automobile-Club de Monaco,
23 blvd Albert 1er,
98000 Monaco

PH: (33) 93 15 26 00
FAX: (33) 93 25 80 08

Location: Center city, Monte Carlo, Monaco (located southern France, 15 miles east of Nice).

Circuit: 2.06 mile road course;16 turns.

Major races: FIA Formula One Grand Prix World Championship.

Monaco epitomizes the whole Formula One show. Perhaps that's why the race is such an permanent fixture of the FIA GP calendar.

Drivers hate the circuit almost to the man. Unlike Indy, where the win is worth so much more in terms of subsequent prestige, to GP drivers Monaco is just another race. To fans, however, Monaco is as much a happening as Indianapolis or Le Mans.

Finding a room in the middle of the madness is nearly impossible. Don't even think about staying in Monte Carlo. If you could afford it any other time, you'll be flabbergasted at what the same rooms go for during the GP; if you can afford the rooms during the race, well, good luck finding one.

Nice, which is some 10 miles west of Monaco, will be booked well in advance, as will Cannes, and Menton. Fortunately there is really only one viable way into Monaco,

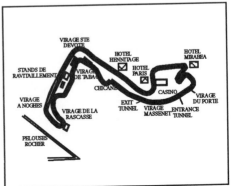

171

and that's by train, so the effort necessary to travel to the circuit is essentially the same, just a longer wait on the train. Staying in San Remo, Bordighera or any of the other small towns on the Italian side of the Riviera is not a bad idea — although it's harder to make arrangements from abroad. There are several small French towns on the Riviera that are as pleasant as Nice, and are generally cheaper: Cagne, Antibes, Cape d'Antibes, Juan les Pins, Golfe Juan or anything as far as St. Tropez are all beautiful, right on the water, and will do a Monaco GP weekend justice.

Remember that this is the beginning of the tourist season; plus, rooms will never be easy to find during the week of the race. Also remember that Monaco lasts one day longer than most GPs because Friday is a free day, with no F1 cars on course. First qualifying gets started Thursday.

Tickets are difficult to find here as well. Getting reserved seats at the race takes serious pre-planning. Like most places, you won't be completely out of luck if you haven't bought tickets in advance. There will be something available up until the day of the race — although don't count on seeing too many racecars from the distance you'll be from the track. Some of the seats are horrible. Some, like the Pelouses Rocher, are literally on the sides of cliffs, a quarter-mile from the track.

This is one race where stepping up is not a bad idea. Try for the stands in the Tabac Corner. From there you'll have a good shot at the cars coming through the tunnel, through the chicane, and past the pool. If not there, try on the dock, where you'll see the entire sequence from Tabac, through the pool area, to the entrance of the slow La Rascasse. Do anything you can to get tickets before you leave! Page and Moy will help you with tickets, or call the ACM in Monaco.

If you can afford to pay more there are lots of ways to see the GP. Balconies all over the city will give you an intimate view of the track. They'll be expensive — $500-2,000 for an average apartment — and you must begin arranging the rental far in advance. Don't expect to show up and find a balcony. It won't happen.

You can watch from several private grandstands. The Mirabeau Hotel, at the far end of the track, has a small private grandstand where you'll watch the corner before the tunnel and the exit of the Lowes Hairpin while being served lunch and champagne. The Rascasse Restaurant (in the corner named, appropriately, "Virage de la Rascasse"), the Cafe de Paris in the Casino Square, and a couple of restaurants on the fast downhill portion of track leading into Mirabeau all have spots on the terrace that literally sit at the edge of the guardrail. You'll spend $500 or so for lunch and a day's view of the cars. Usually the spots are available on race day, but try to reserve in advance if you can.

If you feel like being a high roller, try to get a seat on a boat in the harbor. It won't be cheap. But it will be unique, and you'll have a great view. If nothing else, you'll get to relax in semi-secluded comfort while drivers come and go, visiting the neighboring yachts and all the half-naked beautiful people who are there trying to be seen.

The best place to go for advice on a Monaco weekend is Grand Prix Tours. If you're positive this boat thing is for you, they can help you; if you'd like to watch from the balcony of your room at the Lowes Hotel, call GP Tours; if you need a private balcony, they can suggest where to call.

Also: keep yourself updated on the French tobacco laws. Should the cigarette advertising ban stand up in court, the Monaco race may be in jeopardy since it will be impossible for teams to enter Monaco by airplane from anywhere else besides Nice -- and under the current circumstances some team's equipment is in jeopardy of being seized. Call FISA prior to your departure.

There's a terrific guide book available from the French Office of Tourism which lists all the hotels in the area with prices and phone numbers. Booking from the States is relatively inexpensive if you call during the cheap hours — and provided, of course, that you speak enough French to do the job yourself.

THE NETHERLANDS

Bearing in mind The Netherlands' rivalry with Germany, Holland still feels more like Germany than anywhere else in Europe (except Austria). The countryside screams Holland, with its flat greenery and windmills. But things are German: very orderly and precise.

Roads are some of the widest on the continent, but, as opposed to Germany, speed limits are the lowest in Europe — at 100 KPH on the Autobahns and 80 KPH on the smaller roads. The roads, however, are often six and eight lanes wide.

Getting anywhere in The Netherlands is very easy. Signs are prominent and direct. The Dutch realize that theirs is a language that few endeavor to speak, so they make things easy for travellers. Although signage is not always written in English, the only time you'll have problems will be in the middle of the city (zentrum). Everybody speaks English in Holland. It's almost offensive if you ask if they speak English. Try using Dutch, but you'll find the Dutch speak English better than any country on the continent.

The country is so small, and the difference in speed between the large and small roads is so insignificant, you should really avoid the major highways. The most beautiful scenery in northern Europe is in Holland, and can only be accessed by taking the smaller roads.

Tourist Information: **The Netherlands Board of Tourism** can be found by dropping by any of the 400 VVV information locations around Holland (usually at the train stations and Schipol Airport).

Sporting Authority: **Knac Nationale Autosport Federatie**, Postbus 60, 2380 AB Zoeterwoude, NL. PH: 71 89 2601; FAX: 71 41 45 84.

Circuit van Drenthe,
Assen, The Netherlands

PH: (31) 5920 55000
FAX: (31) 5920 56911

Location: Northern Holland, just east of Dutch Autoroute A28, 70 miles from Amsterdam

Circuit Length: 3.81 miles; 16 turns.

Major races: FIM Motorcycle Grand Prix Championship — 80cc, 125cc, 250cc, 500cc, and Sidecars.

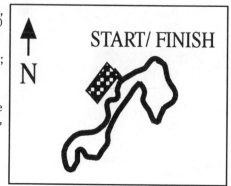

Assen is a good look at Holland, where function and appearance always seems inseparable. The grass at the Dutch track grows right up to the edge of the racetrack, giving a perfect landing area for riders who find themselves accidentally dismounted for their minor errors. The beautifully manicured greenery affords a view of the entire track from most seats, and there are no spectators allowed into the infield. Run-off is wide, but the circuit's viewing areas are not compromised by the safety-wise design.

The track is always packed during the TT, and it is a favorite for riders. With the dominance of the sidecar shows by primarily Dutch and British riders — and the ease of British fans getting to Assen from across the Channel — the Sidecars may just headline the FIM GP weekend. In fact, in 1992 the track hosted the final round of the six-race Sidecar Championship when Italy, Spain, Brazil and South Africa simply abandoned the sidecar championship, flatly refusing to run the pariahed series. Assen stepped in for a second round, thereby deciding the championship.

A bit on the narrow side, action gets tight on this bikes-only track. In the opening stages of a race things can get a bit sticky.

Staying in the area is usually no problem — even during the GP. If you get to the circuit Thursday you should have no problem at all; Friday you can even find a room. Saturday, you'll have to do some driving. But when you consider the distances across Holland — and the terrific train service available — travelling won't be a major headache. Stay in Groningen, some 15 miles north.

Remember that the Dutch TT comprises the last part of the Dutch Speedweek, with European championship racing and other minor formula, and the Dutch TT is actually held on Saturday — not Sunday. Weather in the Netherlands is usually less than perfect. Like Zandvoort, wind can also sometimes be a problem.

Hotel information can be found by going by any VVV office in Holland, which are conveniently located outside the major train stations and airport, or by calling the Netherlands Board of Tourism.

Circuit van Zandvoort

nr 452 Nederlandse,
Autorensport Vereniging,
P.O. Box 132,
Zandvoort, The Netherlands

PH: (31) 2507 18284
FAX: (31) 2507 18262

Location: Western central Holland, on the North Sea Coast between Den Haag and Haarlem, 17 miles from Amsterdam.

From Amsterdam, take A4 to A9 toward Haarlem, following signs to Zandvoort resorts.

Circuit: 1.56 mile road course; nine turns.

Major races: GM Opel Euroseries Championship; Marlboro Masters of Formula 3.

Holland's most notorious circuit was the site of several Championship determining races — and several historically significant racing events. Now, however, Zandvoort is just a shadow of its former self.

The old Zandvoort was where the Cosworth engine first appeared in 1967 in a Colin Champman Lotus; and where the TAG/McLaren engine made its maiden run in 1983. The latest, greatest race at the eastern Dutch track was the 1983 race when Alain Prost and Nelson Piquet touched and spun in Tarzan corner (where else?), and effectively marked the end of the season for Prost, who by then couldn't catch Piquet for the title. Ferrari pleased the Tifosi that year by finishing 1-2 at the hands of Rene Arnoux and Patrick Tambay.

Zandvoort was Tarzan. And although track officials were careful not to disturb the corner when development on the surrounding resort community took place, the run out of Bos Uit has been neutered, so top speeds have been reduced into Tarzan, where braking from 200-mph to 60-mph was done in just a few yards. Even Scheivlak corner, which Niki Lauda claimed was even more exciting than Tarzan, has been changed, so little of the old romance of the circuit still remain. Pity.

The area surrounding it is still noteworthy however. And the beautiful resorts, coupled with Dutch hospitality still make the town worth visiting. If you sit in the dunes and close your eyes perhaps you can still imagine...

The track has seen a resurgence of interest from the mid-summer Marlboro-sponsored Masters of F3, an invitational race comprised of the top six F3 drivers from individual championships around the world. The attendance in the two seasons of its existence have been better than 35,000 spectators per race. As this guide goes to press, there has been no word as to the status of future events, although it's

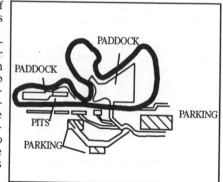

predicted the races will be back. Call or write the track for more information.

Hotel information can be found by going by any VVV office in Holland, which are conveniently located outside the major train stations and airports, or by calling the Netherlands Board of Tourism. You can also try the sporting authority, Knac Nationale Autosport Federatie, at Postbus 60, 2380 AB Zoeterwoude, NL. PH: 71 89 2601; FAX: 71 41 45 84.

Manfeild Autocourse
Manfeild Autocourse Promotions
P.O. Box 1959
Palmerston North, New Zealand
PH: (64 6) 357-7459
FAX: (64 6) 357-7244

Location: On New Zealand's North Island, 90 miles northeast of Wellington, nine miles northwest of Palmerston North, off South Street

Circuit: 1.88 mile road course; seven turns.

Major Races: FIM Superbike Championships

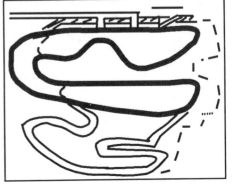

In October 1992, Manfeild hosted the penultimate round of the FIM Superbike season — its first Superbike race.

Like Assen, virtually the entire track can be seen from any seat in the house. Named from the combination of Manawatu and Feilding, the district and township where the circuit is located, Manfeild is the only New Zealand track homologated to run an international motorcycle meeting and is perhaps the best on the calendar for motorcycle fans.

In addition to being within sight of any seat, all corners are banked from 2-10 degrees, making it an extremely fast circuit as well. Currently, spectator embankments offer reserved seating for 4,300 — plus another two thousand or so in hospitality suites — and day gate sales usually allow another 6,000 in the bigger events here. But like pits and paddock -- which are continually being upgraded to appease loud riders who miss the comforts of home -- so are the spectator facilities. The Superbike evens sell out quickly and the organizers are trying to find corners at which to put more grandstands. Currently the only grandstands existing are those along the start/finish straight.

There are only some 80-90 rooms in Feilding, but Palmerston North offers plenty of top and mid-range hotels. The track is located 1.6 miles from Feilding and nine miles from Palmerston North.

Camping is also available at the track, and showers do exist. You can also book you stay with AA Travel Ltd, the track's tour company, just call or fax the track a request and they will help you. Or contact the New Zealand Tourism Board 800 388-5494, 501 Santa Monica Blvd. 300 Santa Monica CA 90401. For more on motorsport call the Motorsport Association of New Zealand, P.O. Box 3793 Wellington, NZ, (64 4)4 723-520; or the New Zealand Auto Cycle Union, P.O. Box 253 Huntly, NZ; FAX: 64 817 87928.

PORTUGAL

Portugal is quaint towns, punctuated by warm, lazy afternoons, and beautiful coastlines, dotted with inexpensive hotels and restaurants.

The Portuguese don't have a great deal of interest in racing — in either the two wheeled or four wheeled variety. The races, in contrast to Spanish races, are well attended, but there's not much for the Portuguese to get behind — except possibly that Brazilians speak Portuguese.

On the road, though, you'd be hard pressed to see the difference between Portugal and any other European country. Portugal's roads feel like French Autoroutes. Speed limits are generally high, with 120KPH being the standard on the major highways, designated by an "N". The local roads are limited to 90KPH, and 60KPH in the cities (although nobody seems to obey the limits).

The Portuguese tend to be aggressive drivers, but once you've conquered Rome, you can intimidate them easily. Not compromising anyone's safety, Portuguese generally will make aggressive moves, perhaps to cut you off, which you'll easily be able to counter by not moving over. It's as simple as that. Unlike Rome, or North Africa, if you get directions wrong and need to make a quick lane change you'll usually be able to accomplish it in Portugal.

Since most of the highways are two lane jobs, passing is prolific. But don't be surprised if overtaking is not completed before the oncoming cars are at the scene of the pass. Usually oncoming traffic tolerates overtaking vehicles over the lane markers. The bolder drivers even begin passes while traffic is coming the opposite direction. Beware.

One of the odd things about Portuguese driving is the tradition where half the traffic passes at once. When a stretch of highway appears where no cars coming the opposite way, literally half the cars on the road pull into the oncoming lane and pass at least one car. If you are one of the faster cars, and don't seize the opportunity to pull left, you'll be passed as well.

Beware the road from Portugal into Spain toward Jerez; as soon as the road crosses into Spain it becomes a nightmare. See the section on Spain for more information.

Tourist Information: **Portuguese National Tourist Office**: 548 Fifth Ave., New York, NY 10036. PH: (212) 354-4403.

Sporting Authority: **Automovil Club de Portugal**, Rua Rosa Araujo 24, 1200 Lisboa, Portugal. PH: (351) 1 563 931; FAX: (351) 1 574 732.

Autodromo Fernanda Pires Da Silva
Estrada Nacional n9-Km6, Ap 4
2765 Estoril Codex, Portugal

PH: (35 11) 469 14 12/469 13 62
FAX: (35 11) 469 12 02

Location: Western coast of Portugal, just west of Lisbon.

From Lisbon, take the Autoroute A2 heading south. Before crossing the Tejo river take the National Route 6 west, following the signs to Cascais and Estoril. The track is four miles north of Monte Estoril on National Route 9.

Circuit: 2.7 mile road circuit; 11 turns.

Major races: FIA Formula One Grand Prix World Championship; GM Euroseries Championship.

Other than Monaco, the Autodromo do Estoril – or more recently titled the Autodromo Fernanda Pires Da Silva -- is probably the best resort-oriented F1 racetrack on the 16-race FIA Grand Prix calendar. Although Paul Ricard was nestled in the mountains on the western edge of the French Riviera when it was on the GP circuit, the track was nearly 45 minutes away by car. The circuit at Estoril, on the other hand, is only a few miles from the beach — and can be walked in 45 minutes. The track, recently renamed after the its creator Fernanda da Silva, is on the outskirts of the city of Estoril, just a few miles north of Lisbon.

Three small resort cities line the beach, and all three are good alternatives to staying as far away as Lisbon. Cascais, which is really more entertaining than Estoril, is to the north, followed by Monte Estoril, then Estoril. At the end of the string, a bluff stops further northward progress, so the three cities are essentially isolated from through traffic, effectively creating an intimate resort area.

Unlike French or Northern Italian beaches, Portugal's beaches

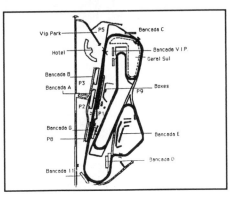

are sandy and user-friendly. Easy to find, a local commuter train goes from the northern end of Cascais to Lisbon. It is cheap, just a few Escudos for a five minute ride. And even if you don't know any Portuguese the ticket windows are set up so anyone can get directions. The same is true for those who find themselves staying less expensively in Lisbon. If you rented a car, it's probably wise to take public transportation, since the area directly around the track will be heavily congested — at least on Sunday.

If you can make Estoril by Wednesday, it's possible to find rooms, although by Thursday evening the prospects are all but hopeless. Prices for rooms may rise during the GP, but, unlike some of the other GPs, rates are still competitive (read: inexpensive) — even close to the track.

If not in Estoril or Cascais, take a train into Estoril, walk under the tracks and across the street to the lines of buses which will have appeared for the Grand Prix, and which, for about a dollar, will take you right to the main entrance of the track.

Finding tickets for the race is, as usual, a well kept secret. Once you arrive in Estoril — hopefully Thursday — you'll find tickets available at the casino. The Casino do Estoril is located just a couple of blocks away from the beach behind the Estoril train station. Follow the directions as if heading toward the bus to the track, but continue to the top of the hill, around front, and to the left of the main entrance to the casino is an office which handles both ticket sales and press accreditation.

There are several good places from which to watch the race, start/finish not being the best of them. Although the stands overlooking the pits are fantastic

for watching the start, and perfect if you need to keep tabs on Senna as he prepares to qualify, you'll have difficulty seeing anything else. The Geral Norte area is probably the best bet if you want to see most of the racing at the same time. Although you won't see the start or the checkered flag, you'll see virtually everything else. The stands sit on a hill, and are built in such a way that with little effort you can see behind you — which seems impossible, but somehow it works.

Estoril has one of the fastest corners in Grand Prix racing, at the entrance to the start finish straight. Nigel Mansell fears the corner is fast enough where drivers will eventually black out from the G-loading — they've been measured at four-and-a-half Gs through there. It's certainly where men are men.

With several sets of grandstands placed in the final turn to witness it all, turn 11 is a good alternative to the start/finish seats. If what's available is in general admission, don't worry, you'll do fine with those tickets as well.

The Portueguese National Tourist office number is 548 5th Ave., New York, NY 10036, and the phone number is (212) 354-4403; the office in Portugal is on Av. Antonio Agusto de Aguiar 86, 1200 Lisbon (01) 575 0911; or Arcadas do Parque, 2765 Estoril, at (01) 268 0113.

SOUTH AFRICA

Sporting Authorities: **AASA Motor Sport Control** (also sanctions motorcycle racing), P.O. Box 9444, Johannesburg 2000, South Africa. PH: 11 403 3160; FAX: 11 403 2580;

Kyalami Grand Prix Circuit
Allandale Road (R561) Midrand
P.O. Box 1603
Halfway House, 1685, South Africa

PH: (27) 11 702 2305
FAX: (27) 702 2372

Location: 15 miles north of Johannesburg, off the N1.

Circuit: 1.82 mile road course; nine turns.

Major Races: FIA Grand Prix World Championship; FIM World Championship for motorcycles; South African Sedan and Motorcycling Championships.

Kyalami, which means "my home" in Zulu, was home for no international championships for six seasons. With the politics as they were in South Africa, things seemed unlikely to change as quickly as they did. Recently, both the political climate and the circuit were completely revamped, hoping for a new look.

There was certainly no shortage of interest in South Africa for a return of the Formula One World Championship. Williams returned to testing at Kyalami in 1989, and the venue quietly slipped back into the testing mainstream via the British team — although actual championship status did not seem likely. It looked like a permanent part of both the F1 and the FIM Grand Prix calendars, until recent problems put the

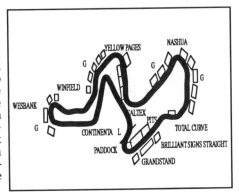

181

circuit into financial difficulties. In 1993, the circuit hosted one of the more glamorous rounds of the F1 Championship, but the FIM finale was cancelled, and the motorcycle GP World Championship was abbreviated.

The circuit has gone through two facelifts since it was abandoned in 1984. Where the old circuit's pit straight was a mind-blowing right-hand kink into a wide, fast, sweeping 180 degree right hander, the new circuit has the start/finish on the back part of the old track, and is entered following a quick left-hander. The old start/finish straight is no longer utilized. The track is considerably slower looking — but as a few teams found, is as fast as the four fastest tracks on the contemporary World Championship Grand Prix calendar. More importantly, there are luxury suites here like no others anywhere in the world, offering cabana-style conveniences with a perfect view of the racing.

Sitting at the top of the Highveld plain, Kyalami is some 6,000 feet above sea level. But thermometers belie the altitude, and the average temperatures are in the high 90s. Although there is little humidity here, late afternoon thunderstorms are typical.

Cosmopolitan Johannesburg is just a few minutes from the circuit and will be the best place to book a room. There are also rooms available in Sandton City. The Jan Smuts International Airport is just a half-an-hour from the track.

For more information on lodging, call or write the South African Tourist Board, or the AASA Motor Sport Control, P.O. Box 9444, Johannesburg 2000, South Africa. PH: 11 403 3160; FAX: 11 403 2580.

SPAIN

The Spanish Grand Prix has played to vacant stands for the past few years, and the FIA World Championship has left the beautiful Jerez circuit for a more accessible (read: profitable) Barcelona circuit. The GP is a big event in Spain, but few locals can afford the race. What's left is a magnificent facility, where anyone who comes has their pick of seats.

Although Spaniards Sito Pons, Juan Garriga and Alex Criville help attendance for bike racing, seats are still available just about anywhere you want them. Jarama and Albacete are no better.

Spain is a relaxing vacation, and an easy race to see. As opposed to an Italian race, or Monaco, Spain is completely effortless. The only problem with Spain is getting to the circuit in the first place.

Highways in Spain are usually good fast roads, which could be compared to any European country favorably. Many, however, are narrow stretches of pavement that are not even suitable as driveways, let alone highways.

Most roads in Spain are two-laned stretches, keeping the average tourist up nights thinking about what the next day's drive will bring. One of the worst roads in all of Europe has to be the 433/260 from Spain to Portugal. The road deteriorates as you leave Spain toward Portugal, so when you reach the Portuguese border and its wide two-laned road on the other side of the frontera, you will be truly thankful.

On the maps it's listed as a major thoroughfare, but as you continue along it from Seville for several miles, you realize how bad things really are. Do not attempt to take this road in a car whose innards are of dubious reliability. The road is rough. The sentence "No hay servicios" takes on new meaning here, and if you do get stuck it can be 30 minutes before another car even comes past.

It becomes as narrow as a sidewalk some places. Be ready, also, to stop for sheep, which will occasionally be meandering in the middle of the road. Understanding the drawbacks of this road is important — because you may have to traverse it if you wish to see races back to back in Portugal and Spain.

Its bad points revealed, there are good things to say about it: It's Spain.

182

Cork trees litter the scenery, and old Spanish castles and churches are sprinkled about. The drive is truly beautiful, but be prepared for a 100 miles to take half a day. In fact, almost all of Spain will be travelled slower than the other parts of Europe.

Tourist Information: **Spanish National Tourist Office**, in Murcia at Alejandro Seiquer #4, Murcia, 30001; PH. 3468 43716. Or at Passeig de Gracia, 35, Pral., Barcelona. PH: 93 215 4477. Or, Passeig de Gracia, 35, Pral., Barcelona. PH: 93 215 4477.

Sporting Authorities: **Federacion Espanola de Automovilisimo**, Avda Menendez Pelayo 67 — local 5, Torre del Retiro, 28009 Madrid, Espana. PH: (34) 1 273 5600; FAX: (34) 1 273 1946; **Real Federacion Motociclista Espanola,** General Pardinas 71-1, 28006 Madrid. PH: (34 1) 562 53 42/43; FAX: (34 1) 561 3507.

Albacete
Crta Ayora KM 3700
02006, Albacete
Office: Apdo Correo 1055.02080
Albacete, Spain.

PH: (967) 24 25 10
FAX: (967) 24 25 62

Track: 2.12mile road course; 13 turns.

Location: South central Spain, two hours southeast of Madrid, two hours southwest of Valencia, three miles outside Albacete on the road to Ayore.

Major races: Superbikes

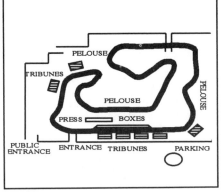

Albacete was opened in 1990 and hosted its first major race, a round of the Superbike World Championship, in 1992. Although it also hosted a round of the FIA F3000 Championship in 1992, all involved seemed to think it should have been left off the schedule. It remains on the calendar for the 1993 season.

With the local Spanish riders spurring interest in the sport, Spain has a well-established fan base in motorcycling and Albacete will likely become the country's favorite motorcycling track. Other than the F3000 race, Albacete's only significant events are of the two-wheeled variety.

The track is very flat, and fairly slow. There are two portions which have slight elevation changes (2% and 9%) but the track is mostly level and featureless. Although there is some vegetation, it is not located around the area of the track. Most of the greenery is on the outskirts, away from the spectating areas. The entire track is visible from almost anywhere. Like much of Spain, it is hot and dry here.

There are stands for 7,000 — four large stands and three smaller stands. Try for seats in turns 3 & 4 , which are the best corners on the track , and from which you can see most of the circuit. Officials say the circuit is completely finished, although timing and scoring buildings are still being erected as well as a cafeteria. Plans also exist to build more stands.

Camping is not available at the track, but there is plenty in the city. This season you should still have no problems staying in or around Albacete. There are many small hotels within a half-an-hour of the track — the best choices will be toward Albacete itself.

For more information on rooms call The Spanish Tourist Office in Murcia at Alejandro Seiquer #4, Murcia, 30001; PH. 3468 43716.

Circuit de Catalunya
Office: Mas "La Moreneta"
P.O. Box 27
08160 Montmelo, Barcelona

Track: Carretera de Granollers,
KM 2
Montmelo, Barcelona, Spain

PH: (34) 3 572 3061
FAX: (34) 3 571 9700

Location: 12 miles north east of Barcelona, on the A7 Autoroute, at exit 13 — the Granollers exit.

Circuit: 2.95 mile road course; 15 turns.

Major races: FIA Formula One World Championship; FIM Grand Prix World Championship motorcycles.

Barcelona's new Catalunya circuit, nicknamed Montmeló (Melon Mountain in Catalan language), is one of the most advanced circuits in the world — and is considered a state-of-the-art facility.

Completed two weeks prior to its F1 Grand Prix in September of '91 and created in time for the 1992 Barcelona Olympics, the new track is still being fine tuned. This is the first time since 1975 — when the Montjuic circuit was closed — that Barcelona has seen a Grand Prix. Unlike its sister in Jerez, Barcelona has attracted a decent crowd — figured at 70,000 or more each season.

Indeed, the track's strengths are its location near Barcelona, and

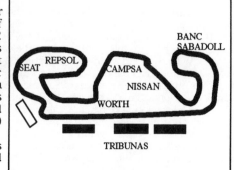

its proximity to transportation. Montmelo is located just a few hundred meters off the A7, making access fantastic — even at the worst of times. And there is a railway station in Montmelo (Circuit de Catalunya Station) that stops 1,400 meters from the front entrance of the facility, making it easy for those without cars.

There are several places to watch racing from. The main grandstands are the most expensive, but there are several other places that are almost as good. For F1, Tribuna F is a grandstand, as is Tribuna C. Each offers good views during the car races. But parts of Tribuna C and all of Tribuna A disappear, making room for what is called "Preferent" admission when the bikes run. An upgraded general admission, the Preferent areas give better views than GA and are not as comfortable as seated areas. This has become a very popular spot for Spanish fans.

The circuit suddenly finds itself with two major races while Jerez hosts a second European GP, and Jarama is quickly fading from the picture. The Superbike Championship, which was last held at Jarama in 1991, has apparently moved to Albacete permanently.

Barcelona has plenty of rooms — from modest to five-star — so finding a place to stay will not be a problem. For more information on rooms contact the Tourist Office, located at Passeig de Gracia, 35, Pral., Barcelona. PH: 93 215 4477.

Circuito del Jarama,
Ctra. Burgos, KM. 28,7
28.700 San Sebastian de los Reyes (MADRID)
Spain
PH: (34 1) 657 08 75
FAX: (34 1) 652 27 44

Location: Central Spain, approximately 20 miles north of Madrid.
From Madrid, take National Route I, and follow the signs to the track.

Circuit: 2.1 mile road course; 15 turns.

Major races: National Spanish motorcycle championships.

Jarama was designed by the same man who invented Zandvoort's Tarzan, and the same effect was desired here in the center of Spain — but it wasn't quite achieved. The arid Spanish terrain makes it a hot and mostly uncomfortable circuit. In addition, run-off was not up to the standards of most FIA venues. Since the success of Jerez and Catalunya, Jarama has slid even further. And the place may eventually disappear completely. The last GP was run here in 1981, the last FIM bike race was here in '88, and although the track had remained on the 1992 calendar for a WSC round, the track refused to run a championship that had less than ten

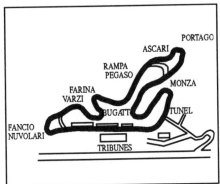

cars in the feature race, cancelling the event. Immediately the FIA followed suit by saying the track did not pass homologation requirements anyway and was not suitable for an international event.

The track starts on a downhill grade — or actually in a bowl — with the first turn being an uphill right-hander. The embankments at the end of the right hander are decent places to watch the racing. Or the hill opposite start/finish offers a good view.

Spanish economy as it is, racing here is generally inexpensive and attractive for foreign travellers, with cheap seats and large expanses of vacant spectator areas no matter where you want to watch. Hotels are inexpensive — unless you must stay in Americanized resorts, and meals are generally both appetizing and affordable. For more information on where to stay, call the Spanish National Tourist Office.

Circuito Permanente de Jerez,
Ctra de Arcos,
Km10, Apdo de Correos 1709,
Spain

PH: (34 56) 349812
FAX: (34 56) 320045

Location: Southern Spain, between Cadiz and Seville.
From Seville, take the Autoroute A4 South, turning west on the Regional Route IV toward Jerez de la Frontera, follow the signs to the track.

Circuit: 2.62 mile road circuit; 15 turns.

Major races: FIA Formula 3000 Championship; GM Lotus Euroseries Championship.

Jerez was absolutely the best viewing track on the Grand Prix trail. Seats were inexpensive, there were always plenty of open grandstands, and from any grandstand one could see at least half the track.

Unfortunately, those reasons were responsible for the abandonment of the track by the FIA in favor of the new Montmelo circuit outside Barcelona. The circuit was one of the best, but was too far from anything. A full day's drive from Madrid or Barcelona, and at least an hour from any major airports, Jerez, in the best light, was a difficult race to attend. Tickets for the GP were still too expensive for the locals, and the sparse crowds did not help the stability of the Jerez GP. Motorcycles will now dominate the calendar.

The circuit is near Jerez de la Frontera, right in in the middle of sherry country. like most of Spain, the area is hot and dry. Although rooms are easy enough to find —even as late as Friday — there is nothing in Jerez itself. The Hotel Jerez is the only game in town, but it will be completely filled with teams come race weekend. The best place to find a room will be in Seville, which is a

START/ FINISH

little over an hour by car. The circuit is off the main road, so getting in and out is easy.

The Spanish GP F1 race may be expensive and unaffordable, but the FIM race is a different story. With tickets at slightly more palatable rates for Spaniards, crowds are larger. There is still not overwhelming attendance at the bike races, but at least there are the hometown heroes —Pons, Garriga and Criville — to cheer to victory.

SWEDEN

Sweden's claim to motorsports fame rests with Ronnie Petersen and Anderstorp. When Petersen was tragically killed in 1978 at Monza, government offices were closed, and schools were dismissed in respect for the talented Swede. Following that race, the Swedish Grand Prix at Anderstorp also ended, and the 1978 race, at which Petersen finished 3rd, was the last for Sweden. Anderstorp didn't run any auto racing of consequence in 1979, presumably paying homage to Petersen. But nothing truly noteworthy ever returned to Anderstorp.

Motorcycling remained, with the 500s running at Anderstorp and the 250s running at Karlskoga. But in '81 the FIM moved the 250cc GP from Karlskoga to Anderstorp, giving Anderstorp a monopoly on what little racing it laid claim to. Although the FIM Grand Prix World Championship has been moved away from Sweden it hosted a round of the Superbike World Championship in 1993.

Sweden has the best roads in Scandinavia, with both the best network and the biggest roads of any of the four -- Norway, Denmark, Finland or Sweden. As in Finland or Norway, the long distances between destinations are filled with incredible scenery.

Roads are generally wide and fast — except, of course, in the winter months. Anyone driving in Sweden is required to have the usual green card insurance, but an International driver licence is not needed here as long as your licence is valid.

187

Speed limits are 110 KPH on the bigger roads, indicated by the "R" preceding the number of the road; or 60-80 on the smaller roads.

Sporting Authority: **Svenska Bilsportforbundet** , Storforsplan 44 Idrottens Hus, 12387, Farsta, Sweden. PH: 8 713 6000; FAX: 250 74681.

Scandinavian Raceway Anderstorp
Box 180, S-33400
Anderstorp, Sweden

PH: (46 371) 161 70
FAX: (46 371) 16177

Location: Southern Sweden, Between Jonkoping and Halmsted on National Route 26, (aprox 70 miles south east of Gothenburg) just a few miles outside Gislaved.

From Gothenburg, take the Autoroute 40 to Boras, then head south on 27 toward Gislaved or Varnamo.

Circuit Length 2.5 mile road circuit; nine turns.

Major races: FIM Superbike World Championships; Swedish Formula 3 Championship.

Since Ronnie Petersen's death, Anderstorp and automobile racing have been out of Sweden's motorsports limelight. However, cars may have been absent from Anderstorp's schedule (except for national championship racing), but it has hosted a World Championship FIM Motorcycle race for the past several years.

The track itself was not well-liked by the GP fraternity, and rumors of boycotts constantly floated through the air around GP time. The track itself was not substandard, but the pit facilities and general conditions of the place were poor. The worst problem was emergency vehicle access. There was no ring road around the circuit for ambulances, so for a few years doctors patrolled sections of the track on motorcycles — which were actually more effective than any enforced safety measures.

The track was also set up wrong for FIM GP racing. Rules concerning the length of the start/finish straight prohibited the GP from using the traditional flagstand to start the event. Bike races were thus started on the backstretch, and the lap distance was increased a half lap, so the finish was recorded at the proper finish line area.

The FIM bikes left in 1990 and were not to return until everything has been completed to FIM standards. It is now back for a round of the FIM Superbike championships,

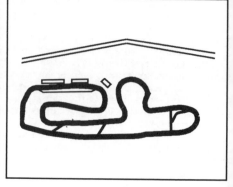

work having been completed to the satisfaction of IRTA and the FIM.

Other than the corrected problems related to rider safety, the track's major problem is its location. It's essentially in the middle of nowhere. The drive to Anderstorp is nice, but it's a very long one. The closest city of any consequence is Gothenburg, but there aren't enough rooms there. The teams all stay at the facility, in motorhomes in the paddock.

There is plenty of camping, although some of the campgrounds can get pretty rowdy. Most riders are afraid to walk through the area. There's no viewing from the infield forest — it's a big bog of mud anyway — and spectator access is limited to the outer ring of the track. One main grandstand area supplies the permanent seating for Anderstorp. The rest is an array of rather nicely laid out earth banks.

Falkenberg Motorklubb

**P.O. Box 156,
31100, Falkenburg,
Sweden
PH: (46) 346 1362**

Location: Southern Sweden, between Helsingborg and Gothenburg, 10 miles north of Falkenberg.

From Gothenburg take the Regional E6 south approximately 60 miles, or, from Helsingborg, take the E6 Regional north 50 miles.

Circuit: 1.3 mile road course; six turns.

Major races: Swedish Formula 3 Championship; Scandinavian Opel Lotus Series.

Looking a bit like a European version of Martinsville, VA, Falkenberg is a short oval, with a set of two dog-legs on the backstretch. It's tight and narrow, but most of the track is visible from any viewing area.

Swedish F3 is its biggest event, but like its peers in Scandinavia, the place has been mostly relegated to instruction and club meetings.

For more information on accommodations and other activities in the area, contact The Falkenberg Tourist Office (Falkenbergs Turistbyra) at Box 293, Sandgatan/Hogersgatan, s-311 01, Falkenberg; PH. (0346) 174 10.

Kinnekule Ring

**Box 79-53321
Gotene, Sweden**

PH: (46 8) 511 580 60

Location: Southern Sweden, between Gothenburg and Orebro, on Lake Vanern.

From Gothenburg, take National Route 45 North to 44 toward Lidkoping. Twenty miles past Lidkoping is Gotene, where the track is located.

Circuit: 1.3 mile road course; seven turns.

Major races: Swedish Formula 3 Championship.

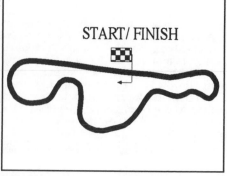

START/ FINISH

Set in a bowl, The natural surroundings of southern Sweden's Kinnekule race track make it especially attractive to race fans, who can see most of the racetrack from the main grandstands. Considering its size, it is a very fast circuit.

The track is only 18 miles from Lidkoping, and sits on the shores of Lake Vanern, just to the south east. Rooms are easier to find than for the races at Anderstorp, and even during the Swedish F3 or Scandinavian Opel Lotus Championship beds will be available in the vicinity. Call the Swedish Tourist Board, at 655 Third Ave., New York, NY 10017. PH: (212) 949-2333, for information on booking before you leave.

Ring Knutstorp,
P.O. Box 112,
S-260 23 Kagerod, Sweden

PH: (46 418) 80044/(46) 418) 80388
FAX: (46 418) 80055

Location: Southern Sweden, Between Malmo and Helsingbord.

Circuit: 1.3 mile road course; 13 turns.

Major races: Swedish Formula 3 Championship; GM Lotus Euroseries Championships.

Knutstorp's small layout has several challenging spots, and is a favorite with the Swedish F3 fraternity. When Anderstorp lost its Grand Prix, Knutstorp became the only Swedish track to host an international automobile race. The Swedish coastline and countryside is worth the visit alone.

Rooms here will be no problem, even for F3. Helsingborg will be closest, just 21 miles southeast; or Malmo will have plenty of places to stay, just a few miles to the southwest of the track, on the coast. For more information contact the Malmo Tourist Office at Hamngatan 2; PH. (40) 34 12 70; or for hotels in the area, call the Hotel Booking Office at (40) 34 12 68.

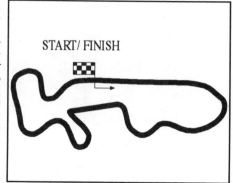

START/ FINISH

Mantorp Park
S-590 20
Mantorp, Sweden

PH: (46) 142 21740
FAX: (46) 142 21195

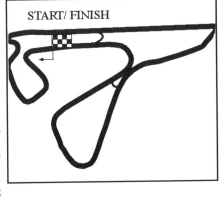

START/ FINISH

Location: South-central Sweden, on the outskirts of Linkoping, about 90 miles from Stockholm.

From Helsingbord, take National Route E4 North to Linkoping; from Stockholm, take E4 South to Linkoping.

Circuit: 2.54 mile road course; nine turns.

Major races: Swedish Formula 3 Championship.

This well designed Swedish track has the versatility of being four different circuits — one of which is a dragstrip. The Swedish Formula Three Championship is, however, Mantorp Park's only major event right now. The season generally gets started around the middle of May.

Rooms will not be as easy to come by here as with the other small tracks in Sweden. Linkoping is closest, but will likely fill up as the Swedish F3 series kicks off the season. Contact the Swedish Tourist Board, at 655 Third Ave., New York, NY 10017. PH: (212) 949-2333, for more information on booking a room in Linkoping or the surrounding areas.

UNITED STATES

The United States has a certain sense of international appeal to racing fans. The fact that the championships do not translate well to other countries, and that they remain very American gives the sometimes odd competition an identity of exclusivity. For example, Winston Cup racing, with its big heavy sedan-based race cars, is hardly attractive to manufacturers outside America. The tight racing, then, is tailor-made specifically for Americans who, manufacturers hope, will buy the products which win on Sunday. With that in mind, the show has always been of primary importance in the United States. For fans, there seem to be fewer subtleties than in, say, Formula One, where the sophistication of the machine is half of the appeal to the fan. In the U.S., almost without exception, the race itself is the appeal. From NASCAR Winston Cup racing to weekly World Of Outlaws sprint car racing, the focus is on the on-track battles.

Racing, for quite a while now, has been the number one spectator sport in the US. The statistic is based mostly on local track turnout, where local drivers with "run-what-you-brung" machinery attract the family and friends from the community each and every week in droves.

Unfortunately, motorsport in the mainstream hardly exists. Unlike in Europe where there is a national consciousness where motorsport is concerned, Americans are often quite ignorant of motorsport — especially international competition.

Media in the south and southeastern United States have always provided good coverage for motor racing; the northeast, and west coast (California being the worst on the left coast) has lacked any in-depth coverage for several years. The nation is geared toward events, not championships. Mention Indianapolis, Daytona, Sebring or Monaco and most Americans can conjure up an accurate image of what cars race there. Ask what championships are contended at those tracks and you'll get blank stares. Indy and Monaco could be the same series; they could be two races with no championship. Such is the understanding of motorsport in the U.S.

This is important information because you will get almost zero help from the person on the street unless you happen to run into a racing fan. Unlikely.

Remember, there is a difference should you attend a Winston Cup race in the south. In that context, you should have no difficulty finding information since the series is one of the most popular forms of entertainment in the south.

But in the best set of circumstances and at the biggest races, there is still a lack of community cognizance. In Britain, at Silverstone for example, ordinary folks in Oxford can tell you the best way to get to the track on a race weekend. At Laguna Seca, most Monterey residents hardly know a race is happening, let alone how to take a bus to the racetrack. It is, then, imperative that you do some advance planning. Perhaps arrive a day earlier than necessary to get your bearings, or contact the track or local chamber of commerce for detailed maps and means of transportation from your hotel.

Bus service information — for all but the urban or near-urban events — is difficult to get. There are often shuttles running, but trying to determine where, when and how is complicated. Car rental is usually the best way to go with most tracks in The States. Expensive, perhaps, but with Americans' penchant for driving everywhere, it is absolutely the easiest way to get around.

Each entry in the following pages will include chamber of commerce and local tourist information. For the championship events you wish to attend, it might be best to call the sanctioning body or track directly. Sanctioning body information is available in the first section.

Huntsville Dragway

P.O. Box 5040
Huntsville AL 35814

Track: 504 Corner Mountain Rd.
Toney AL

PH: (205) 859-0807

Location: Nine miles north of I565 in Huntsville.
From I65 North take I565 East to Highway 53 North or Jordan Lane, to mile marker 328 to Jeff Rd, turning right and following the signs. Or take I65 South to Highway 53 South in Ardmore to Mile marker 329, turn left and follow the signs.

Circuit: Eighth-mile dragstrip.

Major Races: Bama Nitrous Nationals.

Huntsville Dragway sits in small valley, amid slightly rolling green hills, bounded by cotton fields. The track has been in existence since the early fifties and although it started out as a quarter-mile track, it was just exactly a quarter-mile. There was no provision for shut down — which obviously presented a problem for 200+ MPH dragsters. The track was officially shortened to an eighth-mile track.
By the end of the 1993 season the track had repaved the end of the track out into the cotton field (which they just acquired) and the track had become a quarter-mile facility again — this time with a place to shut down....
1993 was Huntsville's second year as an IHRA track, with both years running the Nitrous Nationals. Other big shows are the Quick Eight Pro Modified races and a pair of Quick Sixteen events. In 1993, for the first time, the track hosted a PROSTAR National Motorcycle event in October. The strip holds 8,000 seats and will accommodate 500 racecars filling total capacity to about 15,000 folks.
You can stay in Huntsville with no problem. Or you camp at the Nitrous Nationals (but only at the Nitrous Nationals) if you have a motorhome or other self contained unit. Call the track for more details. For tourist information call the Huntsville Tourist Bureau at (205) 533-5723 24 hours a day.

Talladega Superspeedway

P.O. Box 777
3366 Speedway Blvd.
Talladega, AL 35160

PH: (205) 362-2261
Tickets:(205)362-9064
FAX: (205) 362-3717

Location: North Central Alabama, between Birmingham, and Atlanta just off Interstate I 20.
From Atlanta, take Interstate 20 West toward Birmingham, exiting in Talladega at exit 1#73; from Birmingham, take 20 East, exit at #168.

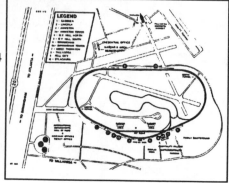

Circuit: 2.66 mile paved tri-oval; high-banked.

Major races: NASCAR Winston Cup — the Winston 500 and the Talladega Die-Hard 500; and the ARCA 500.

Built by NASCAR's Bill France as the ultimate speedway, Talladega Superspeedway is an impressive place. Constructed as the longest speedway in the United States at 2.66 miles (Indianapolis and Daytona are 2.5 miles), it's the fastest stock car track in America (holding stock car speed records of 212 MPH, set by Bill Elliott in 1987 in his Ford Thunderbird). It's the widest, with four lanes of racing and a good sized apron. It has 33-degree banking in the turns — which tower four stories tall — and a 4,000 foot backstretch. In all, it is truly a magnificent piece of work.

Talladega Superspeedway is set on the western outskirts of the Talladega National Forest. Like most of the region, the area is green and alluring during the summer, providing a quiet lazy charm during the humid days. Unlike most tracks which become desolate when abandoned between races, Talladega blends back into the country, and almost looks a natural part of the landscape. But the track is busy year round with testing of all sorts.

Geographically, Talladega is the hub of the south. It is only a day away from most major southern cities including, New Orleans, Daytona Beach, Louisville, Charlotte, Memphis, and Atlanta. In fact, the speedway boasts a 20,000,000 population living within a 300-mile radius, making it one of the most accessible speedways in America.

Entering the facility is all done via Speedway blvd, which is accessible from exits #173 and #168. Once inside you'll be awed at the size of the place, quickly realizing the significance of the motto, "The World's Fastest Superspeedway". After the initial amazement, you'll want to find your seats. Hopefully you'll have reserved tickets. The best view is from tower seats where you can see all the track.

If unable to get reserved grandstands, the infield or backstretch is a good bevy of entertainment, if you're not as picky about seeing serious racing. Do try, however, to get as close to the track as possible — the circuit is so large that the incredible speeds seem less impressive at a distance, and up-close at least you'll be able to get a real feel for the racing.

You can camp on Saturday (only), but the tickets are available on a first-come first-served basis. Once you get into the infield, you can't take your vehicle back outside until the end of the event. Camping is free outside the track, but there are no electrical hookups.

The Talladega Municipal Airport bounds the speedway to the east (just like Daytona, its sister track) and has a 6,000 foot runway. For those who fly their own planes, there's a shuttle from the airport to the track. Birmingham and Atlanta International airports will be the best way to do a weekend if you aren't fortunate enough to own a plane.

Talladega itself has very few hotels and the crews usually book those more than a year in advance. In fact, the entire area has less hotel rooms than it needs. Birmingham or Atlanta are probably easiest for the late-comer; and for those who reserve early, Anniston is a quiet southern city within 20 minutes of the track that may have rooms if you call early.

For Birmingham Hotel information call (205) 252-9825; For Atlanta Chamber of Commerce (404) 586-8403; Atlanta Convention and Visitors Bureau (404) 521-6688; and for Calvin County Chamber of Commerce (Anniston) (205) 237-3536; Pell City (205) 338 3377; Talladega Chamber of Commerce (205) 362-9075.

Firebird Race way

P.O. Box 5023
Chandler, AZ   85226

PH: (602) 268-0200
FAX: (602) 796-0531

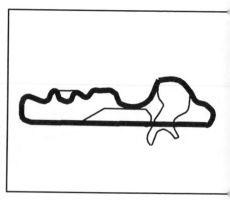

Location: Central Arizona, on the southern fringes of Phoenix, between Phoenix and Tucson.

From Phoenix, take Interstate 10 East toward Chandler, exit Maricopa Rd., approximately 15 miles from Sky Harbor Airport.

Circuit: 1.6 mile road course; 1.2 mile road course; 1.1 mile road course; quarter mile dragstrip.

Major races: NHRA Motorcraft Ford Arizona Nationals; USAC Formula 2000 Championship.

From Bob Bondurant's School of High Performance Driving's 1.6 mile road circuit, to the NHRA caliber drag strip, to Lake Firebird which is on circuit grounds, Firebird International Raceway is as versatile a venue as anywhere in the United States. The three road circuits can be modified to create several variations of layout just by moving cement barriers or by placing some strategic cones in a few critical corners. The complex offers road racing, instruction in road racing, drag racing, and International Hot Boat Association boat drag racing.

Bondurant recently finished construction on his school facilities at the far end of the drag strip, which encompasses the first corners of the existing circuit. Bondurant's track was specially designed with instruction in mind (read: wide run-off, and nothing to hit). The school, which was a fixture at Northern California's Sears Point Raceway for years, moved its base of operations to Firebird in 1990. Its opening in the winter of '89 was a huge success, and the school now offers night instruction as well as weekend classes.

The NHRA Nationals provides Firebird's biggest racing show, filling the stands in February as the second NHRA event of the season. But the IHBA regularly packs in 25,000 fans for boat racing in the watersports complex just north of the dragstrip.

Although the track is actually located in Chandler, southeast of Phoenix, you'll want to be in Phoenix unless you're only there for the racing or instruction. There are several inexpensive hotels in the area, and as with PIR and downtown F1 racing, there are more rooms in Phoenix than necessary. You'll have your pick. Official track hotels offering discounts are listed in the free track newspaper, Firebird Today, which you can receive by calling the track office.

There is little traffic in and around the area — unless you hit rush hour near the downtown area — so anywhere you stay will be just a few minutes away. If you need to be closer to Chandler call the track for more info on the handful of Chandler hotels — or call the Phoenix Metropolitan Chamber of Commerce at (602) 254-5521; or the Phoenix and Valley of The Sun Convention and Visitors Bureau at (602) 254-6500.

Phoenix International Raceway

7602 S. 115th Ave
Tolleson, AZ 85353
Or: 1313 N. 2nd St. #1300
Phoenix, AZ 85004
(office) (602) 252-3833
(Track) (602) 932-0777
Tickets: (602) 252-3833
FAX: (602) 254-4622

Location: Central Arizona, on the western edge of Phoenix, in Avondale.

From Phoenix, take Interstate 10 West to the 115th Ave exit, turning left at the stop. Follow the 115th six miles; From Los Angeles, take I10 through Arizona, exiting 115th just before Phoenix city limits.

Circuit: 1.0 mile oval; 1.5 mile road course, 11 turns.

Major races: Cart Indy Car World Series Championship; NASCAR Winston Cup Series Championship; IMSA Camel GT Series.

During the racing season, Phoenix International Raceway is easy to find; just follow traffic into the facility. But during the week, no matter what you read or see while looking for the circuit, you'll swear you're going the wrong way.

First, PIR is not in Phoenix. Not unusual; most racetracks have homes in areas other than that listed on their letterhead. But PIR feels like Mars. If you like Arizona scenery, with its Saguaro cactus, you'll love PIR. If not, then it'll likely look like one big vacant lot with a circular road stuck in the middle of it.

But fewer facilities could change so much with a crowd.

It transforms from a dusty, barren place into a world of activity. And, as with anything that happens in Arizona, weather is a major factor in its success. For those who like the desert scenery, you'll have come to grips with the climate — probably even liking it somewhat. If, however, you retreat when the mercury climbs to past 75 degrees Phoenix can bite hard. For the Indy Car race, which generally takes place in April, it's likely a hit-or-miss proposition. Still early in the year, with temperatures of 80+ common, it's still possible that some of the 17 days of yearly rain will be spilt — but don't bet on it (in fact, the race hasn't been rained out since its inception in 1964).

NASCAR in November is a different story, however. November, in any other state means the beginning of winter. In Phoenix it means the end of Summer, and there is nowhere on earth with an Indian Summer like Phoenix. It can, and generally does, get hot.

But PIR really is one of the better places to watch a race. Phoenix itself is geared toward tourism probably like no other city in the continental U.S., so when the action on the oval gets dull, discover the delights of the desert. There are at least 75 golf courses in the Phoenix area. If it's hot, and you don't approve of the heat, just cool off in your hotel pool. Besides, as they say in Arizona, "It's a dry heat"....

If you're staying in Phoenix proper, the track is 15 minutes or so to the west. Buses are nonexistent, but there are a few shuttle services from the sixteen hotels and motels affiliated with the track, each of which fills up quickly (and each of which offers racer's rates). Call the track for more information on those. Cars are

197

best for traveling to the track, and there is a good amount of parking outside the racetrack. There is no camping, but if you have a self-contained motorhome you can park it in the track lot for the duration of the weekend.

Once inside the facility, you'll need a seat unless it's race day. There's a general admission area on the hillside to the east of the tri-oval between turns 3-4, but it's only available Sunday. The best seats are the reserved grandstands overlooking start/finish, and there are several levels of quality there. In addition, seats are available on the back straight and third & fourth turns. Seats are best reserved ahead of time, especially for the NASCAR race.

There's infield parking for self-contained vehicles through the weekend at $50.00 a pop, and there are almost 500 of those available on an advance basis. Friday, for Winston Cup, a general admission ticket is available in the infield for $10 — it goes up to $15 Saturday; for Indy Car weekends, the prices are $5-$10. There's also a three-day infield package available — call the track for details.

It would be surprising to find yourself without a room in this city, considering its tourist-oriented economy, but you'll still want to book ahead of time. For more info call: Phoenix Metropolitan Chamber of Commerce at (602) 254-5521; or the Phoenix and Valley of The Sun Convention and Visitors Bureau at (602) 254-6500.

Tucson Raceway Park
12500 Houghton Rd.
Tucson, AZ   85747

PH: (602) 629-0707

Location: Southern Arizona, off highways I 10 & I 19.

Circuit: three-eighths mile clay oval.

Major races: NASCAR interseries (Sunbelt Region).

Tucson Raceway Park is located just east of Tucson's metro area. Once known as Raven Raceway, the track was recently sold and now takes on a new name as well as a different philosophy. Adopting Indy's tight-lipped stance when it comes to attendance publicity, Tucson Raceway Park refuses to publish seating capacities. Officials will say, however, that the biggest race is the Fall Spectacular, which is run in conjunction with the Phoenix NASCAR race. In past years Kenny Schrader, Jimmy Spencer and Dale Earnhardt were invited to the track.

There are plenty of reasonable accommodations in Arizona's other major tourist city. Either call the track for information on the closest rooms, or call the Metropolitan Tucson Convention and Visitors Bureau at (602) 624-1817.

Yuma Speedway
95 and County 15 Highway
Yuma, AZ   85364

PH: (602) 726-9483 9488

Location: In western Arizona, 20 miles from the Mexican border and 20 miles from California. Take Interstate I8 to the 16th St. Highway 95 exit, heading right until you hit Avenue B, then left toward Mexico and five miles to the track.

Circuit: Three eighths mile clay oval.

Major Races: World Of Outlaws Sprint cars.

Yuma Speedway sits atop a steep hill, overlooking Indian land. A Bingo parlor across the street from the track draws from the Yuma area, and feeds the racing occasionally. The Mexican border is also just a few minutes drive from the clay oval.

The place is hot and dry all year long, with 1-2 inches of rain per season. Although flooding may be common to Yuma, it isn't a problem at Yuma Speedway's hillside location.

The 3,800 seat facility is just 3-4 miles away from downtown Yuma, and that's the best place to find rooms. The track averages 1,800 people per race, with the WoO show selling out. Camping is possible in the big parking lot, and rooms are plentiful a few minutes from the circuit.

I 30 Speedway
12297A New Benton Highway - I 30
Little Rock, AR

Mailing: 2900 Old Jacksonville Hwy.
Little Rock, AR   72117

PH: (501) 455-4567

Location: In Little Rock, off Interstate 30 East at the County Line exit, just south of I 30.

Circuit: quarter mile high-banked red clay oval

Major Races: World Of Outlaws.

I 30 Speedway has existed since 1955 as a fixture of the Arkansas landscape in what was the outskirts of Little Rock. Recently, the city annexed the area, and it now has been incorporated and is a part of Little Rock.

The World Of Outlaws is the biggest show of I 30's season, but ranking up there with the WoO date is the October running of the Short Track Nationals. This will mark the seventh running of the event; so far the first four have been won by Steve Kinser, who captured three, and Sammy Swindell, who won once. This season's other highlight, the Short Track Nationals, is usually held late October. Racing is usually held Saturday nights here.

70 acres of I 30 exist, so you can camp if you wish. There is adequate space but no hookups of showers. I 30 has a list of hotels that work with them, and will be happy to give you racer's rates. For more on accommodation information, call the track.

Antioch Fairgrounds Speedway
Office: P.O. Box 430
Antioch, CA   94509

Office: (510) 625-8302
Track: (510) 754-0222

Location: Northern California, in the Sacramento River Delta, 40 miles east of San Francisco, off State Highway 4 at the Summersville off-ramp at 10th and L St.

Circuit: Quarter-mile clay oval.

Major races: NASCAR interseries (Pacific Coast Region).

Antioch Fairgrounds Speedway sits in the Contra Costa County Fairgrounds in Antioch. The quarter-mile dirt track has hosted NASCAR Winston Racing Series events for 30 years, but its biggest race is not a NASCAR sanctioned event. Northern California's NARC series race, run in July, is the largest of the season.

The Antioch area is warm and inviting during the summer, although the breeze coming off the Sacramento Delta can be biting at night. Rooms are available in Antioch, Concord, or Pittsburgh. Camping can be found at Bethel Island and Rio Vista a few miles from the track in the Delta.

Bakersfield Speedway
Bakersfield, CA

PH: (office) (805) 393-3373

Location: Southern California, just north of Bakersfield in Oildale. From Bakersfield take State Route 99 North to SR 65 North, and follow 65 one mile to Standard Rd. Follow Standard Rd. two miles east to Chester, then approximately one mile north to the track.

Circuit: Quarter-mile semi-banked clay oval.

Major races: World of Outlaws Sprint Car Championship Shootout; USAC Midgets; NASCAR Southwest Tour.

Bakersfield Speedway is four miles from downtown Bakersfield, in Oildale, and it can be oppressively hot here, with Summer nights sometimes staying well above the 95 degree mark. Water seems to be an effective means of keeping dust down on the racing surface, although it has to be frequently doused during the brutal summer months.

The track has been in existence some 45 years. Probably its most famous graduates were the Mears brothers — both Rick and Roger each ran here in the pro-mod division. It seats 5,000. For hotel information call the track.

Cajon Speedway

P.O. Box 7
El Cajon, CA   92022
PH: (619) 448-0751

Location: In El Cajon, 20 miles west of San Diego, off Interstate I 8 on Highway 67, next to Bradley Airport.

Circuit: Three-eighths mile paved oval.

Major races: NASCAR interseries (Sunbelt Region); USAC TQ Midgets, Midgets.

Although the area is about as American as you'll find, Cajon Speedway might as well be in Mexico. The terrain is Baja-California-dry. Wing Ave, where the track is located is brown grass with sparse vegetation.

The Southwest Tour or Supermodified show is the biggest of the year, although the facility usually gets close to selling out its 5,500 seats during regular Saturday night shows. There is no camping at the track, but El Cajon has plenty of inexpensive rooms.

Cal Expo State Fairgrounds Speedway

1009 14th St.
Sacramento, CA   95814
Track: 18240 S. Vermont St.
Sacramento, CA
PH: (916) 446-7223

Location: Central California, in Sacramento, at the State Fairgrounds on Arden Wy, just east of Interstate Business I 80, at the Cal Expo exit.

Circuit: One-mile dirt oval.

Major races: AMA Camel Pro Series; USAC Silver Crown Championship.

Located in eastern Sacramento, at the Sacramento State Fairgrounds complex, Cal Expo Fairgrounds Speedway is one of the best one-mile ovals in the state, with the AMA national riders really favoring the place.

The area itself is warm during the racing season, and even the October finale is pleasantly comfortable. The humidity of the Sacramento Central Valley is not usually oppressive, although occasionally it can push the mercury past the 90 degree mark at night — which does become distressing at times. Sacramento has plenty of inns, and even though Sacramento State University is in session during both AMA dates, there will be no problem getting a room nearby.

For more information, call the Sacramento Visitor's Bureau at (916) 442-7644, or call either the Fairgrounds office or the promoter's office.

Calistoga Speedway

P.O. Box 344
Calistoga, CA   94515

PH: (707) 942-5111

Location: In Northern California's Napa Valley, 70 miles north of San Francisco.

From San Francisco, take US Highway 101 to Highway 37 West. From 37, head north on 29 toward Napa, to Fair Way and the Napa County Fairgrounds, where the track is located.

Circuit: Half-mile clay oval; semi-banked.

Major races: World of Outlaws Sprint Car Championship Shootout.

Calistoga Fairgrounds Speedway is located in the scenic Napa Valley, and hosts only a handful of events each year — but all are excellent shows. Northern Auto Racing Club racing dominates the action when the World of Outlaws are not in town. Local racers are talented, but it's the beautiful, warm Napa Valley summer nights that make the visit worthwhile.

Do some wine tasting up the road in St. Helena or Sonoma, or stop in following a day at Sears Point (about 20 minutes away) for a quality dirt track show. Rooms are available in either Napa or Vallejo (see the Sears Point listing).

Carlsbad Raceway

1819 Via Gavilan
San Marcos, CA   92069
PH: (619) 727-1171 (619) 744-1414

Location: In San Marcos, just north of Del Mar, 20 miles from San Diego, seven miles off Highway I 5 on Business Park Drive.

Circuit: 1.7 mile road course; 1/4 dragstrip; 1.9 mile motocross course; one-eighth mile clay oval.

Major races: SCCA Regionals; AMA National Motocross.

Carlsbad Raceway will always be remembered as the home of the FIM International Motocross Championship, hosting the premier series' only stint in the U.S. for 19 years. The race disappeared in 1989, but the AMA still runs National Motocross events here.

The facility has motorcycles on the motocross track every Saturday from 8:00 AM -4:00 PM; drag racing every Saturday from 3:00 PM to 7:00 PM on the quarter-mile strip; dirt oval-track racing every other Saturday night — the 2nd and 4th Saturdays of each month; plus, every Sunday there's either a major off-road race, an SCCA road race, or possibly a large drag race — or a combination of all three. The eighth-mile oval runs just about everything under the sun, from motorcycles, to go-karts, to mini sprints, to full-bodied cars.

The 150-acre facility has no camping, but there are campgrounds on the State Beaches, which are a few miles away from the facility. Several hotels are located off I 5, just a few miles away.

Fresno District Fairgrounds

1125 Chance Ave.,
Fresno, CA 93702
(209) 453-3247
FAX: (209) 453-3226

Location: In Fresno, five miles off I 99 at the Ventura St. exit, following Ventura to the track.

Circuit: One mile dirt oval.

Major Races: AMA 600cc Championship

The Fresno County Fairgrounds hold some 5,000 seats, most of which filled up for the 1991 running of the 600 cc Championship. 1992 marked the second race at the facility, and it has been permanently omitted from the schedule. There is no weekly show here; this race is the only thing of its kind during the season, and it does not run during the fair.

In 1992, the AMA Grand National series made a stop at Fresno, but the track was reportedly considered too bumpy to run. Although practice went fine, and riders felt it would be a decent track for the final, the surface deteriorated, and both Harley-Davidson riders — the top two in the championship — refused to race. The unfolding of that race did not enhance Fresno's image, and it will likely be a while before it recovers.

There is camping at the track, and there are hookups, although they are limited (not all campers will have electricity here). It is located in California's Central Valley, home of most of America's cotton crop, and it is generally hot during the summer.

It will be easiest to stay in Fresno, and the track can give you a list of hotels in the area if you call ahead.

King's Speedway

801 South 10th Ave.
Hanford, CA 93230

Office: P.O. Box 14
Hanford, CA 93232

PH: (office) (209) 584-3318
(track) (209) 582-3478

Location: Central California, mid-Central Valley, roughly between Fresno and Bakersfield, approximately 140 miles north of Los Angeles.

From Bakersfield, take State Route 99 to 198 West to Hanford and 10th Av. exit, following 10th Ave. one mile to the King's County Fairgrounds and the speedway.

Circuit: One-third mile clay oval; slightly banked.

Major races: World of Outlaws Sprint Car Championship Shootout.

Track officials just call it "central valley flat", meaning grapes and cotton may be more at home in the valley heat than racecars. Average summer days range from 100-105 degrees at Hanford's Kings Speedway ... but of course, it's considered dry heat.

Some of the best California sprint car drivers compete here often, including Chuck Miller and Jimmy Sills, who both race cars owned by gentlemen who live in Hanford. The place seats 4,300, and when WoO comes to town it occasionally fills to 5,000. Stay in downtown Hanford, or at the Holiday Inn in Visalia 30 miles from Hanford — which is the headquarters for WoO when they're in town. For more hotel information call the track.

Laguna Seca Raceway
P.O. Box SCRAMP
Monterey, CA 93942

PH: (408) 648-5111
Tickets: 800 367-9939
Or: (408) 648-5100
FAX: (408) 373-0533

Location: Coastal central California, between San Francisco and Monterey. From San Francisco, take U.S. Highway 101 South, exiting at State Highway 68 West through Salinas, and 12 miles to the main entrance; from Los Angeles, take 101 North, exiting same.

Circuit: 2.23 miles, 11 turns

Major races: CART Indycar World Series Championship; FIM World Championship Grand Prix Motorcycle races; Monterey Historic Automobile Races; IMSA Camel GT; AMA Nationals.

Laguna Seca Raceway's latest claim to international motor racing fame has been the FIM International Motorcycling Grand Prix — the most prestigious motorcycle race in the U.S.. Up until the beginning of the '92 season, it was something of a rallying point for Americans who, until 1988, hadn't had an American venue on the championship calendar in some 20 years. Politics ended the successful race, and for 1992 there was no U.S. GP.

But in 1993 the race returned, and its late date on the calendar will make it more popular than ever before. The race, which falls in September, will be the penultimate event of the season, and the World Championship may be decided in California.

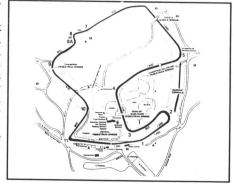

The FIM race will make it five for Laguna: the second AMA Superbike race (mid-April) the IMSA GT (late July); the Monterey Historics (late Aug); the GP; and October's IndyCar finale (early October). Other than the Russell School interseries races there are no other spectator events.

Laguna is located on the outside edge of the Fort Ord Army installation, and was at one time on

land leased from the military — although now it sits atop Parks and Recreation land, and is called Laguna Seca Recreation Area.

The full name is significant since "recreation" connotes camping, which Laguna indeed has. If possible, camping is the best alternative to dealing with the long waits in the car while trying to get into and out of the circuit. Lately, campspots have been very limited and increasingly more popular. So book early.

Keep in mind that Laguna Seca is run on a non-profit basis. Except for the half-dozen permanent office staff, the facility is run completely with the help of unpaid volunteers. All proceeds from the track go to Northern California charities. Bearing that in mind, you will cheerfully overlook some of the problems these temps may cause. Ticket holders are often given wrong information. It isn't done maliciously, nor is it from stupidity. These people are doing the job out of the goodness of their heart, and under the circumstances do a pretty good job — although criticism to the contrary probably keeps the facility from being truly international caliber. With the constant changes in voluntary personnel, traffic is constantly being diverted out of the facility in different directions each season, making a predetermined route nearly impossible.

Sometimes you'll be able to drive straight in, but occasionally you'll be forced to park your car at a parking area at the main entrance and take a shuttle up to the circuit, which is about a half-mile away.

The biggest headache of Laguna is travelling to and from the circuit. In 1991, for CART, Laguna sold out for the first time in its history, and people arriving without tickets were told to go home. Unbelievably, it was also one of the most frustration-free races ever held, and traffic control was excellent. In 1992 the parking was increased and the crowd was bigger, but nobody was turned away.

Although there is only one major entrance to the track there are several other less travelled ways into Laguna. The best way into the facility is probably the back entrance, which actually winds right through the army base storage lot, and into the area behind turns 9, 10, and 11. To get to the rear entrance from Monterey, head north on Hwy 1 to Reservation Road, taking the exit east toward Salinas (coming from Santa Cruz, or the San Francisco Bay Area, take the same exit on the opposite side of the freeway). Approximately four miles down Reservation Road, on the right hand side, there will be a small sign (keep an eye out!) for the track, follow directions from there through the back entrance. From Salinas, take Reservation Road west from Hwy 68 and turn left into the facility about ten miles from the junction.

Once you find your way into the facility, if you've already purchased a ticket, sit down and watch. The grandstands in the new addition — which comprise turns 3,4, & 5 — are great seats. But check out the sparsely populated start/finish straightway. Drivers coming out of turn 11 are intimately close to people in those grandstands. And considering that the pits are right across the track, you'll be able to see everything during a stop. In addition you'll see up the hill into turns 9 & 10, plus a bit of turns 4 & 5. When the bikes are here you'll watch the 500s try to hold down wheelies exiting the corner; for the Indycar race, the entrance of 11 is the main passing zone, and where Rick Mears lost the Marlboro Challenge when his fuel pickup failed in this last corner on the final lap in 1992.

If you like a little bit more adventure, and don't want seats, settle for the top of the infield hill, or the hill overlooking turn two; both are good viewing areas, and you can spread a blanket, eat a picnic lunch, and watch almost the entire track without ever moving. Do, however, go to the corkscrew for a few moments. Television never does it justice; the drop-off is so severe that drivers have to commit to an apex they can't see until they're in it.

Monterey and Carmel are expensive, whenever you go. If you're travelling on a budget, Salinas is the best place to stay — although the innkeepers in Salinas have calendars too, and know what's going on in the area, raising prices accordingly. Since you'll probably want to drive anyway, consider Gilroy, or even farther up 101. It may take you 45 minutes to get to the track, but that's only 25 minutes more than it will take everyone else, and rooms are cheaper, and easier to get.

If you can stay in either Carmel or Monterey the extra funds spent will probably be worth it. Unlike many resorts, where there is always something better which you can never afford, in Monterey and Carmel there are very few outrageously expensive, and ostentatious hotels. Most are rather humble accommodations in serene locations — which is why everyone wants to go there in the first place.

The Monterey Aquarium, Pebble Beach, and the 17 Mile Drive are main attractions. But for those who know their famous roads, Hwy 1 is not to be missed. One of the two sections of Hwy 1 worth driving is below Monterey, which passes through Big Sur's spectacular forests.

Flying into Monterey is as expensive as it is difficult. The airport is just west of the racetrack, and it is only a municipal airport. The best way in is via San Jose, or even SFO or Oakland International — only 20 minutes north of San Jose for each. There's a bus that goes right past the entrance of the circuit run by the Monterey-Salinas Transit System, and recently has been free to ticketholders.

For lodging information for the Monterey area, call the Peninsula Chamber of Commerce at (408) 649-3200; or call Bay Lodging at (408)646-1426; or Roomfinders at (408) 624-1711; or (408) 646-9250.. For more on the bus service to the track call The Monterey Salinas Transit System at (408) 899-2555.

Grand Prix Association of Long Beach
100 W. Broadway
Suite 679
Long Beach, CA   90802

PH: (213) 437-0341
FAX: (213) 436-3703
Tickets: (213) 436-9953

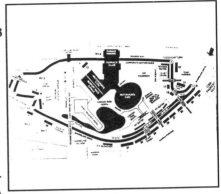

Location: Southern California, 25 miles south of Los Angeles.

From LAX Airport in Los Angeles, take Interstate 405 to I 710 (Long Beach Freeway) bear South to Downtown Long beach, following signs to the Grand Prix circuit.

Circuit: 1.67 miles, 12 turns.

Major races: CART Indy Car World Series Championship; SCCA Trans-Am Championship; Toyota Atlantic; Firestone Indy Lights.

Long Beach was originally designed to be a modern day Monaco. Chris Pook's idea of running a Formula One race through the streets of the then overlookable Long Beach was, in hindsight, a naively ambitious plan. If you want to thank someone — or point a finger at the guy who began the ball rolling toward the U.S.'s proliferation of street circuits — it was Pook. But one has only to look at the changes since the F5000 cars first ran in the streets in 1975 to see what economic impact the street race has had.

Long Beach climbed out of its austere industry-oriented condition to become, indeed, something of a Monaco-West. The new Hyatt Regency Hotel now adorns Shoreline Drive and the man-made lagoon and surrounding grounds add some class to the already fascinating main straightway. Sailboats line the coast during race weekend, and building continues as the Grand Prix returns for its second decade.

Although now run as an Indy Car race, it's certainly a permanent fixture on the calendar, and should remain a money-maker for some time. Long Beach will always be remembered as a Formula One circuit. It's now known as the final tune-up before Indianapolis. Following the opener at Phoenix, Long Beach is the last chance to take a lead in the points, sort out the car, or just plain get used to the new season.

When Indy Cars first came to Long Beach attendance faltered a bit, but the crowds are back, and things are as hectic as ever. As with all street circuits, the best seats are bought and paid for. A general admission ticket at Long Beach is not worth much if you really want to see racing. On the other hand, if you want to party and wander, then go with the GA tickets — plus, you can always sit in the GA bleachers at the shoreline kink.

If, however you are a bit more timid, and take your racing seriously, reserve a ticket. Although the seats on start/finish are the best, there is probably no bad seat at Long Beach, and each will give you a good view of the racing.

Finding a room won't be extremely difficult, providing you have a pocketful of money. If that isn't the case, you might have a tough time. The closest rooms are expensive; the moderately priced rooms are unavailable; and the rest are too far away. And being Los Angeles, driving in and out Friday and Saturday won't be a picnic.

Getting from the nearby regions of Long Beach or surrounding cities is probably best done by bus. Buses stop on Ocean Blvd, and lines connect every part of the LA Basin. For more information call the Southern California Rapid Transit District at (213) 626-4455.

Parking near the circuit is not as bad as somewhere like Detroit, but it is limited. The biggest parking lot — just across from the track's main entrance at Ocean Blvd. and Locust Ave — is open during the race and can be used by race fans. But get there early... you can use the extra time to see the Queen Mary (the Spruce Goose has been moved out of state).

Tourist information can be found by calling the Long Beach Chamber of Commerce, or better yet, the Greater Los Angeles Visitors and Convention Bureau at (213) 629-0711.

Merced Fairgrounds Speedway
Office: P.O. Box 66588
Scotts Valley, CA   95066
Office: (408) 438-3210
Track: (209) 772-6894

Location: Central California, in the Central Valley, off State Highway 99.

Circuit: Quarter-mile clay oval.

Major races: NASCAR interseries (Pacific Coast Region).

Blighted with typical mid-Central Valley fog most of the year, even on the days the fog lifts early at Merced Fairgrounds Speedway it almost always returns by nightfall — just in time for racing.

The quarter-mile dirt track is located in the Merced County Fairgrounds, and the premier division is the Cal-Mod division. NASCAR hosts three major late model stock car shows annually; and a major Figure 8 race takes place in October as well. Accommodations for the 5,000 seat facility are easily located in Merced .

Mesa Marin
P.O. Box 9518
Bakersfield, CA   93389

PH: (805) 366-5711

Location: Southern California, in Bakersfield, 10 miles east of U.S. Highway 99, south of State Highway 178.

Circuit: Half-mile paved oval.

Major races: NASCAR Winston West Championship; NASCAR Southwest Tour; SCCA Formula Mazda; ACRL; and Sports 2000.

Mesa Marin reckons itself the fastest half-mile track west of the Mississippi. The facility has 7,000 seats, most of which are generally occupied when the Winston West or Southwest Tour cars come to the fast track. It is also becoming an oval which is successfully being attacked by road racers, with formula cars running here more and more often. The track is also often used for movie, television, and film production.

You'll be best suited by staying in downtown Bakersfield, or on the outskirts. The track can provide you with more information on the closest lodgings.

Orange Show Speedway

P.O. Box 5749
San Bernardino, CA 92312

PH: (714) 888-5801
Tickets: (714) 884-0178

Location: Southern California, near Riverside off Interstate I 210, and the Orange Show Rd exit, then take E St. two blocks to the speedway.

Circuit: Quarter-mile paved oval.

Major races: NASCAR interseries (Sunbelt Region); USAC full Midget series.

Orange Show Speedway boasts of being the largest of the smallest. The 10,000 seat stadium is one of the biggest in the state in terms of spectator room, but is one of the smallest paved ovals at a quarter-mile. Located in an ex-football stadium, the facility has several different shows, including Super Vs and a unique Model A Clash.

The area around the track is hot and dry during the summer. It's a good place to catch some California sun. For information regarding hotels in the Riverside area call the track, or Riverside Visitors Bureau at (619) 683-7100.

Palm Springs Road Race

Office: 10701 Riverside Dr.
North Hollywood, CA   91602

992 4353
PH: (818) 506-4661
(818) 506-0244

Circuit: 1.3 miles; eight turns.

Location: Downtown Palm Springs, around the Windham Hotel and Palm Springs Convention center area.

Major races: Vintage Road Racing.

Palm Springs' Grand Prix may not be as serious a motorsports event as, say, a Formula One race through the streets of Monaco, but as historic car shows go, however, it's as good as any in the world. And the city planners take it seriously enough, bringing in expensive concrete barriers, and arranging a circuit that would be the envy of most pro racing street circuits.

The race is open to any vintage

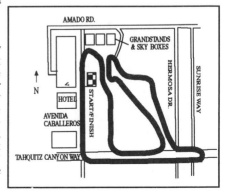

or historic racecars — and any driver, licensed or not, provided he or she has a car that fits a historic classification. Although there were problems with the original promoter, Rick Cole (of exotic car auction car fame) has recently become a five-year promoter of the event, and will help its image by holding a classic car auction during the race weekend.

The race is not the most competitive event on the planet, although racing notables like Bob Bondurant, Brian Redman, Roger Ward, Parnelli Jones, George Follmer, and Denise McCluggage all show up to do some hot laps. Ticket prices have been cheap in the past, and may eventually be free. But the event is for charity, with all the proceeds going to local charitable organizations — so pay if they ask.

The Rick Cole auctions, held Friday, Saturday, and Sunday, are the real attractions here. There are generally three different types of vehicles sold in Palm Springs: Friday's auction is based upon sports and racing cars; Saturday is devoted to motorcycles; and Sunday is for collectable cars, in general.

Obviously, you'll stay in Palm Springs, and rooms should be no problem during the event, but you'll have to make reservations early. For more information on rooms during the race call the Palm Springs Chamber of Commerce at (619) 325-1577. Or call Southern California Hotel Reservation Service (800) 527-9997; Accommodation Host at (800) 347-4678; or PS 800 at (800) 472-3788.

Placerville Speedway
704 Vine Ave
Roseville, CA 95678

Track: El Dorado County Fairgrounds
Placerville Dr., Placerville. CA

PH: (916) 626-3680

Location: 55 miles north east of Sacramento, in the El Dorado County Fairgrounds, a half-mile off U.S Highway 50, on Placerville Dr.

Circuit: Half-mile banked clay oval.

Major races: World Of Outlaws Sprint Car Shootout.

Just an hour from the Casinos of Nevada's Lake Tahoe and an hour from Sacramento, Placerville Speedway sits in the scenic El Dorado County foothills, and is about as rustic a California venue as you'll find off the main highway. The drive to Placerville is worth the time.

The speedway, which will sell-out when WoO comes through, can hold 3,000. In fact, the place is pretty crowded on a weekly basis as well. There are 28 shows per year from April to October. Make sure you head up the hill on Highway 50 to Lake Tahoe for a day at one of the most beautiful gambling resort areas in the world.

There are several hotels in Placerville, but there are also many along the way to the town in either direction. Keep track as you pass them, so in the unlikely event of a fully booked Placerville city, you can backtrack to the one that struck your fancy. The World of Outlaws headquarters is at the Placerville Inn.

Los Angeles Fairplex
Pomona Ca,
P.O. Box 5555
Glendora, CA   91740
PH: (818) 914-4761 FAX: (818) 963-5360

Location: Southern California, 35 miles east of Los Angeles.
From LAX International Airport, take Interstate 405 North to I 10, exiting at the Pomona Exit and following signs to the track.

Circuit: Quarter-mile dragstrip; one-mile dirt oval.

Major races: NHRA Winternationals, and the NHRA Winston Finals; AMA Grand National Dirt Track Championship.

In 1992, the NHRA and the Los Angeles County Fairplex signed a fifteen-year agreement granting the sanctioning body continued use of the strip located at the west end of the L.A. Fairplex. The NHRA plans on stepping up and permanently upgrading what doubles as the Fair parking lot.

Pomona had been the least modern of any NHRA Winston venue on the 20-event schedule. The venerable drag racing facility wasn't outdated by any means, but just wasn't as sparkling-pretty as most of the NHRA tracks.

The venue is the second-oldest in the NHRA series, and hosted the Winternationals since 1959 (the US Nationals at IRP is the oldest). The season finale, the Winston Finals, is also held at Pomona.

Pomona is a major part of drag racing's history. This is one of the tracks that created interest in this uniquely American form of racing. Southern California youths were drag-racing crazy through the '60s — and the two races a year at the Los Angeles Fairplex continue to be a pair of the most successful in the country.

The dragstrip, in actuality, doesn't exist at any other time of the year than February and October. It's really a parking lot of the LA Fairplex, and when the Nationals come through, the place is transformed into a racetrack — complete with lights, press facilities, grandstands, guardrails... and drag racing.

The dirt oval, which the AMA uses for its championship is the horse race track during the fair months, and is transformed into a motorcycle track for bike racing. For two-wheeled racing, the fairgrounds are already set up with parking and seating.

The dragstrip is located just off the Arrow Highway across from a municipal airport — which many drivers use to get in and out of the place. The signs for the NHRA races will change when the tour comes to Pomona, so if you've been to the fair, perhaps for AMA racing, and are determined to use the same parking facilities, well, you'll have a very long walk. Follow the direction as posted — they really will get you closer to the strip.

Hotels are plentiful in the LA Basin, but in the immediate area rooms are rather difficult to come by. But nothing is ever far from anything in LA ... unless you try to get there during rush hour. Try Montclair, Upland, Ontario (near the airport); Covina and West Covina. You'll have no problem finding a room as late as Saturday night.

Bearing that in mind; it's so much easier driving to find a room than hassling with a phone call, and then trying to find the hotel once you're there. But in case you want to do it that way, call the Greater Los Angeles Visitors' and convention Bureau at (213) 689-8822.

Although there are buses in the area (Southern California Rapid Transit — 213 626-4455 — can give you more information), you'll probably want to drive — everyone else does.

211

Redwood Acres Raceway
5503 Walnut Dr.
Eureka, CA   95501

PH: (707) 442-3232
Office: (707) 443-2118

Location: Northern Coastal California, approximately 120 miles south of the Oregon/California border, off State Highway 101.

Circuit: Three-eighths mile oval.

Major races: NASCAR interseries (Pacific Coast Region).

Redwood Acres Raceway, in the heart of California's scenic Redwood Forest, is about 3-4 miles from the coast. It's located on Eureka County Fairgrounds property, and the normal grandstands hold 2,500. The fairgrounds have portable bleachers which appear for the bigger Winston West and Southwest Tour races.

The track is 100 miles south of the Oregon border, and the area is a campers paradise. KOA is just two miles from the track, plus there's other camping in the vicinity as well. If you get lucky, there are 10 RV hookups available at the fairgrounds, and there is abundant tent camping available on the premises as well.

Santa Clara County Fairgrounds
P.O. Box 1239
Soquel, CA 95073

PH: (408) 462-6101

Location: Northern California, just south of the San Francisco Bay Area, in San Jose.

From San Francisco, take U.S. Highway 101 to Tuly Rd, heading west a mile-and-a-half to the Santa Clara County Fairgrounds and the speedway.

Circuit: One-third-mile banked clay oval/One mile dirt oval.

Major races: AMA Camel Pro Series; World of Outlaws Sprint Car Championship Shootout

Santa Clara County Fairgrounds third-mile track is transformed into the country's premier AMA one-mile when the AMA Grand National comes through town. The series used to spin through twice a year, but starting in '92 the famous mile only hosts one event, set for the beginning of the season in April.

The third-mile sits inside the mile oval, and each year the earth moving equipment growls on the front stretch, and out of a week's worth of noise and mess comes the best AMA race of the year.

The Mile attracts 15,000 per event and is famous as being the most exciting race on the Camel Tour. The San Jose mile is famous for its last lap wins, and drafting here is more important than anywhere else. The track is incredibly fast, and it has become one of the toughest and most satisfying races to win. In 1990 there were 49 passes for the lead in the 25-lap main event.

Although the event is a fixture, it was supposed to have had its swan-song

212

in 1988. It somehow survived, and the races are still being run here. 1992 marked the 40th running of the San Jose Mile.

When the big track is not being used, its third-mile little sister hosts some pretty respectable events as well. The biggest show is the World of Outlaws, followed by the Golden State Challenge, Winston Super Sprints and, during the fair, a destruction derby. The regular program is a weekly NASCAR show. The small track still manages to hold 7,200.

Reports at one time were that NASCAR was willing to invest in the Santa Clara County facility, with plans to pave the mile for a Winston Cup race. It seems it was nixed by the locals... although there is still a possibility it may happen.

The San Jose area has plenty of rooms and there is never a problem finding one. There is also camping on the grounds. Contact the fairgrounds for more info: (408) 295-3050.

Santa Maria Speedway
Office: P.O. Box 1270
Morro Bay, CA   93443
PH: (805) 922-2233
Office: (805) 466-4462

Location: Southern California, between San Luis Obispo and Santa Barbara, approximately 110 miles from Los Angeles. Located on Hutton Rd., one quarter-mile north of U.S. 101 and the Bakersfield interchange.

Circuit: One-third mile clay oval; high-banked.

Major races: World of Outlaws Sprint Car Championship Shootout; Golden State Challenge Sprint Cars.

Santa Maria Speedway is located 12 miles from the Pacific coast, one mile from Santa Maria — just past the Santa Maria river (dry). A half-hour south of San Luis Obispo, the track is a nice spot for a California getaway.

Built in 1964, the speedway is located under a coastal mesa. Although water is a problem in the winter, it never floods in the summer months. During the summer the temperatures get up to about 100 degrees, and the clay has to be watered three times a week.

There are 2,000 permanent seats, but the hillsides can accommodate another 1,500 or so — so bring a blanket or lawn chair. Ramada Inn acts as headquarters when the Outlaws come to town, and you can call the track for information on other hotels in the area.

Saugus Speedway
P.O. Box 901
Santa Clarita, CA   91380

PH: (805) 259-3886

Location: Southern California, just north of the Los Angeles Basin, three miles off Interstate 5 at Valencia Blvd..

Circuit: Third-mile oval.

Major races: NASCAR Winston West; Southwest Tour Championship; NASCAR interseries (Sunbelt Region); USAC Sprint Car Championship.

Sitting just a few miles east of Valencia, Saugus Speedway's climate is hot during the summer racing months, with temperatures in the 95 degree range. The heat is less stifling than one would imagine, since the place is cooled by the Santa Ana winds which rush through constantly.

It seats 6,000 racefans, and is generally full during the Winston West and Southwest Tour races. There are plenty of places to stay, since Saugus is just a short drive from Six flags Magic Mountain amusement park where rooms are abundant. If not there, then stay in Valencia or Newhall. Camping World allows a one night hookup for no charge, and is just four miles from the track. For more information call the track.

Sears Point International Raceway
Highways 37 & 121
Sonoma, CA 95476

PH: (707) 938-8448
Ticket Office: 1 (800)870-7223
FAX: (707) 938-8430

Location: Northern California, 25 miles north of San Francisco.

From SFO San Francisco International Airport, take U.S. 101 through downtown San Francisco to San Rafael and State Highway 37, following 37 six miles to 121, where the circuit is located just at the junction.

Circuit: 2.5 miles, 12 turns.

Major races: NASCAR Winston Cup Series Championship; SCCA Trans-Am Championship; NHRA Drag Racing World Championship.

Sears Point International Raceway sits at the southern end of California's beautiful Sonoma Valley, about 40 minutes from downtown San Francisco. Sears Point is one of the few tracks in the United States that has activities nearly every day of the week, and year-round scheduling. The American Federation of Motorcyclists, one of two California amateur motorcycle racing clubs, traditionally schedules 8-10 weekends of racing and instruction, the Northern California SCCA Region uses Sears for school and regional races, and Skip Barber's School of high performance driving has recently replaced Bob Bondurant as the on-track school at the Sonoma Valley venue.

Sears is a wonderful facility for novice fans. The hot California summers are nowhere as predictable as in the Napa/Sonoma Valley, when winemakers depend on the California climate, year-in and year-out. But make no mistake: this is San Francisco's track. Just 45 minutes from downtown SF, this is more a

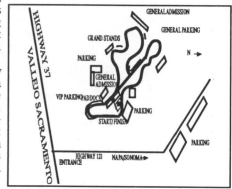

214

track of the Bay Area than of Napa.

The hills turn a golden brown sometime in May, and the circuit which winds through the baked slopes, is 70% visible from most of the general admission viewing spots. These same spots become transformed into sunny picnic areas for those uninterested in the on-track entertainment.

There are several grandstands scattered about — which are most conspicuous at the NHRA California Nationals and May's NASCAR Winston Cup race — but for the most part, the best seats are those created in the grass along the sides of the racetrack. Pit passes are available at most major events.

Turn two is probably the best place to watch. It's where the inevitable bottlenecks occur on the first lap, and from where you can see most of the track.

Seats are nice if you can get one, but don't bother killing yourself. For NASCAR the grandstands overlooking turn #2 are fantastic, but the view from up the hill on the grass is every bit as good, and it doesn't cost extra.

Pit passes are a cheap way to see cars and drivers up-close, and there are no garages, so the set-up is intimate enough where you can talk to the drivers easily. From the pits or paddock, however, there is precious little of the track that can be seen — likewise, from the start/finish grandstands — so try to park yourself somewhere on a hill around the racetrack.

There are several permanent snack bars, but as usual, the food is expensive. There is a scarcity of retail businesses in the immediate Sears area as well, so buy the food and drink you wish to consume from the city where you are staying — each has several large supermarkets. A word to the wise: California Highway Patrol monitors the exits looking for those who imbibe too heartily, so stay sober if you drive.

Although traffic to the track is normally not a problem until mid-morning on race day, it has been bad enough on occasion to have forced delays of two hours. In that case, the extra time spent going farther north and coming through the back via Sonoma on 121 is worth it... and the scenery isn't bad either. At day's end Sunday try to stay clear of the area close to the junction of 37 and 80 — it will usually be congested with Napa Valley tourists trying to get home. A short detour through downtown Vallejo should get you to 80 faster.

Most teams stay in San Rafael or Novato, but the bargains for Sears are in Vallejo, which is actually closer to the facility and easier to get to and from. For the Vallejo Chamber of Commerce, call (707) 644-5551; for San Rafael, call (415) 454-4163; but try beautiful Napa first, by calling the Napa City Hall at (707) 252-7711, or the Napa Chamber of Commerce at (707) 226-7455.

Shasta Speedway

P.O. Box 524
Redding, CA   96099

PH: (916) 221-8008

Location: Northern California, between Red Bluff and Redding, off Interstate I 5 in Anderson.

Circuit: Third-mile paved oval.

Major races: NASCAR Winston West; NASCAR Southwest Tour; Golden State Modified Series; and NASCAR interseries (Great Northern Region).

Shasta Speedway is located in the Shasta District Fairgrounds just south of Redding, Ca. The track has been in existence since 1947, and was updated in 1970 with a new paved surface. It has hosted the Winston Racing Series for 18 years, and is listed as one of the five best tracks of its type in the state. The picturesque Redding area — albeit not easy to get to — is worth the drive. Call the track for accommodation ideas.

Silver Dollar Speedway

(Office) 704 Vine Ave.
Roseville, CA   95825

Silver Dollar Fairgrounds
Fair St. Chico, CA
PH: (916) 891-6535
Office: (916) 969-7484

Location: Northern California, in the Northern Central Valley, approximately 100 miles north of Sacramento, and 170 miles northeast of San Francisco.

From Sacramento, take State Route 99 North (which joins SR 70 and SR 149) through Marysville to Chico to Park Ave, heading west on Park Ave. one half-mile to the Chico Fairgrounds, and the racetrack.

Circuit: Quarter-mile clay oval; high banked.

Major races: World of Outlaws Sprint Car Championship Shootout.

Silver Dollar Speedway is one of Northern California's few stops for the World of Outlaws tour. Those who miss the one day show at Calistoga generally make the drive north for a two or three day WoO show at Silver Dollar Raceway.

216

If the limited appearances of California WoO racing doesn't inspire you to come, then perhaps the Gold Cup — the biggest Outlaws show in California — will.

Although Chico isn't exactly the tourism capital of California, and even though the college's (Chico State University) 14,000 students have inspired hotel construction, you'll likely need to arrive early before an event to find a room (or book by phone).

Things are usually filled in Chico for WoO shows so you might consider staying in Oroville, Marysville, Paradise, or Orland. Camping is also an alternative here. The track can accommodate 144 motorhomes with complete hookups — and on occasion can be changed to accommodate as many as 500. Call the track office at (916) 969 7484 for details.

Stockton 99 Speedway
4105 N. Wilson Wy
Stockton, CA   95205

PH: (209) 463-0456

Location: Central California, off State Highway 99.

Circuit: Quarter-mile paved oval.

Major races: NASCAR interseries (Pacific Coast Region).

Stockton 99 Speedway is another hot mid-California racetrack which offers great summer night racing.

The venue seats 5,000, and the biggest event is the Fourth of July 100 lap main for Late Model stocks. Built in 1946, Stockton 99 Speedway's claim to fame is likely Ernie Irvan, who was a Late Model champion here, and who went on to become a competitive Winston Cup driver. The track is 10 miles from downtown Stockton, and rooms are easy to find there.

Ventura Raceway
2810 W. Wooley Rd.
Oxnard, CA   93030
PH: (805) 985-5433

Location: Southern California, 75 miles north of Los Angeles, just west of U.S. Highway 101 in Ventura.

Circuit: Fifth-mile clay oval.

Major races: USAC Midget Championships.

One hundred feet from the California coast, in the Ventura County Fairgrounds, Ventura Raceway holds a series of popular annual events. Known for its ambience, the area is beautiful; generally cool, with offshore breeze, but very sunny in the summer. The city itself, officially named San Buena Ventura, is very old and quaint. There are several antique shops and a Spanish mission to give it its own character.

The track is literally right on the beach, and from the stands fans can see the ocean. It seats 2,000 people, and racing takes place almost every Friday and

Saturday of the month from March to November. USAC runs once a month, as does Motocross.

A Holiday Inn is within walking distance of the fairgrounds, and an RV park is just two miles away. Camping is abundant at the beach. More information can be had by calling the Chamber of Commerce of Greater Ventura (785 South Seaward Ave, Ventura) at (805) 648 2075; or call the track.

Watsonville Fairgrounds Speedway
Office: c/o CARS Inc.
P.O. Box 729
Soquel, CA   95073-0729

PH: (408) 464-1441

Location: Central coastal California, in the Monterey Bay Area, off State Highway 1.

Circuit: Quarter-mile clay oval.

Major races: Winston NASCAR interseries (Pacific Coast Region).

Watsonville Fairgrounds Speedway entered its 36th year of racing in 1993. Located at the Santa Cruz County Fairgrounds in Watsonville — two miles from the Pacific Ocean — the area is quiet and green. There is camping available at the fairgrounds, and Watsonville is 15 miles from Santa Cruz, where there is not only lodging, but where the Santa Cruz Beach Boardwalk, and famous amusement park are located.

Watsonville was the epicenter of the 1989 California earthquake — and the turn-four grandstands had to be replaced when the tremor shook the structure apart. It was rebuilt with a better seating capacity and will now hold nearly 4,000 people. The biggest show of the year is a stock car event with fireworks around the Fourth of July. You can stay in Watsonville, but the best entertainment is in Santa Cruz.

Willow Springs International Raceway
P.O.   Box X
Rosamond, CA   93560

3500 75th St West
Rosamond, CA

PH: (805) 256-2471

Location: Between Lancaster and Mojave, 75 miles North of the Los Angeles Basin. Take SR14, exiting at the Rosamund exit and proceeding seven miles west.

Circuit: 2.5 mile road course, nine turns; three-eighths mile clay oval; 1.25 mile road circuit, 10 turns.

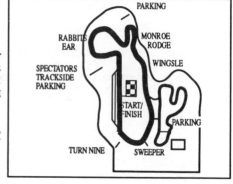

Major races: AMA Nationals; SCCA Nationals and Regionals; WERA motorcycles.

Willow Springs is known mostly as a great motorcycling track, with wide run-off areas and no armco. The hot desert-like climate makes the place a bit austere, and television crews often use it for filming because of that. Testing is also often done here by major sedan and formula car teams. AIS IndyCars, Historic car races, AMA and WERA races highlight a full season of racing. The 24 Hours of Willow Springs bike race highlights a prolific racing season at this popular circuit.

There are no grandstands at Willow, but you can see everything from anywhere on the course. Most spectators seem to congregate in the pit area, from where the entire track can be seen.

A few schools use the track as a temporary base of operations, and during the winter Willow Springs opens up the stadium and from the beginning of December to the end of February the three-eighths mile oval plays host to circle track racing. Camping is allowed at the track, but if you prefer to stay in a hotel, you'll have to go to Tehachapi, Rosamund, Mojave, or Bakersfield. Call the track for suggestions in the immediate area.

Bandimere Speedway
3051 S. Rooney Rd.
Morrison, CO   80465
PH: (303) 697-6001
FAX: (303) 697-0815

Location: Central Colorado, 10 miles from Denver, three miles south of Interstate I70 on Colorado State Highway C470, just north of Morrison, CO.

Circuit: Quarter-mile dragstrip.

Major races: NHRA Mile High Nationals.

Bandimere Speedway, located in the foothills of the majestic Rocky Mountains, caters specifically to drag racing. Unlike most venues that compromise drag racing for road racing, and vice versa, Bandimere concentrates on just the straight-and-narrow, and gives fans and participants a plethora of good drag racing events. Pre-staging is done in designated ten-laned areas, and timing and scoring areas are located directly behind the launching pads, where they should be.

Built 35 years ago by John Bandimere Sr., the track is still operated by Bandimere's son John Jr.. Bandimere's big show is the NHRA Mile Highs, generally held in July, but the track is in use from April to September, with major shows most weekends. In addition, the track is used for many non-racing activities, such as bicycle racing, roller-blade racing, concerts, soap box derbies and general hospitality events.

There is abundant parking, which is free with Pit-Pass purchase, and seating prices are based on how close to staging you wish to be. Virtually all seats offer a panoramic view of both the track and the city skyline of Denver. For '93 a 700-seat luxury box was constructed at a 40 degree angle to the strip along with a 10,000 square foot deck for more prime seating and hospitality tents.

Tickets range from $8 to $27, and the combination pit pass/parking pass is $6. Accommodations are not a problem, and the Mile High Nationals, which attract better than 75,000 people each year, should be an easy booking here.

Booking early is still advisable since the cheaper rooms will go quickly. For ticket prices on any event, along with hotel and attraction information, call (303) 697-4870, and following the recorded message, stay on the line and a representative will answer any of your questions.

For West Chamber of Commerce serving Jefferson County, call (303) 233-5555; for Golden Chamber of Commerce, call (303) 279-3113; for Denver Metro Convention and Visitors Bureau, call (303) 892-1112.

LaJunta Raceway

319 Colorado Ave.
P.O. Box 321
LaJunta, CO   81050
PH: (719)   384-8454/
(719) 384-5976

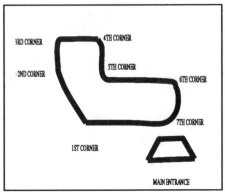

Circuit: 1.7 mile road course; 7 turns.

Location: Eastern Colorado, 175 miles south of Denver, on US 50 in the Airport Industrial Park, 4 miles north of LaJunta.

Major races: SCCA Nationals and Regions; Rocky Mountain Road Racing Motorcycle Championships.

LaJunta Raceway is in what's considered the high plains of Colorado. It's flat, dry, and barren. And in the summer it's hot. The paddock area, where everything is located and where everyone congregates, is a large concrete expanse, spacious enough to accommodate an entire racing field and all the spectators that may accompany a given event. The paddock is important because there's nowhere else to watch the racing.

There are no grandstands; spectator insurance has so far prohibited it. That means no bleachers exist, and there is no access to the course. The only place to watch is from paddock. There is, however, really no need to stray from the area anyway. The place is completely flat, so the paddock is as good as anywhere to watch. Because of its lack of elevation change, the place is exceptionally safe, and good for new racers. There's lots of runoff, and the drivers really get into some high speed cornering — often prompting spins. There is camping at the edge of the paddock; and there are motels in town, at LaJunta.

Pikes Peak Hill Climb Association

135 Manitou Ave.
Manitou Springs, CO   80829
PH: (719) 685-4400

Location: central Colorado, 10 miles west of Colorado Springs, off U.S. Highway 24.

Circuit: 12.5 mile hill climb; dirt surface.

Major races: Pikes Peak Auto Hill Climb

Considering that it's really the only American hill climb with any notoriety at all, Pikes Peak is also probably the most prestigious in the world. European hill climbing is certainly better known to Europeans than it is to Americans, but European manufacturers all want to win Pike's Peak more than any European race.

This unique event requires lots of pre-planning for spectators. To do it right, you should consider getting out to the hill and watching from several different places over the three days of practice — which changes from year to year depending on what day the Fourth of July falls — to find the one place on the mountain that suits you best for the race. Practice is from sunrise until 9:00 AM, and the road is open to traffic the rest of the day. It's only fully closed on race day.

Plan on being on the side of the mountain by 5:00 am each day. Remember, once you've planted yourself on the mountain, there's no getting down until the activities come to an end at 9:00 AM. Teams will be up there and working by 4:00 am.

Each day before the event begins, you can drive your car up the mountain. Once you're parked you can walk about a bit, but strolling is curtailed by the harsh terrain. Practice is done in stages, and on three different parts of the track. Usually each competitor gets about four runs per day. For qualifying half the hill is used. Qualifying is done from the start to Glen Cove, half way up the mountain. The order of quali-

221

fication is then inverted, with the fastest qualifier running last in his division on race day.

The road is closed at 9:00 AM race day, and the race itself begins at 10:00. Race day will always be on July 4th, Independence Day.

There are really two places where most people congregate: the very top of the hill, where you can see quite a bit of the course, including the finish line; and the 11,000 foot Devils Playground — where you'll see most of the mountain and the switchbacks.

Although Devil's Playground is a better area from which to watch, the top of the mountain has its advantages: first, you can take a cog-railway from Manitou Springs to the top — which means you can leave the race early if you'd like; and second, the drivers are stuck there until the road opens again, which means you can talk to them, or at least hear what they have to say after their runs. If you'll be using the cog-railway you'll need to reserve a ticket early.

The event will cost you $8 for practice, $10 for qualifying and $15 for race day (or $20 for the whole enchilada), and you'll pay as you either board the railway or as you begin the drive up the mountain. You can camp on the mountain on Saturday night — the only time during the entire year that you can camp there. For practice, you'll want to stay in Colorado Springs, which is a few minutes drive east of Pike Peak.

If you wish to camp there are several places in the area, including Manitou Springs, and Garden of the Gods, just a few miles from the mountain. For information on lodging, call the Colorado Springs Visitors' Bureau at (719) 635-7506.

The starting line for the race is 9,390 feet and the top is 14,110 high. Be careful with alcohol. Last year 150 people were treated for altitude sickness — which was mostly induced by alcohol. Also: bring a radio and tune in to KRDO AM where you'll hear a broadcast of the runs while you're on the hill.

Pueblo Motor Sports Inc.
3701 Bijou
Pueblo, CO   81002

PH: (719) 545-0878

Location: In north Pueblo, off Highway 50, at Pueblo Blvd.

Circuit: 2.2 mile road course; 10 turns/ quarter-mile dragstrip; 1/20 mile quarter midget; motocross track.

Major races: SCCA Nationals and Regionals.

Pueblo's level, semi-arid surroundings provide a good safe venue for road racers. There are few things to hit on this tight road circuit whose front and back portions are linked by 3,000 feet of dragstrip. Located in flatlands, the track is not completely featureless, rising 30 feet in its 2.2 miles.

The prairie grass grows right up to the side of the racetrack, and

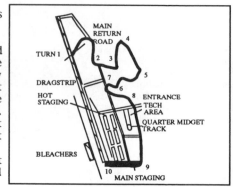

222

provides a nice slow down area for those who leave the asphalt in pursuit of the perfect lap. The armco around the control tower is about the only thing drivers can hit, but they have to do some pretty stupid driving to get that far off-line.

In addition to the road track, there's a dragstrip that has in the past hosted an NHRA Winston Divisional race. The facility also has a radio control track for miniature cars, and is in the process of building a one-half/one-third mile banked clay oval on the property.

There are grandstands on the front straightway which seats 7,000, and a good deal of the track can be seen from there. Camping at the track is free with admission. There are eight motels within three miles of the track, primarily located at the corner of I 25 and Colorado Highway 50 West.

Rocky Mountain Speedway
P.O. Box 1046
Westminster CO 80030

PH (track) : (303) 371-1600
Office: (303) 421-1978

Location: Central Colorado, northwest of Denver, seven miles north of Interstate I 70, off Exit #266 and 88th st., at 96th and Buckley.

Circuit: Half-mile dirt oval.

Major races: World of Outlaws; USAC Midgets; AMA Grand National.

Rocky Mountain Speedway is found about ten miles from downtown Denver. The track is set in the flatlands, in a rural area, and racing takes place here from April through October. The biggest show is the World of Outlaws, but the USAC races draw well. The track seats 10,000.

Headquarters for the WoO is at the Best Western Inn At The Mark during the WoO races. There is camping at the track. For more information call (303) 373-1600.

Second Creek Raceway
Route 1, Box 113
17010 88th Ave
Commerce City, CO   80222
PH: (303) 371-6661

Circuit: 1.7 mile road course; 10 turns. 32 feet wide

Location: Northeast of Denver, in Commerce City, at 88th and Buckley Rd, near the airport.

Major races: SCCA Nationals and Regional; Vintage; motorcycles.

Second Creek Raceway is set at the end of the Denver Airport, in the middle of a wheat field. Considering its surroundings, it would seem to be a fast, level track. It's not a flat track at all, containing some 75 feet of elevation changes.

The rural farming area racetrack is known for its safety, as many of the

223

Colorado SCCA tracks are. Speeds here are usually limited to about 105 mph, and few classes can exceed that mark. Although spectators are not allowed out of the viewing area — located on the west side of the track — most of the racing can be seen from the 1,100 seat grandstands in the viewing area. If the stands fill up — which doesn't happen very often — there's plenty of standing room in the same area.

There is free camping, and you can spend the entire week there if you wish. The nearest hotels are five minutes from the track in Commerce.

Lime Rock Park
Route 112,
Lime Rock, CT   06039/
P.O. Box 111
Lakeville, CT   06039

PH: (203) 435-2571
FAX: (203) 435-2573
Ticket info: (203) 435-0896

Location: Western Connecticut, roughly between New York City and Boston.

From New York, take the New York Thruway North to Exit 17 turning east on Route 84 to Taconic Parkway, turning north to Route 199 East to Route S112. Turn right or east after one mile to Lime Rock Park for both the infield and outfield.

Circuit: 1.53 miles road course, 7 turns.

Major races: IMSA Camel GT Championship; Busch Grand National North.

Racing is generally a Sunday sport — but not at Lime Rock. The park is closed Sunday, and racing only occurs here Saturdays and on three Holidays — Labor Day, Memorial Day, and the Fourth of July. Lime Rock Park is unique.

About a dozen years ago, a small vocal group of summer-home owners filed suit against Lime Rock, complaining of the noise. The vacationers won the suit and effectively stopped weekend racing. The track has been guaranteed a permanence for ten Saturdays a year including the accompanying Fridays. Open practice still occurs on select Tuesday afternoons. Skip Barber and auto club cars run the rest of the week — albeit with serious mufflers.

Lime Rock is a different sort of racetrack. If a wedding takes place at the church across the street during a race weekend the schedule is altered to accommodate the newlyweds. It's well-organized, family oriented, and racing-steeped. Lime Rock is the epitome of sports car racing in the United States. It's one of the oldest continuously run road racing circuits in the U.S., and the New England area has more sports cars than any other in the country. The scenery of Connecticut, and the organization of the facility give it a Silver-

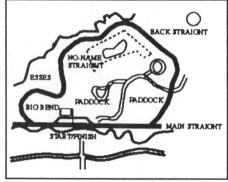

stone-ish flavor.

The area itself looks like a British countryside — or as New Englanders would suggest, typical northeastern scenery. Located in the Berkshire foothills of Connecticut the 36 year old park is known for its intimacy — on the picnic greens as well as on the narrow 1.53 mile circuit.

There are no grandstands so you'll have to create your own seats. The hillside at the "Ss" — at the first corner of the track give you a good view of start/finish. The uphill portion of the backside of the course, near the chicane, is also a good place from which to watch.

Harsh criticism of the track surface from IMSA drivers necessitated a seriously needed resurfacing. A complete re-paving was done during the off-season, and the site appeared on the 1993 IMSA calendar.

Camping is probably the best way to experience a race at Lime Rock. With some 325 acres of park land, a good deal of the area is available for camping — although on raceday track officials compel you to pack up your gear so there's room for more spectators. There are no advance reservations for camping, which is free, and spots are allotted on a first-come first-served basis.

Hotels in the area can be reserved ahead of time by calling B&B reservations (for Bed and Breakfasts) at (203) 364-0505; or call the track. Track representatives will be happy to refer you to hotels in the area — and most hotels give Lime Rock officials updates on room availability. Lime Rock will also send you a copy of the Lime Rock Track Record, which should give you any other information concerning accommodations and restaurants you may wish to know.

Stafford Motor Speedway

P.O. Box 105
Stafford Springs, CT   06076

PH: (203) 684-2783

Location: Northeastern Connecticut, 15 miles northeast of Hartford, on Routes 32 & 190.

Circuit: Half-mile oval.

Major races: NASCAR interseries (Northeastern Region).

Located in mountainous rural northern Connecticut, Stafford Motor Speedway sits in a valley four miles off I 84. Crystal lake Recreation area, which is five miles from the track, supplies most of the entertainment when the track is not in use, but the area in general is sparsely populated and quiet.

The facility seats 11,500, and the biggest show of the racing year — the Modified Tour race — fills the stands. Racing runs from April to October, mostly on Friday nights. There's camping at the track, although there are no facilities. Rooms are available in Vernon, which is 20 miles distant; or call the track for more information.

Thompson International Speedway

P.O. Box 278
Thompson, CT   06277

PH: (203) 923-9591
FAX: (203) 923-9821

Location: North eastern Connecticut, 45 minutes west of Providence, RI, on Rural Route 193.

Circuit: Five-eighths mile high-banked paved oval.

Major races: NASCAR interseries (Northeast Region).

Thompson International Speedway sits in the northeast corner of Connecticut, bordering Massachusetts and Rhode Island. Thompson has typical un-typical New England weather. The rural section of Thompson where the track stands is in farmland country.

The track holds some 11,000 fans, and the biggest show of the year is the Winston 300 World Series in October. Thompson Dam, which is just a few miles away, is good for camping — or fishing or hiking, for that matter. There are other campsites in the area as well. Thompson is located on an 18 hole golf course, which suggests additional recreational possibilities.

Hotels can be found in Webster, and Putnam, and the area is one hour from Hartford, Boston, and Providence. Call the track for more information.

Dover Downs International Speedway

1131 North Dupont Hwy
P.O. Box 843
Dover, DE 19901

PH: (302) 674-4600
Tickets (800) 441-7223
(in DE); 302 734-7223)
FAX: (302) 734-3124

Location: Central Delaware, between Philadelphia and Salisbury, MD.

From Washington, take U.S. Highway 50/301 East to MD 302 to MD 454 to DE 8, turning onto US 13 North after going through the center of town — the track is approximately one mile past city-center.

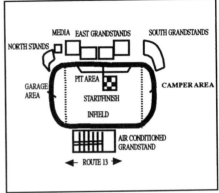

Circuit: 1.0 mile paved oval

Major races: NASCAR Winston Cup Series; Busch Grand National.

During competition weekends there is so much else to do at Dover Downs that racing is almost anti-climactic. Dover promoters deliver a complete range of entertainment over the three-day NASCAR event. The result: great races, and good times.

The "Monster Mile" is one of the best tracks for arduous fans. From any grandstand seat the track is completely visible, and any pass or lead change is observable. The track is less than half the physical size of Talladega, but holds nearly the same amount of seated fans.

The site is used mainly as a harness track for standard-bred horse racing, running about 50 race nights per year. Dover's air-conditioned enclosed grandstand area on the backstretch is actually the main grandstands for harness racing. The track is surrounded by the speedway. During the Winston Cup racing it's converted to backstretch seating and into a stage on Friday night (admission is free) for a live special edition of MRN's "NASCAR Live", with driver appearances and other entertainment. NASCAR certainly highlights Dover's season.

Following the Busch Grand National race, the "Monster Mile Movie" begins at dusk on the grass circle in front of the air-conditioned grandstand (admission is free).

Dover is no longer NASCAR's best kept secret, and tickets sell out earlier each year — even though the track has added seating each season since 1985, building another 5,200 seat stand for '92. Sunday's tickets are reserved so order early. Infield tickets are sold at the gate, and self-contained vehicles (those with permanent toilets) are allowed into the infield area at 5:30 PM Saturday evening (there is a shuttle bus to the movie and back). Sunday at 6:00 AM the infield gates open to cars pickups and vans. Note: no walk-ons are permitted into the infield, and each person must enter in a vehicle. For those who arrive earlier in the week, there is camping available outside the facility.

For hotels and motels call the Chamber of Commerce of Central Delaware at (302) 734-7513.

Charlotte County Speedway
8655 Piper Rd.
Punta Gorda, FL   33982
(813)   575-2422

Location: Off I 75 in Punta Gorda, at exit 28, then east toward Charlotte County Airport which takes you to the track.

Circuit: Three-eighths-mile paved oval.

Major races: World Of Outlaws Sprint Car Championship.

Charlotte County's "retirement community Speedway" runs a weekly show with seven different classes of regular racing and a special guest class each week. Racing generally runs Sunday afternoons until March, then switches to Saturday evenings.
Punta Gorda has a couple of hotels, plus there's a KOA on Golf Course Blvd. There is no camping at the track. You can call the track and they'll be happy to give you the phone numbers of the nearest lodgings.

Daytona International Speedway
P.O. Box Drawer S
Daytona Beach, FL 32015
1801 Speedway Blvd,
Daytona Beach, FL 32914

PH: (904) 253-7223/(904) 763-RACE
FAX: (904) 254-6791

Location: Central Florida, on the Atlantic coast, approximately 200 miles north of Miami.
From Miami, take Interstate 95/Florida Turnpike to Daytona Beach.

Circuit: 2.5 mile tri-oval/3.4 mile road course.

Major races: NASCAR Winston Cup Series Championship (two races); Busch Grand National Series; 24 Hours of Daytona IMSA Prototype and sports car endurance race; AMA Motorcycle Grand National Series Championship; AMA National Championship Road Racing Series Championship; AMA Camel Supercross Championship.

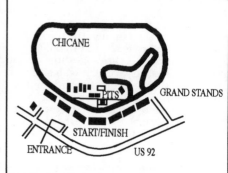

Second only to Indianapolis in terms of prestige in American motor racing, Daytona International Speedway is at least as dear to American racers. But, while Indy only happens once a year, Daytona hosts an eclectic handful of world class events throughout the season.
Daytona Beach is the kind of place that would have become fa-

mous for something sooner or later — racing just happened to be there first. Sunny or cool, the tropical air and the long stretches of beach — which are only minutes from the racetrack — make even the worst race weekend enjoyable.

Daytona has several major event dates — the most impressive being the NASCAR Winston Cup opener in February. Daytona planning constraints change depending on which weekend you wish to attend. The 24 Hours, which usually falls on the last weekend of January or the first weekend in February, is a fairly simple proposition.

For the 24 Hours of Daytona, hotels on the beach are generally still available Friday evening, and at prices from $18 to $33 for decent rooms. Come the 500 mid-February, however, you won't find anything available — or if you do they'll be $70 and up for the same $18 rooms. Pre-planning is essential for the 500.

Likewise, ticketing is something to sort out far in advance. Tickets for the 500 sell out in July of the preceding year. Motorcycle Speedweeks are not as popular as the NASCAR races, but fall during college spring break and pre-planning is wise for those events as well.

Once you've sorted through all the headaches of rooms and tickets, getting to the track can be easy if you do it right. If you're flying in for the day, Daytona Regional Airport actually borders the speedway on the south-east side. If you're staying the weekend you'll probably want to get to your hotel upon arrival, but if not, the airport is literally within walking distance(flying in and out in one day is not a bad idea). AMTRAK trains also service the Daytona area.

DOTS (Daytona Orlando Transit Service) transports passengers from the Daytona airport to their hotels and back, or to and from Orlando International and Daytona Regional Airports (800) 223-1965); VOTRAN, the Volusia County Transit Authority provides a good network of bus systems throughout Daytona Beach area. To get from Daytona Beach Shores, or from Ocean Shore or Atlantic Blvds, take the #10, or #17A, #17B, which become #10 buses as they turn toward the track. For other bus information call VOTRAN at (904) 761-7700.

If you drive, and you like to sleep late, be prepared for a traffic delay in the immediate track area during the days surrounding the races. There are really only two main ways into the track; the infield entrance, via Bill France Blvd; and the Hwy 92 entrance, which then splits into the different grandstand areas. On raceday, the unreserved Backstretch Grandstands are opened, and parking in that area is available — but only on race day. Once you buy tickets, simply follow the signs to the parking area closest to your seats.

Infield parking and admission is done on a first-come, first served basis. Admission prices are $45 per person, plus a per-vehicle charge ($40 for an RV, and $10 for a car). Once in the infield, overnight parking is allowed — but only on Saturday night during the Daytona 500 or Saturday night during the 24 Hours — the remainder of the season, the infield is cleared every evening. There is also RV parking available for overnight stays outside the track at the west end of the facility. The general ticket information number can reserve spots in advance, and they are available beginning in February and going through the end of the August. The track added another 3,400 seats in 1992 near start /finish, bringing the seated capacity to almost 98,000.

The beach itself is an attraction far greater than the track, and the unique tradition of allowing autos on the beach for 10 MPH cruises up and down the coast on the sand still exists. Restaurants are plentiful, in both the inexpensive and fine dining versions, and discos and clubs are also sprinkled along the main streets — typically on Atlantic Ave. Daytona Beach Jai Alai (255-0222), and the Daytona Beach Kennel Clubs (252-6484) are available for those who need a bit more of an investment attached to their entertainment.

Destination Daytona!, the Daytona Beach visitors bureau, is one of the most comprehensive tourist bureaus of any in the nation and will happily brief you on any happenings, or help you in any way they can. The national toll-free number is 800-854-1234, and they can give you a complete rundown of hotel and motel accommodations, as well as a few private residences available for rent (usually on long-term basis only).

Tom Stimus' DeSoto Speedway
Bradenton, FL   34203
PH: (813) 748-2962

Location: Gulf coastal Florida, at the southern tip of Tampa Bay, on State Route 64 at exit 42.

Circuit: Three-eighths mile paved oval.

Major races: NASCAR interseries (Sunbelt Region).

Tom Stimus' DeSoto Speedway, "The South's Fastest Racetrack", is found in typical Florida countryside. It comprises the third leg of the Florida Triple Crown of Sunbelt Winston Racing Series Championship short track championships — with Sunshine and Volusia making up the other two jewels in the crown. There are several events done in stages of three to accommodate the trio of abbreviated ovals in the area. NASCAR full bodied cars are the only things that run here. There are no sprint cars.

There's no camping at Tom Stimus' place, but there are a few motorhomes permitted. Hookups are not available, and they'd prefer you stay in a motel, but in a pinch you can stay in the parking lot. Off Highway 42 there are several motels.

Five Flags Speedway
7451 Pine Forest Rd.
Pensacola FL 32526

PH: (904) 944-0480
Main Office (904) 944-0466

Location: West of Downtown Pensacola, Off Interstate I10 East at Pine Forest Rd. Exit #2, then south 1 1/2 miles to the track.

Circuit: Half-mile paved high-banked oval.

Major races: NASCAR Winston All Pro Series.

Five Flags' Snowball Derby is likely the most prestigious short track full-bodied event in the country, with such notables as Darrell Waltrip, Bobby Allison, Harry Gant and several other top Cup drivers appearing each December. It continues attracting name drivers due to its traditional date: there's really nothing else going on in the first week of December.

Five Flags holds some 5,500 people, and the bigger races sell out easily. The facility offers easy-in/easy-out access, and there is 20 acres of parking on 40 acres of land. It's possible to spend the night in your mobile home — although no hookups exist. Motels are available on Highway 29 or on the Mobile Highway, both of which are only a few minutes away. The Pensacola beach is about 15 minutes from the track.

Gainesville Raceway

Office: NHRA Publicity Dept.
P.O. Box 5555
Glendora, CA   91740
Office: (818) 914-4761
Track: (904) 377-0046

Location: Northern central Florida, in Gainesville, off Hwy 75 and SR 225, 4 miles from the Gainesville Municipal Airport.

Circuit: Quarter-mile dragstrip.

Major races: NHRA Gatornationals.

Gainesville will be long remembered as the track where the magical 300 mile per hour mark was surpassed in the standing quarter mile. On a cool March day early in the 1992 season Kenny Bernstein ran a 301.70, becoming the first man in National Hot Rod Association history over 300. Ironically, he made it to the finals — only to be beat by a record-setting ET put up by Eddie Hill.

Hot and humid in the summer and cool in the winter, Gainesville Raceway can be anywhere on the thermometer for the March NHRA race. Temperatures usually hover in the mid 70s to low 80s, but it's been known to be oppressively hot, or bitterly cold here.

Gainesville holds approximately 30,000 fans, and the NHRA event generally sells out each year, posting four-day totals of 100,000 or more. Up until 1989, the Gatornationals was the only major NHRA race of the Gainesville Raceway season. But the venue now hosts a Super Chevy Sunday show, and a Division 2 Bracket Championship race.

Gainesville is really the beginning of the NHRA racing season. As the first national event on the East Coast, many drivers still may not have their problems ironed out. This may also be the first event for many East Coast racers.

The event gets close to selling out each year, but the track has only turned people away once in its history. Booking hotels, however, is a different story. Only a few rooms exist in the area. To ensure a room in March it's wise to start looking during the summer of the preceding year. If Gainesville is booked, try Ocala or Stark (20 miles north). For latecomers, Jacksonville will surely have rooms — although you'll have at least a 90 minute drive. For more information call the Gainesville Visitors and Convention Bureau at (904) 374-5210. If you stay in Ocala, make sure you visit the Don Garlits museum of Drag Racing, which is a quarter-mile (appropriately) off I75 at Exit 67.

Jax Raceways

6840 Stuart Ave.
Jacksonville, FL   32205

PH: (904) 757-5425

Location: Northeastern Florida, in Jacksonville.

Circuit: Half-mile clay oval/ eighth mile.

Major races: NASCAR interseries (Sunbelt Region).

Jax Raceway has the same distressing southern humidity as Daytona — without the beach. But there are many places to cool off in the immediate area — like creeks, streams, and rivers — including St Johns River.

Located just a few miles outside Jacksonville, the track seats 3,000 and an additional 3,000 can be accommodated for the dragstrip, which holds several annual Funny Car and jet car events. "Speedweek" in Jax, which starts Friday at the same time the 24 Hours begins at Daytona, runs a series of night late model racing. The Jax speedweek runs through the following Saturday, when the other local oval, Volusia Raceway, takes up the night racing.

Jacksonville is the most convenient place to stay, and the track can send you a list of the closest hotels. There is camping at the track's 65 acres, although there are no hookups for RVs.

Miami Street Circuit
Office: 1110 Bricklee Ave., Suite 206
Miami, FL   33131

PH: (305) 379-7223
FAX: (305) 379-8802
Tickets: (305) 379-8802

Location: Southern Florida, in downtown Miami, at Biscayne Blvd and Bicentennial Park.

Circuit: 1.84 mile road course; 11 turns.

Major races: IMSA Camel GT Championship.

Miami's street race got off to a less than auspicious start in 1983, as the first race was literally flooded out. A dry week led to a Sunday downpour — under which a green flag was still waved to a wet field of GTP cars. After only 27 laps the race was mercifully put to sleep, and the late Al Holbert won the inaugural Miami Grand Prix in his Chevy March.

Promoter Ralph Sanchez, although a million-dollars lighter in the wallet, refused to give up on his idea, and re-ran the race in 1984. There was no rain the following year, and the event was a success.

Since that unfortunate start in '83 the race has been a popular event of South Florida's Springtime.

Each year there has been a designated "Spirit of Miami" racecar, symbolizing the winning tradition of the city and the race. Unfortunately, the namesake car had a history of not finishing. Finally, Sanchez put the title on a juggernaut Nissan GTP, and the "Spirit of Miami" won its first race.

The course winds down Biscayne Blvd. and alongside Biscayne Bay and, at least in terms of television, it is a very scenic track. In person, watching is limited to one corner at a time — like most street circuits. But the unreserved General Admission tickets

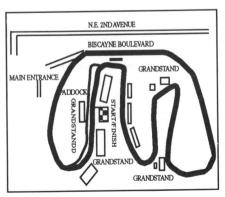

are good — although you'll pay a bit extra to get unreserved grandstand seats (which are worth the extra money). Reserved seats are good if you must see the pit action, although, if you just want to hang out, they're not worth buying.

IMSA regulars call this the circuit with the best atmosphere — and certainly the most entertaining street circuit. There are plenty of things to do besides racing: The Bayside Marketplace, which is right next door to the track, has Miami shopping as well as outdoor restaurants; a five-minute ride from the track and you'll be at the Miami Arena — where you can watch the Miami Heat NBA Basketball team; or four blocks from the track you can be in a small version of Cuba, complete with food and drink.

There are lots of places to stay in Miami, and several hotels are within walking distance. The Intercontinental is where the race headquarters is — but it is expensive and you'll need to book it early.

From farther out, getting to the track is easy. The best way is by using the Miami Metro Rail, which stops two blocks from the track at Government Center, near the entrance to City Hall. Call the Greater Miami Convention and Visitor Bureau at (305) 539-3000 for more information on lodging.

Moroso Motorsports Park

P.O. Box 31907
Palm Beach Gardens, FL   33420

PH: (305) 622-1400

Circuit: 2.25 mile road course; ten turns/quarter-mile dragstrip.

Location: in Palm Beach Gardens, on Route 710 Beeline Highway, across from Pratt & Whitney Aircraft .

Major races: Super Chevy Sunday Weekend; July 4th Jet Cars; SCCA Nationals; AMA Regional Racing.

Moroso Motorsports Park is considered one of the premier testing facilities in the country. Several manufacturers constantly use this road course for tuning and engineer training. In addition, several top SCCA and IMSA teams use the narrow track for race testing.

Moroso is really set up to cater to group rentals and testing sessions. There is, of course, a full calendar of scheduled events, the biggest of which is probably the NHRA Winston Divisional drag races, or the SCCA Nationals. There is a mud-bog for mud racing; Skip Barber has one of his installations here, so it is used for instruction as well; and for more drag racing and skidpad testing Moroso's other facility down the road a few miles in Miami-Hollywood can be accessed. There is also a 200-foot long mud bog created for off-wheel competition.

In 1992 the facility was upgraded with 4,000 feet of new concrete barriers replacing the old guardrails. In addition, 2,400 feet of curbing was replaced and the paddock was raised six inches to avoid flooding that occasionally occurred.

Moroso has almost 200 acres of area that can be used for camping, and shaded paddock area, so it is attractive in a sport that is used to well-tanned personnel. Entertainment-wise, West Palm is as good as Miami. Minutes from downtown West Palm Beach, there are plenty of things to do here. Check out the Palm Beach Polo Club, which you can do Saturday during qualifying. Hotels are plentiful, and can be found by calling Palm Beach Chamber of Commerce at (407) 471-3995.

Sebring International Raceway

113 Midway Dr.
Sebring, FL 33870
PH: (813) 655-1442/
(800) 626-7223 (FLA only)
FAX: (813) 655-1777

Location: Central Florida, near the intersection of Highways 27 and 98, 90 miles from Orlando and Tampa, 110 miles from West Palm Beach.

Circuit: 3.7 mile road course; 17 turns.

Major races: 12 Hours of Sebring IMSA GT Championship.

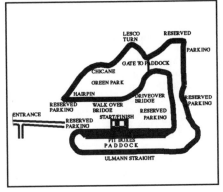

For Europeans, Sebring has a special significance.

In the U.S., however, the reputation is less than tremendous. IMSA drivers generally dislike Sebring. It's rough, bumpy, and dusty. The best machinery gets thrashed. And at 10:00 p.m. the winner is rarely the favorite. Even for the fans, the place is unbearably hot, and very dirty.

But for both fans and drivers, being able to say they've been to Sebring and conquered the place inspires pride enough to do it all again the following year.

Run as part of the Formula One World Championship in 1959 and, of course, as one of the most prestigious endurance races in the world, Sebring has the distinction of hosting some of the best drivers in the history of the sport. Jack Brabham won his first World Championship at Sebring in the final race of the '59

season, as his car ran out of fuel on the final lap and he pushed it 900 yards across the line for the championship. Moss, Von Trips, Shelby, Hill, Fangio, Bonnier, Surtees, Ickx, Donohue, Gregg, Holbert, Stuck, and many others have battled here in open-wheeled and closed-wheeled machinery. It's the oldest endurance race in the country and still has the corner on sentiment in American racing.

Sebring is located approximately two hours from Palm Beach and an hour and a half from Orlando. In other words, it's in the middle of nowhere. If you plan on staying in a room, you'd better book it 6-8 months ahead of time. Sebring has a handful of rooms; Avon Park is another option close to the track; and Lake Placid also has a handful of rooms. But there are far too few rooms. Veterans rent condominiums, which also must be done months in advance.

Because of the hassle of lodging, many people camp at the circuit. But the diehard Sebring-goers do it in one day stints, coming in Thursday for the first round of qualifying which sets the top ten grid spots, then leaving for Disneyworld Thursday night, staying in Orlando, and not returning until 8:00 am Saturday morning for the start of the race (green-flagged at 10:00 AM Saturday). Some, knowing the headaches of driving late on the relatively narrow roads, leave at 8:00

pm before the race ends. But seldom do they leave before sunset, since sunset at Sebring is one of the most beautiful sights in racing, as the sky reddens over the front straight.

Improvements of 1992 have made the circuit better than it has ever been before. Virtually the entire circuit was widened and resurfaced; a new two-laned bridge was installed from the pits to the front gate; and new walkover bridges and spectator mounds were introduced to make the circuit 100 percent viewable. The best places to watch are still from the famous hairpin, the backstretch or from new esses (turns three and four) — but you'll have at least 12 hours to figure that out yourself.

If you find yourself in Sebring on the third Saturday in March and need a place to stay, try Avon Park or farther north off highway 27. For hotel information in the area, try the Sebring Chamber of Commerce at (813) 385-8448 for suggestions... or a prayer or two.

Volusia County Speedway
1500 E. Highway 40
De Leon Springs, FL   32028

PH: (904) 255-2243

Location: in Barbersville, Florida, just north of central Daytona, Atlantic Coastal Florida.

Circuit: Half-mile paved oval.

Major races: NASCAR Busch Grand National; NASCAR interseries (Sunbelt Region).

Volusia County Speedway runs its first major event in the first week of February, coinciding with the start of Daytona's Speedweeks. While Daytona gets ready for the Busch race, Volusia runs 11 straight nights of modifieds.

Barberville itself is 30 minutes northwest of Daytona, in an extremely flat area. As one official put it, "it's not near anything — it's just flat." The area has the same humidity as Daytona, but it's in a wooded area and occasionally has cool weather. It's one hour from Orlando, or Disneyworld.

The facility seats 9,500, and probably the biggest show is the Busch Grand National race which was in its 7th season in 1993. The next biggest is the annual Winston Invitational Showdown — which is an invitational late model race.

There is camping at the track, and showers are available. Or stay in Deland or the Daytona/Ormond Beach area. Call the track for more information, or check the Daytona International Speedway listing in this guide.

Atlanta Dragway
Route 1, Ridgeway Rd,
Commerce, GA   30529

PH: (404) 335-2301
FAX: (404) 335-7135

Location: Northeastern GA, on Interstate I 85 at U.S. Highway 441.

Circuit: Quarter-mile dragstrip.

Major races: NHRA Southern Nationals.

Sixty miles north of Atlanta and five miles north of Road Atlanta, Atlanta Dragway shares the southern charm of each of the other tracks to form one of the NHRA's most prized national venues. The facility hosts racing every Saturday night, and there is one big drag race regularly each month.

Two major NHRA races run here per year — the Southern Nationals, and one major Divisional Championship race. Other major events include the Kudzu Nationals — a Pro-Modified, Super-Stock, Stock, and assorted bracket racing event — which regularly attracts 10,000 or more. The Southern Nationals tops the list with a draw of about 60,000.

Appropriately, the facility seats about 60,000. Based on those figures, that means the event usually sells out. Tickets are available as late as Saturday without any problems, although Sunday morning you may find yourself without a seat. It may be wise to book ahead of time if you only wish to attend Sunday's Eliminator.

Stay in Gainesville, which is 15 miles away; in Suwanee — where the Atlanta Falcons practice — which is 25 miles from the track; or in Oakwood, which is five-and-a-half miles distant. Lake Lanier Island, a 500 acre lake and recreation facility, is close by, and Six Flags Over Georgia Amusement Park is 65 miles from the track. Call the Georgia Department of Industry, Trade, and Tourism at (404) 656-3590 in Atlanta for more information about lodging.

Atlanta Motor Speedway
P.O. Box 500
Highways 19 & 41
Hampton, GA   30228

PH: (404) 946-4211
FAX: (404) 946-3939

Location: In Hampton, 30 miles south of Atlanta, on Highways 19 and 41.

Circuit: 1.522 mile paved oval.

Major races: NASCAR Winston Cup (two races). IMSA Camel GT; NASCAR Busch Grand National.

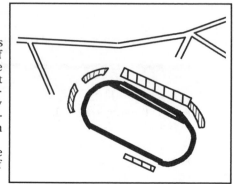

Atlanta Motor Speedway's claim to fame is the annual staging of the final Winston Cup race of the Championship. Probably the most popular race in a season of spectacular events, Atlanta Motor Speedway is known for being the championship-deciding race of the Winston Cup Championship.

It's fitting that the final race should be held here, since it is one of the most accessible tracks on the Winston Cup calendar, as well as being one of the best spectator facilities. There are very few seats at Atlanta Motor Speedway where fans cannot see the entire track. In addition, the infield offers probably the best view in NASCAR racing.

The place does well for its first race in March, but will sell out its 100,000 seats far in advance for the Hooters 500 in November. The March race can be cold, although the rural countryside is known for its hot, humid weather.

But if you want tickets for the grandstands — especially with a view of the pits — you'll have to book tickets early in the season. You can buy tickets by phone with a credit card, or the track will reserve tickets for 10 days until they receive your check. Tickets sell out earlier each year, so act quickly.

There are general admission areas on the north-hill backstretch. People bring lawn chairs, and there are small bleachers there as well. The infield offers a good view, and you can camp there race weekend.

There are several hotels in the immediate area, but the best place to stay is in Atlanta itself. There should be no problem getting rooms — even if you come into Atlanta at the last minute. Call the Georgia Department of Industry, Trade and Tourism at (404) 656-3590 in Atlanta for more information about lodging.

Lanier Raceway
P.O. Box 5145, Highway 53
Gainesville, GA   30501

PH: (404) 967-2131

Location: 40 miles northeast of Atlanta, on State Route 53, five miles north Interstate I 85 off exit 49.

Circuit: Three-eighths mile paved oval.

Major races: NASCAR Busch Grand National; NASCAR interseries (Eastern Seaboard Region); USAC Midgets.

Across the street from Road Atlanta on Highway 53, Lanier Raceway — like Road Atlanta — is very hot and very dry during the season: mid-80s to high 90s. The biggest event of the year here is the Busch Grand National — second biggest is the Budweiser Superbowl, at which all Lanier racing divisions get together on one date to run several endurance-style races.

Lanier seats 4,500 in the grandstands, but has trackside and tiered parking where families can sit and watch from their cars or from picnic areas. Camping is available — but not at trackside.

Lake Lanier Island, a 500 acre lake and recreation facility, is close by, and Six Flags Over Georgia Amusement Park is 60 miles from the track. You can stay in Gainesville, which is 10 miles away; in Suwanee — where the Atlanta Falcons practice — which is 20 miles from the track; or in Oakwood, which is five-and-a-half miles distant.

Oglethorpe Speedway
Route 5, P.O. Box 605
Raymond Rd
Savannah, GA   31408
(912) 964-7069

Location: Eastern GA, 10 miles west of Savannah.

From Savannah, take Interstate I 95 (3 miles) to exit #18, heading east on State Highway 80; proceed three miles to Dublin Rd, turning right and travelling one mile to the track.

Circuit: Half-mile clay oval

Major races: NASCAR interseries (eastern Seaboard).

Oglethorpe Speedway is located in a semi-residential area about three miles from the Savannah International Airport. The 3,500 seat facility runs a weekly NASCAR Saturday evening show, and rarely strays from that formula. The track is some four miles south of a large group of Motels — called "Gateway to Savannah".

Road Atlanta
5300 Winder Highway
Braselton, GA   30517

PH: (404) 967-6143
FAX: (404) 967-2668

Location: Northern Georgia, 40 miles north of Atlanta, on Highway 53 off I 85 in Braselton at exit 49, five miles off I 85.

Circuit: 2.5 mile road course; 12 turns.

Major races: SCCA Trans-Am Championship; SCCA National Runoffs.

In far corners of their closets, Road Atlanta regulars of this track have a designated pair of Road Atlanta tennis shoes. The sneakers, eternally colored with the red dirt of the southern circuit, are virtually unusable for anything else besides race-going. Red Road Atlanta clay clings to anything and anyone who spends a weekend at the famous southern racetrack. The clay covers the area around the 2.5 mile Road Atlanta circuit, giving anyone who's been to the track a permanent souvenir of the place. Race cars get the stuff all over their fenders, as other competitors put wheels off in the dirt, sending plumes of dust into the air.

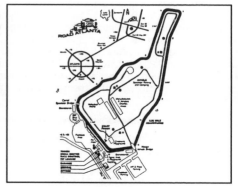

This circuit ranks with Road America and Mid-Ohio as the best spectator road racing circuit in U.S.. Like Road America, the track links two fast portions of road with two slow ones at either end, giving it some good variation, and playing havoc with race set-up.

Unfortunately, the instability with the ownership has caused most of the major series to leave the place. In December of 1992 the property went into Chapter 11 reor-

ganization when Road Atlanta's banks called in the loans and the money wasn't there. That situation led to the sale of the track in July. But by December one of the minority partners bought the major partner out. Three people currently own it, under the business name Road Atlanta Limited.

For a time, even after IMSA's schedules had been published (and Road Atlanta was not on it), track officials felt IMSA would be back. As a death blow, the SCCA pulled its prestigious year-end Runoffs from future seasons. The track was also scheduled for resurfacing, which hadn't been done since 1970 when it was built. The track was to have been slightly reconfigured. Plans to reconfigure have been scrapped, but the repaving plan is apparently still on.

Regardless, there are not many bad places from which to watch racing, although most people seem to end up watching from the Ss past in turns 4-5 or at the Nissan Bridge in turn 11. In both places the track comes very close to where spectators sit, and there is lots of passing. Also, from each section you'll see other major sections of the track. There are only two grandstands -- in turn one and turn 12. In 1991, for the SCCA Valvoline Runoffs, the track added a chicane at turn eight. It was used only for that race, and is not supposed to appear again, but it was also a good place to watch racing while it lasted.

Camping is free in the infield's 300 acres. There are no hookups for RVs, but you can pitch a tent, or sleep in the car. Don't plan on making it a permanent home, though. Most events are slated for Friday through Sunday and that's as long as you can stay. Don't worry about getting a spot — the place rarely fills up completely (although you may not get your pick if you arrive late).

If you need a room, try to stay in Gainesville, which is 10 miles away; or in Suwanee — where the Atlanta Falcons practice — which is 20 miles from the track; Winder, eight miles away, has a few rooms; or in Oakwood, which is five-and-a-half miles distant; the I 85 corridor has several, but if nothing else, Athens and Atlanta will have plenty of rooms. Call The Georgia Department of Industry Trade and Tourism at (404) 656-3590 for more information.

Roebling Road

Route 2, Box 638
Bloomingdale, GA
31302

PH: (912) 748-4205

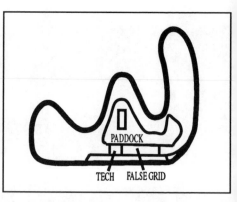

Circuit: 2.0 mile road course; seven turns.

Location: Fifteen miles west of Savannah, off Interstate I 95 and SR 80.

Major races: SCCA Nationals and Regionals; WERA Pro and regionals.

Built in 1958 as a driver's training center, Roebling Road is still used for similar purposes — although the drivers who use it are generally in pro series race trim. The track has a few slight rises, but is essentially flat.

There are sparse spectator facilities here, but Roebling Road is technically open only to participants, so you must be accompanied into the facility by a participant. Once inside, you are free to wander about the facility and watch from the fences. The facility is open during the week for testing and track rental, and on weekends for races.

There is camping at the track, which even includes showers and electricity. If you need a room, Savannah, Pooler or Macon are the best bets.

Blackhawk Farms

P.O. Box 347
Rockton, IL 61072

PH: (815) 389-3323/ (815) 389 -2000
(815) 624-7098

Circuit: 1.95 mile road course; seven turns.

Location: 20 miles north of Rockford, IL, off Prairie Rd, off I 94.

Major races: SCCA National and Regional Championships; AMA Championship Cup regional series.

Blackhawk Farms Racetrack is located in a heavily forested area, and on a relatively flat plateau in northern Illinois. The track itself is very flat with almost no elevation changes. As late as 1989 the venue hosted an SCCA Escort Endurance race, but now its biggest events are WERA and AMA Motorcycle races.

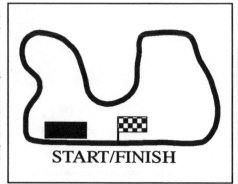

Grandstands are located in turns one and four, but you'll be able to walk to the fences, safely watching racing all around the track. One of the best places for viewing is at the end of the straightway, and in the turn four Carousel.

Camping is free when you purchase an admission ticket, and there is plenty of room. Don't plan on staying the week — you can only camp on the weekends. If you don't feel like camping, stay in Beloit, IL or South Beloit, WI.

Gateway International Raceway

558 N. Highway 203
Madison, IL 62201
PH: (618) 482-5501
(Racing Line) (618) 482-5546
FAX: (618) 482-5595

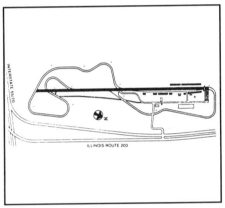

Location: Southern Illinois, five miles from downtown St. Louis, MO., off Highways 55 and 70, on Highway 203.

Circuit: 2.2 mile road course; 12 turns/ quarter-mile dragstrip.

Major races: SCCA Nationals and Regionals; WERA Motorcycle Championships; NHRA drag racing.

Gateway International Raceway is located a few miles east of the Mississippi, and represents one of the few road courses in this part of the country.

The facility is limited to SCCA Nationals now, with its major event, the IHRA Gateway Nationals, having left at the end of 1991. Neither the SCCA nor IMSA run a major event here, although the SCCA regionals are as good as anywhere. It is used often for testing and driving schools, however, and both IMSA and SCCA racers occasionally use the facility to try new equipment. It has recently become an NHRA track and the sanctioning body has held a few relatively large events here.

St. Louis has plenty of rooms, but the track recommends staying in Collinsville, which is east of St. Louis. The track can send you a short list of hotels.

Illinois State Fairgrounds Speedway

2000 E. Cornell
Springfield, IL 62703
PH: (217) 753-8866
Tickets: (217) 782-1979

Location: Central Illinois, north of downtown Springfield, off Business Route 66.

Circuit: One mile clay oval.

Major races: AMA Grand National Championship; World of Outlaws Sprint Car Championship; USAC Silver Crown and Midget Championships.

Illinois State Fairgrounds Speedway is one of the few dirt tracks to host the big three dirt shows, with WoO, AMA, and USAC shows all running at least once during the season. The dirt oval seats 14,000, and the one mile facility is one of the best in the country.

As with most fairgrounds circuits, parking in the wrong place will give you a three-mile hike — and Springfield's fair is no different. Gate seven, off Taintor Rd. is the best way to get to the circuit, and will get you in and out fast. The tunnel to the infield can be reached by using gate six — also off Taintor Rd.

For a concise list of hotels in the area — including prices — call the Springfield Convention and Visitors Bureau at (800) 356-7900 (from Ill.) or (800) 545-7300 (elsewhere).

Peoria Motorcycle Clubgrounds
605 Camron Ln
Peoria, IL   61607

PH: (309) 697-1285

Location: Central Illinois, in west Peoria
From interstate 74 take the 474 bypass and exit 3A to Route 116 two miles.

Circuit: Five eighths mile TT Steeplechase circuit, with both a right and left-hand turn, and a jump.

Major races: AMA Grand National Championship Camel Pro Series.

Peoria Motorcycle Clubgrounds hosts the oldest continuous AMA National race in the country. In operation since 1946, every significant name in U.S. pro motorcycling has at one time graced the venerable Clubgrounds soil. From Kenny Roberts to Dick Mann, the best in the U.S. — the best in the world — have raced the five-eighths mile steeplechase circuit.

The Clubgrounds have the last TT race in the U.S., with both a left turn, a right turn, and a jump — which, for the pros, is hit at nearly 75 mph, sometimes launching them 50 feet or more. This is also the only private club that still hosts an AMA Camel Pro National; the rest are public fairgrounds raceways.

The historic venue is a must-see for die-hard motorcycle race fans. Located on the outskirts of Peoria, it's an easy place to find, and easy area to get rooms. There are no grandstands, so bring a lawn chair and sit under the trees in this unique park.

Make sure at least to walk past the right-left combination on the backside of the track to watch the jump. When they land the bikes get very loose, and only the true talent can keep the power on all the way through.

For more information on hotels in the area, call The Peoria Visitors Bureau at (309) 637-4636, or call the track.

Peoria Speedway
3520 W. Farmington Rd.
Peoria, IL   61604

PH: (309) 673-3342

Location: Central Illinois, on the outskirts of Peoria.

Circuit: Quarter-mile clay oval.

Major races: NASCAR interseries (Central Region).

Located one mile east of the center of Peoria, Peoria Speedway has been in existence since 1964. The Peoria facility's biggest race is the Busch State Championship race near the end of the season. The 4,200 seat arena sees NASCAR driver Kenny Schrader on a fairly regular basis.

Hotels, although plentiful in Peoria, are best had by travelling a few minutes from north of town, about three miles.

Quincy Raceways
Route 1, P.O. Box 236
Quincy, IL 62301

PH: (217) 224-3843

Location: West central Illinois, on the Mississippi river bend,100 miles from St Louis off Hwy 104, three miles east of Quincy.

Circuit: Quarter-mile clay oval.

Major races: NASCAR interseries (Central Region).

Quincy Raceways sits in the country, three miles from the city of Quincy. The track, located in the farm-rich Quincy area, is adjacent to the Bradley Airport. The facility is small, with a seating capacity of 2,500- 3,000. Most of the events get close to filling up, but the annual truck-pull almost always sells out.

You can stay downtown in Quincy, whose population of 42,000 or so needs a few extra rooms from time to time; and there's camping in town. Call the track for more information.

Rockford Speedway
P.O. Box 1000
Rockford, IL 61105

PH: (815) 633-1500

Location: Northern Illinois, north of Rockford.

Circuit: Quarter-mile paved oval.

Major races: NASCAR interseries (Great Northern Region).

Located near Illinois' second largest city, Rockford Speedway runs several programs on a weekly basis. Mainly a late model track, Rockford also hosts a four cylinder U.S stock division, Limited Sportsman, and Road Runners. But the facility's biggest show is the mid-September three-day Winston National Short Track Championship.

Actually located in the city of Love's Park, the privately owned track has only a few rooms in the immediate area. For the National Short track weekend you can camp on the grounds, but the County Health Department considers any area that allows more than six nights of camping a year as a campgrounds; so don't count on camping there the rest of the season. Try 10 miles up the road in South Beloit, or on State St. in Rockford.

Santa Fe Speedway
9100 So. Wolf Rd
Hinsdale, Il   60521

PH: (708) 839-1050

Location: Twenty miles southwest of Chicago, off Interstate I 55 at exit 276-A, then south on County Line Rd to 91st St. and east a quarter-mile to the track.

Circuit: Half-mile clay oval; semi banked/ quarter-mile clay.

Major races: World Of Outlaws Championship; Midgets and Sprint Cars.

When Santa Fe Speedway was constructed in 1952, it was built in the middle of nowhere — 20 miles west of Chicago in a seemingly useless field. But since then residential and commercial installations have sprung up, and the area is now a suburban wonderland.

The track fancies itself a mini-Indy, and doesn't give attendance or seating capacity. Although it hosts both WoO and IRA sprinters, the biggest show is, believe it or not, a Demolition derby — but one of a different nature, with a season long series based on team bashing. Racing takes place Friday and Saturday nights. The best place to stay is Hinsdale, which is five miles from the speedway.

Tri-City Speedway
P.O. Box 3305
Springfield, IL   62708
PH: (office) (618) 931-9965
Track: (618) 931-7836

Location: Southwestern Illinois, near the border of Illinois and Missouri, 20 miles from St. Louis.

From northern St Louis, take Interstate I 270 East to the Granite City exit, and State Route 203, following SR 203 to the track.

Circuit: Half-mile clay oval; semi banked/ quarter-mile clay oval.

Major races: World of Outlaws Sprint Car Championship Shootout; USAC Sprint Cars.

Tri- City Speedway's 31 acres can accommodate 5,000 people on the larger of the facility's two tracks. The facility is open twice a month, and each track is used once a month. On the half-mile oval, the World of Outlaws, USAC Midgets and Late Model full-bodied cars run, while the Econo Late Models and Street Stocks use the quarter mile track.

The best place to stay while in the area is Edwardsville, which is just three miles from the track — where the WoO have their headquarters when they come to town.

Bloomington Speedway
351 Church Ln.
Bloomington, IN   47401

Office: P.O. Box 239
Clear Creek, IN 47426-0239

PH: (office) (812) 824-8753
(track) (812) 824-7400

Location: Central Indiana, approximately 50 miles south of Indianapolis, off State Road 37. South at the Walnut St. exit one mile to Fairplex Road and east a half mile to the track.

Circuit: Quarter-mile clay oval; semi-banked.

Major races: World of Outlaws Sprint Car Championship Shootout; USAC Midgets; All-Star Sprint Cars.

Bloomington Speedway doesn't host a weekly dirt show. There are about a dozen or so races at the circuit per year. But the few races run are set in place with fat purses, and are quality events — like the WoO show. The speedway celebrated its 70th birthday in 1993, and held some premium shows. Bloomington has plenty of rooms, and finding one is not a problem — even when arriving late.

Indianapolis Motor Speedway
4790 W. 16th St.
Indianapolis, IN 46222

PH: (317) 481-8500
FAX: (317) 248-6759
Tickets: (317) 248-6700

Location: Central Indiana, on the west side of Indianapolis, off Georgetown and 16th St..

Circuit: 2.5 mile paved oval.

Major races: Indianapolis 500.

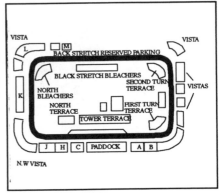

The Indianapolis Motor Speedway is worthy of an entire guidebook of its own. The famous Memorial Day 500-miler is the biggest auto race in the world. In fact, it is the biggest single spectator event on the planet.

Officials at the speedway don't publish seating capacity information, but some members of the press have taken time and counted the seats: there are some 320,000, with the capability of handling nearly the same in the infield.

"The Speedway", as the drivers call it, is richer in history than any other racetrack in the world, and a win here is probably the most prestigious accomplishment in any driver's career. Jimmy Clark and Graham Hill are always remembered for their wins at Indy as much as their dominance in Grand Prix Racing. Even with the feud between CART and Formula One, Indy is still a very special place within the hearts of GP drivers and FIA officials. Although CART drivers do not routinely qualify for an FIA Superlicence, the Indy 500 winner is automatically granted a ticket to race F1.

The 2.5 miles is legendary, and almost any state map has a small figure of the oval on the west side of the city, just north of the Indianapolis International Airport. The Speedway has undergone some subtle changes recently which were not significant for 1993, but likely will be for '94 or beyond. The nine-hole golf course has been redesigned so that it is part of the bigger course located on the outside of the track. Inside, the course is only four holes and the remaining 14 are outside the walls where the old 18-hole course was. Reopened in July of '93, the infield spectator capacity decreased by about 20%.

The height of the wall was raised to 42 inches (although along the front straight it is still 39 inches tall). In addition, there have been warm-up lanes added for drivers coming out of the pits. The lanes extend up to turn two, so drivers actually enter the course much farther up — and at a much greater speed. There are also rumble strips on the apron of each corner. Most notably, there are now three entrances to the pits; the old pit entrance, one just before turn three and one as drivers round turn four. The walls conform to FIA regulations and the gaps created for extra pit entrances can also be utilized for portions of what may eventually be a road circuit. The obvious conclusion is that The Speedway is probably preparing to build a road course in the infield and has eyes on hosting the U.S. Grand Prix World Championship. It also recently tested Winston Cup in preparation for the

first NASCAR Winston Cup race in 1994.

But for now the focus is on the Indy 500. As the biggest race on earth, it is also one of the most flawlessly organized races as well. The month of May in Indiana is geared toward The Speedway. The race is usually held on Memorial Day weekend. For the years with five weekends, the race is usually held on the fourth weekend of the month; first practice usually starts the first Saturday of the month — and the first session starts following the Saturday morning Mayor's Breakfast, usually at about 12:30 PM. Practice runs daily from 11-6, and gates open at 9:00 AM.

The second weekend of May is designated for qualifying, and Saturday is Pole Day. If the entire field gets in a session, the first day of qualification goes into the books. Sunday the remaining qualifiers — those drivers who either waved off their run, or passed their attempt at qualification — will fight for the spots not yet secured. Even if they qualify at speeds faster than those posted by the polesitter, the best they can do is a spot at the tail end of Saturday's provisional grid. So, for example, if 15 cars qualify Saturday, and the rest wave off or pass, the best position available Sunday will be 16th. The same situation exists the following weekend, where the final few 33 starters will be locked in day by day.

There is no practice Monday, Tuesday, or Wednesday following the final qualification. Thursday is Carburation Day, and the track is closed again until Sunday, when the green flag falls for the race.

The first qualification session, and Pole Day will attract some 250,000 people. All tickets for pre-race activities are sold on a first come first served basis, and there will be plenty of seats. Everything is general admission. For $10.00 anyone can attend any of the four qualification sessions, and sit in $100 seats if they wish; for any practice day, admission is $2.00, with the same seats up for grabs.

Other than race day or Pole Day, probably the biggest attendance comes with Carburation Day on Thursday prior to race weekend. During that brief period the entire field appears on the track in two 60 minute sessions. The activities begin around 1 p.m. and end at about 3 p.m..

The Miller Beer-sponsored Pit Stop Competition takes up any slack left by the abbreviated tune-up schedule. The competition matches any crews in the race against one another in a less critical pre-race arena. It usually takes about two hours as the different pit crews try to be the fastest in the field at stuffing a few gallons of fuel in an IndyCar and changing four tires — the reward for being fastest is an extra $25,000 dollar paycheck for a few hours of work.

The Indianapolis City Center volunteers offer one of the most comprehensive tourist hotlines of anywhere in the county. Even Destination Daytona! is not as easy to use as this system. With a toll-free call (800 323 INDY) any visitor can find information on Indianapolis' activities on a given day or week, and can even book a room, all on the same toll-free hot line. The caller simply uses the touch tone pad on the telephone.

After a series of questions, and choices of prices and locations, you'll be connected to the hotel of your choice at no charge. The system can be accessed at any time — although it's best to call during business hours, when the operators can tell you what rooms are available without you going through the hit-and-miss on the phone.

Oddly enough, rooms are often available during Memorial Day weekend. People usually just fail to ask the right folks. Call the Indianapolis City Center and check to make sure. If you get to town Saturday night, you'll probably have a problem. But don't just assume there are no rooms. With some 15,000 rooms in the city you might be surprised. Corporations buy out entire hotels in advance. As a late arrival, what you're looking for is a corporate room that hasn't been claimed.

If you haven't made reservations, and can't find a room in the immediate area, be prepared for a long drive and a long race day. The outskirts of Indianapolis fill up quickly, so all along the I 74, I 65, I 70, I 69 and 465 highways will be completely full. You'll really have a way to go. Terre Haute, 75 miles west, will likely be filled, as will Columbus and Bloomington.

Cincinnati will likely be your best bet, which is some 110 miles southeast, or try Louisville. A two hour drive in any direction will easily yield someplace to sleep. Two hours is a long drive, but remember how many people will be at this race.

Another service the Indy hotline provides is a how-to advisory. They'll certainly be able to tell you about the activities during your stay — and for the month of May there is plenty going on. You can find information on how to participate in the Indianapolis Mini Marathon Sunday morning, or where to eat if you feel like Chinese.

Indianapolis residents are not always as smitten with the race as with the qualifying. Although there is obvious interest in the 500 itself, far more Hoosiers try to make it to The Speedway for the pre-race shows.

Tickets range from $110 in the Paddock Penthouse to $20 for race day infield admission. Tickets are a problem at Indianapolis — but not a major dilemma. Monday morning after the race a line forms outside the speedway ticket office for tickets to the following year's race. About two weeks after tickets go on sale they'll be gone. But The Speedway has never yet sold out an event. If, however, you want to sit in a real seat, you may have a problem.

Stories of tickets being passed down in wills are all true. The day after the race, those who have had tickets for a while, send in a check and are issued the same tickets they had the previous year. If you've only been lucky enough to attend once, you may not end up in the same seats again, but usually the computerized tickets plop you into the same seats. Tickets cannot be applied for until the day following the race — applications postmarked prior to the race date will simply be returned. For an application write the speedway c/o the Ticket Office, and request an application.

Tickets are still available as late as Sunday of the 500 weekend — you just have to know how to find them. Like season tickets for football, baseball or basketball, keeping the ticket is more important than actually seeing the events themselves, and there are plenty of people who bought tickets who can't make the race.

This is the part where you'll need to be a bit resourceful. If you call the volunteers at the Indy City Center, they'll refer you to the Speedway; the Speedway in turn will tell you no seats are available, but that the infield is still open.

If you want seats, try one of the following options: Call the Indianapolis News or the Indianapolis Star (same number — 317 633-1240); or try the ad section in your local newspaper. Even as far away as the west coast, ads will appear in local papers advertising Indy seats; try the National Speed Sport News under the classified heading listed as TICKETS. All of these options are viable as long as you have a month or so of planning.

If you wind up in Indianapolis by accident on race weekend and need to see the race, call Tickets Up Front. They won't be cheap but they will have tickets. Prices range from $50-$300. There are also usually some folks around the track who sell tickets, and that is an option available on Sunday — albeit, not a very good one.

But remember where the biggest blocks of tickets go: to corporations, for promotion. Many companies buy blocks of tickets and for one reason or another cannot use them all. If you're in town Thursday, do some discreet checking. Although the bellman in your hotel may be able to tell you where to find a ticket, your best bet is to ask someone not usually accosted by race fans. Ask the guy at the grocery store; the clerk in the department store — get creative.

If you are neither assertive nor wealthy, spend $15 dollars and head to the infield. "The infield is the greatest deal in all of sports", says one veteran journalist. You may not see much action. In fact, some people don't even see the race! And some people *can't* see the race. But the infield is a happening like no other infield at any other oval. The "Snakepit" no longer exists as it once did, but the partying still persists. Once primarily located in the first turn, it was the test for the true party-goer. Most fans in the Snakepit are not there for the racing as much as for the partying itself, and it can get pretty wild, although the speedway will eject any real derelicts.

You can use the infield to park your car, even if your seat is outside in the grandstands; or park your car and sit on top and watch. Some families come to the race each year with a picnic lunch, and never even see the event, settling instead to hear the cars and see the crowd.

If you drive, there are several options. The Coca Cola Parking lot, between 25th and 30th on Georgetown Rd is probably your best bet, and is easiest to find a way out following the race. There are lots all along Georgetown Rd, between 30th and 38th, and several on 34th between Lafayette Rd. and Moller Rd. The two biggest parking areas are the infield and the North Forty Parking. Or you can park your car at the airport or downtown and take a shuttle to the track.

The Metro 500 Express takes passengers to and from the track on most qualifying days and race morning. Buses leave from three downtown areas: the first is on the east side of the Hoosier Dome, off Capitol Ave; the second is outside the Pan Am Plaza off Georgia St; and the last one is on Illinois St., between Market and Washington. The service begins at 8:00 and leaves every hour, on the hour. Returns from The Speedway are on the half-hour. The service runs as long as there are passengers.

In addition, there is a shuttle from the airport — located at the main terminal's lower level — which begins at 6:30 AM, and continues all day until the service is no longer necessary for outbound passengers. The service is only available on the first Saturday of qualifying and then again during the race.

Tickets for the shuttle are available in-advance, through Metro 500 Express Tickets, P.O. Box 2383, Indianapolis, IN 46206 (317 635-3344). Shuttle tickets can be purchased the day of the scheduled event at METRO's Downtown Customer Service Center, 36 North Delaware St. (on the first qualifying weekend); at the Union Station's Grand Hall Information Desk (second qualifying weekend); and booths on Capitol Ave. at the Hoosier Dome, Illinois St. at Union Station and Market St. on race day.

Tickets for the express bus are $2.00 one-way on the first and second qualifying weekends; Sunday's tickets are $7.00 one way or $12.00 round trip. The buses will let you off in front of the main gate on 16th (the front stretch, where the majority of the grandstands and the pits are, actually parallels Georgetown Rd.).

Indianapolis Raceway Park

P.O. Box 34300
Indianapolis, IN 46234

PH: (317) 291-4090
FAX: (317) 291-4220

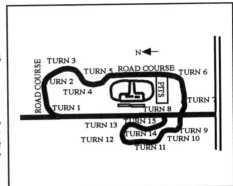

Location: Central Indiana, about five miles west of the Indianapolis Motor Speedway, one mile west of Clermont on U.S. Highway 136.

Circuit: .686 mile paved oval/quarter-mile dragstrip/ 2.5 mile road course; 14 turns.

Major races: NHRA U.S. Nationals; NHRA Winston Drag Racing Series; NASCAR Busch Grand National Series; USAC Silver Crown and Midget Championships; SCCA National Road Racing Championships; WERA Motorcycle Road Racing Championships.

Indianapolis Raceway Park is mostly known for its .686-mile oval track, which has served as the cornerstone of ESPN's popular series, Saturday Night Thunder, since its inception in 1988. The ESPN production has an average of 1.1 million viewers per show, making IRP the most televised short track in motorsports.

But the park is far more than that. Located five miles northwest of Indy, the 300 acre facility holds the world's largest and most prestigious drag race, the annual NHRA U.S. Nationals. First appearing on the NHRA trail in 1961, The U.S. Nationals boast a million-and-a-half dollar purse, 1,000 entries, and 150,000 spectators. It has been held at IRP for over 30 years, and the dragstrip was the site of the first 200 mile-per-hour run posted in 1964 by Connie Kalitta. The strip also attracts thousands of relatively local drivers for the Winston Drag Racing Series and the Good Guys Hot Rod Happening plus some 500 bikes to the Fall's ProStar Motorcycle Drag Racing competition

But there's even more to it than that. Three facilities make up IRP. The two-and-a-half mile road course, which is not used for any major series (except SCCA National events) is as good as any in the country. Several major teams use the road course for testing, and WERA motorcycles race here; Skip Barber also uses the track occasionally for instruction.

The oval hosts NASCAR's Busch Grand National series and USAC Midget and Silver Crowns. The Budweiser Night Before The 500 is one of the best USAC shows in the country. There is also a Skoal Classic on Indy Pole Night, which often attracts drivers from the 500.

The oval alone holds 20,000 — which is full for special events like the Busch GN. The first race on the IRP paved oval was in 1961. A young Texan named AJ Foyt won that first IRP race — then promptly went to Indy the following day and won his first 500.

Except for the nights in May, which for obvious reasons will be full, the area around IRP will be easy enough to find rooms. See the Indianapolis section in this guide, or call IRP for more information.

Indiana State Fairgrounds

5106 E. 65th St.
Indianapolis, IN 46201

PH: (track): (317) 923-3431
Fairgrounds: (317) 927-7500

Location: Central Indiana, in northwest Indianapolis, on 38th St.

Circuit: One mile clay oval.

Major races: USAC Silver Crown, and midget Championships.

Indiana State Fairgrounds Speedway hosts two USAC Silver Crown races. The first is traditionally run one week before the Indy 500 to a packed house, and the second takes place around Labor Day. On the final Saturday of the State Fair the track also hosts a AMA Camel Pro race.

Located on the northeast side of Indianapolis, and just off I-65, I-74, I-70, and U.S. Highways 40 and 31, it is easily accessible. The venue offers 170 RV campsites, with modern amenities. For more information see the Indianapolis Motor Speedway section in this guide or call the track.

Indianapolis Speedrome

P.O. Box 301
Greenwood, IN 46142
PH (track): (317) 888-7265

Location: Central Indiana, in southeastern Indianapolis, at U.S. Highway 52 and Kitley Ave.

Circuit: Fifth-mile paved oval.

Major races: USAC Midget Championships.

Indianapolis Speedrome, located in oval-rich Indianapolis, hosts several midget races through the year, but the major event is a non-sanctioned three-hour figure-eight race with pro-stock cars. The cars are high tech racers; tube framed, and often costing in excess of $25,000 each. The regular show is run Friday nights and is run with full-bodied and open wheeled cars. The facility seats 7,000.

John Andretti became a Midget Champion at this track, as did the late, great Rich Vogler. Rooms can be found a mile up the road — or downtown, or see the Indianapolis Motor Speedway section in this guide for more information.

Kokomo Speedway

P.O. Box 448
Kokomo, IN 46901
PH: (317) 459-3877
Location: Central Indiana, about 50 miles north of Indianapolis.
From Indianapolis, take State Route 31 into Kokomo, then west on Morgan St. one-and-a-quarter miles to Davis, and north on Davis to the track.

Circuit: Quarter-mile clay oval; slightly banked.

Major races: World of Outlaws Sprint Car Championship Shootout; and USAC Midgets.

Racing at Kokomo Speedway is mostly done in sprinters and midgets. One noteworthy item concerning Kokomo is their reluctance to allow winged sprint cars to race here. Track officials don't run any races — with the exception of the WoO — with winged cars. The biggest show of the year, however, is the WoO show.

The track holds 3,000 in the grandstands and another 2,000-3,000 in the bleachers located in the pits and on the top of the hill. You can camp at speedway, but there are no hookups for RVs. Kokomo, which is actually just north of the track, has plenty of rooms.

Lawrenceburg Speedway
Lawrenceburg, IN   47025

PH (track): (812) 537-3599

Location: South western Ohio, 20 miles west of Cincinnati, one mile east of Lawrenceburg on U.S. Highway 50.

Circuit: Quarter-mile dirt oval.

Major races: USAC Sprint and Midget Championships.

Lawrenceburg Speedway features several sprint car shows, including open-wheel nights with non-winged USAC midgets and IMCA modifieds. The weekly show pays $1,000 for a Midget win. Recently a change of format at the track now runs the racing on Saturday nights. There are rooms in western Cincinnati, or stay in Aurora or Burlington, KY.

Putnam Park
County Road 550 E.
(317) 526-2290

Office: 7776 Moller Rd.
Indianapolis, IN   46268
Office Phone: (317) 875-7417
FAX: (317) 875-7460

Location: 35 miles southwest of Indianapolis, off I 70 West at the Cloverdale Exit #41, then north on U.S. 231 to Rte 40 east to Mt Meridian, and right on Road 550.

Circuit:1.8 mile road course;10 turns.

Major Races: WERA and AMA motorcycle regional championships.

This new road course outside Indianapolis, designed, financed and built by Dick Diasio, was created when Diasio, as the President of the local Porsche Club, was unable to get any dates at IRP. He changed that by building his own track.

This Field of Dreams racetrack, which actually does sit in an Indianapolis cornfield, has been only open since Labor Day of 1991, and the track managed to book most weekends of 1992. Things continue doing well, and prolific testing has been going on here, most notably with Bobby Rahal, Scott Goodyear and Raul Boesel from IndyCars doing shakedowns, and Buz McCall's Trans-Am team doing a driver test for the seat relinquished by Scott Sharp.

This is probably the only hilly part of Indiana, and the track contains 45 feet of elevation changes. The surface is glass-smooth via laser technology. It is 30 feet wide everywhere, and all corners are fairly fast sweepers. The toughest part of the course is the turn 9-10 combination, which is a pair of corners starting with a very fast off-camber right-hander with a hump in the middle which leads to turn ten which is another very fast right hander. The one corner not known by a number is not as ominous as it sounds: Dead Bear Turn, a long 180 with a few degrees of banking, was named when they found a dead bear while laying out the track.

There is a minimal amount of guardrailed areas and lots of run-off. When the track appeared, there was only one tire wall, now three tire walls exist and the other guardrails are surrounded by haybales. There are no gravel pits yet... but are expected eventually.

Since the place was built entirely with private funds, things will proceed slowly at first. A three-year plan is in place that will eventually render the facility suitable for pro racing.

In 1992 spectators were allowed in free, and there were no gates. As one official explained, "It's hard to charge someone to stand in the mud". But there is no longer any mud, 150 acres were planted with grass and there is now a paved paddock and staging area, complete with a restroom and flush toilets. Can ticketed admission be far behind?

There are plenty of hotels in the area. Greencastle, the biggest town, is just eight miles away and has a very capable tourist board. The Covered Bridge Festival, held every October, is a big deal in these parts, and several State Parks close by add to the allure of the area. Greencastle is also home to De Paul University.

There is no camping at track this year, but there probably will be in a few years. Campsites exist in Cloverdale, at the KOA Campgrounds, which are 3 miles from track. For more information call the very amiable track office, or for hotel info call the Greencastle Development Center at (317) 653-2474.

Salem Speedway
P.O. Box 466
Salem, IN 47167
PH (track): (812) 883-6504
Location: Central Indiana, 100 miles south of Indianapolis, on Highway

56, just outside Salem.

Circuit: Half-mile paved oval.

Major races: USAC Sprint Car Championships; ASA Championships; USAC Midgets; and ARCA.

Salem Speedway re-opened in 1987 after a six year layoff with some substantial changes, making it one of the finest half-mile paved ovals in oval-rich Indiana.

The 52 acre facility was purchased by Don Gettelfinger, who immediately put buckets full of money into new guardrails, new catch fencing, a new paint job, and upgraded grandstands. The track, which originally opened in 1947, was torn apart by a tornado in 1981, and had been only haphazardly repaired. As soon as Gettelfinger bought the facility, he completely repaired and immediately reopened it.

This track boasts of being the place that Mario Andretti won his first USAC race in 1964, and where Darrell Waltrip held a winning streak of six straight races. This is also the track where Rich Vogler lost his life. NASCAR once used this track, and where Benny Parsons won several races here on the 33 degree half-mile banking. Salem has plenty of rooms.

Tri- State Speedway
Rural Route 2
Haubstadt, IN   47639

PH: (office) (812) 768-6025
(track) (812) 768-5995

Location: Southwestern Indiana, approximately 145 miles from Indianapolis.

From Indianapolis, take Interstate I 65 South to I 64 West to State Route 41, heading north — the track is on SR 41, three miles from the junction of I-64 and Highway 41.

Circuit: Quarter-mile clay oval; semi- banked.

Major races: World of Outlaws Sprint Car Championship Shootout; USAC Sprint cars.

Set in the flat, rural surroundings of western Indiana Tri- State Speedway's 5,000 seat facility hosts an Outlaw show — the biggest of the year — and usually fills the place to capacity. There is camping here, but there are no RV hookups. You can stay in Princeton, which is some 10 miles from the track, or Evansville, which is 15 miles away.

Winchester Speedway
P.O. Box 31
Winchester, IN   47394

257

PH: (317) 584-9701

Location: Central Indiana, 70 miles northeast of Indianapolis, off State Highway 32, just west of Winchester.

Circuit: Half-mile paved oval.

Major races: USAC Sprint Car and Midget Championships; ARCA Championship.

Winchester Speedway is the second oldest purpose-built facility in the country — only Indianapolis has a deeper history. The track boasts of 13 regular drivers who went on to win the Indy 500.

Winchester's paved surfaces recently joined ESPN's Speed World show and looks to appear again on an ESPN in the future with the USAC Midgets or ARCA cars. Winchester has a few rooms; or call the track for a better idea of where to stay.

Adams County Speedway
P.O. Box 8
Nodaway, IA 50857

PH: (712) 785-3271

Location: Southwest Iowa, 90 miles southeast of Omaha, on hwys 34 & 148.

Circuit: Half-mile clay oval.

Major races: NASCAR Winston Racing Series (Central Region).

Adams County Speedway is located at the Adams County Fairgrounds in the northeast section of Corning. Adams is the smallest county in the state, and the track is set in the largest residential area of mostly rural Corning. The county seat is only 2,000 strong.

The facilities were recently upgraded with new lighting, and can accommodate 2,500 spectators. Once a horse racing track, it was modified, banked and has been used as a motor racing track for 40 years. It joined the Winston Racing Series in 1984. Staying here is not the easiest thing to do. There are a few rooms out in Nodaway... but there is no Hilton.

Des Moines
Greater Des Moines Grand Prix Association
2201 Ingersoll
Des Moines, IA 50312

PH: (515) 243-5515

Location: Downtown Des Moines, between Third and Fifth Avenues, bounded by Crocker Ave, which is the longest straight on the racetrack.

Circuit: 1.8 mile 12 turns

Major races: SCCA Trans-Am Championship.

1990 Ruan Greater Des Moines Grand Prix Course Map

Crossing the Des Moines River twice, the Des Moines Grand Prix is the only street circuit in the U.S. that traverses water..

The Des Moines community really gets behind this SCCA road race, and the enthusiasm shows. Support comes not only from local race fans, but from corporations. Corporate interest here is probably better than any race in the U.S., with some 160 hospitality suites rented to businesses during the 1992 motorsports event.

As with any street circuit, viewing is really limited to a couple of corners at a time. One of the best places to view racing is along the start/finish straight on Crocker. There are reserved grandstands in corner-two, which also provide a look at the best action at start/finish and the final corner. If you don't feel like being sedentary, buy the GA tickets and have a look from the GA grandstands on Second Ave. — that area gives you a view of both bridges.

So far, this race has been plagued by odd weather. Although crowds have been large, officials believe when things get back to the normal 80-85 degree mark (in 1989, the mercury hit 110 degrees, in '90 it poured down rain, and in '91 and '92 it was hot once again) the crowds will increase.

The track is, of course, located downtown, and there are several hotels within walking distance. There are six gates around the track, so from any direction, one can get trackside with relative ease. Hotel information can be found by calling the Des Moines Convention and Visitors Bureau at (515) 286-4960 (or call the Greater Des Moines Grand Prix Association for a listing of the hotels in the immediate area).

Dubuque Fairgrounds Speedway
14583 Old Highway Rd
Dubuque, IA   52011

PH: (319) 588-1406

Location: West Iowa, seven miles from the border of Illinois, 220 miles from Chicago.

From Dubuque, take highway 20 to Old Highway 20, or 416 to the track entrance.

Circuit: Three-eighths mile clay oval.

Major races: NASCAR interseries (Central Region).

Just a few short miles west of the Mississippi River — in the same area where river boat gambling is starting to explode, Dubuque Fairgrounds Speedway

259

is located. Already five miles from the dog track, it is certainly about to see a boom in interest with the explosion of gamblers coming through the area. Who knows, by the end of the decade you may be able to get odds on Steve Kinser.

Built in 1966, the oval has seats for 10,000, and fills most of them with a good series of weekly shows. You can camp at the fairgrounds, and there are a handful of hookups. For real beds, call (319) 557-9545.

Farley Speedway
2044 Washington Ave
Cedar Rapids, IA   52403

PH: (319) 744-3620

Location: Northeastern Iowa, 20 miles from Dubuque, on Highway 20.

Circuit: Half-mile high banked clay oval.

Major races: NASCAR interseries (Central region)

Farley Speedway, which recently reopened after a multi-year hiatus, only ran USA sprint cars in 1989. When the USA folded, the WoO allotted a date for the new speedway. But late in the WoO planning stages for the 1990 calendar, the Farley schedule couldn't be met, and the tour didn't make race at Farley. For some reason, it was also left off the schedule again in '91 and '92.

The 5,000 seat facility is 20 miles from Dubuque, 60 miles from Cedar Rapids, in the heart of farming country. The track itself is a high banked clay racetrack just on the edge of town. Racing is a Friday affair, with late models, modified pro stock, Outlaw Stock Cars, and two annual Busch All-Star NASCAR races filling the card. There is camping at the facility. And just up the road, the Mississippi River is surrounded by camp grounds. Call the track and they'll give you more info.

Hawkeye Downs
P.O. Box 549
West Burlington, IA   52655
Track: (319) 365-7777

Location: Eastern Iowa, just outside Cedar Rapids, off Interstate I 380 at exit B-16, a half-mile west to sixth street, and north to the track.

Circuit: Half-mile paved oval.

Major Races: USAC Midgets.

Hawkeye Downs, Iowa's only asphalt racing oval, is located in West Burlington, just a few miles from the Mississippi River and the Illinois State border. The track has some 6,500 seats, and has a versatile schedule, running open-wheeled, full-bodied, and a handful of motocross races. Burlington is just east of West Burlington and the city of 28,000 has plenty of lodging.

Knoxville Raceway

Marion County Fair
P.O. Box 347
1000 N. Lincoln
Knoxville, IA   50318

PH: (515) 842-5431/ (515) 842-3220
FAX: (515) 842-2899

Location: Central Iowa, approximately 40 miles from Des Moines, on State Route 14 in the Marion County Fairgrounds.

Circuit: Half-mile dirt oval; semi-banked.

Major races: World of Outlaws Sprint Car Championship Shootout; Knoxville Nationals.

Knoxville has a full calendar of events, with racing usually occurring four days a week, and with everything from motorcycling to sprint cars racing here. The weekly features are, appropriately, sprint car races, with two sizes of cars (410 CID and 360 CID).

The season starts in April and features racing every Saturday through August. The World of Outlaws tour stops in Knoxville once a month April through September. The 17,600-seat facility often has televised races, and most top racers have been on Knoxville's banks at one time in their career. This is a premier sprint car oval — and is touted as absolutely the best in the country. And if the on-track action is not enough to spur a pilgrimage to Knoxville, the National Sprint Car Hall Of Fame Museum recently opened, overlooking the second turn, surely will.

Although the area gets crowded when the bigger shows come through — and will likely be packed to the gills for the Knoxville Sprint Car Nationals, held mid-August, and the WoO Hawkeye Fall Harvest Race (late September), which will wind up the Knoxville season — there should be plenty of rooms even if you have to travel as far as Des Moines. Knoxville has several hotels, but if booked try: Newton, which has seven hotels; Pella, which has three inns; Chariston, with three; Oskaloosa's five lodgings are conveniently located; and there is at least one hotel each in Indianola, Prairie City, and Albia.

West Liberty Raceway

2044 Washington Ave
Cedar Rapids, IA   52403

PH: (319) 627-2414

Location: Eastern Iowa, 40 miles southeast of Cedar Rapids, five miles south of I 80, at the West Liberty exit.

Circuit: Half-mile clay oval.

Major races: NASCAR interseries (Central Region).

West Liberty Raceway is located in the town of West Liberty, at the Muscatine County Fairground. The grassy rolling hills around the facility belie the fairgrounds layout, which, like most, is completely level. The biggest race of the year is the Spring Championships for late model cars.

There are campgrounds in the area, although nothing is available at the fair. Call the track for more information on where to stay.

Heartland Park
7530 S. Topeka Ave
Topeka, KS   66619/
1805 SW 71st St
Topeka, KS   66619

PH: (913) 862-4781
FAX: (913) 862-2061
Tickets: (913) 862-7223/ (800) 43 RACES

Location: Eastern Kansas, just south of Topeka on Highway 75.

Circuit: 2.5 mile road course; 14 turns/ 1.8 mile road course; quarter-mile dragstrip.

Major races: IMSA Camel GT Championships; NHRA Heartland Nationals; ARCA Stock Cars.

When construction on Heartland Park's multipurpose facility began five years ago the Mid American Pipeline Company was just one of many entities which challenged the construction of the racetrack. Mid American Pipeline Company's natural gas pipeline ran across what is now the south portion of the racetrack, and the company objected to having their pipe covered over by soil and an occasional racecar. But judges, in what turned out to be only the first in a series of court rounds, decided for the track and building went on as proposed.

Three years later, however, the pipeline company won its appeal in the 10th District Court in Denver and the decision was reversed. For a while, the south portion of the 2.5 mile track was in jeopardy, while the possiblity of tearing up the track in order to expose the pipeline (which is apparently covered by a major highway, and which also reportedly runs beneath several major suburbs in Kansas City) existed. The pipeline never affected the dragstrip or the 1.8 mile short course. Although IMSA could have run the 1.8 mile track they chose not to do so..

In the meantime, the president of the pipeline company and the track president, sat down and discussed the possibilities, ultimately reaching an agreement. As it turns out, the entire fight concerned pipelines which were not yet built, and which would be in jeopardy if the track were to win their case. So the track agreed to allow future construction of pipelines on the south side of the facility as long as the existing lines can be covered — as they currently are.

Regardless, racing continues. Heartland Park will likely be associated

START/ FINISH

more with drag racing in the years to come than with road racing. Not that it's not a great road course — in fact it was one of the best. But the facility is the first since the Texas Motorplex to design a purpose-built dragstrip.

When the NHRA was first founded by Wally Parks in the early 60s, the first national event was held in Kansas. Kansas, because it was the exact geographical center of the country, does cater to drag racers. But oddly enough, one of the major instigators of the track in the Heartland of America was the SCCA, which only held one Trans-Am race at the facility since the gates opened.

The track was heralded as a prototype for multi-purpose motorsports facilities. At nearly every grandstand spectators can see the majority of the road course. The staging for the drag racing is done as if it was a drag-racing-only track. And parking for both drag racing and road racing is plentiful.

But the emphasis recently has been toward stock cars. As this guide goes to press an announcement is expected concerning an ASA race at Heartland Park. Heartland officials hope to have Busch Grand National and perhaps Winston Cup after that.

It is, however, Kansas. Dorothy and Toto may have wanted to get back there, but some drivers don't. It's very difficult to get to, timewise. The nearest airport for a commercial flight is in Kansas City, MO.

The drivers have no problems getting rooms, since the teams make certain they're booked far in advance of the race. But Topeka is only 118,000 strong, and there aren't that many places to stay. Unlike many cities of that size, there's nothing around Topeka. If the race gets 50,000 and they're all local fans, that means that almost half the city is at the track — and obviously that's not going to be the case. Even though several new hotels opened in the past year, rooms still fill up early, so make arrangements as soon as possible.

There is some camping at Perry Recreation Area, 16 miles northeast of Topeka on Highway 24. It would be wise to call the parks and recreation dept at (913) 295-3838; for information on Lodging call the Topeka Chamber of Commerce at (913) 234-2644.

Hutchinson Raceway Park
207 So. Mohawk
Hutchinson, KS   67501

(316) 662-2213

Location: South west corner of Wichita, off Highway 50 North, at 4th st, west to the track.

Circuit: Three-eighths mile clay oval, with a one-eighth mile Quarter midget track inside the larger oval.

Major Races: World Of Outlaws Sprint Cars.

The annual Fun Valley National Baseball Tournament is Hutchinson's claim to fame. The Hutchinson Raceway Park was actually built to be a part of the baseball season and was originally called the Salt City Speedway. In November of '90, Gary Mussatto bought the track and re-opened it in 1991 as a serious race track.

Regular racing is now held on Friday, and the biggest race is Wheatshocker National, held last weekend of September or the J-Hawk Classic, which runs the third weekend in October. Outlaws race in May. And although the place holds 8,000 in Grandstands, there have been no sellouts yet, and 2,500 is so far the biggest crowd.

The 55 acres facility offers camping, but has no hookups or showers — yet. There is electricity in the pits, and there may be showers by the time the Outlaws roll around in May, so call first before bringing the port-a-potty. The track has a list of motels, and some give racers' rates. The track will send or fax you a list if you give them a call.

Lakeside Speedway
5615 Wolcott Dr.,
Kansas City, KS   66109

(913)   299-2040
(913)   299 1105

Location: On the Kansas side of metropolitan Kansas City area, five miles north of I 70, at I 435 exit No. #18, Wolcott Dr., a half-mile west of the exit.

Circuit: Half-mile semi-banked paved oval.

Major Races: World Of Outlaws Sprint Car Championship.

Lakeside Speedway permanently etched itself into Outlaws history books by becoming the first track ever to host Outlaws Sprint cars on pavement.

In April of '92, World Of Outlaws driver Doug Wolfgang crashed hard between turns four and five in practice. Wolfgang had glanced off a tire barrier which shot him straight out to the retaining wall, and with no steering, he hit the wall hard and knocked himself unconscious, the car bursting into flames. Steve Beitler, Mark Kinser and Lee Brewer Jr. all stopped, risking injury, and pried Wolfgang out of the car. Wolfgang was taken to the hospital, burned over 30% of his body. He remained in the Kansas hospital for two months, and had been in therapy up until the end of the season. Due to the accident, World of Outlaws officials are taking a second look at asphalt tracks, and certainly will be critical of Lakeside — even though the track was not at fault.

This NASCAR Mid America Region track normally seats 5,000 for regular weekly Friday night racing, but filled out to 8,000 via temporary grandstands for the first-ever pavement race. Previews of the upcoming season include ARTGO Stock Cars, and a July 10th feature..

The track offers campsites, and the place has never been full so you'll be able to spread out. The grounds can accommodate 200. There are no hookups, but showers are available. You can stay in Kansas, KS, and the Outlaws use the Riverview Inn at I 70 at fifth St. as their base of operations; that number is (800) 542-2983. Or call the track for more information on rooming.

Thomas County Speedway
P.O. Box 372
Colby, KS   67701

PH: (913) 462-8860

Location: Northwestern Kansas, one mile north of Interstate I 70, on U.S. Highway 24.

Circuit: Three-eighths mile clay oval.

Major races: USAC Midgets.

Thomas County Speedway is located inside the Thomas Country Free Fair fairgrounds, which has its annual gathering at the beginning of August. But from April to September Saturday night racing is the program. The grandstands hold some 4,500.
Located in northwest Kansas 30 miles east of the Colorado border — it's typical Kansas: flat. The western wheat and cornfields don't inspire use for many hotels, but there should be no problem finding rooms in Colby unless the fair is in town.

Florence Speedway
Office: P.O. Box 12807
Cincinnati, OH   45212

PH (track): (606) 485-7591

Location: Northern Kentucky, 15 miles from the Ohio River, nine miles south of Florence on U.S. Highway 42.

Circuit: Half-mile clay oval.

Major races: USAC Sprint Car Championship; NASCAR interseries.

Florence Speedway hosts a regular NASCAR Saturday night show with late models, sport stocks, stocks, and the Bomber division. The 4,500 seat racetrack has only a few special shows a year which do not occur Saturdays — the Fourth of July fireworks show being the biggest. Rooms are available in nearby Cincinnati, by calling (606) 621-2142.

Louisville Downs
P.O. Box 32457
Louisville, KY   40232

PH: (502) 964-6415

Location: South end of Louisville off SR 264 .

Circuit: Half-mile dirt oval.

Major races: AMA Grand National Championship Camel Pro Series.

Louisville Downs is a Kentucky harness racing track which is transformed into an AMA Grand National track once a season for its only deviation from four

265

legged racing during the whole year. The half-mile is a favorite of the riders (AMA riders, that is), and the 8,500 seat facility is generally packed when the AMA boys come through. The track itself is opened most of the year — although it shuts down several times through the 12 months.

The Louisville area is rich in accommodations, but the AMA riders generally stay at the Executive Inn, which is the closest at three miles from the track. For more information on lodging in the Louisville area, call the Louisville Visitors' Bureau (800) 626-5646; or, in Kentucky, call (800) 633-3384.

Louisville Motor Speedway
P.O. Box 19678
Louisville, KY   40219

PH: (502) 966-2277

Location: North Central Kentucky, in Louisville, on Outer Loop Road, one mile west of Interstate I 65's exit 127.

Circuit: Three-eighths mile paved oval.

Major races: NASCAR interseries (Mid-America Region); USAC Midgets.

Louisville Motor Speedway is found four miles from Churchill Downs, Kentucky's famous horse racing track and the home of the Kentucky Derby. The Motor Speedway is set at the end of the Stanford Field Airport, a few miles from downtown Louisville. The track, which opened for business in 1987, seats 12,000 fans.

The place runs some 50-60 events a year, including several non-racing shows. The biggest race is the Bluegrass 300 — a set of three 100-lap events for late model stocks; the next biggest is the Mid-South Figure 8 Championships; or the Granger's Race of Champions, another race that's beginning to gain in popularity with several name Winston Cup drivers competing in a match race.

There are 10 motels within two miles of the track, and accommodations, in general, are no problem. Call the track for the names and numbers of those inns, or call the Louisville Visitors' Bureau at (502) 582-3732 to make your own lodging arrangements.

Richmond Raceway
1221 N. Main
London, KY   40741

PH (track): (606) 623-9408

Location: Central Kentucky, 25 miles south of Lexington, on State Road 52, in Richmond, KY.

Circuit: Quarter-mile clay oval.

Major races: USAC Sprint Car Championships.

Richmond Raceway runs several USAC winged and non-winged shows throughout the year, and usually draws a full house for the bigger shows, filling all 5,500 seats. The regular show is held on Saturday night. The track is located out of the mainstream, and hotels, although there are a few in the area, are not the easiest to find. Call the track for names of the closest.

Grand Prix Du Mardi Gras

601 Loyola St.,
Suite 214
New Orleans, LA   70113

PH: (504) 581-RACE/ (800) RACETRK
FAX: (504) 581-7276

Location: Downtown New Orleans, just off Interstate I-10 at the Poydras exit adjacent to the New Orleans Superdome.

Circuit: 1.5 miles road course; 10 turns.

Major races: IMSA Camel GTP.

Louisiana, being as sports-barren as it is, certainly lacks no interest in motorsports, and the Grand Prix du Mardi Gras has been met with great success by both drivers and fans.

The '91 circuit was comprised of downtown streets around the historic New Orleans Warehouse District. Start/finish was on Canal Street, the technical boundary of the French Quarter, and the track ran past the old World Expo site. The first year's temporary layout was really temporary.... The current site was actually agreed upon prior to the 1991 season, but an arena football game at the Superdome coincided with the inaugural race date. In 1992 the race was moved about four miles away to the Superdome where it remained for 1993 and beyond.

While trying to create an aesthetically pleasing racetrack, the Crescent City Motorsports organization, the organizers of the race, set start/finish in '91 on a very short few hundred feet of asphalt along Canal St.. IMSA expressed a distaste for the layout from day one, and the start was eventually held on the back portion of the track, on the longest straight on the track on Poydras St..

The new circuit has a 1,000 foot front stretch, which is located on Poydras St. The track winds counter-clockwise around the Superdome via Poydras St., then West Access Rd., Girod St., Loyola Ave, Peridido St., La Salle St., and back onto Poydras St..

The organizers have tried to establish ticket prices as low as possible, and the apparent result has been the lowest general admission tickets in IMSA street racing at $15.00 (was $12.50 originally), which includes the 14% tax levied on everything sold in New Orleans.

There are also some fantastic GA areas here (which have been enhanced at the new circuit). Grandstands, likewise, are

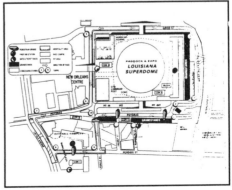

inexpensive, with the most costly reserved seat going for just $50.

Staying in New Orleans should be no problem — even during the race. But for the best spots you'll need to book early. DMI Inc. will be handling bookings for the event, and a toll-free call will likely get you set up pretty quickly. For more information call DMI at (800) 366-8882; or call the New Orleans Convention and Visitor's Center at (504) 566-5011.

State Capitol Dragway
11436 Highway 190 West
Erwinville, LA

PH: (504) 627-4574

Location: South eastern Louisiana, in Erwinville, 10 miles west of Baton Rouge on U.S Highway 190.

Circuit: Quarter mile dragstrip.

Major races: NHRA Cajun Nationals.

State Capitol Dragway, Louisiana's only major permanent racetrack, is a purpose-built dragstrip which has hosted a national Championship NHRA event since 1977. The southern stop on the NHRA tour is now one of the favorites of the NHRA pro regulars.

The facility essentially it sits in the middle of swampland, ten miles from Baton Rouge, and a few miles from the Atchafalaya River. The dragstrip is run in a north-south configuration, with the north side being the finish line. To the east is the pits, and to the west is parking.

The surroundings are littered with cypress trees, and an occasional bog. The track is beautiful when it's dry, but is not dry all the time. The Cajun Nationals have been rained-out several times in the past, and the parking lot turns into a quagmire. The substantial rains have been bad enough in recent years where the water has come through the track. Like most of areas near the gulf, Erwinville is hot and generally humid.

The few bad points aside, State Capitol Dragway offers the best ambience of almost any racetrack in the U.S.. Here, that famous southern hospitality is mixed with some of the most sensational and unique food in the country. The area is world-famous for Cajun cooking. May's Cajun Nationals date also coincides with the Crawfish season, and local crawfish dishes abound.

Louisiana racefans get behind the event, and the Baton Rouge City officials promote the race with Cajun bands and several publicity tours. Even at the track, Louisiana traditions transcend typical racetrack thinking: hamburgers are not the staple here — jambalaya and fried crawfish are more along the tradition of snack bar food.

Baton Rouge is the closest town of any size. The magnolia and cypress lined streets are worth the short drive. There are plenty of rooms in Baton Rouge and the I 10 Corridor, but if you prefer it, New Orleans is only 75 miles from the track. For the Baton Rouge Visitor's Center, and information about rooms, call (800) LA-ROUGE or (504) 383-1825 (in Louisiana).

Oxford Plains Speedway
Route 26
Oxford, ME   04270

PH:(207)   539-8865

Location: Southwestern Maine, about 50 miles from Portland in Oxford, 20 miles off I 495 on Highway 26.

Circuit: One-third mile paved oval/ eighth-mile dragstrip.

Major races: NASCAR Busch Grand National Series; NASCAR interseries (Eastern Seaboard Region).

Oxford Plains Speedway's third-mile paved oval was built in 1949 — as a slightly longer dirt circuit. Revitalized in 1965 with new grandstands and a paving of the clay surface, the track gained notoriety with the old NASCAR Limited Sportsman circuit which ran for the first time in 1966.
Bobby Allison won his first Winston Cup race here, and such notables as Geoff and Brett Bodine, and Richard Petty also won races at Oxford.
The Limited Sportsman series at Oxford evolved and changed, and with the addition of several other NASCAR series Oxford finally got a break and lured the Busch Grand National series to its short track in 1987.
In 1992 the Oxford show expanded to feature two more classes of regulars, which essentially developed the endurance series into a weekly competition.
The track is located in one of the few flat areas of the Oxford Hills, the foothills of Maine's Western Mountains. The track is some 20 miles from ski country, and 20 minutes from Lewiston or 45 from Portland. It is 1-2 hours from three major metro shopping areas. For more information on hotels call Oxford Hills Chamber of Commerce at (207) 743-2425.

Hagerstown Speedway
Office: P.O. Box 712
McConnellsburg, PA   17233

PH: (office) (717) 425- 5141
(track) (301) 582-0640

Location: Northwestern Maryland, approximately 70 miles from Washington DC, in Hagerstown.
From Washington DC, take Interstate I 270 to I 70 North to Hagerstown — the track is just off I 70 in Hagerstown.

Circuit: Half-mile clay oval; semi banked.

Major races: World of Outlaws Sprint Car Championship Shootout.

Amid rolling greenery and scenic forests of western Maryland, Hagerstown Speedway looms like a hilltop citadel. The track is enclosed on all but one side by woods (the side not bounded by trees is dominated by grandstands) making it a unique place to watch a dirt race. It is one of the best dirt tracks in the country,

269

hosting both motorcycles and cars (WoO, sprinters, ARCA, and late model stockers).

Track owner Frank Plessinger was the first in the country to offer a $50,000 prize for a dirt track win. Later he created a speedweek worth $200,000. Hagerstown is constantly being updated, and its modernization — as well as its large prize money — make it a regular favorite on television.

The track also holds a handful of interesting races you won't see elsewhere — like big-rig truck racing on the dirt. The track has been a long time host of World Of Outlaws, and in '87 began running Camel Pro Grand National events. Hagerstown has a handful of rooms, and you should have no problem there, or try Frederick, which is 28 miles away.

For information on local hotels call the track, or call the Visitors Information Bureau at (301) 837-INFO.

Maryland International Dragway
8904 Centerville
Manassas, VA 22110

Track: Route 234
Budds Creek, MD

PH: (703) 368-8445
FAX: (703) 631-2945

Location: Southern Maryland, 10 miles north of the Potomac and Wicomico Rivers.

From I95, take exit 7A 30 miles south to the flashing lights and Rte. 234, turing left on 234, proceeding seven miles to track, which is located on the right hand side.

Maryland International Dragway's quarter-mile strip is located in a flat tract of land, surrounded by rural scenery and neighbors the Potomac Raceway and a motorcross track named Budd's Creek Raceway. A few times a year the dates conflict but there never seems to be a problem between the three circuits. Occasionally the lines into the track extend a way back along the single lane road for the bigger shows.

The track runs a weekly street car bracket series on Friday nights, and then a non-street legal race on Saturday. Funny Cars, Jet Cars, Wheels Standers and Nitrous Pro Stock make appearances throughout the season on Sundays, preempting Friday races. Sometimes Monday nights will host an occasional event. The biggest race of the year, the Pro Stock Open, is usually held mid-July.

The track added bleachers recently on both the spectator and pit side so there are quite a few more seats. If you get to Maryland Dragway late, you'll still be able to get in — even if you don't have a reserved seat — and can almost stand next to fence. So far, it has never sold out.

Campsites are available for special events (but not for fans ; racers only). Fans can stay in La Plata, which is 15 minutes north or Waldorf, also north. You can also call the track for a list of hotels.

Riverside Park Speedway
P.O. Box 307
Agwam, MA 01001

PH: (413) 786-9300

Location: Connecticut/Massachusetts line, four miles northwest of Springfield, in Agwam, MA on State Route 159.

Circuit: Quarter-mile paved oval.

Major races: NASCAR interseries (Northwest Region).

Riverside Park Speedway can be found inside the grounds of the Riverside Amusement Park. The amusement park is complete with roller coasters and several other thrill rides. The 8,500 seat facility hosts the Modified Tour and Busch Grand National North together at the end of August — which is the biggest race of the year.

There is plenty of lodging in the area, since Springfield is just 15 miles north of the track, and Hartford is close as well. Hotels can be located on Route 5, which is also known as Riverdale Rd..

Detroit Renaissance Grand Prix, Inc.,
100 Renaissance Center #1760
Detroit, MI 48243

PH: (313) 259-5400
FAX: (313) 567-8355
Ticket info: (313) 259-7749

Location: Two miles east of Downtown Detroit, on Belle Isle, on the Detroit river.

Circuit: 2.1 mile road course; 14 turns

Major races: CART IndyCar World Series Championship; SCCA Trans-Am.

In 1988 a plan to move the over-criticized Detroit Formula One Grand Prix street race to a permanent replacement site on Detroit's Belle Isle Park surfaced. It died quickly. And so did the Grand Prix.

Before even a decent wake, Indy Cars came to the Motor City. The event has since become a showcase for American manufacturers, with the American SCCA Trans-Am at least as popular as the Indy Car race.

But with the new fascination with Detroit — which was truly generated by auto racing — new con-

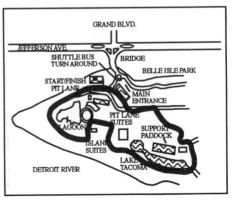

struction downtown threatened again to kill the downtown race. So the plan to move to Belle Isle Park resurfaced. This time it was not stillborn, and on June 7th, 1992 the 11th annual Detroit Grand Prix was held on Belle Isle Park, two miles east of the old circuit at the Renaissance Center.

Originally in 1988, concerns existed that the island would be a nightmare for ingress and egress. There is, after all, only one bridge on and off the island. But the management crew of the race have done a careful job of planning the event and have studied ways to move the expected 50,000-75,000 people per day.

The Unlimited Hydroplane races attract upwards of 500,000 people, 200,000 of whom watch the races from the island. And Detroit Police are not as evident there as they are for the GP.

A purpose-built shuttle turnaround was constructed for shuttles carrying people onto the island. From the drop off spectators just follow signs to their seats. In addition, the walkway across the five-laned bridge is open for those who choose to walk the 3/10ths of a mile onto the circuit.

The shuttle pick-up points are located at Cobo Hall, the site of the old Motorsports Expo and F1 garages; the second pick-up is at the entrance to the Renaissance Center on Jefferson just 200 yards from the Windsor Tunnel exit; the third is at Chene Park, which is a mile east of the Ren Cen on the Detroit River; and the last is right at the entrance to the bridge. Additionally, there are waterbound shuttles running from St Aubin Park landing to the Belle Isle Boat Club and the southern side of island near hospitality suite area via a portable pier.

Up river there are not nearly as many places to stay as there were when the race ran downtown. So staying in Detroit is still as it was in '91 — around the Ren Cen. But rooms at the hotels in the area around the old circuit are expensive and difficult to come by. The cheapest rooms in Detroit are not in Detroit. In fact, the best rooms in Detroit are not even in the U.S., but in Windsor, across the river.

The bridge is one way to travel to the Canadian city (which, from Detroit, is south across the river!), but the best way through the tunnel is by border shuttle bus (the drop of of the bus is located just to the right of the front of the Westin Hotel in the Ren Cen where the shuttle will pick you up for the Belle Isle ride). With your car safely parked in the Canadian hotel parking lot, these shuttle buses run frequently during race weekend, and once things get hectic, customs is a breeze. The rooms are just a tad less expensive in Windsor. In addition, there are more of them, and there are always buses to the Canadian entrance of the tunnel where you'll find a border shuttle.

The Westin in the Ren Cen is still tentatively slated as race headquarters during the weekend. But the Riverplace Inn, an old warehouse which was converted into an upscale hotel, has a good chance to take over the honors of being the center of race activity.

For the past few years, general admission tickets in Detroit gave you a good look at the snack bars, so it was best to try to reserve a seat. Things have changed, but start/finish seats are still the best seats available and are probably worth the money. You should see everything that happens up and down pit lane, and can see the start perfectly.

The only flaw of the new circuit was following the race itself Sunday, when the entire island tried to leave at the same time. It would have been the same whether it was baseball or racing. Fans waited a little longer Sunday than they did any other day, but other than that — and the criticism by Michael Andretti from the racer's point of view — it has been remakably well run.

For hotel and other tourist information, call the Detroit Chamber of Commerce at (313) 964 4000. For general information call (313) 259-5400.

Gratten Raceway

7200 Lessiter
Gratten, MI 48809
PH: (616) 691-7221

Circuit: 2.0 mile road course; 10 turns.

Location: 10 miles north of Grand Rapids Michigan, in Gratten, MI.

Major races: SCCA Nationals and Regionals; WERA Nationals and Regionals; AMA Nationals.

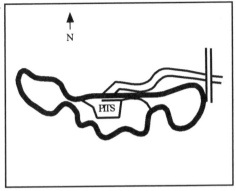

If nothing else, Gratten Raceway is probably the most beautiful racetrack in the United States. The circuit is located in a scenic area, complete with several ponds naturally stocked with Canadian Geese and Pike. Racers can camp and fish at this picturesque track for $15 per person — unfortunately, spectators are not allowed to spend the nights — so try to do some grunt work to get the racers' camping spots. Either way, you'll still be able to enjoy the place during the day.

The track winds around the forest, past two of the ponds. The first cars on the track will likely wake the geese up that occasionally sleep on the warm asphalt. The track may not be as safe as it could be, with guardrails coming right up to the track's edge in some spots, and streams running next to the pavement.

There are several spectacular corners. One, in particular, gets the cars airborne: past the first three turns, where all the corners are slightly banked, the track gives drivers a fast ride into a quick-rising turn-four, where all four wheels generally leave the road. The best place to watch an entire race is from the hill on the far side of the track, where you'll see almost everything. There are no grandstands.

If you can't hook up with a team, you'll have no problems staying in Belding, which is 10 miles away; if not there, try Grand Rapids.

Kalamazoo Speedway

3006 30th St, Route 1
Allegan, MI 49010
PH: (616) 349-3978

Location: Southern Michigan, just west of Kalamazoo.

Circuit: Three-eighths mile paved oval.

Major races: NASCAR interseries (Great Northern Region).

Kalamazoo Speedway is one of the few NASCAR Winston Racing tracks in Michigan. In addition to NASCAR late model cars, Kalamazoo also hosts some non-sanctioned full bodied racing, with Super Late Model Sports Cars and Factory Stocks. Call the track for information on lodging in Kalamazoo.

Michigan International Speedway

12626 U.S. Hwy 12
Brooklyn, MI 49203

PH: (517) 592-6666
Ticket info: (517) 592-6671

FAX: (517) 592-3848

Location: Southern central Michigan.

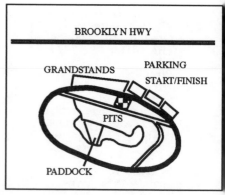

Circuit: 2.0 mile banked, paved oval.

Major races: NASCAR Winston Cup (two events); NASCAR Busch Grand National; PPG CART IndyCar World Series Championship; International Race of Champions; ARCA Championship.

Often overlooked in Talladega's large shadow, and never the equal of Indy, Michigan International Speedway is one of the finest ovals in the United States. MIS has to struggle for respect, although it is every bit the track either of the other two are. Roger Penske's MIS has the distinction of being the fastest speedway in the U.S. — Rick Mears' 233.934 MPH speed, set in 1986, still stands. Richard Petty had his 1,000th start as well as his 500th consecutive start here. And Al Unser Jr. holds a record speed for any race, set here in the 1990 Marlboro 500 Indycar race — 189.727 mph.

Michigan is certainly the biggest Indycar oval race after the Indy 500. The track is a great spectating venue, and you'll see almost the entire racing surface from anywhere in the stands.

The infield opens Friday after practice. Admission is $20 dollars per person. There is MIS camping outside, directly across the track from the main grandstands. It opens Monday of race week and costs $20 for the week.

Located in Brooklyn, the area is not exactly a hotel mecca. It is 35 minutes from Ann Arbor, and there are lots of rooms available in Ann Arbor, even as late as Saturday. Brooklyn is a quaint little town... with nowhere to sleep. Jackson is larger, with 50,000 people, but there is little free there either, as the teams snatch those rooms up quickly.

There are several campgrounds in the Irish Hills area and there are lakes and lake cottages scattered about. There is also camping in the track's infield and outside the facility.

For more information on lodging, call the Ann Arbor Area Convention and Visitors Bureau at (313) 995-7281; or call the track for more on ticket prices.

Brainerd International Raceway

17113 Minnetonka Blvd
Suite 214
Minnetonka, MN 55345
Track: Highway 371 North

Brainerd, MN 56401

Track: (218) 829-9836
Office: (612) 475-1500
FAX: (612) 475-2149

Location: Central Minnesota, approximately 100 miles northwest of Minneapolis.

From Minneapolis, take Interstate I 94 to St. Cloud, following signs across the Mississippi River to U.S. Highway 10 North. At Little Falls, head north on State Route 371 to Brainerd, following signs to the track.

Circuit: Three-mile road course, 10 turns/ quarter-mile dragstrip.

Major races: NHRA Champion Auto Stores Nationals; FIM Superbike Championships; SCCA Nationals.

With a longstanding association with the SCCA, Brainerd had hosted a Trans-Am race for 16 out of 20 years from 1969 to 1988. But it has not held a Trans-Am since 1990, and seems now to be sliding toward drag racing.

Brainerd's 22,000 grandstand seats are contained to start/finish for the NHRA Nationals, which draws the circuit's biggest crowds. It is, however, a beautiful road racing facility with wide, green run-off areas running through nicely forested areas. Relatively flat, spectators really have no place to watch the entire track. But the up-close views from any of the general admission areas are good.

The FIM held a Superbike race here for several years, but the event was suddenly cancelled due to an increase in costs. It is not likely to return anytime soon.

The track is situated on 500 acres, so camping is abundant — either in motor homes or in tents. For hotel information, call the Brainerd Chamber of Commerce at (800) 432-3775/(218) 829-2838 (Minnesota only), or the Nisswa Chamber of Commerce at (218) 963-2620.

Capital Speedway
P.O. Box 100
Holts Summit, MO 65043

PH: (314) 896-5500

Location: Central Missouri, just north of Jefferson City, off Highway 54.

Circuit: Three-eighths mile clay oval.

Major races: NASCAR interseries (Central Region).

Capital Speedway hosts a weekly NASCAR late model program with a NASCAR Busch All Star Tour race as its season feature event. The three-eighths mile oval is considered one of the best in Missouri.

Located just south of Mark Twain National Forest, there are places to camp close by; Holts Summit has a few rooms; or try Jefferson City; or cross the Missouri River and stay in Frankenstein...(no kidding).

I - 55 Speedway
P.O Box 614
Pevely, MO   63070

PH: (314) 479-3219

Location: Eastern Missouri, thirty miles from St. Louis.
From St. Louis, take Interstate 55 South past Pevely to exit 178.

Circuit: Third-mile clay oval; high banked.

Major races: World of Outlaws Sprint Car Championship Shootout.

I 55 Speedway sits between two hills in the midst of lots of greenery, and would be secluded.... except it's right off the Interstate. The track runs mostly late model stocks on Saturday nights, but it holds one round of the WoO Sprint car championships.

The 6,500 seat facility has camping for those who wish to follow the Outlaws, or you can stay in Festus, which is two miles south of the track.

Eagle Raceway
Office: P.O. Box 30532
Lincoln, NE   68503

PH: (office) (402) 467-4222
Track: (402) 781-2929

Location: Eastern Nebraska, 11 miles from Lincoln, and 45 miles from Omaha.

From Lincoln, take U.S. 34 to State Route 63 — the track is at the junction of SR 63 and U.S. 34.

Circuit: Third-mile clay oval; high banked.

Major races: World of Outlaws Sprint Car Championship Shootout.

Eagle Raceway's Friday night regular racing is punctuated with a round of the World of Outlaws, and several weeknight racing events. There are also a few Winged Prototype Modified races. Lincoln is the best bet for accommodations.

Nebraska Motorplex
13116 Lockwood Plaza Circle
Omaha, NE 68142-4245

PH: (402) 238-2900
FAX: 402 238 2774
Track: (402) 664 2577

Circuit: Quarter-mile dragstrip.

Location: Approximately 50 minutes north of Omaha.
From Omaha, take Highway 275 about 45 miles past Hoover, turning left on Raceway Rd., then south (left) two miles to the track, located in Scribner.

Major Races: IHRA Nationals.

Built on the Scribner Airfield, Nebraska Motorplex is comprised of one edge of the huge triangle that made up the Midwestern WWII airbase. The airbase is now mostly a weather station, and two thirds of the triangle have been sold off — with one going to Nebraska Motorplex. Each leg was 7,700 feet long, but the Motorplex only owns 5,000 feet of it. 1980 marked the strip's first years of operation.

As one would image, it is very flat — on the track and in the immediate area. From the top of the grandstands you can see for miles. The biggest towns — Hooper and Scribner — sit in a very slight valley, and as you leave the highway you go up a hill about 100 feet to a very wide plateau.

The Motorplex seats 14,000, but the largest crowd has been 10,500 fans. With the new series sponsorship, the IHRA Nationals may help post record attendance for Nebraska Motorplex as it becomes popular.

The closest town is Fremont, which is 20 miles on Hwy 275 heading back to Omaha or Blair, which is 30 miles east (Scribner or Hooper have populations of about 900). There is also camping at the track, primarily in the pit area and in the parking lot. Showers are available as well.

Sunset Speedway
6201 N. 132nd St.
Omaha, NE 68164

PH: (402) 493-5491

Location: Eastern Nebraska, in Omaha, two miles off Interstate I 680 at Exit Six.

Circuit: Three-eighths mile clay oval.

Major races: NASCAR interseries (Central Region).

Sunset Speedway is located on the outskirts of northeast Omaha, in the Nebraska farmland that bounds the city. The facility seats 5,000 in all-new grandstands. Racing is scheduled for Sunday nights, with a few special events dotting the calendar. The biggest crowds appear near the end of the season as several NASCAR Winston Racing specials are held in conjunction with three other tracks in the area. Sunset also holds some special sprints races - but no WoO racing. Hotels are plentiful in the Omaha area, but call the track for the nearest inns.

Las Vegas International Speedway
6000 N. Las Vegas Bld.
Las Vegas, NV

(Office) 5370 E. Craig Rd., #1425
Las Vegas, NV   89115
(702) 643-3333

Location: Nine miles north of the Las Vegas strip, on Las Vegas Blvd.

Circuit: 1.6 road course 9 turns/ three-eighths mile high-banked oval/ quarter-mile dragstrip.

Major Races: NHRA Divisional Drag Race; NASCAR Winston West, Southwest Tour.

A few miles down the road from Las Vegas Speedway the thermometer outside Neiman-Marcus usually reads in triple digit numbers during the summer months. The track is not spared from the heat, which often gets past 110 degrees.

Even so, the track has had a decent amount of success in its 50 years. The grandstands seat 4,000 for the oval track fans; the dragstrip holds another 6,000; and the road course, although it has no grandstands, can accommodate about the same as the combined total of both of the former. The paddock is in the center of the road course, and most of the action can be seen from there.

The road course, although it is not used for any major series other than AMA Superbikes, was actually a favorite for testing for some of the major road racing teams like Nissan and Toyota GTP teams. The flat circuit is located on the back part of property so teams test here because of its privacy.

Road course runners bring RVs, but most of the time the track is locked up for the drags and the oval, so staying on the property will be mostly limited to road racers. There are hotels closer than the strip, just two miles from the facility near Nellis Air Force Base (home of the Thunderbirds). You will have absolutely no problems finding a room in Las Vegas, but if you wish to book ahead, call the track for more information on the closest rooms.

Silver State Raceway
P.O. Box 3014
Carson City, NV   89702

PH: (702) 883-1009

Location: Western Nevada, 20 miles east of Lake Tahoe, near State Highways 50 & 395, a mile south of Snyder Av. and Carson.

Circuit: Quarter-mile paved oval.

Major races: NASCAR interseries (Pacific Coast Region); USAC Midgets.

Located inside the city limits of Carson City, Silver State Raceway offers a nice diversion from the blackjack tables of Nevada.

Silver State holds a Saturday night oval show, with the biggest event of the season being the South West Tour or USAC Midget races. Motocross runs on Friday night in a separate stadium on the property. The oval seats 4,000, and the motocross track can accommodate some 1,000.

Just down the street from the facility is the Ormsby House casino — which is also race headquarters (and where you can get a free drink with your ticket stub, and almost half-off room rates when you ask for racer's discount). There are plenty of other accommodations in Carson City, or you can also camp outside the track. So if you lose all your money on the games of fortune, there's always racing...

Monadnock Speedway
137 Fair Oak Rd.
Springfield MA   01128

PH: (603) 239-4067

Location: In eastern New Hampshire, in Winchester, NH.

Circuit: Quarter-mile paved oval.

Major races: NASCAR interseries (Northeast Region).

Self-named the "fastest high banked quarter-mile in the east", Monadnock Speedway holds a handful of special events in addition to the regular Friday night racing. The big show is the Budweiser Firecracker on Fourth of July, with NASCAR Winston Racing Series regulars running 200 lap races. Hotel information can be found by calling the track.

New England Dragway
P.O. Box 1320
Epping NH   03042

Track: Route 27, Epping NH

PH: (603) 679-8001
FAX: (603) 679 1955

Circuit: Quarter-mile dragstrip.

Location: Off Route 27, in Epping.

Major Races: IHRA North American Nationals; IHRA Northeast Nitrous Nationals.

New England Dragway runs a packed weekly schedule from April first to October 31, with racing Wednesday, Saturday and Sunday, with special shows occurring about once a month.

The major races are the North American Nationals, which are held at the end of July; the Spring Funny Car Classic in April; the Cars Under the Stars shows — one in May and one in June; and the Jet Cars Under the Stars event; and the Northeast Nitrous Nationals in early September.

The facility holds about 15,000 people. For accommodations, you can stay in Hampton or Portsmith, both 15 minutes from the track. New England Dragway officials will be happy to provide you with a list of hotels. There is also camping at the facility for self-contained vehicles.

New Hampshire International Raceway
Route 106 P.O. Box 7888
Louden, NH   03301

PH: (603) 783-4744
FAX: (603) 783-9691
Tickets: (603) 783-4931

Circuit: 1.058 mile paved oval/ 1.65 mile road course; 13 turns.

Location: Central New Hampshire, 10 miles north of Concord, 80 miles north of Boston, on Route 106.

Major races: Cart IndyCars; NASCAR Winston Cup, Busch Grand National, Busch Series North Grand National, Winston Modified Tour; AMA Pro National Road Racing Series; SCCA Nationals and Regionals; WKA Nationals and Regionals.

New Hampshire International Speedway opened on May 26th, 1990 with an inagaural SCCA race. Previously called Bryar Motorsports Park, owner Bob Bahre, who at one time owned Oxford Plains Speedway in Maine, completely leveled the old facility and started from scratch.

The facility is dual purpose, with both a top-notch superspeedway oval (the first new facility since Talladega) and a challenging 1.65 mile road circuit.

The oval is 80 feet wide, and flat — except in the turns, which are banked at 12 degrees. With those figures — and an excellent turnout for every race held here — officials lured Winston Cup to the facility in 1993.

NHIR becomes one of only three tracks in the nation to host top level bikes, IndyCar and Winston Cup racing at the same facility. The Winston Cup race is mid-July, and the New England 200 IndyCar race is scheduled for early August — both run the oval; the AMA race utilizes the road course.

The backstretch of the oval is elevated six feet, enabling fans on the front straight to see all the action from their seats. There are 12 VIP suites, which can each accommodate 60 people. The lone grandstand seats 59,000 people, and the same grandstand also serves as the primary viewing area for the road course, which utilizes the same front straightway and start/finish area.

Additionally, the road course is certainly the country's most innovative. Designed with spectators in mind, it is not just an afterthought of an oval, but an honest-to-goodness road circuit. The track winds away from the oval on each end, as well as straying out in the middle of the backstretch. Interestingly, where it winds outward from the backside of the circuit, it runs up a hill, so from anywhere in the grandstands every inch of the track can be seen. The stadium-style thinking doesn't seem to have compromised the road racing.

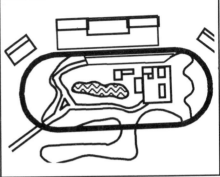

This is a difficult place to get a room during a regular race weekend. What with the relationship with CART, and with the general interest in the new speedway, it will become even more difficult. You'll need to book rooms very early. For more information on where to stay, call the Concord Vacation Information office of New Hampshire at (603 271-2343), or better yet call the chambers of commerce for Concord (603 224 2508), Loconia (800 531-2347), Manchester (603 666-6600) or Nashua (603 881 8333).

Star Speedway
P.O. Box E
Epping, NH   03042

PH: (603) 679-5306

Location: Southern New Hampshire, eight miles east of I95 in Epping on Route 27 East.

Circuit: Quarter-mile paved oval.

Major races: NASCAR interseries (Northeast Region).

Star Speedway's charming green countryside location is quiet most of the year. But when Star hosts racing on its 11 Saturday nights throughout the season the place becomes a hotbed of activity. The biggest event is the Star Classic, run just after Labor day. The facility seats 6,000. Stay in Exeter, Seabrook, or Manchester. There is limited camping at the track, but there is a good deal of public camping less than an hour away.

Atco Raceway
Office: P.O. Box 182
Atco, NJ 08004

Track: Route 534 & East Jackson Rd.,
Atco, NJ

(609) 768-2167
Fax (609) 753-9604

Directions: Fifteen miles east of Philadelphia and 15 miles west of Atlantic City, five miles east of route 73.

Circuit: quarter mile dragstrip.

Major races: IHRA Summer Nationals.

Atco Raceway has returned to IHRA competition after several seasons of hiatus. The 1993 Summer Nationals at Atco were once named the IHRA Eastern Nationals. But however titled, the track is back with a major event for the new season.

Located at the very edge of Wharton State Forest, Atco's surroundings are green and placid. Pine trees loom all about, providing some shade during the hot and humid summers.

The track has an altitude which is 30 feet above sea level, but conditions can make it appear to the barometers, altimeters and other various meteorological instruments as if it is 1,200 feet below sea level! It is a good place for drag racing. It is 4,200 feet long and 60 feet wide, with steel guardrails on both sides running the length of the strip. It seats 9,000 people, but holds 15,000 including the standing room along the fences and in the paddock.

Only closed three weeks of the year, the track is generally open Tuesdays for a Gambler's race; Friday nights, for street racing nights (which is usually attended by 300 drivers, and organized with help from the community for youth participation); Saturday is slated for regular bracket racing, with the first races beginning at 1 p.m. and run into evening; and Sunday's races for motorcycle begin at 9 a.m. until 12, with eliminations at 1 p.m.. A few special shows are held on Wednesday eves during the summer, with the Jet Car Nationals being the premier event. The Anniversary show in August will have nitro cars, and the Fourth of July show generally has John Force and his Funny Car on hand. In fact, Atco is only one of two IHRA tracks this season which will have Nitro Funny Cars competing.

On the property outside the main gate 5,000 people can camp. There has been no charge for admission in the past, but there may be a charge in '93 with the coming of IHRA. The campgrounds usually fill for the Harley-Davidson Races, usually held in early June and mid-September. Check first for details on camping at the facility. Regardless, there will be camping available at the Wharton State Forest campgrounds. If you are at your campsite during the race, be sure to listen to AM 530 for race broadcasts. There is also a weather hotline (609 768-0900) for those who have an aversion to camping in the rain.

A dozen or so hotels exist at the junction of where highway 73 comes together with the turnpike, at exit 4 or Mount Laurel. The track will be happy to supply you with a list. Or you can stay at Atlantic City and arrive, perhaps a bit poorer, to the races.

Bridgeport Speedway
P.O. Box 493
Bridgeport NJ 08014

PH: (609) 467-4407

Location: South New Jersey, a few miles east of Atlantic City.

Circuit: Three-eighth mile clay oval.

Major races: World Of Outlaws.

Bridgeport Speedway, which is just a few minutes away from the blackjack tables at Atlantic City, hosted its first WoO event in 1990. The track hosts an open-wheeled and full-bodied regular show on Sunday evenings. Located on fairgrounds, the 6,500-seat stands usually fill when bigger events come through.

Flemington Speedway
P.O. Box 293
Flemington, NJ   08822

PH: (track) (201) 782-2413

Location: Western New Jersey, approximately 35 miles from New York City, just north of Flemington, on State Route 31 — the track is one mile northeast of U.S. 202 on State Route 31.

Circuit: Five-eighths mile paved oval; semi-banked.

Major races: NASCAR Modifieds.

Flemington Speedway is found in a rural, very green, warm, and very comfortable area outside Flemington. The regular show is a modified stock event, which takes place every Saturday from April through October.

The deviations from the standard program usually pack the 10,000 seat stands. A Monster Truck show brings in lots of spectators, but the WoO racing is the biggest of the season. The Outlaws usually run on weekdays here. The best places to stay are in Clinton, where the Outlaws stay at the Holiday Inn during a race. There are also rooms in Flemington.

Old Bridge Raceway Park
230 Pension Rd,
Englishtown, NJ   07726

PH: (201) 446-6338
FAX: (201) 446-1373

Location: Central New Jersey, about 40 miles south of Newark, off highways 18 and 527, located on Pension Rd., two miles north of Englishtown, in Old Bridge.

Circuit: Quarter-mile dragstrip/ motocross track

Major races: NHRA Summernationals; Jet Car Nationals.

Old Bridge Raceway Park is nestled in New Jersey's scenic Middlesex county. Although the area around the track is gently-rolling, rural, and green, the area is actually a winter ski resort. Englishtown is a ski area (Englishtown is where the office can be found — and not, as most magazines suggest, where the track is located).

In the Summer Old Bridge plays host to NHRA Winston Drag Racing and the NHRA Summernationals, and the 20,000 permanent seats are enhanced by an additional 25,000-30,000 bringing the grand total up to 50,000.

The facility has a regular ET bracket racing night every Wednesday, Friday, and Sunday evening. Besides the NHRA and Jet Car Nationals, there is a Budweiser All Pro Funny Car Championships.

There's also a small motocross track, which is used occasionally for small events, and which, for the Summernationals, doubles as a parking lot.

This race is easy to attend. The area is rich with rooms, and anywhere you stay will be just a few minutes away from Old Bridge. The tickets shouldn't sell out either, and unless you want seats right next to staging you should have no problems getting good seats. If you phone the track, they'll gladly send you a list of hotels in the area. You can stay in Englishtown, Old Bridge, Perth Amboy, or even Trenton or Newark. Atlantic City is about 100 miles from the track.

Bridgehampton Racing Circuit
c/o Dennis Macchio
Business Trend Analysts
2171 Jericho Turnpike
Commack, NY   11725

PH: (516) 462-5454/ (516) 725-0888
FAX: (516) 4621842

Circuit: 2.86 mile road course; 13 turns.

Location: At New York's south fork of eastern Long Island, in the Hamptons, just off Highway 27 in Bridgehampton.

Major races: SCCA Nationals; Regionals.

Bridgehampton's days of glory are gone, but there looks like a resurgence of interest in the classic circuit, as the track begins a renovation process in hopes of luring major series back to its challenging 2.86 racetrack. The SCCA's return to Bridgehampton after a multi-year absence is significant, and the ambitious plans make the circuit look like a major player in the future of northeastern racing.

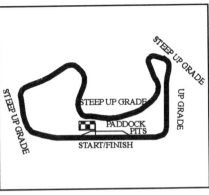

The track completed construction of grandstands along the main straight in 1992, their first grandstands ever. The structure seats around 500 people. The good fortune of the lucky 500 with real seats notwithstanding, there are plenty of areas where fans can watch the racing from alongside the racing surface. The "downhill" is probably the best for viewing.

The beautiful track has some very fast corners, and in days past had limited run-off areas — in fact, drop-offs in some fast corners that were deadly at speed. That situation is being changed without losing the original flavor of the old Bridgehampton circuit.

The area is a resort community, and there are plenty of accommodations in nearby Sag Harbor, Southampton, and East Hampton.

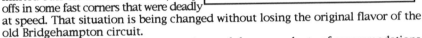

Canandaigua Speedway
Office: P.O. Box 240
Weedsport, NY 13166

PH: (716) 394-0961

Location: Northern New York State, 40 miles east of Buffalo, and approximately 155 miles from New York City.

From Buffalo, take Interstate 90 East to State Route 21 South toward Canandaigua, turning east SR 20 to Town Line Rd., where the track is located.

Circuit: Half-mile clay oval; semi banked.

Major races: World of Outlaws Sprint Car Championship Shootout.

Ontario County Fairgrounds, in the Finger Lakes region of New York, is the home of Canandaigua Speedway. It's located north west of Watkins Glen, in the picturesque area just off Canandaigua Lake. The track holds a regular modified show on Saturday nights, with sportsman racing following up the successful modifieds each evening. The speedway's season high spot comes with the World of Outlaws lone race in June. Accommodations can be found on SR 20 in Canandaigua, or farther up on the New York State Throughway.

285

Erie County Fairgrounds
5600 McKinley Parkway,
Hamburg, NY   14075
(716) 649-3900

Location: 13 miles south of Buffalo, off the New York Throughway exit #56.

Circuit: Half-mile dirt oval.

Major Races: AMA 600cc Championship.

Located in the scenic Lake Erie area, Erie County Fairgrounds holds fewer motor sports events than most, counting on 150 nights of paramutal harness race betting per year to make its money. The fair, which is open late August, sees good traffic, and during the ten-day spell when the fair is open attendance climbs -- mainly for the country music concert held in the center of the oval.

An occasional demo derby is held at the oval, but the 600 AMA race is the biggest of the season. Niagara Falls is only 40 minutes away from the 8,000 seat facility, and there are hotels in the area (Holiday Inn in Hamburg is the AMA head-quarters). Camping is also possible.

Holland International Speedway
2 North Main
Holland, NY   14080

PH: (716) 537-2272

Location: Northeastern New York, 25 miles south of Buffalo, on State Route 16.

Circuit: Three-eighths mile paved oval.

Major races: NASCAR interseries (Northeast Region).

Holland International Speedway seats 6,000 amid the scenic rolling hills country of upstate New York. Annually, the biggest show is the Modified Tour Busch Grand National North, but racing happens here every Saturday night. In 1992 there was an emphasis on more getting more cars to the track and some rules and class restrictions were relaxed to fill out the fields. There is nowhere to stay in Holland, but you can stay in Buffalo, South Wales, or Chaffee. Darien Lake Amusement Park is 20 miles away.

Lebanon Valley Speedway
Route 20
W. Lebanon, NY   12195

PH: (518) 794-9965/ 794-9606

Location: Central eastern New York State, eighteen miles southeast of Albany on U.S. 20.

Circuit: Half-mile clay oval; high banked.

Major races: World of Outlaws Sprint Car Championship Shootout.

Lebanon Valley Speedway is basically a series of dragstrips: a paved quarter-mile strip which acts as a true dragstrip; and two dirt stretches that comprise each of the main straightways of the oval. The clay at Lebanon is very quick, and the turns are a tad tighter than normal, giving it an appearance of having gigantic front and back stretches.

The track is located in a green secluded area, and gives the often dusty world of dirt racing a bit more class than one might expect to see. The oval portion seats some 20,000 so it's a noteworthy facility in that respect alone.

The dragstrip, on the outside of the oval, also is set up to seat some 10,000, and the drag racing show — although not hosting an NHRA National event — does have some excellent nitro-methane, and jet-powered car shows.

For a brief list of nearby hotels, call the track, or call the Department of Economic Development Division of Tourism at (800) 225-5697.

New York International Dragway
office P.O. Box 296
Leicester, New York 14481

Track: 2011 New Road
Leicester, NY

PH: (716) 382-3075
FAX: (716) 382-9061

Circuit: Quarter-mile dragstrip.

Location: Southwest of Rochester and southeast of Buffalo.

Major Races: IHRA Empire Nationals.

Just seven miles from Lechworth State Park, nicknamed the Grand Canyon of the East, New York International Dragway is just a few minutes from the park's beautiful waterfalls and gorges.

The track is open from April to November, and the Empire Nationals is the biggest event of the year. With 8,000 seats and far more standing room, the Empire Nationals never gets close to selling out.

Starting in April, racing happens on Sunday afternoons, then in mid-May the weekly show moves to Saturday night until mid -September, when it moves back to Sundays until the season finale. In addition, the track also runs Wednesday night from May until end of September.

There is no camping at the facility, although camping exists at Lechworth State Park. The track will provide a hotel/motel list with a majority of the hotels available (most are 27 miles away — although one hotel is within 7 miles of the track). Try Henrietta, toward the Rochester direction, or Batavia toward Buffalo.

New York State Fairgrounds Speedway
State Fair Blvd.
Syracuse, NY   13209

PH: (office) (315) 834-6606
Track: (315) 487-7711
FAX: 834 9734

Location: Central New York State, just west of Syracuse.
From Syracuse, take Interstate I 90 west to I 690 South (exit 39) and take the Fairgrounds exit to the fairgrounds, the site of the track.

Circuit: One mile clay oval; semi banked.

Major races: World of Outlaws Sprint Car Championship Shootout.

New York State Fairgrounds, on Syracuse's west side, holds a lone WoO event, which is the track's biggest event. Super Dirt Week (usually the first week in October) is almost as popular, bringing in 30,000-40,000 over the course of the multi-day racing. Local races are held with Modified Championship cars, which qualify for the major events during the summer as they race the regular Saturday night program. The main grandstands hold 15,000, and grandstands exist in the infield as well.
    The track sells out often, so for the AMA and the WoO shows you'll want to get tickets ahead of time. Call the track for information on rooms in Syracuse.

Orange County Fair Speedway
239 Wisner Ave.
Middletown, NY   10940
PH: (office) (315) 834-6606
Track: (914) 342-2573

Location: Southern New York State, approximately 50 miles northwest of New York City.
From New York City, take Palidades Parkway North to State Route 6, and West through Harriman State Park, then north on SR 17 to Middletown. Take exit #120, and head west on SR 211, turning southwest on local 96 to the track, which is a half-mile from the junction of SR 211 and 96.

Circuit: Five-eighths mile clay oval; semi banked.

Major races: World of Outlaws Sprint Car Championship Shootout.

Orange County Fair Speedway, at the Orange County Fairgrounds, is located just outside Middletown, 55 miles from NYC. The track is set in a commercial area, surrounded by shopping centers, housing developments, and light industry.
    Racing occurs Saturday nights from April to October, and is sanctioned and promoted by the successful eastern DIRT organization. The biggest race of the season, outside the World of Outlaws race, is the Eastern States 200 in October. The track office will give you more information on where to stay in the area, or call the New York Division of Tourism office at (800) 225-5697.

288

Riverhead Raceway
1732 Great Neck Rd.
Copiague, NY   11726

PH: (516) 842-7223

Location: Coastal New York, eastern Long Island, off Highway 24.

Circuit: Quarter-mile semi-banked paved oval.

Major races: NASCAR interseries (Eastern Seaboard Region).

On the east end of Long Island in the "Hamptons", just before Long Island splits into its famous north and south forks, Riverhead Raceway appeals to wayward race fans. The paved oval attracts the tourist crowd during peak season, and the NASCAR Winston Modified Tour race (held usually in the last week of July) generally helps fill the place to near capacity. The facility holds 5,000 spectators, including pit viewing. The track was repaved in 1992 — the first time since 1951, and the pace of racing at Riverhead increased since then.

There is camping outside the track, although there are no services, nor are there hookups for RVs. If you want a room, there will be plenty in the area, but Riverhead has a few that will be the closest to the racing.

Rolling Wheels Speedway
Route 5
Elbridge, NY   13060

PH: (office) (315) 834-6606
(track) (315) 689-7809

Location: Central New York State, eight miles from Syracuse.
From Syracuse, take Interstate I 90 West to State Route 31C to Elbridge, then SR 5 west two miles to the track.

Circuit: Five-eighths mile clay oval; semi-banked.

Major races: World of Outlaws Sprint Car Championship Shootout.

Rolling Wheels Speedway sits in a forested area eight miles from Syracuse, in Elbridge, off Highways 5 & 20. WoO is the biggest show of the season. There are only 13 races a year here, but most races are at least 50-lappers. The most frequently run classes are Street Stock, Sportsman, and modifieds. Rooms are available in Syracuse.

Shangri-La Motor Speedway
3 Perry Dr.
Apalachin, NY   13732

PH: (607) 687-1251

Location: Southern New York, roughly between Binghampton and Elmira, just north of State Highway 17.

Circuit: Half-mile clay oval/ quarter-mile dragstrip.

Major races: NASCAR interseries (Northeast region).

Shangri-La runs two shows on two tracks two nights each week. On Fridays Shangri-La holds NCC street drags, where anyone with a helmet can race their car on the the strip. Saturday evenings the oval is utilized, with ARCA Pro and NASCAR racing.

Spencer Speedway
288 Jefferson Ave.
Fairport, NY 14450

PH: (315) 589-2310

Location: Northern New York, five miles south of Lake Ontario, and eight miles east of Rochester, on State Route 104.

Circuit: Half-mile oval.

Major races: NASCAR interseries (Northeast Region).

Spencer Speedway operates a Friday night late model program on its half-mile paved oval, and hosts IHRA races on its dragstrip on Wednesdays, where, for a few dollars, you can race your own car. The track is actually located in Williamson, which is some 10 miles east of Rochester. There are plenty of rooms in the area.

Watkins Glen International
P.O. Box 500
500 County Route 16
Watkins Glen, NY 14891

PH: (607) 535-2481
FAX: (607) 535-7508

Location: In the Finger Lakes area of central New York State, approximately 160 miles from New York City, roughly between Elmira and Syracuse, off State Route 17, on Route 14.

Circuit: 3.4 mile road course; 11 turns/2.45 mile road circuit; 11 turns (NASCAR).

Major races: NASCAR Winston Cup Championship; NASCAR

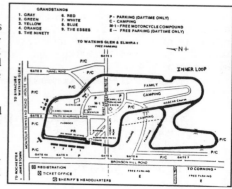

Busch Grand National SCCA Trans-Am; SCRA Vintage; IMSA Camel GT; Firestone Firehawk

Watkins Glen is in the midst of a renaissance. Since the France family reopened the track in 1984 following its '81 bankruptcy, the famous road course has been one of the most popular on the NASCAR, IMSA and Trans-Am circuits. For the 1992 Winston Cup race 130,000 fans made the migration to northern New York state, and the attendance is expected to continue to rise.

Although it temporarily stumbled in 1991 when J.D. McDuffie was killed and Tom Kendall was seriously injured at the end of the long straight, the corner has been de-fanged by an infield loop. More grandstands have been built and viewing berms have been added in turn one. In general, greater attention is being paid to quality viewing and fan comfort (the track has also totally rebuilt restrooms and family camping roads). The track has also added a fifth-mile oval near the inner loop and will experiment with Midget races.

"The Glen" will always be remembered first and foremost as the U.S.'s permanent home of the FIA Formula One Grand Prix. From 1961 to 1980 the U.S. Grand Prix was held at Watkins Glen. The loss of the F1 circus in 1981 truly sacrificed a home for the GP in the U.S., and there has never been another circuit that's had the distinction of being a true American GP track — even though the streets of Detroit saw the event for seven years.

The major problem of F1 is the biggest concern for fans as well. Where do you stay? Although 12 new hotels have been built since the departure of the F1 tour, this beautiful area of New York has serious accommodation problems when racing comes to town. During the GP years, teams used to rent private houses for the week. These days, with NASCAR, it's probably not much different — although most of us can't afford the option of renting a house.

Camping is probably the best way to spend a weekend at Watkins Glen, and there is camping at the circuit. Except for the NASCAR weekend (when campers

are allowed into the circuit at 5:00 PM Thursday) vehicles are allowed into the camping areas at 6:00 Am Friday of each event. The charges are per vehicle, which includes a towed camper or tent trailer. You'll be forced to buy at least a general admission ticket too. You'll be able to camp in most of the parking areas, but if you enter late or try to stay without a pass, you'll eventually be charged — so save yourself the embarrassment and do it right.

Tickets for Watkins Glen vary greatly depending on which races and where you want to watch. If you want pit roof seating, or reserved camping spots (which are advisable) call for information and/or reservations. There is a handicapped viewing and parking area at Watkins Glen, and more information about those passes can be obtained by calling the office.

For Watkins Glen or Schuyler County Chambers of Commerce, call (607) 535-4300; for Elmira, call the Elmira/Chemung Chambers of Commerce at (607) 734-5137; for Corning Chamber of Commerce, call (607) 936-4686.

Bowman Gray Stadium
4537 Country Club Rd
Winston-Salem, NC   27104

(919) 765-1027

Location: Northern North Carolina, in Winston-Salem, on Martin Luther King Blvd.

Circuit: Quarter-mile clay oval.

Major races: NASCAR interseries (Eastern Seaboard Region).

Bowman Gray Stadium is nestled in a hilly area of North Carolina that, oddly, becomes dry and brown early in the normally humid North Carolina summers. But there is not much humidity here, making the race-watching a bit easier. The fifty-two year old quarter-mile track is built around a football stadium, which is city owned, and used during the fall and winter by the Winston-Salem State University, Reynold High School, and Parkland High School football teams. The stadium seats 17,000. The racing surface is wide, but completely flat. Racing doesn't interfere with football, although sometimes as rain-outs occur the cars run past the goal posts at rescheduled events!

The regular show is run with Modified Street, and Buzz Bombers, and is occasionally sprinkled with a demolition derby or two. The biggest event is the Winston 200, followed by the Goodys 150 — all run with modifieds. There are plenty of rooms in the Winston-Salem area, which can be had by calling (800) VISIT NC.

Charlotte Motor Speedway
P.O. Box 600
Highway 29 South
Concord, NC   28026

PH: (704) 455-2121
Ticket info: (704) 455-3200
FAX: (704)455-2547

292

Location: Southern central North Carolina, 12 miles north of Charlotte, in Concord.

From Charlotte, take Interstate I 85 to state Highway 12, following signs on Hwy 12 to the track.

Circuit: 1.5 mile paved, banked oval.

Major races: NASCAR Coca-Cola 600 Winston Cup; Mello-Yello 500 NASCAR Winston Cup; The Winston; NASCAR's All Star Race.

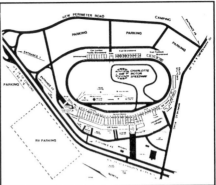

In the grand scheme of things, Charlotte Motor Speedway is the most colorful on the NASCAR's Winston Cup calendar. If Talladega has a corner on being the fastest NASCAR track, and Daytona has the distinction of being the oldest, Charlotte is definitely the loudest.

"Humpy" Wheeler's idea of racing was right along the lines of what Bill France saw as the essence of NASCAR: a good race, and a great show. Come Memorial Day, the race is no longer accepted as Indy but Charlotte. The biggest spectator event in the country may still be Indy, but the Charlotte Coca-Cola 600 is second.

Charlotte has built more on marketing than any other track in the U.S. — and the attendance suggests it has been worth the effort. To this day it's still run like a last-ditch effort at survivability — even though it is much more permanent than any NASCAR venue.

The land, described by CMS Public Relations people as "the worst piece of real estate in Charlotte", was transformed into a racetrack following some heroic construction. The first event was a disaster, as the uncured track broke up so badly during the first race that the cars were brought in for bolt-on metal windscreens to keep asphalt chunks from flying through the windshields. The next two years were not too great either, and the original owners were forced into chapter 11 bankruptcy. During that time, Wheeler was hired for PR. When the dust had settled, only one of the original owners remained, and the track relied upon Wheeler's shrewd marketing for spectators — a relic of those days which has remained, and helps in the allure of Charlotte.

A feud between Bill Elliott and Dale Earnhardt in 1988 inspired one of the most clever campaigns in NASCAR history. To keep interest going, the media folks at the speedway sent out press releases — along with bent Coors cans and broken wrenches (signifying the possibility of a crunch duel between the aptly sponsored stock cars).

Entertainment in recent years included: motorcycle stuntmen who jumped a football field's worth of junk cars; a 100 foot tall robot that eats cars; and a re-enactment of the U.S invasion of Panama — complete with helicopters and troops! To just say Charlotte is exciting racing is to have missed the point completely.

The track boasts an incredible 107,000 grandstand seats, plus VIP and other suite seating, allowing better than 170,000 viewers. Remember that Winston Cup happens twice a year here and there are several other attractions, so the speedway effectively pumps better than $200 million into Charlotte's economy annually.

As one could imagine, getting into Charlotte can be a zoo. Track officials allow three hours time to finally clear the facility following a race. There are nine gates, and on race day there's a rear entrance for backstretch grandstands.

Infield tickets can be reserved. The $15 per car, and $30 per person infield tickets offer decent viewing, and are great if you can get close to the fence. The best spots are in turns 3-4, where you can see most of the track, including start/finish.

You can buy a $45 two-day ticket to park in the infield, but the area is cleared following Saturday's final qualifying, and you must wait in line again for Sunday. By the way, vehicles begin lining up Saturday evening.

Getting into and out of the area is easy from Interstate I 85. Traveling to the track is simple, and there are four freeway exits each way which will take you north of Charlotte to highway 29 — all are well-marked. The track is two miles off highway 29. Unfortunately, there are no buses to the track, so you must find a ride somehow. There is plenty of parking.

Hotel and motel rooms in the Charlotte area are plentiful. Most teams are based here, so rooms normally booked for other races are available in Charlotte — so even late arrivals should have no problem finding something. For more information call: Charlotte Convention and Visitors Bureau at (800) 321-4636, or the Charlotte Chamber of Commerce: (704) 378-1332.

Dixieland Speedway
1818 Turners Ave.
Elizabeth City, NC   27909

PH: (919) 771-5151

Location: Northeastern North Carolina, on State Route 17 in Elizabeth City.

Circuit: Three-eighths mile clay oval.

Major races: NASCAR Interseries (Mid Atlantic Region).

Like most North Carolina tracks, Dixieland Speedway is set in a rural locale, and is green, humid, and hot. Located just outside Elizabeth City, NC, the stadium seats 2,000, and the show is generally contained to 100-lappers which occur every Friday night — except the first and last races of the season, which are held on Saturdays.

Elizabeth City has several hotels, and is only nine miles from the track, which is actually just outside the city limits.

Hickory Motor Speedway
P.O Box 1749
Hickory, NC 28603

PH: (704) 464-3655
FAX: (704) 465-5017

Location: Central-western North Carolina, in Hickory, on Route 70, just off Interstate 40 at exit 128.

Circuit: Two-fifths mile paved oval.

Major races: NASCAR Busch Grand National; NASCAR Interseries (Mid-Atlantic Region)

294

Hickory Motor Speedway lays claim to some of the best racing NASCAR history of the region.

Junior Johnson began his career on the red clay banks of Hickory. So did Ned Jarrett, Ralph Earnhardt, and Harry Gant. Of the newer breed, Dale Jarrett, Dale Earnhardt, and Morgan Shepherd began racing careers at Hickory — which was finally paved in 1969.

Located in the Piedmont Foothills, the area is famous for its furniture and textile industries. One hour away from the Blue Ridge Mountains — and several skiing areas — the track is also central to the majors of NASCAR racing (Charlotte, Darlington, Rockingham, North Wilkesboro, Martinsville, and Bristol). Rooms are available in Hickory, but you must book early. Call the Catawba County Chamber of Commerce at (704) 324-0754. If not Hickory, Charlotte will have plenty of space.

New Asheville Speedway
Route 3, P.O. Box 1208
Asheville, NC   28806

(704) 254-4627

Location: Western North Carolina, in Asheville, off I 40.

Circuit: Third-mile paved oval.

Major races: NASCAR interseries (Mid-Atlantic Region).

New Asheville Speedway sits within Asheville city limits in an attractive industrial area. The 4,500 seat venue, which was rebuilt recently after several years of abandonment, hosts the North Carolina State Championship, New Ashville's biggest of the racing season. The event is a 200-lap race for late model cars. The regular program is held on Fridays. There are several places to stay, but the best and closest are located on Highway 40 and I 26 in Asheville.

North Carolina Motor Speedway
U.S. Highway 1 North
Rockingham, NC   28379
PH: (919) 582-2861
FAX: (919) 582-3324

Location: Southern central North Carolina, fifteen miles from the SC border, at the junction of Highways NC Highway 74 and U.S. Highway 1.

Circuit: 1.07 mile paved oval.

Major races: NASCAR Winston Cup Championship (two races); NASCAR Busch Grand National Series Championship (two races); NHRA Winston Invitational.

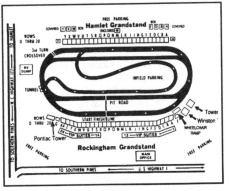

Rockingham is not just famous for racing, it's also one of the country's foremost golf resort areas. Located in the middle of what is essentially a golf mecca, the track is the clubhouse in a 10,000 hole greenery. The entire area is surrounded by country clubs, with such notable golf resorts as Pinehurst just up the road from the track.

For those who play golf, race week at Rockingham will be perfect — play a few rounds and watch a few laps. If, however, you aren't a golfer you won't understand why it costs so much to stay near a course — and won't have much choice when trying to find a room close to the track.

You either pray for a Motel 6 near the track, or you get stuck paying for a country club room. The teams avoid the hassle by commuting back and forth from Charlotte where most of them are based. It is, likewise, about two hours from Darlington (and teams also drive from there as well). Florence is the best bet when booking early, but is a bit small, and can't handle all the traffic. New hotels have been built in Southern Pines, and a few in Cheraw, SC, and the drive to each is not bad. Many people — including almost all the drivers — fly in, using Rockingham's dragstrip/airport to land.

As far as the track itself, Rockingham doesn't have the aura of some of the other NASCAR Winston Cup tracks. Not that there is anything wrong with it, it just is not as steeped in tradition as, say, Darlington.

Pits on both sides at "The Rock" make either side of the track good for viewing. But you'll want a view of turn two. As cars come out of turn-two the surface rises slightly. But as it begins to flatten out there is a small lip in the last foot of pavement next to the wall. In qualifying, the faster cars use the whole racetrack, and get spectacularly loose there as they try to keep the unsprung suspension settled with some full-fledged drifts.

Tickets are difficult to get for Rockingham. The VIP suites are above main grandstands, which limits the seating on the front straight. The new L.G. Dewitt Grandstand is located in turn-two and will give 1,800 people another view of the place. To secure tickets to any of the stands you should book far in advance. There's always infield if you get there late, but it's better to watch from a real seat.

For drag racing, things are much easier. For the strip you can call (919) 582-3400 — it changed hands in 1992, and is no longer a part of North Carolina Motor Speedway. The strip is located across the street from the oval. The entire parking area of the oval — which was upgraded in 1991 with several acres of new parking behind the Hamlet Grandstand — is accessible during an NHRA event. The NHRA event is one of the biggest in the south, but doesn't bring in the same business as the NASCAR racing does. Neither track's schedule coincides with golf tournament play.

Call the track for ticket information. For accommodations, try the Rockingham chamber of Commerce at (919) 895-9058; for the Darlington Chamber of Commerce, call (803) 393-2641; and as a last resort try the Florence area, at (803) 665-0515.

North Wilkesboro Speedway
General Office and Ticket Office:
P.O. Box 337
North Wilkesboro, NC   28659

PH: (919) 667-6663
or Winston-Salem Public Relations Office (919) 724-7932
FAX: (919) 722-3757

Location: 50 minutes west of Winston-Salem, off U.S. 421, on Speedway

Road near North Wilkesboro.

Circuit: Five-eighths mile paved oval.

Major races: NASCAR Winston Cup Series Championship (two rounds).

North Wilkesboro Speedway is the oldest track in Winston Cup racing. Built in 1947, by Enoch Staley, who drove pace car for the France family early in NASCAR's history, the track has been an intimate place to watch stock car racing for better than 40 years. North Wilkesboro is probably best known for being Junior Johnson's home track. Johnson has won nearly one third of every race he, or one of his drivers, have entered, and is always the guy to beat here.

Average attendance has been about 40,000 per race. Although long term goals are to double deck the front stretch grandstands, for now spectator space is at a premium. Race tickets sell out quickly, but there is still decent availability considering the limited seats. If you find yourself in the area without a ticket and wish to see the race, have no fear; on raceday 5,000 unreserved seats and infield admission are placed on sale.

Once the additional seats are built — if the additional seats are built — it's anticipated that public admission to the infield may be discontinued, as at Martinsville and Bristol (which no longer sell infield tickets).

The Speedway has a lot of property, so the free camping outside is great for those who have motorhomes or campers. You can show up as early as Tuesday or Wednesday and wait for the action to begin. However, the infield is closed to the public until Sunday at 7:00 am, and there is no camping inside the track at all.

As far as seating is concerned, you can generally see from anywhere around the grandstands. Most seats give almost a full view of the action, although, like most ovals, the lower seats don't offer a great eyeful. The best seats are in the south grandstands in the first and second turns.

Motels are not exactly abundant, but are available in Wilkesboro, or anywhere in Wilkes County, Winston-Salem, Statesville, and Hickory. Wilkes County Chamber of Commerce phone number is (919) 725-2361; Winston-Salem or Forsyth County Chamber of Commerce is (919) 838 8662. Greensboro Piedmont Triad International Airport is closest to the track, and is located on I-40 between Greensboro and Winston-Salem.

Orange County Speedway
Office: P.O. Box 759
South Boston, VA   24592

PH: (919) 364-2232

Location: Central northern North Carolina, 20 miles north of Durham, NC, off U.S. Highway 501, in Rougemont.

Circuit: Three-eighths mile paved oval.

Major races: NASCAR Busch Grand National Series (two races); NASCAR interseries (Mid Atlantic Region).

Orange County Speedway is found between Roxboro and Durham on State Route 57. It is set in a beautiful green hills area of picturesque North Carolina in the middle of nowhere. The closest town is Rougemont — which is 1 1/2 miles away.

The three-eighths mile paved oval is one of the best places to watch a Grand National Race, and the Winston Cup drivers try to race here when their schedules allow it. The place seats 8,500 "If everyone has an 18-inch fanny", says track owner Bud Wilkins.

Come raceday, everyone seems to fit those measurements, and the track always gets just over 8,500 on a GN weekend — of which there are two during the year. Seats are not sold on a reserved basis here, but you can buy tickets by mail to ensure that you won't arrive to a sold-out event.

Camping on the grounds is permitted on race weekends. The area has a grove of oak trees where people can pitch tents and enjoy the southern weather. If you don't fancy camping you'll have a bit of a drive. There's no place to stay in Rougemont. You can stay in Durham, where Duke University has almost ensured there will be hotel space available; or try Roxboro. Hyco Lake has 7,000 miles of shoreline, so camping — as well as fishing, swimming, and boating — is available in abundance at places other than the track. For more information on rooms, call the Travel and Tourism Division of North Carolina at (800) 847-4862.

Rockingham Dragway

P.O. Box 70
Marston, NC   28363

(919)   582-3400
(919)   582-8667

Location: Southern central North Carolina, fifteen miles from the SC border, at the junction of Highways NC Highway 74 and U.S. Highway 1, across the street from the North Carolina Motor Speedway.

Circuit: Quarter-mile dragstrip.

Major Races: NHRA Invitational.

In February of 1992, Steve Earwood and Roy Hill bought the dragstrip portion of the North Carolina Motor Speedway, and proceeded to give it some life. For the past three seasons prior to the Earwood/Hill partnership the track only hosted one event per year — the NHRA race. Before the NHRA's arrival at the strip the season's race weekends had been twice as exciting — running two IHRA races a year.

Now, it has gone from one lone event to 48 in their first year, and plans are eventually to have 90 events. The season consists of a weekly Saturday show (with time trials starting at 3 p.m. and eliminations at 7:30 p.m.) which is punctuated by seven big races. Racing is scheduled to start up again in March. In addition, Hill has a Pro-Stock drag racing school at the track.

The strip seats 26,000, but with the space in the pits the track will accommodate a lot more. For 1992's Invitational, 52,000 attended over the three days, with Sunday's attendance set at 28,000. The split was harmonious, and the strip is still used as the airport for the two Winston Cup races at The Rock per year, and the parking lot across the street from the Dragway is still used by the strip on big weekends.

For more information on lodging, see the North Carolina Motor Speedway entry.

Tri-County Speedway
Route 2, P.O. Box 517
Hudson, NC   28638

PH: (704) 728-7223

Location: Central western North Carolina, 15 miles north of Hickory, NC, on State Route 321.

Circuit: Three-eighths mile paved oval.

Major races: NASCAR interseries (Mid-Atlantic Region).

Tri-County Speedway is located on farmland, in a flat area of western North Carolina. The biggest race of the season is the Larry Smith Memorial with late model stocks, limited sportsman, mini stocks, street stocks, and Bud Cup racing. The regular program takes place on Friday nights. Accommodations can be found at Lenoir, which is a few miles from the track.

Red River Valley Speedway
Office: Route 2
East Grand Forks, MN   56721

PH: (office) (218) 773-2120
Track: (701) 282-2200
Ticket info: (218) 773-9221

Location: Eastern North Dakota, just west of Fargo.
From Fargo take Interstate I 94 to exit 85, then a quarter-mile east on SR 10 to the track.

Circuit: Half-mile clay oval; high banked.

Major races: World of Outlaws Sprint Car Championship Shootout.

Red River Valley Speedway, in the Red River Valley Fairgrounds, sits in the western city limits of Fargo. Set in a nice rural, open, grassy area, with sparse buildings, the track hosts some terrific racing. The 27 year old facility seats 6,000 people, and the place fills up for the Outlaws, which is the speedway's biggest event of the season. There is camping at the track, or Fargo has plenty of rooms.

Allen County Fairgrounds Speedway
P.O. Box 6935
Toledo, OH 43612

PH: (419) 476-2312

Location: In Lima, OH, between Dayton and Toledo at I 75 and SR 309.

Circuit: Half-mile dirt oval.

Major races: AMA Grand National Championship Camel Pro Series.

Allen County Fairgrounds Speedway is a horse racing facility that occasionally sees AMA Grand National racing. Located in the industrial area of Lima, this is probably the favorite half-mile of the AMA Camel Pro circuit. The track never grooves as the racers abuse it, so the racing is usually four wide, and no one way is fastest.

There are at least 50 hotels in the Lima area, and rooms are never a problem here. Call the track office for more information.

Attica Raceway Park
450 W. Country Rd 6
Tiffin, OH 44883

PH: (419) 448-9800/(419) 426-8911

Location: Central northern Ohio, roughly between Columbus and Toledo. From Columbus, take Interstate I 71 to U.S. 60 North, then 60 to 224 West. The track is less than a half-mile from SR 4, on Lemmon.

Circuit: Third-mile clay oval.

Major Races: World of Outlaws; USAC Sprint Car Championship.

Attica Raceway Park, located in the farmland of Ohio, seats 4,500. Its major event of the season is not the WoO show, but the 4th leg of Ohio Speedweek — which is a seven-race series held at seven different tracks, and sanctioned by the All Star Circuit of Champions. The seven include: Millstream Speedway; Buckeye; Speedway 7; Attica; Sharon Speedway; Fremont Speedway; and concluding at Eldora Speedway.

Attica has racing every Friday night with Sprints, Street Stock, and Econo Sprints — which is the newest open wheeled division invented by Attica to keep the costs of a sprint car team manageable. The racetrack, which opened in May of '88, is already proving a valuable asset as a racing facility.

Barberton Speedway
3363 Clarkmill Rd.
Norton, OH.

PH(track): (216) 753-8668

Location: Southern Ohio, one mile southwest of Barber road, two miles from Interstate I 76.

Circuit: Quarter-mile paved oval.

Major races: USAC Midget Championships.

Barberton Speedway is a small racetrack that once hosted a USAC Midget track, but its biggest races are now regional non-NASCAR sanctioned events. The track holds 1,200 people. It is located 10 miles from Akron in the farmlands west of the city.

Buckeye Speedway
8848 Ely Rd.
Apple Creek, OH   44606
PH: (track): (216) 682-7435; (216) 682-5235.

Location: 75 miles south of Cleveland, between Canton and Wooster on Rte 30.

Circuit: Three-eighths mile clay oval.

Major races: USAC Sprint Car Championships.

Set in rural Amish country, Buckeye Speedway is flooded with tourists during the warm summer months. The Amish towns and the spillover from tourism from the biggest Swiss Cheese producing area in the country adds to Buckeye's already impressive reputation.

The track's regular program is a Saturday night event, with sprints and outlaw-sprints. The biggest races of the season are an August $12,000- purse, non-sanctioned, winged sprint race called the Outlaw Sprint Challenge and the Ohio Speedweek — which is a seven-race series held at seven different tracks, and sanctioned by the All Star Circuit of Champions. The seven include: Millstream Speedway; Buckeye; KC Speedway; Attica; Sharon speedway; Fremont Speedway; and concluding at Eldora Speedway.

The facility seats 4,000. You can stay in Wooster, or you can camp outside the track — there are no facilities for RVs. Wayne County, where the track is located, is a half-hour away from the Pro Football Hall of Fame.

Burke Lakefront Airport
Cleveland, OH

Office: Indycar Grand Prix
c/o Motor Marketing
1 Erieview Plaza Suite 1300
Cleveland, OH   44114

PH: (216) 522-1200
FAX: (216) 522-1145
Ticket info: (216) 781-3500

Location: At Burke Lakefront Airport, on Lake Erie, in downtown Cleveland.

Circuit: 2.369 mile road course; ten turns.

Major races: CART Indy Car PPG World Series Championship.

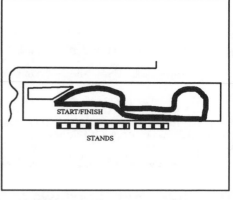

Burke Lakefront Airport has been the site of the Cleveland Grand Prix for a decade and has always had success and enthusiasm each and every year.

It made no sense, then, when the CART Board of Directors voted to remove it from the calendar for the 1992 season. In an extraordinary show of force, Cleveland's Mayor pled his case before the CART board in October of '91. His mission was successful and the board, impressed with the interest from Cleveland, put the race back on the schedule — for 1993. Eventually, it was granted a date for 1992 as well.

Now, according to Cleveland Grand Prix brass, the race is back with a new promoter. Roger Penske reportedly had a date problem with the '93 running of the Cleveland GP, and was forced to pull out. The International Management Group people, who organized the stillborn Manhattan Grand Prix, had a date that needed filling and purchased the rights from Penske.

The race now seems a permanent part of the series, and it has reportedly been contracted to ABC TV for the first time ever.

The Cleveland Grand Prix is next door to Cleveland Municipal Stadium where the Cleveland Indians play baseball. The track is an operating airport until the beginning of July, its traditional date, when it's transformed into an Indycar track.

As far as temporary circuits go, this is one of the better ones for fans. Completely flat, spectators can see the entire racing surface from the stands. Laid out on airport runways, the only barriers are on the start/finish straight. Racing is fast and passing is prolific. There may be one fast line through here, but there's more than one way to pass, and drivers do anything to overtake here. The track is wide and the surfaces are good. For the benefit of both drivers and sponsors, landscaping was added in 1993 in the form of signage and sculpted temporary earth and grass mounds. The drivers complained of no reference points for braking and turning.

In 1990, the track, which had been recently resurfaced except for one area just past the start/finish line, was changed during the race weekend. The cars were hitting some large bumps in the first sequence of two corners, which began to cause the track to break up even more. Eventually, following Friday's first practice, the first two turns were simply omitted altogether, and the track was shortened — the race distance subsequently lengthened. The drivers liked the changes, and it has become a permanent feature of the track.

The city has had a great deal of success with this event. It has grown a great deal in terms of popularity over the years. Tickets for the event will probably be no problem, although it is still wise to buy in advance. All tickets are for stands along the south side of the track, and there is no access to anything north of the grandstands by spectators. In any event, there's no need to get out onto the track — you can't see any better from out there anyway. The best seats are in front of start/finish, but don't worry if you can't get them there. You don't need them. A view from any of the stands is good enough to see everything.

Lodging is easy to find in Cleveland, with several places close to the track. Access is just off I 90 and both entry and exit is simple. For rooming in the Cleveland area call the Cleveland Division of Tourism at (800) 321-1001.

Cloverleaf Speedway
**3403 Chickasaw Ct
Sidney, OH   45365**

PH:(216)   524-4400

Location: Northern Ohio, in Cleveland, off exit 21 from Interstate 480, on Canal Road.

Circuit: Quarter-mile paved oval.

Major Races: USAC Midgets.

Cloverleaf Speedway, located in Valleyview, seven miles south of Cleveland, has some odd ideas about motorsports. Although racing is held every Friday and Sunday night, the big show, which is always on or around the Fourth of July, is comprised of the Mid -Season Championships and a series of demolition derbies. Not just any demolition derbies. First, there is an auto demolition derby; followed by a truck and van demo derby; then a motorcycle demo derby; and finally, a boat demolition derby in the infield lake!

The track, built in 1960, is now in an industrial area 10 minutes from the city. There are hotels two miles from the track on Rockside Rd. off 77th and Independence.

Columbus Grand Prix
**Office: 325 E. Broad St.,
Columbus, OH 43225**

**Office/ Tickets (614) 221-7223
FAX: (614) 221 PRIX**

Circuit: 1.8 mile road course; 12 turns.

Location: Downtown Columbus. From central Columbus, take 70 West to 71 North to the 17th ave/Ohio State Fairgrounds turnoff, where the fairgrounds will be to the left.

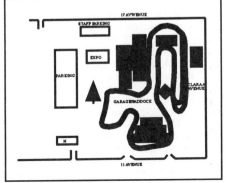

Major races: SCCA Trans-Am Championship.

Columbus' racecourse is

completely different from the configuration utilized between 1985 and '89; and the race cars are now Trans-Am sedans rather than IMSA sports cars. But the Columbus Grand Prix has returned to the motorsports calendars. Scheduled for mid-May, the Columbus Grand Prix has returned for another shot at a temporary race through downtown Columbus. But this time things are different.

The new organizers saw the wisdom in having a race during football's off-season. Ohio, as crazy as it is about college football, was not about to get behind a race while the season was in full swing. So the new promoters took a shot at a race just one week prior to the Indy 500 — and they got it from the SCCA. The organizers signed a three-year contract with the SCCA.

Addressing the problems of downtown viewing access, it is now run at the Ohio State Fairgrounds, giving most seated fans the opportunity to view almost 50% of the racetrack at one time. It also allows parking for 120,000 people. So far, there are four grandstands planned, with the possibility of more. All four sit on the main straight.

All structures and pavement already exist, so it was just a matter of directing the circuit through the Fairgrounds complex. The circuit does not use any public roads. The track is a good array of four straights — the longest topping out at about 2,000 feet — and a pair of hairpins mixed with a few medium fast corners. It will put a premium on braking.

The fairgrounds are downtown and easily accessible. Four million people a year come to the fair, so the area is ready for the rush. Camping is available close to the fairgrounds. For accommodation and camping information you can call the track at (800) 860-7223; or call the Columbus Convention and Visitor's Bureau at (614) 221-6623.

Eldora Speedway
**Office: 13929 State Route 118
New Weston, OH 45348**

PH: (513) 338-3815

Location: Southeastern Ohio, 50 miles northwest of Dayton, and 100 miles northwest of Cincinnati.

From Cincinnati, take Interstate I 75 through Dayton to I-70 West to State Route 49 North to Greenville. From Greenville take State Route 118 North fifteen miles to Rossburg. The track is two-and-a-half miles north of Rossburg on SR 118.

Circuit: Half-mile clay oval; high banked.

Major races: World of Outlaws Sprint Car Championship Shootout; USAC Sprint Cars, Midgets, and Silver Crown Championships; King's Royal Sprints.

Eldora Speedway is one of the most impressive dirt tracks in the county, and is certainly the best in Ohio. The farm area around it belies its stature, as the little track has purses of $50,000 for a King's Royal Sprint car race win. The wide, high-banked track hosts all facets of the USAC Championships series, as well as a couple of WoO shows.

The King's Royal, aptly named for the king's ransom the track pays for the win, has become the biggest race of the Outlaws season, eclipsing even the Knoxville Nationals as competitors will do just about anything to win. Coincidentally, fans will do almost anything to get a chance to watch. In fact, other tracks in the area shut down during the King's Royal so they can attend!

304

Another big event here is the World's 100 for Sprint cars, which attracts the WoO drivers. But the Ohio Speedweek — which is a seven-race series held at seven different tracks, and sanctioned by the All Star Circuit of Champions — is the most popular of the Eldora season. The seven include: Millstream Speedway; Buckeye; Speedway 7; Attica; Sharon Speedway; Fremont Speedway; and concluding at Eldora Speedway.

Fifteen miles south of Eldora is Greenville, and most stay there for a race. Other places to stay include Versailles, Salina, Sydney, Piqua, Troy and Dayton.

K-C Raceway
2535 Blain Highway
Waverly, OH   45690
P.O. Box 1645
Chillicothe, OH   45601
PH: (614) 663-4141

Circuit: Three eighths mile clay high banked oval

Location: Southern Ohio, between Columbus and Portsmouth, off State Route 23, on Blain Highway.

Major Races: All Star Pro; USAC Sprint.

Race fans know Chillicothe. It's where Junior Johnson spent time in the Federal Penitentiary for moonshining, and where he was inspired to take his fast driving to the legitimate arenas of NASCAR.

K-C racetrack is now Chillicothe's racing claim to fame, and the track, which has been in existence 38 years, may have seen Johnson race a stock car on its high banks once or twice.

In a tranquil setting in the Chillicothe hills, K-C is very easy to get to. The track sits in a valley, and is often the victim of odd weather, where rain can attack the valley, and the surrounding area can be clear. K-C officials suggest you call before travelling to the track. The place seats 3,500.

Camping is free at the 41 acres of K-C and there is plenty of space for you to pitch a tent. If camping is not your preference, 12 miles from the track in either direction will yield plenty of rooms.

Kil-Kare Speedway
1166 Dayton Xenia Rd
Xenia, OH   45385
PH: (513) 426-2764

Location: South central Ohio, 10 miles east of Dayton, on State Route 35.
Circuit: Three-eighths mile oval/ quarter-mile dragstrip
Major races: NASCAR interseries (Great Northern Region).

Kil-Kare Speedway hosts both a weekly dragstrip and an asphalt oval program. The oval racing is restricted to Friday night with the exception of special events and NHRA drag racing, which is held Saturday evenings. Racers usually stay in Xenia.

Marion County Int'l Dragway

2454 Richwood Larue Rd.,
Larue OH   43332

PH (614) 499-3666
FAX: (614) 499 2185

Circuit: Quarter-mile dragstrip.

Location: Roughly one hour from either Lima or Columbus. From Marion, take SR 95 West to La Rue, then take SR 37 left and proceed three miles to the track.

Major Races: IHRA Sportsman Nationals.

Bill Guthry's family settled here in 1887, plowing the fields and creating a farm out of the flat land. A little over a hundred years later Guthry's family still farms the land, but from April to October racecars run through the fields.

Marion County Dragway sits on farmland, the asphalt strip has the distinction of being one of the longest in the world at 6,200 feet. But if you manage to travel past that distance — as Gene Snow did some 20 years ago when his chutes failed to open — you'll run off into Guthry's bean field. In that case, the normally amiable Guthry won't be too happy.

On either side of the track, beans, corn and wheat grow in planted rows. Guthry likes it that way, and takes pride in the fact that everything sold from a Marion County Dragway concession stand is fresh and homemade. Racers generally like to come here to race. It has become a pretty quick track too. More national records have been set on this track than any other IHRA track.

The weekly show is held on Saturdays, and the gates open at 3 p.m.. America's largest sportsman race, the IHRA Sports Nationals, is traditionally held mid-August. The stands hold 4,000 fans, and the paddock can accommodate 550 cars. The bleachers are up on a dirt embankment, so people can stand between bleachers and the fence without disturbing any of the seated folks.

Staying in Marion is easiest for travelling fans — it is within a half-an-hour of the strip, about 15 miles away. Or try Marysville, where the Honda plant is located. You can call Bill for an idea of where to stay.

Mid-Ohio Sports Car Course

Truesports Inc.,
4355 Davidson Rd.,
Hilliard, Oh   43026-
9699

Track:
Steam Corners Rd
P.O. Box 3108
Lexington, OH 44904

PH: (419) 884-4000
FAX: (614) 884-0042
    Ticket info: (419) 884-2295/
(800) MID OHIO

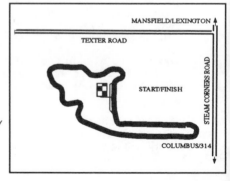

Location: Central northern Ohio, 60 miles north of Columbus and 70 miles south of Cleveland.

Take Interstate I 71 to exits #151 (SR 95; turn right or Rte 95 following 95 to the first light, turning left on Rte 314 to Steam Corners Rd, then right one mile), 165 (SR 97; turn right on 97 through Lexington, turning left on Steam Corners Rd., proceeding two miles to the track) or exit 169. then take on Steam Corners Rd. to the track.

Circuit: 2.4 mile road course; 15 turns.

Major races: CART PPG Indycar World Series Championship; IMSA Camel GT Championship; AMA National Road Races.

Mid Ohio was purchased by the late Jim Trueman in 1981, and the track has continued to move forward as one of the country's best road racing circuits.

Although it has hosted an Indycar race for ten of the past 12 years, and has been on the Camel GT calendar for the past 21 consecutive seasons, the track is narrow compared to most world-class venues. Even though the track was resurfaced in 1989 and widened, passing here is almost as difficult as passing on a street circuit.

Not so many years ago, Mid-Ohio was considered Bobby Rahal's property. The Ohio resident lives a few miles away in Dublin. And as a longtime driver for Trueman and Truesports he has logged thousands of miles on the hilly racetrack.

Although only posting two wins through the eight years of Indycar racing at Mid-Ohio, Rahal has usually led here, and, were it not for late-race bad luck, would probably have won several more races than he actually did. He's still considered the guy to beat. This track will long be remembered as the one and only Indycar win for Porsche, which came in 1989, at the hands of Teo Fabi.

The track has several good places to watch racing. The Keyhole, in particular, is a great area from which to watch, as you sit on a hill, looking down upon the cars as they race past. There are also good viewing places on the hill past the Ss. From drivers' right you can watch the 90 degree right-hander which leads onto the fastest part of the track. Unfortunately, catch-fencing is going in all over the circuit in preparation for the NASCAR Winston Cup Series, so you must now look through a fence.

Mid-Ohio is a long way from anything (an hour from Columbus) so you must book early if you expect to get a room in Lexington — but don't count on it. For more information, call the track, or call the Greater Columbus Convention and Visitors Bureau at (513) 221-6623 or (out of state only) 1 (800) 821-5784.

Millstream Speedway
13929 State Route 118
New Weston, Oh 45348

PH: (office) (513) 338-3815
Track: (419) 423-4386

Location: Northwestern Ohio, approximately 100 miles from Dayton and 150 miles from Cincinnati.

From Cincinnati, take Interstate I75 to Findlay, turning west on U.S. 224 just past Findlay. Take U.S. 224 to Township Liberty Rd North and proceed one-and-a-half miles to the racetrack.

Circuit: Half-mile clay oval; semi-banked.

Major races: World of Outlaws Sprint Car Championship Shootout.

Millstream Speedway is located in a bowl, in the middle of Ohio farm country. The track only has grandstands for 2,000, but its location allows at least double that number to park on tiered hillsides and watch from along the sides of the track.

The Sunday night regular show is highlighted by two WoO races per season — which, at least occasionally, also run on Sunday. There are also two All Star Sprint races, and several late model and econo-stock shows. Another big event here is the World's 100 for Sprint cars, which attracts the WoO drivers. The Ohio Speedweek — which is a seven-race series held at seven different tracks, and sanctioned by the All Star Circuit of Champions — is one of the most popular at Millstream. The seven include: Millstream Speedway; Buckeye; Speedway 7; Attica; Sharon Speedway; Fremont Speedway; and concluding at Eldora Speedway. There are hotels in Findlay, which is three miles west of the track.

Nelson Ledges
3709 Valacamp
Warren, OH   44484

PH: (216) 548-8551

Location: Northeastern Ohio, near Cleveland, off the Ohio Turnpike at exit 14, and 10 miles to the track.

Circuit: 2.0 mile road course; seven turns.

Major races: 24 hours of Nelson Ledges; SCCA Nationals; WERA Championships.

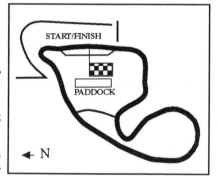

Nelson Ledges is considered the fastest permanent road course in America. Atlantics are the fleetest cars regularly running here, and can complete the two miles in some 1.08 minutes.

Although the track is very narrow, and there is not lots of run-off, it is considered relatively safe. With a reported 8,000,000 tires lining its racing surface, it's forgiving in the event of a track departure. In fact, in 1974 track officials were given an award from Lloyds Insurance for Outstanding Contribution to Automobile Safety, mostly for the innovative tire walls. Nowadays, however, long stretches of earth run-off and gravel pits are the standard of safety more likely to win an award.

Areas from which to watch racing are near the BF Goodrich Barn and Station 13. Since there are no grandstands anywhere anyway, you'll want to look around for your own spot. Bring your own chairs and sit on the dirt embankments.

In addition to the SCCA racing which highlights the motorsports season here, WERA motorcycling also holds a few races. There are two national WERA sprint races, and a 24 hour WERA Enduro.

You can stay in Warren, Niles, or Youngstown. For more information about hotels in the area, call the track, or call the Convention and Visitors Bureau of Trumbull County in Niles at (800) 672-9555; or in Youngstown, call the Youngstown Mahoning County Convention and Visitors Bureau at (216) 747-8200.

Norwalk Raceway Park

P.O. Box 708
Norwalk, OH 44857

Track: 1300 State Route 18 EAST
Norwalk, OH

PH: (419) 668-5555
FAX: (419) 663-0502

Circuit: Quarter-mile dragstrip.

Location: At the junction of state Route 18 and 601.
From Cleveland take the Ohio Turnpike 45 miles to exit 7, then head south five miles on Route 250 and follow signs.

Major Races: IHRA World Nationals.

In the rural and flat farmland of Ohio, Norwalk Raceway Park stands quietly much of the year. From April to October the silence is broken twice a week for the regular weekly Wednesday and Saturday night shows, with an occasional appearance by a major series.

Ranked as one of the "Top Five Tracks in the Country" by Drag Racing Magazine in 1991 (from information gathered on everything from best traction to cleanliness to most congenial track personnel), Norwalk is the only IHRA track in the bunch of NHRA circuits. It is the biggest IHRA track in existence, with the biggest national event drawing 60,000-70,000 people in three days. In addition to the Nationals, the Night Under Fire Jet Cars and Wall of Fire fireworks show is touted a pair of the best pyro shows in racing. The shows will be held at the end of June this year.

The track has been around since 1959, and has been affiliated with the IHRA since 1981. The quarter-mile dragstrip hosts the World Nationals IHRA race and also the Quarter Mile Bracket Finals. It seats 15,000-20,000 at the major events, with the ability to hold many more at the fences and in the paddock.

There is camping at the back of the property at certain events (like the Halloween Classic — world's largest bracket race), but no hookups are available. You can find rooms near the turnpike in Avery or Norwalk, or near the Sandusky Speedway.

Sandusky Speedway
614 W. Perkins Ave.
Sandusky, OH   44870

PH: (419) 625-4084

Location: Northern Ohio, on Lake Erie, between Cleveland and Toledo, off State Route 4, on Route 250.

Circuit: Half-mile oval.

Major races: NASCAR interseries (Great Northern Region).

Sandusky Speedway is just three miles from Cedar Point Amusement Park, home of the world's biggest roller coaster. You can swim, boat, and picnic within a few minutes of the track, and there are plenty of hotels.

Sandusky seats more than 5,000 now that the new bleachers are in place (built at the start of '92). The half-mile paved oval hosts the High Miler Nationals — an invitational supermodifieds, sports stock, and street stock race with cars coming from all over the country to compete. The regular NASCAR show is a Saturday night affair.

Toledo Speedway
5639 Benore Rd.
Toledo, OH   43612

PH: (419) 729-1634

Location: Northern Ohio, near the Michigan border, off Interstate I 75 at exit 210.

Circuit: Half-mile paved oval.

Major races: USAC Sprint Car Championships.

Racing at Toledo Speedway draws quite well from Ohio's metro area. Located just off I 75 — just a few minutes away from Toledo — it is easy to find, and has several good races a season. The 900 Series, which is a nine-race series around a series championship which pays $150,000, is quite popular; or the ARCA Permatex 125 does well as a feature event for the racing season. There is also a quarter-mile oval in the center of the half-mile high banks, plus a figure eight track. All the racing happens Sunday night.

The facility sits on 52 acres of open field, so there is free camping, although there are only a couple of hookups for RVs. Toledo has plenty of rooms if camping is not your style.

Hallett Motor Racing Circuit

2232 South Nogales
Tulsa, OK   74107
PH: (918) 356-4384
Office: (918) 583-1134

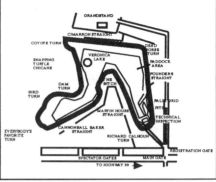

Circuit: 1.8 mile road course;
10 turns

Location: 35 miles northwest of Tulsa, at the Highway 99 exit of the Cimarron Turnpike.

Major races: SCCA Regionals and Nationals; WERA Motorcycle Championships; AIS Championships; International Kart Federation Mid-America Road Races.

New owners took possession of Hallett Motor Racing Circuit in 1989, and are currently attempting to attract some major teams (IMSA, SCCA, and Indycars) for testing — with an eye on luring a major series here in the near future.

Although the place is short on spectator facilities — with grandstands only accommodating 1,000 people or so — the track itself is challenging and safe. It has 80 feet of elevation changes, and some very quick combinations. It has good runoff, and where the runoff is at a minimum, it is stuffed with tires. Track officials are quick to point out that there is no armco and almost no concrete barriers.

Located in eastern Oklahoma on the western edge of the Ozarks, the area is all rolling hills with sand and Scrub Oaks. The track has several picnic areas. From the grandstand you can see 70% of the track, but the combination in turns 7,8, and 9 — nicknamed "The Bitch" — is one of the best places to watch. The high speed third gear corner is blind at the top, so drivers can't tell where they're going. If they miss it, the uphill loses lots of time as speed diminishes quickly. So most guys go through fast, prepared to miss the exit.

The track boasts of being able to move wanna-bes into real racers through the Stephan School of High Performance Driving, whch sponsors SCCA style road races. The school uses Shelby Can-Am or GT1 cars.

You can camp free here, and the 168 acres has several good places to pitch a tent. If you don't wish to camp, stay in Cleveland, OK, which is 10 miles away. Or head to Tulsa. The track will give you advice if you wish to know about accommodations, so don't hesitate to call.

Oklahoma State Fair Speedway

Office: 4437 W. Liberty
Oklahoma City, OK   73107
PH: (office) (405) 946-1122
Track: (405) 946-0422

Location: Central Oklahoma, off Interstate I 40 on may Ave.

Circuit: Half-mile clay oval; semi-banked.

Major races: World of Outlaws Sprint Car Championship Shootout.

Oklahoma State Fair Speedway is located off I 40 at May Ave., a half-mile north of city-center. The 9,000 seat grandstands are filled for the two WoO races per year. The track also holds an AMA Supercross and a CRA Sprint Car show — although Friday night's four-division racing is the staple.

Lodging is available at I 40 and Meridian area, where there are several choices of motels.

Tulsa Expo Raceway
1141 South 83rd East Ave.
Tulsa, OK   74112

PH: (918) 838-3777

**Track: ITE Bldg,
Tulsa Expo State Fair**

Circuit: Third-mile clay oval.

Location: In Tulsa at 21st Street and Yale, at the Tulsa Square.

Major Races: Chilly Bowl Midget Racing.

The Tulsa Expo Raceway is located inside what is known to be the largest free standing structure in the nation — and probably in the world. It is ten acres of space indoors.

Six times a year, within a period of a few weeks, the building at Tulsa Square plays host to motor racing — with the featured event being one of the best midget races in the country. Running in early January, it is not sanctioned by any major auto racing body. The event is just a free-for-all that has tended to attract some of the best drivers in the country. John Andretti, Kenny Schrader, Sammy Swindell and many other top name drivers compete in this one for fun.

The two-level building has a 60,000 seating capacity, and the viewing is also two level, with some seats on the second floor overlooking the action. In addition to the midget race there is a motocross and go-kart show. But the biggest is still the midget event.

There is camping at the fairgrounds and there are some hookups. Or you can stay in Tulsa. For more information on lodging call the track office or the Tulsa Square Fairgrounds at (918) 744-1113.

Tulsa Speedway
Office: P.O. Box 76
Hwy 75 North & 66th
Owasso, OK   74055

PH: (office) (918) 272-6120
Track: (918) 425-7551

Location: Northeastern Oklahoma, on the outskirts of Tulsa.
From Interstate I 75 North, take the 66th St. exit and head east to the track.

Circuit: Three-eighths mile clay oval; high banked.

Major races: World of Outlaws Sprint Car Championship Shootout.

Tulsa Speedway, located six-and-a-half miles north of downtown Tulsa, is hot and dry. Friday is factory stock night, with full-bodied racecars, while the open wheeled sprints run Saturday nights. The Outlaws race twice a year in this 4,500 seat facility.

Although the track is closer to downtown than to the Tulsa International Airport, which is just east of the track, the only motels downtown are the high-dollar business type. Try around the airport first.

Portland International Raceway

P.O. Box 3024
Portland, OR   97208/
Global Events Group
4242 SE Milwaukie
Portland, OR 97202

PH: (503) 232-3000
FAX: (503) 232-2336
Ticket info: (503) 236-8006

Location: North western Oregon, one mile from the Washington border, five miles north of downtown, in West Delta Park, northern Portland.

Circuit: 1.95 mile road course; 12 turns.

Major races: CART Indycar World Series Championship; IMSA Camel GT.

At the split of the Columbia and Willamette Rivers, in the middle of West Delta Park, sits Portland International Raceway. Host to year-round activity from driving schools to go-karts and motorcycle races, PIR is best known for hosting the Pacific Northwest's only IndyCar and IMSA events.

Flying into Portland International Airport, you'll likely see the inconspicuous track on your approach; you will certainly see it as you leave, since it's in the flight pattern for outbound jets. The track is only four miles west of the airport.

The track winds through typical Pacific Northwestern scenery. There's a lake on the city-owned park, and the track meanders past the water. In the old days, frogmen stood by waiting for drivers who overcooked it into the water.

Racers generally like the place, since it's mostly flat, with forgiving corners and lots of runoff. One of the most challenging places on the track is the combination of turns-7,8,9. Coming

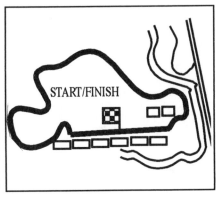

313

off the fast back part of the track, the jog left is very difficult and fairly slow. Cars are never completely straight under braking, which means they have to tiptoe through the left-hander and sneak up to the tight right-hander.

Turn-nine is bounded by a large grass area, which is usually where the drivers who didn't get the combination right end up. From the grandstands in turn-nine you can see both the combination of 7,8,9 and the pits. Originally, pit lane was located at the beginning of turn 8 (it is also the launching pad for drag racing). But the true pits are too small for both Indycars and IMSA, so a new pit lane was constructed for IMSA and CART use only. Now, on drivers right at the exit of turn-nine, there's an entrance to the pit lane. Club racers still use the old pits.

Probably the best place to watch racing is from the turn-nine grandstands; or try the hillside overlooking seven, eight, and nine; or take a look from the chicane on straight which has been unrelenting on brakes and transmissions as drivers sometimes downshift to first gear (the chicane now appears for the Indycar and IMSA weekends, with most other series using the entire length of the straight).

The one major problem with Portland is spectator access. There's only one bridge in the whole place — it goes from the far side of the pits to the other side of the track. From wherever you are, getting to the other side of the track is difficult. If you're in the pits and want to go to the outside of turn-three, well, you'll have a long walk.

Staying in Portland is often difficult. Usually, Portland has enough rooms, but it is becoming a popular place to hold conventions, and rooms are becoming increasingly hard to come by. In addition, the Pacific Northwest is crazy about motorsports and fans from all over the area come to see races here. In recent years, some Indycar teams had to drive 40 miles for a room when a major convention conflicted with the race weekend.

There is RV parking all the way outside turns 2,3,4, and 5. For more information on rooms, call the Portland Oregon Visitors Association at (503) 222-2223.

Portland Speedway
9727 N. Union Ave.
Portland, OR   97211

PH: (503) 285-2883

Location: Northern Oregon, on the outskirts of Portland.

Circuit: Quarter-mile paved oval.

Major races: NASCAR interseries (Great Northern Region).

Portland Speedway runs a Friday night racing program with late model NASCAR Winston Racing Series cars headlining the season. The track sits just across the highway from PIR and is actually easier to see from I-5 than the bigger road racing facility. It runs a weekly show and has occasional destruction derbies as well. The Winston 50 races are the most popular here. Set in the green Pacific Northwest, Portland has inexpensive rooms outside the big Pacific city, many of which are just minutes from the track. See PIR for rooming information.

Grandview Speedway
218C Wilt Rd
RD1, Bechtelseville, PA   19505

PH: (215) 754-7688

Location: Eastern Pennsylvania, on State Route 100, 20 miles north of Pottstown, on Passmore Rd.

Circuit: Third-mile clay oval.

Major Races: USAC Midgets.

Grandview calls itself the "Greatest Show on Dirt". And as the home of the biggest and richest short track modified stock car race in the Tri-state area, the claim may not be far from the truth. The purse for one race is over $35,000.
   Saturday evening racing is the staple here, and the track boasts of every seat being close to the action, and racing which can be clearly seen from any seat in the place. There is also a non-drinkers seating section. The track is minutes from Allentown Reading, Wilmington, Norristown, and Philly — all of which have rooms.

Jennerstown Speedway
Route 1, P.O. Box 228
Hollsopple, PA   15935

PH: (814) 629-9615

Location: Western Pennsylvania, 75 miles east of Pittsburgh, 15 miles off Interstate I 70, on U.S. Highway 30.

315

Circuit: Five-eighths mile paved oval.

Major races: NASCAR interseries (Great Northern Region).

Jennerstown Speedway hosts a Modified Tour race as its seasonal feature event, but its main staple is the NASCAR Winston Racing Series. The track is fast, at five-eighths of a mile, and hosts some great racing — usually on Saturday nights. There are a few rooms in Jennerstown, or you can stay in Jenners or Boswell.

Lernerville Speedway
Office: 278 N. Pike Rd,.,
Sarver, PA   16055
PH: (office) (412) 353-1511
Track: (412) 353-1350

Location: Western Pennsylvania, 20 miles north of Pittsburgh.
From Pittsburgh, take Interstate I 79 to State Route 68 North, then take SR 356 South 11 miles to the track.

Circuit: Half-mile clay oval; semi-banked.

Major races: World of Outlaws Sprint Car Championship Shootout.

Lernerville Speedway officials boast of being more successful than both the Pittsburgh Pirates and the Pittsburgh Penguins on a per-night basis. With five divisions of racing weekly, the oval has plenty of variation — and a lot of activity. World of Outlaws headline the season, but the 9,000 seat grandstands usually fill close to capacity every week — making the purses lucrative, and the driver rosters full of top hotshots. The outskirts of Pittsburg have plenty of rooms, with several just a few minutes from the track.

Lincoln Speedway
Office: 765 Carlisle
Hanover, PA   17331
PH: (track) (717) 637-1101

Location: Southern Pennsylvania, 20 miles south of Baltimore, MD.
From Baltimore, take MD State Route 30 to the state line (where it becomes PA SR 94) and go east eight miles past the state line on U.S. 30 to the track.

Circuit: four-tenths of a mile oval; semi-banked.

Major races: World of Outlaws Sprint Car Championship Shootout.

Lincoln Speedway is located in eastern Pennsylvania farmland in an open field. The track is a D-shaped oval which makes for an interesting show, while playing havoc on race set-up — especially when the WoO racing comes to town. The track is actually in New Oxford, where there are rooms. Also try Hanover.

Maple Grove Raceway

R. D. 3, P.O. Box 3420,
Mohnton, PA   19540

PH: (215) 856-7200
Track: (215) 856-7812
FAX: (215) 856-1601

Location: In southeastern Pennsylvania, in Mohnton, 15 miles south of Reading off of Route 10.

Circuit: Quarter-mile dragstrip

Major races: NHRA Drag Racing.

Judging Maple Grove Speedway by its surroundings, one gets a feeling of peace and serenity. The place doesn't seem like anywhere two drivers could post a smoking sub-five second at the same time on the normally quiet 1,320.

But it was. And Shirley Muldowney and Joe Amato have the records (and a spot in the four-second-club) to prove they were the first side-by-side sub-five second run in history.

Even so, the place doesn't seem very awe-inspiring. Located on 550 acres of rich Berks County farmland, Maple Grove is surrounded by rural country farmland. It is Amish country, and about the biggest thing in the vicinity is the nearby factory outlet shopping (where manufacturers sell their wares wholesale to the public).

The speedway takes up the slack let out by the easy going neighborhood. There are several good events throughout the season beside the Keystone Nationals. There is a Budweiser Super Stock National event; the Ford Motorsport Nationals; Pepsi Olympics of Drag Racing; Super Chevy Show; VW Super Jam; and the Mopar at Maple Grove Nationals (any more car companies want a date?).

In their 31st year of NHRA Drag Racing in 1993, the place pulls in some 100,000 people for the NHRA Nationals alone. Although it doesn't sell out in advance, it does sell out eventually. Don't plan on showing up Sunday for the Final Eliminator with the intention of getting a good seat. Any day you attend, however, children under 16 years of age are admitted free.

Not only do the rooms sell out near the track, but camping, which is run by Maple Grove, is also a hot item here too. The spots in the camping areas are reservable, and will be snatched up well in advance, so book early. Prices vary according to the event. Rooms are available in Reading, Lancaster, Morgantown, and Denver. Although the better places (ie, the closer places) will be gone early — even as far in advance as a year ahead of time — there are still lots of little inns in the area. You may have a drive, but you should be able to find something.

The track will be happy to give you a listing of hotels in the immediate area, or can reserve campspots for you.

Pennsylvania International Raceway
Nazareth Speedway (renamed)

P.O. Box Drawer F
Hwy 191
Nazareth, PA   18064
PH: (215) 759-8000
TICKETS (215) 759-8800

FAX: (215) 759-9055

Location: Eastern Pennsylvania, in the Lehigh Valley, eight miles from the New Jersey border, eighteen miles north east of Allentown.

From Newark, take Interstate I 78 to U.S. 22. From there, take U.S. 33 North, heading east at State Route 248. There are entrances on 248 and SR 191.

Circuit: One mile paved tri-oval.

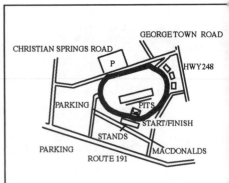

Major races: CART Indycar PPG World Series; NASCAR Busch Grand National Championship series; and NASCAR Winston Modifieds.

Pennsylvania International Raceway was purchased by Roger Penske in 1986 when it was a dirt track of a different name. It was completely refurbished, paved, widened, fenced, and just generally upgraded into a top-notch racetrack. It still retains its unique layout, which is a tri-oval, with a slight dog leg before the short start/finish straightway. The facility opened in 1987, and is now a permanent fixture on the Indycar circuit, earning the privilege of being called the world's fastest mile oval. For the new season the name will be changed to Nazareth Speedway, since the initials PIR already exist in two other IndyCar races (Phoenix and Portland) ... and nobody ever called it "Pennsylvania"; the track has always been referred to as "Nazareth".

The Lehigh Valley area is old Pennsylvania. And, although great for sightseeing, its very allure makes it difficult to find places to stay. There is really almost nowhere to stay in Nazareth itself. Bethlehem and Allentown have a few rooms, but the crews usually roll over reservations to the following season in preparation for the next race, so finding a room there will not be easy either. Phillipsburg, NJ, or Clinton, NJ, which are just over the Delaware River, are other possibilities; or try Quakertown, or the Poconos, which are about an hour away.

Tickets range from $20 - $50 and there is no set amount of seats available, since the grandstands are removed and rebuilt following or prior to an event. Penske, remember, owns MIS, and the grandstands are shuttled back and forth — and in addition, the seats are also used at the Cleveland Indycar race. Most of the seats here offer a view of the entire track, so don't become preoccupied with where you sit.

Infield overnight parking is permitted following time-trials — for Grand National events, that's Friday night — and Indycar race fans can enter Saturday. You can watch from your vehicle, or wander around by foot. Although there is really no general admission ticket, anyone can enter the infield. Unfortunately, you'll have to pay the same price as someone who goes by car, which is $10 for the vehicle and $10 per person overnight — so you pay $20 even if your vehicle is just a pair of tennis shoes. In all cases, children 12 and under are admitted free with a paying adult.

The Allentown/Bethlehem/Eastman area does have an airport, named aptly, ABE Municipal Airport. There are commercial flights, and 727s do land there. For the Chamber of Commerce of Nazareth, call 215 759-9188; for Bethlehem, call (215) 867-3788; in Allentown (215) 437-9661. Or call the track and ask for a short list of the area's hotels.

Pocono Raceway

P.O. Box 500
Long Pond, PA 18334
PH: (717) 646-2300
Ticket info: (800) 722-3929
FAX: (717) 646-2010

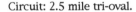

Location: Eastern Pennsylvania, in the Pocono Mountains, 20 miles from the Delaware River, and New Jersey.

From Newark/New York City, take 280/95 to Interstate I 80 West into Pennsylvania, following I 80 to Exit #43 to Route 115, and to Hulman Rd into the speedway.

Circuit: 2.5 mile tri-oval.

Major races: NASCAR Winston Cup (two events).

Pocono Raceway is located in the Pocono Mountain resort area of Northeastern Pennsylvania, and its recent claim to fame has been the running of a pair of annual NASCAR Winston Cup events.

Pocono's 2.5 mile tri-oval is a challenging circuit that presents drivers with three different radius turns with three different degrees of banking and three variations of radius. The first turn is 675 feet long and has the sharpest rake, with a 14-degree tilt; the second turn is 750 feet long and is banked eight degrees; and the third turn is 800 feet long and has a slant of six degrees. The back straight is 3,055 feet long, the short straight is 1,780 feet and the main straightway is 3,740 feet long. From the upper seats in the grandstands you'll be able to see the entire track. There is only one section of grandstands, located on the front straight.

The placid greenery of Pocono has been more and more attractive to fans as the Winston Cup now has two events. In fact, grandstand tickets for Pocono's NASCAR Winston Cup races have recently been sold out two to three weeks in advance, so grandstand tickets must be purchased early. If you manage to miss the opportunity for tickets at Pocono, you can always watch from the infield. There is no general admission grandstand.

There is little in the Pocono Mountains in terms of large hotels so pre-planning for this one is essential. The roads are fairly narrow, so even the drive to the track requires some forethought. The track issues instructions for traveling to and from the area. For speedier entry, track officials suggest avoiding the standard I 80 to 115 route, instead coming from the south or east into Route 115 and Hulman Rd.. For the complete list of suggested alternatives, call or write the track.

You can stay at the track if you have a self contained vehicle. Sunday the infield is open to any vehicle starting Friday night. Spots are available in advance, and are cheaper when purchased ahead of time. The infield opens up at 5 a.m. Sunday for the general public. For infield parking, you must proceed through the tunnel, which is located to east of the main entrance, on Long Pond Rd. (nothing over 7' 10" will clear the tunnel). There are also about 60 VIP RV camping areas on the outside of the short straight, but you'll need to move quickly. More information on those, as well as any other questions you may have, is available by calling the track. Information for lodging is available by calling (800) 762-6667.

Williams Grove Speedway
1 Speedway Dr.
Mechanicsburg, PA   17055

PH: (717) 766-4778

Location: Central Pennsylvania, roughly between Williamsport and Harrisburg, seven miles southwest of Interstate I 80, off U.S. 15 at State Route 74.

Circuit: Half-mile clay oval; semi-banked.

Major races: World of Outlaws Sprint Car Championship Shootout; USAC Midget Championships.

Williams Grove Speedway's 8,500 seat facility hosts a regular Friday show which is headlined by late model full-bodied cars. The track also has a World Of Outlaws race and two USAC Midget races per year. In addition, the September Fram-Autolite National Open is one of the biggest races in the state — featuring invitational sprint car racing, and attracting some of the country's best drivers.

The green Pennsylvania farmlands racetrack is directly across the street from the Williamsport Amusement Park, and there are plenty of places to stay in the area. The best are in Mechanicsburg, or up the road in Carlisle. Call the track for more information on lodging.

Anderson Speedway
P.O. Box 1026
Salem, SC   29678
PH: (803) 226-5481

Location: North western South Carolina, 2 miles north of Interstate 85.

Circuit: Three-eighths mile paved oval, semi-banked

Major races: NASCAR interseries (Mid-America Region).

Anderson Speedway's three-eighths mile paved track is in the heart of NASCAR country, just two hours from Atlanta and three hours from Darlington. The Friday night NASCAR racing is supplemented by several Budweiser-sponsored late model races and a tractor pull. The 31 year old circuit also boasts a VIP tower which seats 250 people.

Just off I 85 accommodations are fairly easy to find, but call the track for the closest places.

Darlington International Dragway

1813 South Fifth St.,
Hartsville, SC 29550
Track:
2056 East Bobo Newsome Hwy.(South Carolina Highway 151)
Hartsville, NC

PH: (803) 332-0123 (for fax dial ext. #242)

Circuit: Quarter-mile dragstrip.

Location: On South Carolina Highway 151, halfway between Hartsville and Darlington.

Major races: IHRA Winternational & IHRA U.S. Nationals.

In the middle of a cattle farm, about four miles west of the famous Darlington International Raceway, Darlington International Dragway lies dormant. It sees action only twice a season — with a pair of IHRA National events.

Built in 1971, the 65-feet above sea level quarter mile dragstrip is all that is left of the ambitious three-stage plan. The project was supposed to encompass the creation of a strip, a road course and a museum. The former partner finished the strip and started on the road course, but stopped as it was about halfway finished. Half of it still exists, and every once in a while car clubs or magazines rent it to test cars.

The facility is ready for serious racing, seating 25,000 and usually filling to around 55,000 for three days of racing. Even so, it has never been so full that they were forced to turn folks away.

You can call the track for information on accommodations — good motels exist in Hartsville or Florence at the intersection of I195 and 52— or you can camp. Camping is free, encompassing 35 acres for parking and camping. Getting in and out is no problem since there are six exits.

Darlington Raceway

P.O. Box 500
Highways 151 & 34
Darlington, SC 29532-0500
PH: (803) 393-9592

Location: Northeast South Carolina, just west of Darlington, on Highways 34-151, six miles north of Interstate I 95.

Circuit: 1.366 mile paved oval.

Major races: NASCAR Winston Cup Series Championship (two events); NASCAR Busch Grand National (two events).

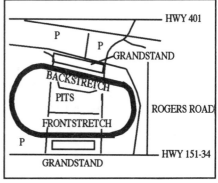

Nicknamed the track "too tough to tame", Darlington Raceway has taken its toll on many Winston Cup drivers. Darlington has the distinction of being the first superspeedway in the U.S.. Opened for business in 1950, Darlington now has a blend of old and new which both elicits images of past days of stock car racing, and offers a glimpse of the technology in the series now which makes it one of the toughest in the world to dominate.

This is yet another International Speedway Corporation track, under the wings of the France family, and it has the same allure about it as Talladega or Daytona.

The "Darlington stripe" is one of the interesting aspects of Darlington. The stripe was formed as someone realized long ago that the fastest way around Darlington's quick 1.366 miles was to smack the right rear quarter-panel into the wall outside turn four. To run 400 perfect laps, drivers needed to hit the wall 400 times.

Resurfacing neutered the corner, and the stripe is not as significant a feature as it once was. But the layout is still a challenge. Originally built as a 1.25 mile oval, it was repaved and altered slightly in 1953 to its present configuration. The slight changes affected only one end of the circuit, so the banking and turn geometry is different on each side — which is a nightmare for car set-up. Turns one and two are banked at 23 degrees, and turns three and four are banked at 25 degrees, making chassis tuning a compromise, at best. In addition, the high banks — which are 60 feet wide — only allow a true racing surface of 30 feet or so, really allowing only a one-car-groove in the turns — and tight racing for those who chose to try to make it a two-car groove. Those who try to pass in the turns at Darlington don't usually see the end of the race.

The old Darlington is infield madness and tin-roofed grandstands; the new circuit is the upgraded access roads, seating, and rejuvenated spectator facilities. There are still only 44,000 seats in the place, although it fills to 70,000 including infield tickets.

Camping in the infield is permitted, provided the vehicles are self contained. The spaces are sold on a first-come first-served basis or as a two-weekend package at the track. There are commercial camping facilities about 20 miles from the track for those who wish to pitch a tent.

Rooms are not overly abundant in the Darlington area. There are about 3,000 in the area — obviously far short of what's needed during a NASCAR weekend. Myrtle Beach and Columbia are good choices, if a 75 mile drive doesn't scare you, and Charlotte is also worth a look — at about the same distance.

For Darlington Chamber of Commerce, call (803) 393-2641 and for the Florence area, call (803) 665-0515.

Florence I-95 Speedway

P.O. Box 1527
Hartsville, SC   29550
PH: (803) 346-7711

Location: Central-eastern South Carolina, between Florence and Charlotte, NC, roughly 20 miles from Darlington, in Hartsville.
Circuit: Three-eighths mile oval.
Major races: NASCAR Interseries (Eastern Seaboard Region).

Florence I-95 Speedway is primarily a Saturday night NASCAR race venue that also hosts a series of twin-purse/twin-race events. There are also some lucrative $1,000 winner's purses for Florence demo-derbies, which attracts lots of bombs.

322

Greenville Pickens Speedway

P.O. Box 5206
Greenville, SC   29606

PH: (803) 269-0852

Location: Northern South Carolina, at the junction of SRs 183, 3, and 178, just east of Greenville, in Pickens.

Circuit: Half-mile paved oval.

Major races: NASCAR Interseries (Mid-Atlantic Region).

Where most speedways are on fairgrounds land, Greenville Pickens Speedway is privately owned, and lets the county fair committee use the land for two weeks a year to hold the county fair. The 8,000 seat grandstands are used for the live entertainment at the fair, and tents are set up in the infield with the exhibition areas.

The biggest show — when the Fair is not in town — is on Labor Day weekend, but there is always racing on Saturday nights, with additional events on holidays. There are places to set up RVs at the speedway, but hotels can be found in Pickens, or Easley, a few miles away.

Myrtle Beach

456 Sea Mountain Highway
Little River, SC   29566
Track: 4300 Highway 501
Myrtle Beach, 29577, SC
PH: (803) 236-0500

Location: Coastal South Carolina, just west of Myrtle beach on U.S. Highway 501.

Circuit: Half-mile paved oval.

Major races: NASCAR Busch Grand National Series Championship. NASCAR interseries (Eastern Seaboard Region).

Myrtle Beach Speedway is five miles from the famous beach town of the same name. It has recently become a tennis and golf oasis, with new resort areas popping up each year. Although the place was rocked by Hurricane Hugo several years ago, repairs from the devastation have been finally completed and the resort town is again a quaint place to go spend a few summer days... and a good place to watch racing.

The 14,000 seat racing facility fills up for the Grand National, and the NASCAR Dash races are also very popular. There is open-wheeled Modified All-Pro racing here, as well as ASA Sportsman racing. Most of the competition, however, is limited to full-bodies NASCAR racing, which is normally here on Saturday nights. The track has gone from dirt to paved and back again four times — now running as a paved oval.

Head down Highway 501 East for rooms at the Beach. Call the Myrtle Beach Chamber of Commerce at (800) 722-3224 (or 800 692-2472 in SC) for more information on accommodations.

Summerville Speedway
330 Robin St.
Moncks Corner, SC   29461

PH: (803) 873-3438

Location: Eastern South Carolina, 25 miles northwest of Charleston, two miles from the southern end of Lake Moultrie.

Circuit: Two-fifths mile paved oval.

Major races: NASCAR Interseries (Eastern Seaboard Region).

Summerville Speedway hosts the NASCAR Winston Racing Series on Saturday night for a regular racing card. The big show is the Budweiser NASCAR Dash which is held mid-July in conjunction with the regular five Summerville racing divisions. There are a few hotels around Lake Moultrie, and rooms should not be a major problem.

Black Hills Speedway
Office: 2467 E. 39th St.
Rapid City, SD   57709

PH: (605) 393-2122

Location: Western South Dakota, a half-mile east of Rapid City on SR 44.

Circuit: Half-mile dirt oval; high-banked.

Major races: World of Outlaws Sprint Car Championship Shootout.

Black Hills Speedway, just 16 miles from Mt Rushmore, is alluring — in the middle of the beautiful Black Hills. The rolling green of South Dakota and the track is situated just outside Rapid City to the east.
The facility had in the past hosted a round of the WoO Championship was left off the schedule but now reappears and looks permanent. Starting its 40th season in 1993, racing happens at Black Hills Speedway weekly on Friday nights with four major classes, including sprints, Late models, modifieds and Black Hills Speedway Grand Nationals.
Black Hills Speedway seats 8,500, and inexpensive accommodations can easily be found in the tourist-oriented countryside. Camper space makes overnight parking easy and handicapped facilities aid those in wheelchairs or on crutches.

Huset's Speedway
Sioux Falls, SD
Office: P.O. Box 130
Brandon, SD   57005

PH: (605) 332-2999

324

Location: Eastern South Dakota, east of Sioux Falls.
Take Interstate I 90 East to exit #406, then head south three miles on State Route 11 to the track.

Circuit: Three-eighths mile clay oval; high-banked.

Major races: World of Outlaws Sprint Car Championship Shootout.

Huset's Speedway is located in the arid high plains of South Dakota, and is one of the biggest attractions of the immediate area. The WoO show is the biggest of the year, generally filling the 4,500 seat facility as the open-wheeled cars come through. There are plenty of rooms in Sioux Falls, and more information regarding accommodations can be found by calling the Sioux Falls Convention and Visitors Bureau at (605) 336-1620.

Jackpine Gypsies MC Clubgrounds
P.O. Box 627
Sturgis, SD
(605) 347-6022
(605) 347-3418

Location: 30 miles east of Rapid City at exit 30 off I 90, then toward Deadwood, SD, turning south at the signs to the track, which is 3/4s of a mile down the service road on the east side.

Circuit: Sixth-mile clay oval/ sixth-mile TT track, with left turn right turn and a jump.

Major Races: AMA 600cc Championship.

Unlike most local tracks, Jackpine Gypsies doesn't have a season-long championship. Certainly, championships are contended over the course of the season, but they're more like two-to-three race mini series championships.
The big race here comes during August which is not just a race, but a week's worth of events. This season's week-long Black Hills Rally and Races will be the first week of August. The week's racing usually attracted some 80,000 people — all flooding into Sturgis, which has perhaps 5,000 residents.
There are actually four types of events held at Jackpine — or three at the facility and the fourth being a half-mile event run at a different venue under the auspices of Jackpine Gypsies: there's a hillclimb on the backside of the facility; the TT on the small TT track; the short oval dirt track, which is headlined by the AMA 600 Championship; and the half-mile Pro-Am race, held down the street at the Sturgis Fair, which sits in the center of Sturgis.
Jackpine Gypsies holds approximately 7,000 in the stands, but many more can watch from the hillside overlooking the track. And although the AMA 600 is the major race, the hillclimb seems to attract more people annually.
Of the 53 years in operation, 52 have had the blessing of the AMA. The club is actually a non-profit organization which is funded completely from private money, and the Indian Motorcycle Convention and annual motorcycle tours are at least as popular as the racing here.
Staying in Sturgis may be a problem. Camping is not available at the track, although campsites can be found in the immediate area.

There are only a handful of rooms in Sturgis, but lots of rooms exist in Spearfish or Rapid City. For more information call the track or call the Black Hills Motorcycle Consortium at (605) 347-6570; Fax (605) 347-3245.

Blankenship Motorsports Park
Office: P.O. Box 280 885
Memphis, TN   38168-0885

PH: (901) 358-7223

Location: Southwestern Tennessee, northeast of Memphis, at the corner of Raleigh-Millington Rd and Fite Rd.

Circuit: Half-mile clay oval; high-banked.

Major races: World of Outlaws Sprint Car Championship Shootout.

Blankenship Motorsports Park is located in a picturesque farming area in the Memphis area countryside. The greenery around the track provides World Of Outlaw racers with a nice rest from the quick paced world outside the sleepy universe called Memphis... at least until the racing starts.

The area is saturated with lodging, and there should be no problem finding a room for Outlaws racing as late as Saturday — although you may be a way away. Try Millington first or call the Memphis Convention and Visitors Bureau for more information at (901) 576-8181.

Bristol International Dragway
P.O. Box 729
Morehead KY 40351

Track: Highway 11E
Bristol, TN 37625

PH: (606) 784-8013
FAX: (606) 784 4520

Location: Bristol International Speedway is to the left of NASCAR track; see Bristol International Raceway for directions.

Circuit: Quarter-mile dragstrip.

Major Races: IHRA Spring Nationals; IHRA Fall Nationals.

Bristol International Dragway is the oldest track on the IHRA trail, running their 29th national season in 1993. Located four miles from the city limits of Bristol, the dragstrip lies just behind the NASCAR oval. The track owner, Larry Carrie, once owned the IHRA itself as well, and the relationship is still obvious — the IHRA office is still located at the front gate of the dragstrip.

Sitting between two mountains, the track is about 80 feet wide — wide for a dragstrip — and is 4,400 feet long. Nicknamed the "Thunder Valley Dragstrip" because of the noise it creates, the strip sponsors a bi-weekly bracket series of 20 races throughout the season, determining a series champion.

The Spring Nationals, Fall Nationals and South Eastern World Bracket Finals are the three biggest shows of the year, and the Super Chevy Sunday attracts some 1,100 entries. Super Chevy Sunday will be held on one of the last two weekends of June in 1993 (call the track for exact dates).

Bristol seats about 16,000 people, and at the Spring Nationals the place comes close to selling out. But since there is standing room, it never does. Grandstands will go quickly though. The Spring Nationals is the biggest and weather is generally good — although there was some rain in '92 (the event was rained out Friday). The Fall Nationals are quite often rained out.

There is camping available, which both NASCAR and Dragway fans use. It is $15 a weekend and will be available for any of the Dragway's events as late as Friday of the Nationals.

If you wish to stay in a hotel, try Kingsport, Johnson City, Elizabeth or any of the other small towns in the area (see Bristol International Raceway for more details).

Bristol International Raceway
Highway 11 East & Volunteer Parkway
P.O. Box 3966
Bristol, Tn 37625

PH: (615) 764-1161
FAX: (615) 764-1646

Location: Northern Tennessee, five miles from the Virginia border, off Interstate I 81 in Bristol.

Circuit: .533 mile paved oval.

Major races: NASCAR Winston Cup (two races); NASCAR Busch Grand National (two races).

Touted as "The World's Fastest Half Mile", Bristol is the home of the only permanent night race in NASCAR Winston Cup racing's 29 race calendar — which makes the track unique right off the bat. But Bristol is also remarkable in that it truly is an ultra fast half-mile circuit — mostly credited to its 36 degree banking.

The entire circuit is visible from anywhere in the stands, so any ticket will do the job. The work, however, is getting the seat in the first place. The inexpensive tickets, and the scarcity of bleachers at the facility make this track — and especially August's night race — the most difficult in the series. Long time fans reserve permanent seats a year in advance, and are on the waiting list for the following year, making life for one-timers difficult.

Staying in Bristol is not easy either. The hilly forested area of north-

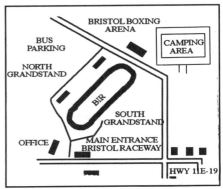

ern Tennessee is very attractive, making the event even more difficult to see, since tourists who often have only a passing interest in racing will come to Bristol while vacationing in nearby Cumberland National Park areas.

There are several hotels in Bristol, but they are quickly snatched up by teams. Camping exists outside the track, but there's nothing in the infield. In fact, you can't get into the infield at all.

Knoxville will have rooms, but is almost two hours away; or try Roanoke. Camping is probably the best way to do it.

Bristol's Chamber of Commerce is (615) 968-4399; for camping and cabin rental call the Tennessee Department of Conservation Division of Parks at (800) 421-6683; or call the Tennessee Department of Tourist Development at (615) 741-2158.

Crossville Raceway
RT. 4, Box 673
Crossville, TN   38555

PH: (615) 456-0222

Location: Central Tennessee, between Nashville and Knoxville, five miles south of I 40, on State Route 127.

Circuit: Third-mile clay oval.

Major races: NASCAR interseries (Eastern Seaboard Region).

Crossville Raceway is set in a well-populated area of central Tennessee noted for a recent boom in tourism. It has a plethora of resorts and golf courses in the area — at least nine courses within a few minutes of the racetrack.

The Cumberland County track is operated in a bowl, and the tiered parking offers a change from the ordinary grandstand-style viewing — it does, however, have grandstands in case you fancy that kind of race-watching. You can cookout on the hills around the oval while you watch the regular Friday night show.

Rooms are plentiful in the area, but for more information, call the Nashville Chamber of Commerce at (615) 259-3900 or (615) 242-5606.

Memphis Motorsports Park
5500 Taylor-Forger Rd.,
Memphis, TN   38053

PH: (901) 358-7223
FAX: (901) 358-7274

Location: Southern Tennessee, in North Memphis.

From Interstate I 240 North, take Warford/New Allen Rd exit north to Ral-Mill Rd, then go three miles, heading left on Ral-Mill, then left on Fite and a half mile to the track.

Circuit: Half-mile clay oval/eighth-mile midget track/quarter-mile drag-strip/ 2.0 mile road course; nine turns.

328

Major races: NHRA Mid-South Nationals; SCCA Regional Road Racing Championships; WERA Motorcycle Racing Championships.

Memphis International Motorsports Park has all the bases covered with its variety of circuits. For some reason the place is just not a household name — even among people who talk motorsports in the house. The May NHRA Nationals are certainly noteworthy, but with all the activity, and all the things that could be going on here, it's just not a well known venue.

Although the facility has only been in existence since 1987 it has already pulled in about 200,000 people per year — but few people other than the drag racers know about MIMP. The NHRA is far and away the biggest event of the season, but it hosts a handful of quality races as well. A tractor pull is also scheduled to find its way to MIMP (... which may not be the ideal way to help the anonymity problems).

Tennessee was in dire need of a facility like this, but for now the closest the big road race machines of IMSA or SCCA will get to racing here is testing, which they do on occasion.

NHRA's Mid-South Nationals is the biggest show of the MIMP year with attendance of nearly 80,000. Contact the Memphis Convention and Visitors Bureau at (901) 576-8181 for hotel information.

Nashville Motor Raceway
Tennessee State Fairgrounds.
P.O. Box 101585
Nashville, TN 37210-1585

PH: (615) 726-1818
FAX: (615) 244-5235

Location: Southern downtown Nashville, at the Tennessee State Fairgrounds, off I 65 at exit 81 Wedgewood Ave.

Circuit: Five-eighths mile high-banked paved oval, with flat quarter-mile paved oval inside.

Major races. NASCAR Winston All-Pro racing (two shows); ASA; ARCA Supercars.

Nashville Motor Raceway is located within the Tennessee State Fairgrounds, a few minutes of downtown Nashville. Regular racing is a Saturday night program which runs from April through September in the warm Tennessee heat.

Nashville has become increasingly more tourist-oriented in the past few years, and although there is no lodging within walking distance of the track, there are plenty of hotels in the area. For more information, call the Nashville Chamber of Commerce for reservation information at (615) 259-3900. Camping spots are available about $15, with hookups. The track is accessible to the handicap. Call the the track for more information.

Big H Speedway
11620 Lake Houston Parkway
Houston, TX   77044

(713) 458-1972

Location: Five miles east of Hwy 59 North. East Mount Houston Exit, five miles east on E. Mount Houston Rd.

Circuit: Quarter-mile dirt oval.

Major races: World Of Outlaws Sprint Cars.

In the middle of the woods, in the Wetlands of Lake Houston, Big H Speedway hosts a handful of quality shows and a weekly Saturday night show of seven racing classes. The lake's edge is just a few hundred feet down the street from the track, and the track is surrounded by high trees and greenery.

Big H seats 4,000 for Outlaw racing, and seats do sell out, so you'll want to reserve in advance. If you'd prefer to watch from your car or from an RV, you can sit in your motorhomes on the hill which overlooks the backstretch. There, you can BBQ or picnic while watching the action on the track.

Camping is available, but there are no hookups or showers. Two motels are just a short drive from the track, and the Travel Lodge is the HQs for the Outlaws when the series sweeps through — and where you'll get a discount if you say "Big H Speedway".

Grand Prix of Dallas
14875 Landmark
Suite 200
Dallas, TX   75240

(214) 701-9091
FAX: (214) 701-9093

Location: Central Texas, in Dallas, around the Reunion Arena, off the I35 Freeway.

Circuit: 1.6 mile road course; seven turns.

Major races: SCCA Trans-Am Championship.

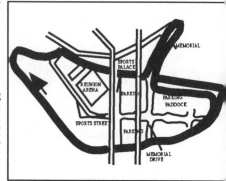

Dallas is a study in racing enthusiasm. Detroit may be the most conspicuous Trans-Am race for manufacturers, but Dallas is the favorite of SCCA officials. Even under stormy skies in the past, the temporary road course has still pulled in over 100,000

fans in bad weather to watch three days worth of racing.

The only other recent motorsports event in Dallas' history was the unsuccessful — but lucrative — Formula One race in 1984, which was doomed by heat and a fragile track surface which cracked as the turbo F1 horsepower was applied to it. A shame. The F1 drivers liked the visit to the hospitable Texas city, and fans turned out in droves for the one-off Grand Prix.

But Dallas has Trans-Am now, and is making it every bit as successful as an F1 race could have been. The old track wound out onto the Addison Airport and around a few of the streets in the immediate area. In 1993 the race moved to the Reunion Arena — where it was supposed to be located when the race was first conceived in 1986.

The race runs around the stadium where the Dallas Mavericks play basketball. It winds through the parking lot and on the streets around the complex. The Trans-Am circuit will make a large loop around the arena, then take a quick dog leg — similar to the old loop at the first Long Beach layout — toward downtown's Convention Center.

There was always plenty of parking at Addison, but most of it was in grass lots, and when the weather was bad so was the parking. the Reunion area allows for 8000 cars to park right on the outside of the track and more within a few blocks of the circuit. In addition, there are more than 35,000 rooms and 11 downtown hotels — the Hyatt is right on the track, sitting outside the circuit.

Since the race has always been packed in the past, tickets for the grandstands will need to be purchased early. Rooms in the area are easy to find, and should be easy to come by as late as Saturday, since most of the spectators are locals. Many of the hotels within walking distance of the track offer discount rates during the GP if booked early. If you want to ensure a spot, call the Dallas Chamber of Commerce at (214) 746-6600.

Devil's Bowl Speedway
1711 Lawson Rd.,
Mesquite, TX   75181

PH: (214) 222-2421
FAX: 214 222-8901

Circuit: Half-mile clay oval

Location: 20 miles from downtown Dallas. Take Highway 80 east from Dallas, taking the Lawson Road exit, then heading right on Lawson Road three miles to the track.

Major Races: World Of Outlaws.

Devil's Bowl Raceway originally stood closer to Dallas, but was moved to where it stands now in Mesquite some 25 years ago. For the past 20 years it has been owned by Lanny and Beverly Edward. Devil's Bowl now sits west of the Mesquite Municipal Airport, adjacent to both a fish reserve and a shooting range.

Racing takes place here on Friday nights with sprints and late models and street stocks. Its regular show is from March to Labor Day , and then it runs special events thereafter. The biggest races are the 600 Nationals in June and the Outlaws show in October.

You can stay in Mesquite, where there are quite a few motels, but the track has agreements with a pair of hotels in Garland where you can get racer's rates. Try the Ramada Inn at (214) 279-6751 and the Hampton Inn at (214) 613-5000. There is also free camping available on the 19 acres of blacktop parking lot. There are no hookups.

Heart O' Texas Speedway
203 Trailwood Ave.
Waco, TX 76710

PH: (817) 829-2294

Location: Central Texas, about 100 miles South of Dallas, off Interstate I 35.

Circuit: Quarter-mile clay oval.

Major races: NASCAR interseries (Sunbelt Region).

Heart O' Texas Speedway hosts a four class series of NASCAR Winston Series Racing on Friday nights with Hot Stock, Modifies, Street Stock, and Bombers. A handful of rooms are available in Waco.

Houston Raceway Park
P.O. Box 1345,
Baytown, TX 77522

PH: (713) 383-2666
FAX: (713) 383-3777

Location: East of Houston, 25 miles south of Interstate I 10 at exit 798, then right following the signs.

Circuit: Quarter-mile dragstrip.

Major races: NHRA Supernationals; Winston Drag Racing Divisional.

Houston Raceway Park has had a few problems with weather in its first few seasons. The Houston skies area dumped water on the track for the first two years, raining the events out.
Even with the poor weather the place has been attracting good crowds. So far there are 20,000 permanent seats — which increase with temporary seating during the Nationals. But with the interest in racing in Texas, there will likely be more built.
The facility already has some noteworthy records under its new belt: Houston's Raceway Park already has the distinction of being one of the quickest dragstrips in the world, with the quickest 4.90 ET of the era, set in '89 by Darrell Gwynn. It also held records in six of the top 12 categories. Some of the records came as a result of its construction: the first 400 feet of the strip is concrete, including of course, the launching pad.
Stay in Baytown if possible, or go back up to Houston, where you won't

have a problem finding accommodations. Call the Greater Houston Visitors Council at (713) 523-5050 for more lodging information.

North Texas Motor Speedway

Royce City, TX
Office: 3306 W. Walnut
1st City Bank Bldg.
Suite 405
Garland, TX   75042

PH: (office) (214) 272-6999
(track) (214) 635-9737

Location: Northern Texas, 30 miles east of Dallas, at Interstate I 30 and FM 2642.

Circuit: Third-mile clay oval; semi banked.

Major races: World of Outlaws Sprint Car Championship Shootout.

Humid, but not uncomfortable, North Texas Motor Speedway is some 32 miles from downtown Dallas. Located on I 30 east of Dallas, 25 miles from 635, the speedway is located in the green rolling hills of North Texas.

The WoO is the track's only special event — NASCAR Modified, late model, hot stocks, and street stocks make up the normal Winston Racing Series' Saturday evening racing. The facility seats 6,000. For lodging try the Greenville area — Royce City has a motel, but little else.

Texas Motorplex

7500 W Highway 287
Ennis, TX   75119

PH: (214) 875-2641
FAX: (214) 875-1848

Location: Central Texas, 35 miles from Dallas, between Highways 35 and 45 on U.S 287 in Ennis, TX.

Circuit: All-concrete quarter-mile dragstrip.

Major races: NHRA Chief Auto Parts Nationals; Bud Light Night of Fire; Super Chevy Show.

The Texas Motorplex will always be remembered as the place where drag racing's first sub-five-second run was posted. Laid down by Eddie Hill in 1988, the run was the first ever in a Top Fuel dragster, and has been credited to the all-concrete construction of the strip. In the season since that run, it has seen many other records, and many other sub-five runs. In fact, in October of 1992 15 of the 16 finalists qualified in the fours.

The facility has only been open since 1986, and is surely the premier drag racing facility in the country. In just the first few years of operation the track already boasts of drawing crowds of better than 300,000 per year. The modern VIP and media suites highlight the already impressive venue.

Being near Dallas, things are simple when it comes to finding rooms, although the drive from anywhere in Texas to anywhere else in Texas always seems to take all day. Don't expect to find anything near the track if you arrive late. But there are a few hotels in the area; try Ennis, Waxahachie, or Palmer, or call the Dallas Visitor Information Center.

Texas World Speedway
P.O. Box 10070
College Station TX 77842

PH: (409) 690-2500
Tickets: 1 (800) 299-TEXAS
FAX: (409) 690-0575

Location: 70 miles northwest of Houston, off Texas 290 to Hempstead then exiting at Highway 6 North through Navasota, where the track sits between Navasota and College Station.

Track: 2.0 mile high-banked paved oval; 1.8 & 1.9 mile road courses.

Major Races: SCCA Trans-Am Championship; ARCA; AMA Championship Motorcycles.

Texas World Speedway appeared on the trail of the Winston Cup from 1969 to 1981, but faded from sight in 1982. The track has recently been renovated and is back in the hunt for a major NASCAR race, although it may be a while until it gets a Winston Cup race again.

The track was slated for a bevy of events in 1992 — most notably the SCCA Trans-Am race. But problems forced the cancellation of the SCCA's featured class. Partially due to that, the track has earned itself a bad reputation. Unfortunate, since it is a great facility.

The track sits in the flat and hot brushland of eastern Texas. Although east Texas is generally humid as a sauna, the College Station area is generally dry and arid — probably a blessing.

Not noted on the map is the road course. Just before turn-one of the oval is a "D"-shaped ninety degree turn, and a snake bend, then a 180 degree wide hairpin. On the way back down the backstretch the track makes another excursion into the infield, veering off just prior to the entrance of turns three and four and looking a lot like Daytona. TWS holds some 30,000 and is slated for expansion in the near future. For now seating is not a problem.

College Station is aptly named for the school that provides

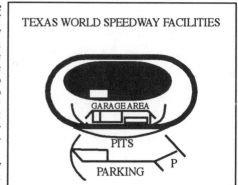

TEXAS WORLD SPEEDWAY FACILITIES

GARAGE AREA

PITS

PARKING

P

the raison d' etre for the place: it is the home of Texas A&M. There are more than 30 hotels in College Station, so staying here should be no problem even if you come late.

Langley Raceway
Office: 3200 W. Moore St.
Richmond, VA 23230

PH (track): (703) 865-1992

Location: In CIA country, outside Langley AFB in northeastern Virginia, on the Potomac River.

Circuit: Two-fifths mile paved oval.

Major races: NASCAR interseries (Mid-Atlantic Region).

Even the racetrack sounds official: "Langley Raceway". In the shadow of the famous air force base — and the infamous CIA headquarters -- Langley Raceway hosts a Saturday evening full-bodied show, and occasionally hosts a NASCAR Dash. Langley has only a few rooms, but there are rooms in the area, heading across the Potomac to Bethesda.

Martinsville Speedway
P.O. Box 3311
Martinsville, VA   24115

PH: (703) 956-3151
FAX: (703) 956-2820)

Location: Southern Virginia, 10 miles north of the North Carolina border, 40 miles North of Greensboro.
From Greensboro, take Route 220 North into Virginia, toward Martinsville, taking the 220 South Business loop to the track.

Circuit: Half-mile paved oval.

Major races: NASCAR Winston Cup (two races); NASCAR Busch Grand National (two races).

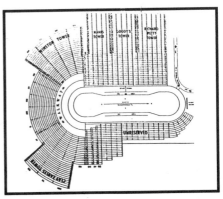

The shortest track on the Winston Cup calendar, Martinsville Speedway's roots are obvious: the dual set of pits — one on either side of the oval — shows the dirt track history of the circuit. This great little facility has all the big VIP hospitality areas in turns 1-2, leaving the grandstands pretty much left open to race fans.

The place is relatively flat so folks in the lower seats won't see directly across onto the backstretch. But because of the mostly level playing surfaces there's plenty of slipping and sliding, which makes for some exciting racing.

It's a popular short track with the Charlotte crowd, many of whom travel three hours to Martinsville for the racing. It's an easy place to get into and out of, and because of the physical limitations of a half-mile track, the crowds are not gigantic.

Tickets for Martinsville will be a problem, and you'll have to book far in advance. There's no infield viewing, so that option won't be open to you on race-day. There's an unreserved section for folks who show up late, but seats there are obviously limited.

Martinsville is a small city, but has a good amount of rooms. With the size of the track, it's possible to find lodging here if you book at the same time you buy tickets. You may have to drive a bit to either Roanoke, or Winston-Salem, where you'll be sure to find a room. There is some camping outside the track.

A word to the wise: watch out for the Virginia Police. You can't use radar detectors in Virginia, and if caught with one in operation it will be confiscated and you'll be fined. Keep it in the trunk while you're here.

Call the track for hotel information, or the Virginia State Chamber of Commerce for more information at (800) VISIT VA.

New River Valley Speedway
Route 2, P.O. Box 278
Radford, VA   24141

PH: (703) 639-2000

Location: Western Virginia, 50 miles from Roanoke, four miles north of Interstate I 81, on U.S Highway 11.

Circuit: Two-fifths mile paved oval.

Major races: NASCAR Goody's Dash.

Now named New River Valley Speedway, the old Pulaski County Speedway was originally opened in 1949 as a half-mile oval, but was closed in 1968, remaining dormant for nearly 20 years until it reopened in 1988 again as a Winston Racing Series .416 mile paved track. The 12,500 seat venue now hosts the Busch Grand National Series, as well as the NASCAR Dash.

New River Valley Speedway is located 50 miles from Roanoke in the New River Valley, of the Blue Ridge Mountains. Just 45 minutes from the track is Mountain Lake — where the movie "Dirty Dancing" was filmed. The track is also 15 miles from Virginia Tech, located in Blacksburg.

For hotel information call the track, or the Virginia State Chamber of Commerce for more information at (800) VISIT VA.

Old Dominion Speedway
10611 Dumfries Rd.
Manassas, VA   2211

PH: (703) 361-7753

Location: 20 miles west of Washington DC, in Manassas, VA, five miles south of Interstate I 66, off State Route 234.

Circuit: Three-eighths mile paved oval.

Major races: NASCAR interseries (Mid-Atlantic Region).

Old Dominion Speedway hosts a regular group of five racing divisions each Saturday night. The NASCAR sanctioned oval also has a dragstrip on the property and holds divisional and bracket drags frequently. An IHRA sanctioned event runs here as the biggest show of the drag racing season. The area has plenty of rooms — although they may be a tad expensive. Call the track for numbers of the cheaper inns.

Richmond International Raceway
P.O. Box 9257
Richmond, VA   23227

PH: (804) 329-6796
FAX: (804) 329-5029

Location: North Richmond, at 600 E. Laburnum Ave, between I 64 and I 95.

Circuit: .75 mile paved, banked oval.

Major races: NASCAR Winston Cup (2 races); NASCAR Busch Grand National Series.

Richmond International Raceway is one of the easiest races on the Winston Cup circuit to attend. Richmond's large metro area makes finding a room an easy proposition — even if arriving late.

Richmond, like Milwaukee and Indycar racing, has the unfortunate (or fortunate, depending on how you wish to look at it) distinction of being the race after the biggest of the year. Run as the second event of the season, Richmond's first of two in the season is held right after Daytona. It's really where the season gets down to business. If at Daytona the drivers are racing for the win, at Richmond they're going for the points.

There's a huge difference between the first and second races at Richmond: the first is held in February

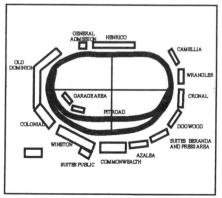

and the second is run in September. As one could imagine, September in Richmond is hot and humid. But February in Richmond can be cold. In fact, for the 1990 race, the green flag dropped on the field in zero-degree temps!

The track is located on the Virginia State Fairgrounds, and was once called the Richmond Fairgrounds Speedway. The land upon which it stood was purchased by Paul Sawyer, who renamed the facility Richmond International Raceway — with the intention of divorcing the track from the image associated with being a fairgrounds event. He probably didn't need to worry — it is far from a fairgrounds race.

The Tri-oval is a fantastic spectating venue — with 60,000 seats and not a bad seat in the house. Its brevity gives fans an intimate look at the racing, but it's fast enough that it makes for quick laps; it is slightly banked, so fans at each end can see the action on the far side easily; the pits wind around at each end, so you can actually see some of the pits from 75% of the seats. The grandstands are continually being upgraded, and eventually the entire place will be encompassed by seats.

Staying in Richmond is a breeze. There are plenty of hotels within a few minutes of the raceway, and even the more distant accommodations are easy to get to and from during a race. There is also some camping outside the track. Call the track, or the Virginia State Chamber of Commerce for more information at (800) VISIT VA.

South Boston Speedway

P.O. Box 186
South Boston, VA   24592

PH: (804) 572-4947

Location: Southern central Virginia, 10 miles from the North Carolina border, in South Boston, off Highways 501 and 58.

Circuit: .357 mile paved oval.

Major races: NASCAR Busch Grand National Series; NASCAR interseries (Mid Atlantic Region).

Located in Southside Va, just outside the city limits of South Boston, is South Boston Speedway. South Boston's Halifax County, which is home to 35,000 people, is in the green rolling hills of Virginia.

The track can accommodate some 11,000 people — although the grandstands only hold 7,000. The remainder sit mostly in an area around turn 3-4. The Grand National races are the best draws, but there's normally a very good crowd for regular shows, averaging 5,000 a week. There are only general admission tickets here, and nothing can be reserved, nor are there any advance ticket sales.

Other than the GN, the biggest race is the mid-September 100 mile race for late model stockers — which touts a purse of $20,000.

You can stay in South Boston, Danville, Clarksville, or Roxboro, NC. There is also camping available at Buggs Island Lake, which is a State Park 25 miles away; or camp in Halifax at the Staunton River State Park. For more information on rooms, call the Virginia State Chamber of Commerce at (800) VISIT VA; or the North Carolina Travel and Tourism Division at (800) VISIT NC.

Southside Speedway

P.O. Box 9606
Richmond, VA   23228

PH: (804) 744-1275

Location: Central eastern Virginia, in south Richmond, off Highway 360 West.

Circuit: Third-mile paved oval

Major races: NASCAR interseries (Mid Atlantic Region).

Just south of Richmond in Chesterfield, Southside Speedway is known as the "toughest track in the south". The narrow oval is almost completely flat, which makes for some good bumping and jostling on any given race night. Its biggest event is the NASCAR Dash series, and for that one most of the 6,300 seats are filled. The regular Friday night shows are run with NASCAR late model stocks and minis.

There are probably 50 motels within 20 miles of the track, but Chesterfield and Hanover are the closest. Some people camp — although there are no formal camping facilities — for the Dash.

Evergreen Speedway

P.O. Box 879
Monroe, WA   98272
PH: (206) 776-2802

Location: 20 miles northeast of Seattle, a few miles east of Puget Sound on U.S. Highway 2 in Monroe.

Circuit: Five-eighths mile paved oval/ three eighths mile paved oval.

Major races: NASCAR Winston West; NASCAR Northwest Tour; NASCAR interseries (Great Northern Region).

Evergreen Speedway was designed with versatility in mind, and it can be transformed from the big five-eighths mile oval where the serious NASCAR cars race, to a three-eighths miler, a one-fifth miler, and a figure eight circuit — all paved. The track offers a great selection of different entertainment, from NASCAR Winston West racing to Destruction Derbies.

The mild Pacific Northwest climate is no problem for fans, who have a chance to weather the storms in the track's 10,000 covered seats. Racing takes place rain or shine in this track which is located at the Evergreen Fairgrounds.

Seattle International Raceway

P.O. Box 506,
Kent, WA   98035

Track: 31001 - 144th Ave S.E.

Kent, WA   98042

PH: (206) 631-1550

Location: Northern Washington, just west of Puget Sound, 25 miles south of Seattle.

From Seattle, take Interstate I5 South to I405 West to U.S. 167 South, taking Auburn Way to Kent, and the Kent Kangley Highway to the track.

Circuit: Quarter-mile dragstrip/2.25 mile road course; 9 turns.

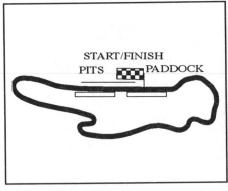

Major races: NHRA Northwest Nationals; SCCA Regionals.

Seattle International Raceway, or what was once called Pacific Raceways, is now mostly used as a quarter-mile dragstrip. But in its heyday, in the late 50s and early 60s, Pacific Raceways saw the likes of Mark Donohue, Peter Revson, and Parnelli Jones race the 2.25 mile road course in the early Trans-Am cars.

The nine-turn circuit winds through the scenic forests of Kent, just outside Seattle. Alas, the circuit has yet to do a major resurfacing since its opening in the 50s. It is narrow, bumpy, and provides little runoff, relegating it to amateur status for road racing and testing.

The quarter-mile track, however, is one of the finest on the west coast, and has become a permanent fixture on the NHRA's premier drag racing calendar.

There are hotels in the immediate area, but Seattle and its outskirts have a large section of cheap rooms. The Salish Lodge offers an incredible view of Snoqualmie Falls, and finishes off a perfect Pacific Northwest weekend — if not too expensive. It is just a short drive away.

For more information on where to stay, call the Seattle/King County Visitors Bureau at (206) 461-3888.

South Sound Speedway
7012 220th St.
Mountlake Terrace, WA   98043
PH: (206) 273-6420

Location: In Tenino, 10 miles south of Olympia.

Circuit: Third-mile paved oval.

Major races: NASCAR interseries (Pacific Region).

South Sound Speedway sits on an atypical prairie in western Washington. The 5,000 seat facility's biggest show of the racing season is the NASCAR Northwest Tour and the Uhlmann Motors 200 Winston West. Saturday nights see the regular program with full-bodied cars from the NASCAR Winston Racing Series regulars. For the closest inns, head 3-5 miles south to Chehalis or Dentralia. There is camping at the track — at least for over-nighters during the major events.

Wenatchee Valley Raceway

825 11th Ave
East Wenatchee, WA   98802

PH: (509) 884-8592

Location: Central Washington, across the Columbia River from Wenatchee, in East Wenatchee.

Circuit: Quarter-mile paved oval.

Major races: NASCAR interseries (Great Northern Region).

Wenatchee Valley Raceway hosts some interesting shows beside the NASCAR Winston Racing Series Saturday night racing program. Probably the best non-NASCAR race is the Old Time Racers Association races — done in 1930s cars. There are rooms available in the area.

Pennsboro Speedway

Office: 8848 Ely Rd.
Apple Creek, OH   44606

PH: (216) 682-7435
PH: (Track): (216) 683-3085

Location: In West Virginia on Route 50, halfway between Parkersburg and Clarksburg, north of Charleston.

Circuit: Half-mile clay oval.

Major races: Dirt Track World Championships.

Pennsboro Speedway hosts just two races during the entire season — but both are heavy hitters. The first is the Hillbilly 100, which in 1993 was in its 25th year. The Hillbilly, which runs every September, pays a measly $11,000 (!), but October's Dirt Track World Championships pays $50,000 for a win, making it the richest race in the country for late model dirt track stock cars.

The half-mile clay oval sits in the Ritchie County Fairgrounds, and the facility fills to capacity when the World Series comes through town. Rooms can be found in Parkersburg or Clarksburg.

Summit Point Raceway

P.O. Box 190
Summit Point, WV   25446

PH: (304) 725-8444
FAX: (304) 728-7124

Location: Near Charles Town, West Virginia, in Summit Point on Route 13.

Circuit: 2.0 mile road course; 10 turns.

Major races: IMSA GTO/ GTU Championships; SCCA Regionals and Nationals; WERA Championships.

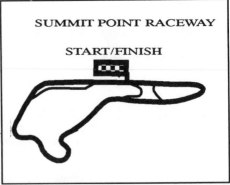

Seventy miles from Baltimore, and the same distance from Washington DC, in a remote part of the Shenandoah Valley farming country, Summit Point Raceway gives West Virginia a bit of road racing excitement.

The track is quite challenging, with 70 feet of elevation changes in its two miles. Wagon Bend, which is essentially a reverse of Laguna Seca's Corkscrew is probably the toughest on the circuit, and it must be hit just right to make time.

You can watch from there, or check out the Carousel, turn five, where you'll see most of the track from the same corner. There are grandstands which can accommodate some 6,000 people — and larger grandstands are assembled for bigger races, holding up to 12,000 people. But it's just as easy to sit in the hills and watch.

You can stay in Winchester VA, which is 14 miles away; or in Charles Town or Harpers Ferry WV, which are both about eight miles away. You can also stay in either Baltimore or Washington, although both will be more expensive. There is free camping at the track, but there are no hookups — although showers exist — and stays are limited to Friday and Saturday nights.

West Virginia Motor Speedway
P.O. Box 107
Mineral Wells WV   26150

(304)   489-1979
(304)   489-1889

Location: Just off Interstate I77 at exit #170 in Mineral Wells.

Circuit: Five-eighths of a mile red clay oval.

Major Races: Camel Pro AMA.

Mineral Wells' importance notwithstanding, the town is not exactly a metropolis. But the racetrack does just fine. And although it has never sold out, it brings in a good crowd. The AMA Camel Pro Series brings the biggest event here, and there is a regular Late Model show.

The track is located in a hilly area and is on the side of a terraced hill from which spectators can watch racing. Between the hill and the cement bleachers on the backstretch, almost 14,000 can attend racing here. Lodging is best found eight miles away in Parkersburg, which has a population of 50,000. Or information can be had by calling the track.

Cedar Lake Speedway
New Richmond, WI
PH: (715) 248-7119

Location: Western Wisconsin, 60 miles east of Minneapolis, MN.
From Minneapolis, take Interstate I 94 to State Route 65 to SR 64. From SR 64, go four miles east to County Route C to Country Route CC, then two miles west to the track.

Circuit: Half-mile clay oval; high banked.

Major races: World of Outlaws Sprint Car Championship Shootout.

Cedar Lake Speedway's annual World of Outlaws race regularly packs in upwards of 8,500 people, and the quiet farms are transformed into a race mecca. There are not only bleachers in the facility, but spectators can sit in their cars in tiered parking areas and watch racing from there as well.
The best place to find rooms is in Richmond, or you can camp by the side of the track, or in the parking lot under the shade trees. There is running water and bathrooms, but no hookups for RVs are available.

Hales Corners Speedway
P.O. Box 22
Hales Corners, WI   53130
PH: (414) 529-1328

Location: Eastern Wisconsin, on the outskirts of Milwaukee.
From Downtown Milwaukee, take Interstate I 43 to State Route 100 and Hales Corners. The track is a half-mile from Hales Corners on SR 100.

Circuit: Half-mile clay oval; semi-banked.

Major races: World of Outlaws Sprint Car Championship Shootout.

Hales Corners is located in a wooded suburban/commercial area, which sits, appropriately, between two auto dealerships. The city is a suburb of Milwaukee. It is a very peaceful area, with Whithall park a couple blocks away, and a flower garden just a few hundred yards away from the track entrance.
Racing is held on Saturday nights, with a half-dozen special events held at the 10,000 seat track, enhancing the season action. The WoO show is the biggest of the season.
You can stay near the airport which is 10 miles away, or four miles away on Highway 10 where there are several motels. The track is about four miles from West Allis, and the Milwaukee State Fair Park Indycar track.

La Crosse Fairgrounds Speedway
P.O. Box 853
West Salem, WI   54669
PH: (608) 786-1525

Location: Western Wisconsin, 12 miles from the Mississippi River, on Highway 16, in West Salem.

Circuit: Five-eighths and quarter-mile paved ovals.

Major races: NASCAR interseries (Great Northern Region).

La Crosse Fairgrounds Speedway hosts a regular show of NASCAR late model racing, with street stock, and Powder Puffers racing as well. Racing is generally done on Saturday nights, although recently there has been more racing on Wednesday evenings. Rooms are plentiful in La Crosse.

Milwaukee Mile
West Allis, WI
7722 West Greenfield Ave.,
West Allis, WI 53214

PH: (414) 453-8277
FAX: (414) 453-9920
Ticket info: (414) 453-8277

Location: Central Milwaukee, just off Interstate I 94, in the Milwaukee State Fairgrounds.

Circuit: One mile oval, slightly banked.

Major races: CART IndyCar World Series Championship; NASCAR Busch Grand National; ASA Championships; USAC Silver Crown and Midget Championships.

Milwaukee is known as the first real event of the CART season, and has been the traditional race following Indy for seven decades. Oddly, in 1992 it had moved to the third race following Indy, and the seventh in the championship. In 1993, it returned to its traditional date following Indy, in June.

Originally opened in 1933 for Indycar racing, Milwaukee is where the season usually gets down to business. Phoenix, Gold Coast, and Long Beach are tune-up races for May's Indy 500, which is almost a separate event from the rest of the CART PPG Championship. The facility marked its 100th anniversary as a racing venue in 1991, with horses being the original competitors. Its first auto races began in 1903, and the track celebrated its 90th season as an auto racing facility — in fact, predating the Indianapolis Motor Speedway by eight years.

The track is nearly as rich in history as the Indianapolis Motor Speedway. Almost like baseball's Wrigley field, the circuit is in the middle of the city — a place you

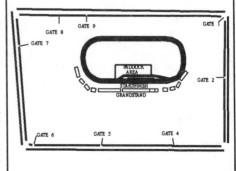

rarely find a racetrack these days. The Interstate (I 94) bounds the north side of the speedway, and on the back-stretch, 60 to 80 yards from the track, is a row of suburban Milwaukee houses. Due to its unique location it does not host a weekly show, and only has racing an average of once a month.

Some 35,000 seats are housed in the West Allis facility. The USAC and ASA races are popular, but fail to get the crowds the IndyCars pull in. Last season Milwaukee sold out, breaking an attendance record at 43,260 ticketed. And the track will likely post more records now that management of the track has been taken on by Carl Haas. For the '93 season — in anticipation of the Busch series race (the first NASCAR race in 10 seasons) — the track constructed 900 feet of new retaining wall in turns three and four.

Ten minutes from downtown Milwaukee, hotels are available there, but Brookfield has more rooms, and is only five minutes away. The strip where Wisconsin Fair Park is located follows I 94 west which, by travelling either direction, will have plenty of hotels; 84th St. also has lots of hotels.

Although the circuit is located in a congested area, parking is not a problem. You can, however, take a bus to the entrance of the track on Greenfield Ave. if you like. For bus information on routeing and times, call (414) 344-6711 for the Milwaukee County Transit System. For more information on lodging, call the Greater Milwaukee Convention and Visitor's Bureau at (414) 273-7222.

Road America
Office: Box P
Elkhart Lake
WI, 53020

Track: N7390 Highway 67
Elkhart Lake, WI 53020

PH: (414) 892-4576
FAX: (414) 892-4550
Ticket Info: (800) 365-7223

Location: Eastern Wisconsin, 18 miles from Sheboygan, approximately 65 miles from Milwaukee.

From Milwaukee, take Interstate I 43 North to Highway 57 North, heading west on County Trunk "J" to Highway 67. Follow 67 North to the track, which is on 67 near Elkhart Lake; Chicago Historic Vintage Races; SCCA June Sprints and Club Racing.

Circuit: Four-mile road circuit. 14 turns.

Major races: CART PPG Indy Car World Series Championship; IMSA Camel GT; SCCA Trans-Am; AMA Pro Road Racing Series Championships.

Road America is arguably America's finest road racing facility. From the standpoint of spectators, Elkhart Lake offers spectacular scenery, on a circuit big enough to accommodate

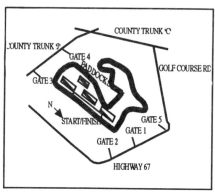

the largest crowd without the traditional claustrophobia caused by the overpacking of spectators. From the drivers' point of view Road America is a fantastic challenge, with ultra-fast areas, as well as some tight, challenging corners. Is it any wonder that whenever a permanent site for a Formula One Grand Prix is considered, the name Road America generally follows?

The 175 feet of elevation changes make for good viewing as well as great racing. There are several good spots in the 525 acre facility from which to watch the racing: turn five is a 90 degree left-hander at the bottom of a slope (which now has grandstands that offer a great view). The corner, called Morraine Sweep, forces cars to slow from 130MPH or so down to 35 or 40 for the 90 degree turn, then accelerate back up again to top speed — it's not unusual to see cars go off-course here; or go to Camel Pavilion on top of the hill between turn-five and the back of the course. You'll see the whole valley.

A $1.1 million renovation was completed in time for the start of the '92 season. The old pagoda in the paddock was finally torn down and in its place the paddock has been expanded 1,200 X 200 feet. An infield press room was added, a new medical center was constructed and Winner's Circle was moved out to the main straight. The long walk between the VIP center and the paddock was eliminated via a $275,000 tunnel under the main straightway. The new tunnel is to the left of the VIP center as you walk out. Once on the other side, it brings you to the southern edge of the paddock. Now crews and teams can walk to both Winners Circle or the press room with relative ease, and general admission or grandstand fans can get into the paddock more quickly. An off-road track, built inside the Carousel area, was also inaugurated in July of '92, and the track hosted an AMA Motocross race in September.

There is no camping at the facility, but there are campgrounds on Highway 67, and there are camping areas across the street from the main entrance of the track. For more information on camping you can call Road America (ask for Gail Bartlett). An hour from Milwaukee, the best places to stay are 19 miles away in Sheboygan, five miles from the circuit in Plymouth, or in Kohler, also close to the racing. During the Indy Car races, you may have to stay farther away, in either Milwaukee or in Green Bay.

For more information, call the Lodging Information Hotlines: for Sheboygan, call (414) 457-9495; for Milwaukee, call (800) 231-0903; for Fond du Lac, call (414) 923-3010.